102

The Long Recessional

Other books by the author

LEBANON: THE FRACTURED COUNTRY

THE TRANSFORMATION OF SPAIN: FROM FRANCO TO THE
CONSTITUTIONAL MONARCHY

THE LAST LEOPARD: A LIFE OF GIUSEPPE DI LAMPEDUSA

THE HUNGRY GENERATIONS

CITIES OF SPAIN

CURZON

The Long Recessional

The Imperial Life of Rudyard Kipling

DAVID GILMOUR

Farrar, Straus and Giroux

New York

To Sarah, with love and gratitude

Farrar, Straus and Giroux
19 Union Square West, New York 10003

ISBN: 0-374-18702-9
Library of Congress Control Number: 2002100585

www.fsgbooks.com

1 3 5 7 9 10 8 6 4 2

Contents

Contents

Illustrations

The author and publishers would like to thank the following for permission to reproduce illustrations: Plate 3, Kipling Papers, Special Collections, University of Sussex © National Trust; 4, 13, 16, 17, 20, 24 and 31, Mary Evans Picture Library; 5, 25, 28, 29, 33 and 34, Topham Picturepoint; 6, The Royal Photographic Society, Bath; 7, Library of Congress; 8, British Library; 9, The Art Archive/Eileen Tweedy, reproduced by permission of Elizabeth Banks; 11, National Trust Photographic Library/John Hammond; 12, 19, 21, 22, 23, 26, 27 and 32, Hulton Archive; 15, The Art Archive/The Art Archive; 18, National Portrait Gallery, London.

Preface

———————◆———————

The *Struwwelpeter Alphabet*, an Edwardian children's book, has a drawing under the letter K of Rudyard Kipling and Lord Kitchener, at that time the Commander-in-Chief in India. The soldier stands very tall with a drawn sword and a massive moustache; the writer appears small and dumpy beside him, holding a quill pen as if it were a sword. Beneath the caricatures is the verse:

> Men of different trades and sizes
> Here you have before your eyeses;
> Lanky sword and stumpy pen,
> Doing useful things for men;
> When the Empire wants a stitch in her
> Send for Kipling and for Kitchener.

Indifferent though the lines are, they reflected a common perception of the two Ks as the chief imperial icons of the age. Lord Esher, that shrewd and feline eminence at Court, argued that Kipling had earned the Order of Merit for having accomplished as much for the British Empire as Kitchener or Lord Cromer, who had ruled Egypt for twenty-four years.[1]

Kitchener remains an imperial symbol although he was certainly not one of the Empire's best generals. But Kipling's role has been derided by detractors, who accuse him of jingoism, and neglected by admirers, who are embarrassed by his imperialism. The intrepid Bengali writer, Nirad Chaudhuri, insisted that Kipling's politics were 'no essential ingredient of his writings', while Charles Carrington, Kipling's official biographer, argued privately that his subject was really neither a Tory nor an imperialist.[2] The prevalence of such views among admirers has resulted in a curious imbalance in their treatment of Kipling in their writing. Most of their work has concentrated on the prose, much of it on the life, a little on the poetry, and virtually none on his public role. This is the first volume to chronicle Kipling's political life, his early role as apostle of the Empire, the embodiment of imperial aspiration, and his later one as the prophet of national decline.

Imperialism and conservatism were in fact essential ingredients of Kipling's life and of much of his writing: some three-quarters of the forty-five poems in *The Years Between*, which he regarded as his most important collection, have political or imperial themes. Kipling himself knew that his politics could not be disentangled from his work: for nearly forty years, he told a French friend in 1919, the Empire had been 'of the fabric of [my] physical and mental existence'.[3] He needed the stimulus of imperial labour, to preach and to exhort and to prophesy. He was a great artist but he had – and required – other roles as well.

Kipling lived the first half of his life in the reign of Queen Victoria. He was a child of her Empire – and of imperial self-confidence. As a young man in India he neither questioned British rule nor suspected its impermanence. While he recognized its absurdities – and mocked them in his work – he became convinced that it was a force for good, a conviction that grew after he left the Subcontinent at the age of 23 and travelled to other territories of the Empire. He incarnated the Victorian sense of imperial mission and preached its merits to an audience he found exasperatingly inattentive. In 'The White Man's Burden', which he published in 1899, he urged the United States to share with Britain the role of 'civilizing' the backward regions of the Earth.

Kipling's message gave him an audience and a status that no other British poet, not even Tennyson, has enjoyed in his lifetime. By his range of imperial experience and his anticipation of public moods, he made himself an essential figure for people who did not normally read poetry. Although he refused all honours offered by the

Government, he was widely and enthusiastically acknowledged as the unofficial laureate of the British Empire. His influence on the nation is of course difficult to quantify, but it was obvious at the time. The poem 'If' had a palpable moral influence on his contemporaries within the Empire and beyond, including the American president, Woodrow Wilson, who regarded a newspaper clipping of it as one of his 'treasured possessions'.[4] According to a BBC poll, it is still Britain's favourite poem, the one most often displayed in people's homes, framed and illuminated in medieval script, hanging balefully on the wall as an exhortation to self-improvement.

Queen Victoria celebrated her Diamond Jubilee in 1897, an event that Kipling commemorated in his great poem 'Recessional'. In retrospect the year seems to represent the apogee of the British Empire – and Kipling's recognition of its mortality. Soon after he had perceived its potential, he became aware of the Empire's frailty and of the growing threats to its health and even to its existence. Survival, he began stridently to insist, depended on the implementation of certain policies: Tariff Reform and Imperial Preference, compulsory service and an expansion of the armed forces, an alliance with France and resistance to Germany, and a halt to all concessions to Indian and to Irish nationalists. These were imperatives, and he demanded them imperatively.

The Liberal Government, which came to power at the end of 1905, adopted none of these policies except, belatedly in 1914, the alliance with France against Germany. Kipling thus found himself in the role of Cassandra, condemned to utter prophecies that no one would heed, though in his later, even more despairing, moments, he assumed the mantle of Jeremiah: the Empire will fall, Britain will fall, civilization will topple into a new Dark Age. At the end of his life, when Hitler's intentions stood revealed, his concern was simply the survival of Britain. The trajectory of imperial decline thus coincided with the trajectory of his life, a synchronism that explains the bitterness of those decades as a disregarded prophet. The man who had celebrated the Empire's zenith was dying with the expectation of its imminent demise.

Acknowledgements

People writing about Rudyard Kipling inevitably accumulate debts around the world: to the archivists who have preserved and catalogued his papers and who assist the student in his or her researches; to the band of scholars who have written so effectively on different aspects of their subject's life and works; and to Kipling's own literary agents, A.P. Watt Ltd, who, on behalf of the National Trust, have given me and many others permission to quote from the books and papers.

In the first category I would like to thank Elizabeth Inglis of Sussex University, Karen Smith of Dalhousie University and innumerable other librarians in Britain and the United States. In the second I am especially grateful to the works of the early biographers, Charles Carrington, Angus Wilson and Lord Birkenhead, and to the authors of more recent lives, Harry Ricketts and Andrew Lycett. I am also obliged to many specialist scholars including Peter Keating (*Kipling the Poet*), J.M.S. Tompkins (*The Art of Rudyard Kipling*), and Michael Brock (for his essay ' "Outside his Art": Rudyard Kipling in Politics'). My principal debt, however, is to Thomas Pinney, the world's leading scholar in the field and the editor, among other things, of four volumes of Kipling's letters.

I am also extremely grateful to Thomas Pinney for reading the manuscript and giving invaluable advice. All or part of the text was also read by my father, Ian Gilmour, and by Jan Dalley, Roy Foster,

Acknowledgements

Ramachandra Guha, Sunil Khilnani and Xan Smiley. I am much indebted to all of them for their comments and suggestions.

I have been very fortunate with my editors on both sides of the Atlantic, with Lauren Osborne at Farrar, Straus and Giroux, whose rigor and enthusiasm I have greatly appreciated, and with everyone at John Murray, especially Grant McIntyre, a model of patience and general encouragement, and Gail Pirkis, whose incomparable and almost telepathic skills have once again much improved a book of mine. I am grateful to all of them and to my literary agent, Gillon Aitken, as always a pillar of sagacity.

Finally, and above all, I must thank my wife Sarah, to whom the work is dedicated, for her special contribution to the making of this book.

Edinburgh
September 2001

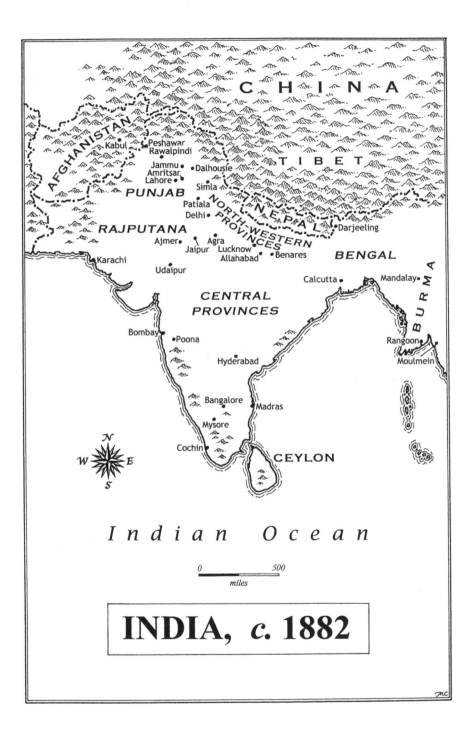

INDIA, c. 1882

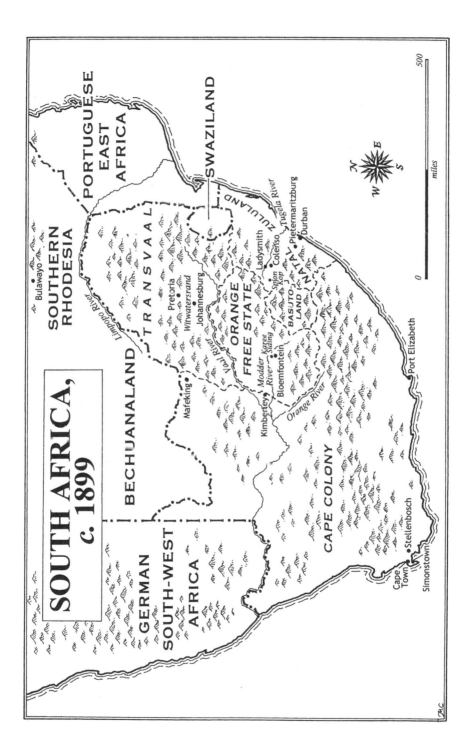

SOUTH AFRICA, c. 1899

PORTUGUESE EAST AFRICA

SOUTHERN RHODESIA

Bulawayo

BECHUANALAND

GERMAN SOUTH-WEST AFRICA

TRANSVAAL

Limpopo River

Pretoria

Witwatersrand

Johannesburg

Vaal River

Mafeking

Kimberley

Modder River

Karee Siding

Bloemfontein

ORANGE FREE STATE

Orange River

SWAZILAND

ZULULAND

Ladysmith

Spion Kop

Colenso

Tugela River

BASUTO LAND

NATAL

Pietermaritzburg

Durban

CAPE COLONY

Port Elizabeth

Stellenbosch

Cape Town

Simonstown

N
E
S
W

miles

0   500

Part One

Child of Empire

I

Ejections from Paradise

RUDYARD KIPLING NEVER wasted time investigating his roots. He was 'not a bit interested' in his ancestry, he reflected in old age, and only wished that a pestering inquirer would desist from hunting down his 'pedigree'.[1]

Rootlessness is in the essence of Kipling's work. He lived in four continents and wrote about six. He crossed the great oceans; he knew the Mediterranean on all its sides; his favourite landscapes were in adverse angles of the Pacific (New Zealand and British Columbia) and in opposite corners of the Atlantic (New England and Cape Colony). At the halfway point of his life he planted laborious roots in Sussex, but it was illness rather than the forests of the Weald that restrained his enthusiasm for travel. In the popular imagination he became – and remains – an English jingoist with his heart in India. Yet it would be as accurate to think of him as a citizen of the world in love with France while sometimes still yearning for a previous mistress, South Africa.

Kipling took occasional pride in being a Yorkshireman, a 'tyke' whose family had lived for 200 years in the West Riding. Yet even though he enjoyed hearing 'the good meaty Yorkshire tongue', he was seldom moved to visit the paternal homeland. He believed his ancestors included clock-makers, bell-founders and yeoman farmers, but he knew nothing else about them except that their sons were christened John and Joseph in alternate generations. He was happy in principle to be identified as a Yorkshireman so long as he was not required to assume that identity.[2]

He was not happy, however, to be identified as a Celt. Celtishness suggested affinities with Lloyd George or Irish nationalists, two of Kipling's least favourite organisms. Yet his mother's family were Jacobite Macdonalds who had left the Hebrides after 1745 and settled in Ulster. Inspired by John Wesley, his great-grandfather James joined the Methodist Church and went to England, where his son married Hannah Jones, thereby introducing Welsh blood into the family, a detail about which Rudyard did not boast.

In middle age Kipling became Rector of St Andrews University where he commended the traditional East Coast, non-Celtic Scottish virtues of thrift, common sense and hard work. He could never have been a Calvinist, either in doctrine or in temperament. But he admired the society he believed Presbyterianism had created in Scotland: the system of education, the making of a 'portentous, granite-gutted, self-sufficient community'.[3]

Kipling's innate romanticism, never as submerged as is sometimes thought, surfaced as soon as he saw the heather or read Stevenson and remembered the Jacobites. Although he was incurious about the origins of his Macdonald forebears, he was a partisan of their clan's historic feud with the Campbells. His mother, he told a Highlander during the Boer War, had 'taught [me] never to like a Campbell', and he followed her precept half-seriously ever after: travelling in the 'enemy' territory of Argyllshire in 1919, he found himself 'cursing all Campbells' and admitting that, despite their scenery, he could never love them.[4] If it was strange to dismiss roots yet accept rooted ancestral prejudice, at least he was consistent in the matter. Attempting to explain his highly partisan stance on Ireland in 1911, he wondered half-humorously whether it had anything to do with his 'great-great grandfather buried at Ballynamallard in a grim methody churchyard'.[5]

Methodism flowed into his veins from Yorkshire as well as from the Celtic fringe. Both of Kipling's grandfathers were Methodist ministers. So were his mother's brother and her grandfather: their Macdonald ministry lasted unbroken for three generations and 144 years. Yet these were relaxed strains of Methodism. Kipling's uncle, Frederic Macdonald, may have become President of the Wesleyan Methodist Conference, but his four married sisters all had Anglican weddings. Alice Macdonald, Kipling's mother, is even said to have thrown a lock of John Wesley's hair on to the fire with the cry, 'See! A hair of the dog that bit us!'[6] Kipling's father, Lockwood, was equally disrespectful of his religious heritage, a sceptic who found it 'grievously demoralising' to meet parsons, especially at teatime with their wives.[7] The result was that Rudyard was no more a Methodist than he was a Calvinist. In his adult poems he often invoked a Divinity – whom he vaguely believed in – and certainly he respected other people's religions. But he was never, in any real sense, a practising Christian.* Whatever bigotries he may have collected in the course of his life, religious ones were absent.

Alice Macdonald was an attractive, vivacious and mildly mischievous girl. She was also a flirt: her youngest sister remarked that she seemed unable 'to go on a visit without becoming engaged to some wild cad of the desert'. Impetuous, musical and tartly humorous, in personality she was very unlike Lockwood, the serene, tolerant, slow-moving man whom she married in March 1865. But as friends pointed out, they had 'congenial tastes and contrasted temperaments'; they shared similar interests, were 'most excellent company' and could 'see persons and events from the humorous side'.[9]

As a matrimonial catch, Lockwood was not in the same league as her sisters' husbands: the painters Edward Burne-Jones and Edward Poynter, and the wealthy ironmaster Alfred Baldwin, the father of Stanley. But this short, bearded and prematurely venerable man had much charm and wisdom. A friend used to refer to him as Socrates because he resembled sculptures of the Athenian philosopher, although she later felt that his 'intense interest in the world of man and nature' made Chaucer a more appropriate comparison. A sculptor and craftsman of skill and diligence, he was dispatched to Bombay soon after his wedding to teach at the School of Art and Industry. As a natural ally of the Arts and Crafts Movement in Britain, he was well suited to a post intended to preserve and rejuvenate the crafts of India.

Rudyard inherited far more from his father than from his mother. Poor Alice had no success in transmitting her musical talent to a boy who admitted near the end of his life that Allah had excluded all music from his 'make-up except the brute instinct for beat, as

---

*In 1908 he described himself as 'a godfearing Christian Atheist', long anticipating Graham Greene's self-identification as a 'Catholic atheist'.

necessary for the manufacture of verse'. But from Lockwood, Rudyard acquired a love of craft skills and the belief that craftsmanship is the essential basis of all great art. 'He treated me always as a comrade,' Kipling recalled in old age, 'and his severest orders were at most suggestions or invitations.' No doubt it was this approach that made his son so receptive to his ideas: the love of animals and France and India; the dislike of Germans and missionaries; the sceptical views on religion and the conservative opinions on politics. Most of Rudyard's tastes and prejudices were in the blood. After his parents died within a few weeks of each other in the winter of 1910–11, he wrote: 'Dear as my mother was, my father was more to me than most men are to their sons: and now that I have no one to talk or write to I find myself desolate.'[10]

At the beginning of his autobiography, *Something of Myself*, Kipling quoted the Jesuits' demand, 'Give me the first six years of a child's life and you can have the rest.' Some time earlier he had told a French admirer that he had lived in Bombay during 'those terrible first years of which the Jesuits know the value'.[11] The implication, that India was the crucial factor in his childhood development, approaches the borders of myth-making. It was influential, of course, much more so than ancestral roots, yet his crucial experience of India did not end when he went to England in his sixth year but started on his return there at the age of 16.

Joseph Rudyard Kipling was born in Bombay on the penultimate day of 1865. His first impressions, he recalled seventy years later, were of 'daybreak, light and colour and golden and purple fruits'. He was in the Bombay market at dawn with his native *ayah*, who used to kneel before Catholic shrines, and a Hindu bearer, who took him into wayside temples. Sometimes they walked to the 'edge of the sea where the Parsees waded in and prayed to the setting or rising sun'.

> Our evening walks were by the sea in the shadow of palm-groves ... When the wind blew the great nuts would tumble, and we fled – my *ayah*, and my sister in her perambulator – to the safety of the open. I have always felt the menacing darkness of tropical eventides, as I have loved the voices of night-winds through palm or banana leaves, and the song of the tree-frogs.

In old age he tried to communicate his infant enthusiasms to a young godson in Bombay. Did he like mangoes? Did he eat sugar-cane? Had he 'tasted red peppers yet on the [plants]? I did once and it made me howl and my Daddy spanked me for it.'[12]

His *ayah* used to remind him to speak English to his parents because, like many Anglo-Indian children, he spent most of his time with servants and spoke Hindustani as his first language. Since he was below the age of Hindu caste restrictions, he could accompany members of the household wherever they went, becoming 'as wise as any native child' about the 'elementary facts of life' and on good terms with 'Hindu deities with garlands round their necks'. Few children remembered their native servants without intense affection. As Kipling's friend Walter Lawrence later recalled, their parents' Indian employees crooned incomparable lullabies, invented endless games and played 'patiently for hours with the *baba log* [the sahib's children], never reproaching them for their desultory, changing moods'.[13]

Such indulgence naturally made the *baba log* rather spoilt and, as one of Lockwood's acquaintances put it, 'badly in need of a basting'. Rudyard's father tried to be more philosophical. 'We are willing slaves to our small emperors,' he wrote, 'feeling that the best we can give them is but poor compensation for the loss of their birthright of English air.'[14]

The Macdonalds were less philosophical when his wife brought their 2½-year-old son to England for the birth of her daughter Alice ('Trix') in 1868. The pampered little sahib with his blue eyes and dark, podgy, strong-jawed face, was loud, aggressive and prone to tantrums. In Bewdley, the village of his maternal grandparents, he walked down the street shouting, 'Out of the way, out of the way, there's an angry Ruddy coming.' One of his aunts called him an 'ill-ordered child', another blamed him for hastening their father's death, and his grandmother complained that he was a 'self-willed rebel'. After several months of disruption, 'screaming tempers' and turning their houses into a 'bear garden', they were happy to see him return to Bombay. His mild and charitable Uncle Fred hoped that Lockwood would become 'very firm with him for dear Alice [is] as wax in his small fists'.[15]

The cure turned out to be firmer than anyone could have intended: Ruddy and Trix were exiled to England at the ages of 5 and 3, and prevented from seeing their mother for over five years and their father for nearly seven. Exiles and separations were usual in Anglo-India, for it was claimed that the climate was unsuitable for children of Rudyard's age. If that had been the only reason, children could have been sent to boarding-schools in the hill stations. But Kipling implied there were other considerations when recalling later that it was thought 'inexpedient and dangerous for a white child to be reared [in India] through youth'.[16] It was 'inexpedient' to create little orientalized pashas coddled by servants, enervated by the climate and thinking of India as 'home'. Expediency required them to be sent to real 'Home', learn austere Victorian virtues and get the stuffing knocked out of them at boarding-school.

The unusual feature in this case is that the Kipling children were not sent to either of their grandmothers or to any of their eight aunts. One of Alice's sisters offered to have Trix, another suggested sharing Rudyard with her brother, but nobody volunteered to have both together or to keep the 'self-willed rebel' all the time. Perhaps Alice was too embarrassed to inflict him on her relations again; perhaps she was reluctant to become dependent on her richer and younger sisters. In any case, insisting that Ruddy and Trix should not be separated, she took them to Southsea on the south coast of England and deposited them at a grim boarding-house. It was a terrible mistake, swiftly compounded by another. In November 1871, after six months in Britain, Alice and Lockwood returned to India without explanation, thus leaving, besides the anguish and loneliness, a sense of uncomprehending betrayal.

The boarding-house, Lorne Lodge, became the House of Desolation in Kipling's memoirs, a place 'smelling of aridity and emptiness' inhabited by a couple called Holloway and their son. Rudyard liked 'Captain' Holloway, a retired midshipman and coastguard officer who took him for walks to look at ships. But the old sailor died midway through the children's Southsea exile, leaving them entirely in the hands of his wife, a tyrant who ran her establishment with the 'full vigour of the Evangelical as revealed to the Woman'. Mrs Holloway reacted to Rudyard, who was doubtless still rude and undisciplined, by beating him at the slightest provocation and ordering him to his bedroom where her son, a bullyboy twice his age, continued the treatment. Once she sent him through the streets to his day school with the placard 'Liar' between his shoulders – a punishment that some authors, despite corroboration by

Trix, have suggested Kipling invented on the grounds that a similar humiliation was inflicted on David Copperfield. But there is no reason why Mrs Holloway should not have read Dickens and been inspired by this imaginative torture. Lord Curzon's governess had been similarly inspired when she made the future Viceroy of India parade around his ancestral village in a conical cap and a calico petticoat with the words 'liar', 'sneak' and 'coward' attached to the costume.[17]

Kipling recalled his five and a half years in the House of Desolation in his autobiography and in 'Baa Baa, Black Sheep', a bitter and harrowing story that understandably upset his parents. He may have exaggerated his degree of abandonment and the relentlessness of his persecution – some Macdonalds did occasionally visit the children at Southsea. But the essence of the narratives is true, and the experience marked Kipling forever. As one acute critic observed, it did not leave him a cruel man but it gave him an 'emotional comprehension of cruelty and an intellectual interest in it'.[18] It must also have been at least partly responsible for his most endearing quality – his deep understanding of the vulnerabilities of children.

Each December Rudyard was allowed to escape Hell and spend a month in Paradise, The Grange in Fulham, where his Aunt Georgy Burne-Jones lived with her Pre-Raphaelite husband. On arrival he had to jump to reach its iron bell-pull, 'a sort of "open sesame" into a House Beautiful', a world of cousins and rocking-horses and 'wonderful smells of paints and turpentine' wafting down from his uncle's studio. He climbed the mulberry tree with his cousins, he listened to his aunt reading Scott or *The Arabian Nights*, he encountered poets and artists all willing to talk to him and play except an 'elderly person called "Browning", who took no proper interest' in the children skirmishing in the hall. Each January Paradise ejected him, and he returned to 'misery and Evangelical brutality and childish fears'. But the bell-pull remained a combination of 'Rosebud' and 'madeleine'. Many years later, when the Burne-Jones family left The Grange, he begged for it to hang on his own front door 'in the hope that other children might also feel happy when they rang it'.[19] It is still at his house at Bateman's.

Rudyard later recognized that the artistic ambience of The Grange had been important to him, even the austere presence of William Morris, the self-absorbed and humourless holder of views that he later came to detest. He adored his Burne-Jones uncle for his warmth, his zest, his 'glorious sense of humour', announcing after his death that Uncle Ned had been a god to him. Infected by their enthusiasms, the small boy loved to hear the two men 'talking and laughing and painting and drawing and playing with coloured glass'. He absorbed their lessons in craftsmanship, applied them later to his own craft and later still passed them on to his mother's sister. Poetry was 'jeweller's work, remember', he told his Aunt Louisa Baldwin, who aspired to write and requested advice; or rather it was 'like grinding diamonds to show the most light in the smallest facet'.[20]

Yet political bitterness at the end of his life made him denigrate Morris, Burne-Jones and their fellow craftsmen. Their influence on interior decoration, he granted, had been salutary; they had arrived in time to destroy a hideous world of horsehair chairs and glossy red lambrequins. All the same, they were essentially 'purveyors of luxuries', dependent on the prosperity of the society that supported them. They opposed wars and defence costs and anything else which threatened that prosperity. They knew nothing about life that did not 'directly touch their own emotions and prettinesses' – and their attitudes consequently 'helped to bring and to continue trouble'. But the reaction had set in years earlier, after his second stint in India, after his exposure to Wilde and the aesthetes in the early 1890s. A scholar, he wrote in 1893, might 'get more pleasure out of his life than an army officer, but only little children believe that a man's life is given him to decorate with pretty little things, as though it were a girl's room or a picture screen'.[21]

Rudyard was too frightened of Mrs Holloway to tell anyone about his maltreatment at her house. But at the beginning of 1877 Georgy Burne-Jones at last noticed what should have been obvious long before: her nephew was miserable, and so blind that he needed strong spectacles. She wrote to tell her sister, who hurried back from India and removed her children from the House of Desolation. Afterwards Alice told her son that, the first time she went up to his room to kiss him goodnight, he 'flung up an arm to guard off the cuff that [he] had been trained to expect'. That was in his memoirs, written (and never revised) at the end of his life. But the boy in 'Baa Baa, Black Sheep', composed only a decade after the experience, admits that not even the fictional Mrs Holloway ('Aunty Rosa') tried to hit him in the dark.

Alice remained in England for nearly four years and was joined by Lockwood for eighteen months in the middle. Contrite and indulgent, she took the children to Epping Forest for the summer, allowing Rudyard to run 'wild as a colt' on a farm with his cousin Stanley, and only drawing the line when he came into the house with boots muddied and bloodied from the farmyard. Later holidays were spent with 'three dear ladies', who lived in Kensington in a house full of books, peace and kindliness. And in the summer of 1878 he was at last reunited with his father, who had returned to Europe to supervise the Indian display at the Paris Exhibition. Lockwood took him to France, gave him a free pass to visit the Trocadero, and helped inculcate a love of French things.

Earlier that year, at the age of 12, Rudyard had gone to boarding-school in Devon. The United Services College at Westward Ho! was a recent foundation intended to attract the sons of naval and military officers who could not afford the fees of the great public schools. But it was not a predictable mid-Victorian establishment. It had no uniforms, no cadet corps and no school chapel; its teachers were not in holy orders; and its headmaster, Cormell Price, was only a reluctant and intermittent flogger. In fact Price was not only good-tempered and liberal but also a friend of Morris and Burne-Jones. Rudyard liked 'Uncle Crom' ('one of my numerous deputy "Uncles"') but, as is the usual fate of schoolteachers, only really appreciated him after he had left the school. Then he came to realize that Price was a '*very* great man' who had done 'miracles on unpromising stuff'. But his own later experiences seem to have affected his memories of the school's ethos. Gratitude to the Headmaster persuaded him to return to the place in 1894 for the 'doleful job' of making a 'funeral speech' at his retirement. 'All that the College', he declared, ' – all that Mr Price – has ever aimed at was to make men able to make and keep empires.'[22] Price must have been surprised. He had also aimed to educate boys.

Rudyard was miserable during his first term. He had been with Alice for nearly a year, he had come to depend on her again, and now he had been sent away once more. He wrote to her constantly – once she received four letters in a single day. 'It is the roughness of the lads he seems to feel most', she wrote in a sensible letter to Price, adding that, as he had a 'great deal that is feminine in his nature … a little sympathy from any quarter will reconcile him to his changed life'.[23]

He became happier when he acquired some rather strange pets – jackdaws, shrews and blindworms – and still more so when he began to appreciate the school's expansive outdoor life, especially swimming in the sea off Pebble Ridge. In *Stalky & Co* he later immortalized (and exaggerated) his japes with Lionel Dunsterville (Stalky), who evolved into a two-dimensional soldier-hero out of John Buchan, and the acidulous George Beresford (M'Turk), who became a photographer and author of a sardonic and unreliable volume, *Schooldays with Kipling*.

Kipling later admitted there had been bullying at the school but 'nothing worse'. On reading the manuscript of *Stalky's Reminiscences* in 1927, he urged Dunsterville to stress the 'amazing "cleanliness"' of 'the Coll' compared to the homosexual 'beastliness' and scandals of more famous schools. He believed that the boys had been 'saved' by Price's policy – 'send us to bed dead tired' – and by the system of 'open dormitories and the masters moving about at all times'. Although in his memoirs he claimed there had been 'no cases of even suspected perversion', he himself had actually been a suspect. When Dunsterville told him in 1886 that their housemaster had made him change dormitories for this reason, he became 'rabidly furious' and wrote an angry letter of denial to another master, W.C.Crofts, his inspirational teacher in English and Latin. He was 'conscious of a deep and personal hatred' of the housemaster whom, in revenge, he was going to put in a novel. Forty years later, long after he had realized he could not write novels, he wrote a short story about a ridiculous master who believed that smoking led to homosexuality.[24] At 'the Coll' Kipling had been an ardent smoker.

Price and Crofts recognized a talent and nurtured it in an infertile environment. Crofts provoked, ridiculed and made his pupil think. The gentler Price encouraged by opportunity: he made Rudyard editor of the school magazine and allowed him the run of his large and diverse library. The boy had learned tardily to read at Southsea: one of his punishments had been learning the Collects and passages from the Bible. Now he read enormously: the English novelists, the American poets, the spread of verse from Chaucer to Matthew Arnold. He also began to write in other men's styles, parodies of Tennyson and Browning, 'unpublished fragments' of Pope and Keats and Shelley. These and other poems so impressed his parents that in India they published a collection, *Schoolboy Lyrics*, without his knowledge. On finding a copy on his return to the Subcontinent, Rudyard was furious and sulked for two days.

While most of his verses are clever and facetious, some aspire to solemnity. 'The Battle of Assaye' is a conventional narrative of Wellington's victory over the Marathas, but 'Ave Imperatrix' presents an unsolved literary puzzle. It is ostensibly a profession of imperial loyalty to Queen Victoria after a lunatic attempt to assassinate her in 1882. That is how it was read at the time, how it has subsequently been read by most people, and how Kipling himself had come to regard it forty years later when he claimed to André Chevrillon that it 'set the key' for the rest of his writings. While the French writer took this to mean that 'Ave Imperatrix' was an anticipation of 'Recessional' and similar work, and that 'the general direction of his life-work was [thus] determined', contemporary evidence suggests that Rudyard may have composed the verses with no high-minded intentions. He and the rest of the school, he told a correspondent, were 'intensely amused' at the assassination attempt – perhaps because it was such a hopeless one – and were 'scarcely loyal and patriotic'. Beresford, who knew that Kipling was then far from being an imperialist, believed the poem had been written 'tongue in cheek'. But probably it was no more a 'loyalist spoof' than a sincere and portentous ode. It was merely Rudyard experimenting with form and expressing views suited to that experiment.[25]

At school and afterwards, he also wrote poems for Florence Garrard, a slender, beautiful girl with 'hair like Rapunzel', who later became an artist. 'Flo' had followed Rudyard as an inmate of the House of Desolation, where she befriended Trix, who had been relatively unharmed by Mrs Holloway and who had returned to Lorne Lodge while her brother was at boarding-school. Although the poet and his muse do not seem to have met very often, 'Flo' inspired more passion in Kipling than any other woman in his life. He was distraught when he lost her photograph and distracted himself by frenetic writing when their 'affair' broke down in 1882. The relationship was naturally chaste and, because Flo was unenthusiastic, never very close. Even so, Rudyard later wrote her poems and letters from India and went to see her on his return to Europe at the end of the decade. As he failed to detect her latent lesbianism, he remained bewildered by her coolness towards him.

Rudyard was not widely popular at Westward Ho! Two subalterns in India, his contemporaries at the school, testified that he had been 'so brilliant and cynical that he was most cordially hated by his fellow students'. A clever and sophisticated boy, who preferred the library to the rugger pitch, was not a natural chum of young hearties preparing for their Indian commissions with the 28th Punjabis, the 54th Sikhs or the 129th Baluchis. Uncomfortable in his presence, they consoled themselves with disparagement. Kipling was a 'bookworm', recalled one of them, 'entirely absorbed in the life of books, unathletic, unsociable, and sad to say – decidedly fat'.[26]

He himself retained happy memories of 'the Coll' and followed the careers of its old boys with sentimental interest. He was delighted to meet them as they passed across India and proud later to discover that so many were in command of native regiments. And he was always glad that the school had concentrated on turning out men who did 'real work' rather than men who wrote about their own thoughts or about other men's work.[27]

In the summer of 1882 'Crom' Price told him he would be going to Lahore in the autumn to work as a journalist. Expense ruled out a university education, and bad eyesight eliminated a more physical profession. Lockwood, who had been with his son for only a few months in the last eleven years, was anxious to find him work in Lahore, a city he loved and to which he had moved in 1865 to become Principal of the Mayo School of Industrial Arts and Curator of the city's museum. He contacted a newspaper proprietor in India, an interview was arranged with the schoolboy in London, and the offer of a job soon followed.

The opportunity of work and family unity were reasons enough to bring Rudyard to Lahore, but Lockwood had another motive: the safeguarding of his son's morals. The Punjabi capital was the best place for him, he told a confidante, because there were 'no music-hall ditties to pick up, no young persons to philander about with, and a great many other negatives of the most wholesome description'. Everything that made Lahore 'so profoundly dull' made it 'safe for young people'. Like Rudyard with his own son many years later, the normally broad-minded Lockwood was desperate to preserve his boy's virginity.[28]

2

A Newsman in Lahore

———————◆———————

IN OCTOBER 1882, after an absence of eleven years, Rudyard returned to the city of his birth. The sights and smells of his childhood were so familiar that he found himself speaking sentences in Hindustani, although he could not remember their meaning. He visited Bombay only once more in his lifetime but he always regarded it as the finest of Indian cities – 'the queen of all' as he wrote in *Kim* – more beautiful even than Lucknow.

A few days later he travelled by train to Lahore, dismaying his mother with a display of side-whiskers that she immediately removed – though he was permitted to grow them back. Perhaps she was alarmed by his very adult appearance. He was only 16 yet, even if his eyebrows and moustache were not as large or as bristling as they later became, he looked many years older. The most notable feature of his head was the combination of prominent chin and receding forehead: one friend in India remembered him dashing about 'with his protruding cleft chin out-thrust, as though it were leading him'.[1] Intense blue eyes penetrated through thick-lensed spectacles that misted over when he laughed, and his skin was sufficiently dark to provoke a rumour that his real father was an Indian. Suspecting that he owed his pigment to the Macdonalds, he once playfully asked his mother to shake out her family tree to dislodge 'the nigger in the woodpile'.[2]

Rudyard was happy to live in his parents' bungalow, which was dustier than others in this very dusty city because his parents refused to have a garden that might attract disease-carrying insects. There he had a room of his own, a servant, a groom, a horse and cart, and in hot weather at least one punkah-wallah. He was also happy with his parents' company, enjoying once more their contrasting styles, his mother 'all Celt and three-parts fire' with a caustic and quick-moving wit, his father 'with his sage Yorkshire outlook and wisdom' and a slower, quizzical, sometimes cynical sense of humour.[3] In old age Kipling claimed that there was no friction between any of them, and the evidence suggests that, while Lockwood was irritated by his wife's occasional disenchantment with India, they were a contented and self-sufficient unit – especially when Trix returned from England in December 1883 to reform what they called 'the Family Square'. Rudyard seldom had a serious disagreement with either of his parents, though Alice complained about her adolescent son's moods, his untidiness and his graceless social manners. She also chaffed him for being self-centred and uninterested in anyone but himself.

Shortly after his arrival in Lahore, Kipling began work as assistant editor of the *Civil and Military Gazette*, a sister newspaper of the larger and very profitable *Pioneer* at Allahabad. Although the *Gazette* had a tiny circulation and operated at a loss (profits were made from its printing press), it enjoyed considerable prestige because it was the only daily paper in the Punjab and was read by the Lieutenant-Governor. Some seventy Indians worked under Kipling, physically producing each issue, but he represented, as he put it, 50 per cent of the editorial staff. The other 50 per cent consisted of the editor, Stephen Wheeler, a peevish and disgruntled individual who left his assistant in no doubt that his job was to subedit other men's work and not to indulge his fantasies of becoming a poet. Kipling therefore embarked on a dutiful routine of précis-writing, proof-reading, preparing telegrams for the press and other kinds of scissors-and-paste work. After performing these tasks with sufficient competence, he was allowed to write a few reviews and editorial notes, and at Christmas, when Wheeler fell off his pony and concussed himself, he briefly took over the newspaper.

Kipling's working hours, originally from ten in the morning until a quarter past four, quickly expanded as he took on more work. Soon he was spending at least ten hours a day on the job, often returning to the office after dinner and receiving visits from the printer on Sundays. Like most other Anglo-Indians, he took exercise in the early mornings, especially in the hot weather, cantering down to the racecourse on a roan stallion called Joe, a former cavalry horse that Lockwood had given him. He attempted to play polo and to shoot partridge, but he did not excel at either sport. He derived more pleasure from his dogs, a bull-terrier and then a fox-terrier, the two most popular breeds of Anglo-India. The fox-terrier was an essential part of his routine, waking him to share chota hazri (the early morning snack), breakfast and the inside of the day's post, accompanying her master in his victoria to the office, where she slept, returning home in the evening for a rat hunt and a saucer of milk, before going out again with the coachman to take Kipling to dinner and later retrieve him from the Club. From his tone of voice, she always knew whether to throw herself into his lap and 'croon' or whether a nap under his chair was 'the sounder policy'.

In the cold weather Kipling sometimes played tennis in the Lawrence Gardens, where the British community used to congregate and dance in the Montgomery Hall before dinner. During the summer months, when his parents were in the hills and the civil 'station' was reduced to eleven people, he drank iced drinks in the Hall before the 'terribly dull ceremony' of dinner in the Punjab Club where a few desiccated bachelors ate 'meals of no merit among men whose merits they knew well'.[1] In that inexorable season everyone felt bored, unwell and disinclined to talk about anything except his particular work. Kipling sometimes stayed for a game of whist or billiards and then went home to bed.

Most of his social life was confined to Simla, the summer capital of the Raj, which he visited each year except 1884 when the family went to Dalhousie. Lahore winters supplied him with some dancing and the opportunity to participate in amateur theatricals. More congenially, his membership of a masonic lodge enabled him to meet men of different religions on an equal footing: his 'brethren' there included members of the Islamic, Sikh, Christian and Jewish religions.*

---

*Kipling was never a very active mason, either in India or later. But he appreciated Freemasonry for its sense of brotherhood and its egalitarian attitude to diverse faiths and classes.

In the hot weather the only respites from the Hall and the Club were moonlit picnics in the Shalimar Gardens, a paradise of exquisite terraces laid out by the Mughal Emperor, Shah Jehan, the builder of the Taj Mahal. Kipling, who was the host on one of these occasions, found the setting quintessentially romantic: a full moon illuminating sheets of still water and inlaid marble colonnades, while acres of night-blooming flowers scented the air and his female guests began to sing, their voices coming 'across the water like the voices of spirits'. The scene reminded him of Tennyson's description of the garden of the Princess Ida.[5]

Kipling hoped that the setting, which contained a dak bungalow often occupied by couples on their honeymoon, might ignite some great love affair, for the adolescent wanted to be a romantic figure with passionate longings. He often claimed to be in love or to be falling in love, but it seems unlikely that he ever was, either then or later on. Sometimes the claims were jocular – he had fallen, he announced in an article, 'deeply and irrevocably in love with a Burmese girl'; sometimes they were self-delusion – nothing came of his fixations with 'a golden haired beauty' glimpsed in a window in Mussorie and a chaplain's daughter with 'the face of an angel, the voice of a dove and the step of the fawn'.[6] And sometimes they seem to have been pure invention. For weeks he sent a female friend bulletins of his unrequited love for a woman he referred to as 'My Lady' but, unless she was a concealed means of describing his affection for the unwitting recipient, she seems to have been imaginary.[7] The significance of these and other declarations lies not so much in their unreality as in Kipling's need to make them.

His inability to fall in love with women would be explicable if a previous biographer's allegations of homosexuality could be sustained.[8] But the evidence for the case, based almost entirely on a later friendship in London, is meagre. Besides, even if Kipling's Indian love life was non-existent, he appears to have had some sexual encounters, probably with prostitutes. In one letter to a friend he observed that neither of them could 'put aside the occasional woman which is good for health and the softening of ferocious manners'. And some exiguous notes in a diary he kept in 1885 suggest that a visit to a brothel had left him terrified that he had caught a venereal infection.[9]

The hot weather reached Lahore in April, sending Alice and Trix to the hills and the thermometer up to 108 degrees in the shade. Each year Kipling experienced that 'sinking feeling when the heat shuts in and the women folk go off'. Although he always joined them for a time, he returned alone to the 'utter desolation' of a 'plains station' in August and September. By employing several men on the punkah and keeping them contented with sticky sweet cakes, he usually managed to maintain his bedroom under 90 degrees, but he was often ill with fever, prickly heat and stomach cramps, which he tried to combat with opium. Sometimes, when it was too hot to sleep, he became a noctambulist, wandering the alleys and bazaars of the old city, that 'prodigious brick honeycomb' as Lockwood described it, dropping in at opium dens and gambling haunts, strolling with Indians or listening to the 'long yarns' they spun in the men's quarters of their homes. At dawn he found a carriage that smelt of jasmine, sandalwood and hookah fumes, and came home quizzing the driver about the native life of the city. He became fascinated by opium and later visited a factory to learn how it was made. The drug, he maintained, was 'an excellent thing in itself' and in moderation was beneficial for Indians because it worked as both a guard against fever and a stimulus for hard work.[10]

Lahore in Kipling's time was an Anglican see (the brick and sandstone cathedral was built in the 1880s), the site of a large army cantonment, and the capital of a province of British India. Yet its population of 150,000 (excluding the native and European soldiers in the barracks at Mian Mir) contained only 1,200 Britons. A majority of the city's inhabitants were Muslims, but there was a substantial minority of Hindus and a small community of Sikhs.

Lahore had been under British rule for barely a generation. Before 1849 it had been the capital of a powerful but short-lived Sikh empire, and before that it had been, with Agra and Delhi, one of the three great Mughal cities. In the 1880s the principal landmarks were still the monuments of the last four Mughal emperors, the fort of Akbar and Shah Jehan, the mausoleum of Jahangir and the Badshahi Mosque of Aurangzeb. The taste of Lahore's most recent conquerors was poorly represented – apart from the 'Mughal-Gothic' Government College, the best British buildings had not yet been constructed – and the civil station was still a raw and dusty place, its unwatered streets lined by squat brick bungalows and ugly tamarisks. The military station at Mian Mir was even worse: hot, dusty and unhealthy (it had been constructed on and among old graveyards), it was one of the most unpopular cantonments in India.

Lahore's province, the Punjab, was, apart from Lower Burma, the newest in British India. At the time it included the North-West Frontier as well as the traditional features of a frontier existence: a strong military contingent, a shortage of Englishwomen, and a habit of frequently transferring officials to new posts. The senior men in the administration saw themselves as descendants of the generation that had pacified the Punjab and then kept it loyal during the Indian Mutiny of 1857: the Lawrence brothers – Henry who died at Lucknow, John who became Viceroy – and the legendary figures of Herbert Edwardes and John Nicholson (who was killed storming the walls of Delhi). Pre-Mutiny traditions survived, especially the belief that officials should be mobile and travel light, living alone on a camp bed and ruling from the saddle rather than from a desk or a textbook. On learning that one district officer had brought out a piano, John Lawrence vowed to 'smash' it for him: the wretched man was subsequently transferred five times in two years.[11]

Yet if the style of the old days lingered, the quality of administration had declined. Lord Curzon, who became Viceroy in 1899, criticized the Punjab Government for being an instrument of obstruction and procrastination on frontier matters and its officials for being ignorant of the tribes and ill-equipped to handle them. Its five previous Lieutenant-Governors had visited the Frontier so seldom that their inexperience, which was shared by the chief secretaries and other officials, led to delays and indecisiveness in an area which usually required prompt action.[12] Lord George Hamilton, the Secretary of State for India, agreed with him. For many years, he said, the Punjab had been the 'spoilt child of India', its civil service trading on the reputations of Nicolson, Edwardes and the Lawrences. But in recent times it had produced hardly anyone of 'exceptional ability or strength of character', and its officials carried out their frontier duties in a 'wooden and unintelligent spirit'.[13]

The officials of the Indian Civil Service (ICS) with whom Kipling dined at the Punjab Club belonged to the group criticized by Curzon and Hamilton. In his memoirs Kipling referred to them and their colleagues in other Government services as 'picked men at their definite work' who talked 'shop', gave him a taste for technical knowledge – and sometimes bored him. At the time they struck him as people who were always either working or thinking and talking about working: most of them were tired and discontented, with no leisure or enthusiasm for anything. In a private verse from 1884 he wrote:

> Who is the Public I write for?
> Men 'neath an Indian sky
> Cynical, seedy and dry,
> Are these then the people I write for?
> No, not I.[14]

And yet they were. ICS officers (known as Civilians), engineers, forestry officials, men who built bridges and canals, doctors of the Indian Medical Service – these were the men he encountered in the Club and who read his work in the *Gazette*. They were not an ideal audience: ill health, overwork and disillusionment had robbed many, especially the older men, of the inclination to read much beyond official reports. Young Civilians were different. Fresh from Oxford, they brought out books and, in a doomed effort to stay in touch with their previous lives, besought friends and former tutors to send out new literary works. But this passion was usually quenched by middle age, so that they came to resemble their predecessors, 'cynical, seedy and dry'. The wife of one Civilian in the Punjab complained that their compatriots in India could not forgive the couple because they read books, they avoided club gossip, and her husband had gone to Eton (an unusual nursery for ICS officers). Another Civilian observed that if Shakespeare had been writing for an Anglo-Indian public, he would have earned barely enough to pay for his pen-nibs.[15]

It is difficult to assess Kipling's degree of unpopularity at the Club. A bumptious, opinionated teenage journalist was unlikely to be appreciated by men who had just spent the monsoon repairing a bridge over the Indus. Yet, considering the drawbacks of age, personality and profession, surprisingly few incidents of active hostility have been recorded: an elderly Civilian who snubbed him, a couple of men who once threw him out of the building, and a young officer who wanted to 'thrash' him for his rudeness but was restrained by other members.[16] The only example of general animosity came one evening in 1883 when he was hissed by everyone in the Club dining-room. Asking the reason, he was told that his 'dam' rag [had] ratted over the [Ilbert] Bill' – that is, it had supported an unpopular Government measure. Kipling was not responsible for the *Gazette*'s position – he seldom wrote the leading articles and was scarcely consulted on the editorial line – but he did not come out well from the evening's sequel either in his writings at the time or in his memoirs where he misrepresented the nature of the Bill and unfairly ascribed the paper's 'ratting' to one of its proprietors' desire for a knighthood.[17]

The Ilbert Bill, named after Courtenay Ilbert, a lawyer and Oxford Fellow who had recently joined the Viceroy's Council, was one of the liberalizing measures of Lord Ripon, whom Gladstone had sent out with vague instructions to promote greater Indian participation in the running of the country. Ripon, the son of a most unremarkable Prime Minister, Lord Goderich, was a Roman Catholic convert with ministerial experience at the India Office in the 1860s. Earnest and high-minded, yet cautious and verbose, he was a zealous though not energetic proponent of reform in the Subcontinent. Like Gladstone, Morley and others of their brand of Victorian liberalism, he was unable to formulate a clear aim or a final destination for his party's policy in India. For the time being it was enough to be liberal and tolerant, to avoid wars and to foster some kind of political consciousness among educated and Westernized Indians. 'I get more Radical every day', wrote Ripon, 'and am rejoiced to say that the effect of despotic power has so far been to strengthen and deepen my liberal convictions.'[18] The Viceroy's increasingly radical tone sometimes provoked consternation in London as well as in Anglo-India. His Government's Resolution on extending local self-rule, which referred to 'that desire and capacity for self-government which all intelligent and fairly educated men may safely be assumed to possess', certainly encouraged educated Indians to believe that they also possessed them.[19]

Neither the Viceroy nor his Council nor the provincial governors foresaw serious problems with the Ilbert Bill, which was designed to correct an anomaly in the legal system. Until 1872 all British-born subjects facing criminal charges had been tried in the High Courts of the Presidency towns (Bombay, Madras and Calcutta); in that year the Criminal Procedure Code was amended so that they could be tried in their own provinces by British sessions judges and district magistrates;

and in 1877 the restrictions on Indian magistrates trying British subjects in the Presidency towns were removed. By 1883, when a few Indians in the ICS were reaching the ranks of sessions judge and district magistrate, it was logical to end the discrimination that prevented them trying British subjects outside the three major cities.

But it was not logical to Anglo-India, especially when Ilbert, a conscientious liberal, proposed to extend such jurisdiction to a broader category of Civilians, Indian as well as British. The non-official community was universally indignant. The Calcutta Bar, already incensed by a reduction in judicial salaries, started the agitation, its barristers denouncing the proposals in the city's main newspaper, the *Englishman*, and in the columns of the London *Times*. Businessmen joined in: banks and shops were closed, protest meetings were held and a Defence Association was quickly organized. Outrage in the countryside stemmed mainly from planters, especially the tea growers of Assam, a rough and rapacious body of men who habitually maltreated their coolies in the knowledge that they would be dealt with leniently by British magistrates. Now they contemplated the unwelcome possibility of a coolie bringing a trumped-up charge against his employer, the Indian magistrate believing it, and the planter going to jail.

Among officials the Bill had some support, especially in the higher ranks, but almost everywhere else the cry went up that the liberties of British subjects were at risk, that business investment was being threatened and – most emotive of all, designed to resurrect memories of the Cawnpore massacres of 1857 – that the Englishwoman was in danger. If Hindus kept their women in purdah and in virtual slavery – so ran the argument – they should not be in a position to judge free white women.

The Kiplings participated in the general hysteria. Even Lockwood, usually the most phlegmatic of men, regarded Ripon as a 'terrible calamity' and claimed that his replacement the following year prevented 'poor Anglo-India' from going 'crazy with vexation and apprehension'.[20] Rudyard himself, who was only 17, was implacable, telling his former Headmaster that he could not write calmly about the Bill and warning him that race feeling was running high enough to provoke an uprising.[21] In his memoirs he reflected the panic and repeated the prejudice of half a century before. The Bill had been introduced by Ripon, 'a circular and bewildered recluse of religious tendencies', because it was 'a matter of principle that Native Judges should try white women' despite the fact that most judges were Hindus whose 'idea of women [was] not lofty'.[22]

The Viceroy was astonished and upset by the vehemence of the opposition. Allergic to any form of confrontation, he refused to force the measure through the Legislative Council. Instead he dithered, wondering how to modify the Bill, gaining time by asking the provincial governments for their views, hoping desperately that the Secretary of State and the House of Commons would relieve him of the problem and solve it themselves. In March 1883, as Ripon left Calcutta for Simla in search of a compromise that would placate Anglo-India, Kipling published a poem in the *Gazette* suggesting that the British community considered him an ass who was running away from his responsibilities.[23] By the end of the year, after feverish discussions in the Viceroy's Council, a compromise had been found, though it was heavily weighted in favour of the opposition. Ilbert's more far-reaching proposals were dropped and, while the principle of Indian magistrates trying British subjects was maintained, it was largely negated in practice by the concession that the accused could insist on trial by a jury, at least half of whose members would be British.

In spite of this victory, Kipling continued his denunciation of Ripon. In September 1884, when the Viceroy announced his retirement (so that another Liberal could be appointed before the next general election), he published 'Lord Ripon's Reverie', a parody of Tennyson's 'Locksley Hall' containing attacks on two of his favourite future targets, Liberal politics and Bengali babus.* Accusing the departing Viceroy of 'playing skittles' with men's rights, Kipling mocked his impractical idealism:

> There I sketched my swart Utopia, nourishing the Babu's pride
> On the fairy-tales of justice – with a leaning to his side.

A year later, on learning that Ripon had made a speech in England appealing to the people of India to vindicate his administration, Kipling turned more savage, calling him 'Pedantry set on the throne'

---

*A babu is a clerk in Hindustani, but Anglo-Indians also used the term, often disparagingly, when referring to middle-class Hindus with some English education.

and asserting that, by failing to make the natives richer or to 'charm black want' from their fields, he had done nothing for India. His legacy had merely been unrest and racial tension:

This was his 'policy', – turmoil and babble and ceaseless strife,
Seeds of dissension to sprout when the sower's name is forgot.

('A Lost Leader')

In the spring of 1886 Kipling became abusive in prose, insulting the former Viceroy in the *Gazette* by calling him 'an unmitigated bore – a rhetorician whom it would be gross flattery to call sophisticated'.[24] And in 'The Head of the District', a story written some years later, he turned to sarcasm, referring to Ripon (though without naming him) as 'the Very Greatest of All the Viceroys', whose administration was based on principles that must be enforced at all times, and who decided to appoint a timorous Bengali to take charge of a rough tribal district on the North-West Frontier. The vendetta was an early example of Kipling's capacity for sustained hatred of people repre-senting a cause he disliked. It was also a manifestation of one of his most unpleasing characteristics – his almost total inability to forgive.

Ripon was not the only Liberal target of his acerbic pen. In one issue of the *Gazette* in 1887, Kipling mocked Sir Mountstuart Grant Duff, the outgoing Governor of Madras and a former Liberal MP, as a 'discredited failure' who was proof of the 'extreme necessity of giving bloated presidencies'* governors from the ICS; and in the next he jeered at the distinguished Civilian, Henry Cotton, for comparing Burmese resistance to British forces to 'Hereward of old in the Fens of Lincolnshire' holding out against the Norman conquerers.[25]

Most of Kipling's contributions, however, were less derisive. In fact the bulk of his work on the paper remained mechanical: proof-reading, dealing with the printer, cutting down unwieldy articles on questions of Revenue and Assessment delivered by a long-winded Civilian. Everything in the *Gazette* between the end of the leading article and the beginning of the advertisements was his responsibil-ity. Most of his writing took the form of 'scraps', short items describ-ing events or commenting on issues in the news. His editor once

---

*That is Madras and Bombay, whose governors, like the Viceroy himself, were political appointments.

complained that he was averse to routine and idle about producing 'scraps', but this is not borne out by his diaries, his letters, his large crammed cuttings books or the testimony of Wheeler's successor. A diary entry for a January weekend in 1885 records that, although he felt 'abominably seedy and queer in the head', Kipling not only wrote 'scraps' on Formosa, Calcutta and a ploughing match in Madras but even visited the Lahore Serai to see if he could find anything else to write about.[26]

Without proper reporters and with very limited foreign news, he had to find a great many things to write about simply to fill up the paper. The topics of his 'scraps' were a mixture of the serious and the frivolous, ranging from accidents on Indian railways to a horse fair in Jallalabad to the vegetarianism of Allan Octavian Hume, the ornithologist, former ICS officer and organizer of the Indian National Congress. Sometimes he produced items on France and Russia, the two European empires with territories closest to India. But his favourite subjects, which he brought up again and again in his 'scraps' and which became minor crusades for him, were Indian political claims (especially in Bengal), the failings of various municipalities (especially with regard to sanitation), and the iniquities of certain Hindu customs, especially child marriage and its usual unfortunate consequences, widowhood and prostitution.*

After a couple of years in the job, Kipling was allowed to publish more literary work so long as he continued to fulfil his editorial duties and produce the requisite number of 'scraps'. He had a lot of hack writing still to do – reviewing amateur theatricals, describing a fancy dress ball (and listing the costumes worn by each guest), reporting the results of race meetings at Ascot and Goodwood (places he had never been to, hosting a sport he cared nothing about) – but in the course of 1884 and 1885 a number of his poems, stories and comic sketches appeared in the *Gazette*. So too did some long descriptive articles on Indian subjects such as municipal elections in Lahore, the city's milk supply and the disgusting conditions in which it was produced, and the religious festivals of the Muslim and Hindu communities.

About once a year Wheeler allowed him to act as a special correspondent reporting an important public event outside Lahore. These

---

*Kipling's attitudes to these issues are discussed in Chapter 4.

expeditions gave him a taste for travel that eventually took him to all the world's continents and across almost every major sea. It was 'good beyond expression', he wrote later, 'to see the sun rise upon a strange land and to know that you have only to go forward and possess that land – that it will dower you before the day is ended with a hundred new impressions and, perhaps, one idea'.[27] His first excursion was to Patiala, a Sikh native state hosting a viceregal visit, where he was offered an elephant to ride and a bribe (which he angrily rejected) to write nice things about the Patiala Government. But however decadent the place, he enjoyed 'the blaze of jewels and colour' which showed him what India had once been.

In subsequent years he went to Amritsar for the horse fair at the Diwali festival, to Ajmer in Rajputana for the opening of Mayo College, and to Jammu for the installation of the Maharaja of Kashmir. But his most important assignment came in 1885 when he attended a durbar in Rawalpindi held by the new Viceroy, Lord Dufferin, for Abdur Rahman, the Amir of Afghanistan. Although largely ceremonial in intent, the meeting assumed political importance because it coincided with a crisis on the very indistinct frontier between Afghanistan and the Russian Empire. Dufferin was initially bellicose and, heedless of Britain's history of disasters in Kabul, talked of marching through Afghanistan and confronting the Russians in Herat. He was supported by some Civilians as well as by army officers eager to do something virile to efface the humiliating memory of Khartoum where General Gordon had recently been killed. But conflict was averted. Dufferin cooled down, the Amir indicated little concern for the bit of land occupied by Russia, and the governments in London and St Petersburg showed no inclination to fight.

It was a testing period for the young correspondent desperate to find subjects about which to write: while incessant rain limited his range, the Amir's delayed arrival obliged him to conjure copy from elsewhere – eventually he was able to muster thirteen very padded articles. After waiting for the Amir in Rawalpindi, Kipling went up to Peshawar and had a glimpse of the Khyber Pass, his sole experience of the frontier that later featured in several of his stories. In his memoirs he recalled that he had been shot at in the Khyber, but this must have been a trick of memory; a contemporary letter reveals that he was threatened by an Afghan with a knife.[28]

In 1886 Wheeler took five months' leave and in the following year he left the *Gazette* altogether. His replacement was Edward Kay Robinson, a more congenial character who believed Wheeler had done his best to turn his assistant into a 'sound second-rate journalist'. Ten years later Kipling reminded Wheeler how he had suffered 'no end of a gruelling' for four years but conceded it had done 'a heap of good' to his self-discipline. Even so, he was delighted by the change of editor. Robinson appreciated his enthusiasm, his writing and his knowledge of the castes and religions of India; he also left a memorable portrait of his assistant splashing so much ink about that in summer, clad in a thin vest and white cotton trousers, he resembled a Dalmatian dog.[29] Told by the proprietors 'to put sparkle' into the paper, the two Englishmen set about changing its appearance and its contents. The most notably sparkling new items were Kipling's verses and fiction; at the end of 1886 a series of stories, printed under the title 'Plain Tales from the Hills', began to appear in the paper.

Even before becoming editor of the *Gazette*, Robinson had recognized his assistant's talents and advised him to go to Britain where he could win fame and perhaps wealth. But although Kipling often pined for England, writing with nostalgia about Putney and Kensington and the Sussex Downs, he did not want to abandon India or his career there. The country may have been hot and unhealthy, but his family and friends and interests were all there. He loved India, he told Robinson, and was 'deeply interested in the queer ways and works of the people of the land'. He liked to 'hunt and rummage' among them, especially in Lahore, 'that wonderful, dirty, mysterious ant hill', a city he knew 'blind fold' and which he loved to wander through 'like Haroun Al-Raschid in search of strange things'. Robinson, he thought, should eventually return to Fleet Street, where he had worked on the *Globe*, but he himself needed to stay in his 'own place' where he found 'heat and smells of oil and spices, and puffs of temple incense, and sweat, and darkness, and dirt and lust and cruelty, and, above all, things wonderful and fascinating innumerable'.[30]

3

The Anglo-Indian Chronicle

─────────────◆─────────────

IN THE HEAT of Lahore Kipling day-dreamed of his month in Simla, planning idle days smoking cheroots, lying in the sun and sleeping under two thick blankets. He longed to be up there in the Himalayas, 7,000 feet above sea level, among the cliffs and deodar forests and great 'grass-downs swelling like a woman's breasts', where the 'wind across the grass, and the rain among the deodars say, "Hush-hush-hush".' Eventually the day came that began in heat and discomfort in a train and ended in the cool of the evening with a wood fire in his bedroom and the assurance that his mother would bring him a cup of tea in the morning.[1]

Simla, strung out along a narrow ridge with bazaars dropping from its side and mountains in every direction, was the summer capital for both the Indian Government and the Punjab. Like Lahore, it was going through an extensive phase of construction in the 1880s, erecting the Town Hall and the Ripon Hospital, two vast new offices for the Army and the Civil Secretariat − structures ugly enough to remind people of warehouses in Liverpool − and the neo-Elizabethan Viceregal Lodge on Observatory Hill. Most viceroys and senior officials, obliged to spend half the year there, disliked Simla. Curzon complained that he felt isolated not only from the world but even from India; he might almost have been living in a German spa. His chief objection, however, was the monotony of living six months on a single hilltop chained to a sort of middle-class suburb where cultural interests had been 'sterilised by the arid breath of a semi-court and purely official existence'.[2]

Yet the place was much loved by Civilians who had spent the previous eleven months in remote districts and who needed a holiday of revels and recreation with their compatriots. As a young Punjabi Civilian, Walter Lawrence regarded Simla society as 'the brightest, wittiest and most refined community' he had ever known; but when he returned in middle age in the viceregal entourage, he felt disinclined to take part in its rowdy and frivolous 'high jinks'.[3] Being a very young man, Kipling was naturally susceptible to 'high jinks', and he spent his first leave at picnics, dances and theatricals, flirting 'with the bottled up energy of a year' and claiming implausibly to have left 'the lacerated fragments' of his heart with 'half a dozen girls'. It was comforting to feel cut off from the plains, just as it was amusing as well as reassuring to see a senior Civilian 'tobogganing' down the staircase of the Simla Club on a table top. He spent much of his time riding along the Mall, usually with an older woman because he did not want to risk 'entangling alliances' with girls. According to a confidante, his lack of money and his 'grimy trade' did not suit the matrimonial plans of their mothers.[4]

In the summer of 1885 Kipling spent several months in Simla as special correspondent of the *Gazette*. As his principal duty was to report the highlights of the 'season', he was ordered by his proprietors to improve his dancing. He did so, acquiring in the process a passion for waltzing, but he soon tired of the role of '*chroniqueur* of a Gay Season in the hills': the 'best way to sicken a youth of frivolity', he thought, was to pitch him into the thick of it and make him write descriptions of every dance and 'frivol'. Fortunately he was allowed to write about other subjects, urging the authorities to install a proper sewage system and even questioning the whole purpose of Simla. Much as he loved the place, he doubted whether any other nation would have pitched its seat of government a hundred miles from a railway, 'on the wrong side of an irresponsible river' and liable – with the collaboration of a steady downpour and the mildest of earthquakes – to be cut off from the land it ruled as effectively as if 'separated by a month's sea voyage'.[5] As in Lahore, he thoroughly explored the bazaar, describing it in *Kim* as a rabbit warren in which 'a man who knows his way . . . can defy all the police of India's summer capital, so cunningly does veranda communicate with veranda, alley-way with alley-way, and bolt-hole with bolt-hole'.

Much of the pleasure of Simla was derived from the reassembling of the Family Square, though Kipling found it so difficult to work in the same room as his father that he sometimes stayed with one of the *Gazette*'s proprietors. But the main problem for him and Lockwood was the menace of Trix's admirers attempting 'to smash' the Square. Rudyard adored his pretty and spirited sister, whom he called 'the Maiden', but he admitted he was 'savage' to other men who also adored her. One suitor, who made the mistake of confessing his feelings to him, was dispatched with an 'exceedingly unpleasant' letter. Another, Captain Jack Fleming of the Queen's Own Scottish Borderers, proved more obdurate. He was disliked by Kipling, who tried to obstruct the match, and by Lockwood, who regarded him as a 'disturber of domestic peace, separator of companions and terminator of tranquillity'.[6] They had good grounds for their opposition, recognizing that the couple were temperamentally incompatible, but the relationship stuttered along, interrupted by a broken engagement, and culminated in a marriage that was unhappy and childless.

Before Trix became embroiled in amorous crises, she collaborated with her brother in literary projects. At Dalhousie in 1884, where social life was duller than at Simla, they wrote a collection of verses printed later that year by the *Gazette* press under the title *Echoes*. The contents, mainly written by Rudyard, were mostly clever and mildly witty parodies of Browning, Swinburne and other senior poets of the period. More interesting was the volume produced at the end of the following year on which their parents also co-operated. Entitled '*Quartette: The Christmas Annual of the Civil & Military Gazette* by Four Anglo-Indian writers', it includes Rudyard's most remarkable early story, 'The Strange Ride of Morrowbie Jukes', a powerful and harrowing tale illustrating the vulnerability of the Englishman when he strayed beyond the protection of Anglo-India.

The Kiplings did not rank very highly in the hierarchy of Simla society until Lord Dufferin put them on his hospitality list, a policy soon followed by General Roberts, the Commander-in-Chief of the Indian Army, and by the Lieutenant-Governor of the Punjab. Dufferin frequently dropped in at the Kiplings' house for tea and a visit to their sketching-room, where his daughter attended Lockwood's class. He enjoyed talking to her tutor about art and to

Alice about anything – 'Dullness and Mrs Kipling cannot exist in the same room', he once said; he also appreciated their son's verses, praising his combination of satire and delicacy as well his ear for rhythm and cadence. Completing the Dufferin admiration for the Kiplings, the Viceroy's son, Lord Clandeboye, became so enamoured of Trix that he had to be sent home.[7]

Lord Dufferin was far from being Kipling's ideal administrator. The most indolent of all viceroys ('a dead lazy fellow' according to one member of his Council), he had charm, humour and a vanity that he usually managed to conceal. He enjoyed Simla for its parties, even its fancy dress balls, and made twice-daily visits to inspect the construction in progress at Viceregal Lodge. For Kipling, who once observed that a certain woman was as 'sincerely insincere as Lord Dufferin',[8] he had several other drawbacks: he was a Liberal (though not a zealot like Ripon), he neglected domestic issues for foreign affairs, and he sympathized with the early aims of the Indian National Congress. In his favour he had nothing of the pedant or the preacher about him, he conquered and annexed Upper Burma, and he had a wife who set up a fund, for which Kipling wrote some verses, to supply female medical advice to Indian women.* But it was probably the family connection that spared him from the rather spiteful satire directed at his predecessor and some of his colleagues. On his departure Kipling wrote a long poem, 'One Viceroy Resigns', a dramatic monologue in the style of Browning and reminiscent in tone of 'Bishop Blougram's Apology'. It is a clever work, written as Dufferin's reflections on his rule and advice to his successor (Lord Lansdowne), but it contains some curious and derogatory lines about both Congress and Indians ('You'll never plumb the Oriental Mind, / And if you did, it isn't worth the toil'). As Harold Nicolson rightly pointed out, Kipling did not 'accurately reflect the habits, manners or phraseology of the proconsul whom he was describing'.[9] The views expressed belonged more to Kipling than to Dufferin.

The young journalist had complained that it was 'the dullest of dull things to be *chroniqueur*' of the Simla season for the press. But it soon dawned on him that it would not be at all dull to be the *chroniqueur* of Anglo-India both in fiction and in verse. The position was vacant – it almost always had been vacant – and Kipling was well placed to fill it.

---

*See below, p. 61.

Anglo-India had produced a handful of weak novelists, some mediocre satirists, and Sir Alfred Lyall, one of the ablest Civilians in the history of the ICS. Lyall was an anthropologist, a historian and a poet who, believing that Anglo-India could produce neither a writer nor an audience, devoted his best verses ('Land of Regrets') to the homesickness of the exiles abroad. But in any case Kipling was better fitted for the role: he did not share Lyall's self-doubt or his ability to see both sides of a question; and his versatility allowed him to write in various styles and with various voices so that he could chronicle Anglo-India as effectively with light satire as with smoking-room realism.

All his life Kipling was able to move easily between different classes within different nationalities. As one observer remarked, he talked equally well to a scientist and a judge of the High Court.[10] And the Viceroy's partiality for his family certainly gave him the chance to extend his knowledge of gossip in high places. Soon after one of his arrivals in the hills, he spent an afternoon loping alongside his mother's rickshaw learning 'most of the scandal in Simla'. One friend thought him rather blatant in his continual quest of copy. From a Mrs Napier, who was cynical and lied 'like a fiend', he acquired 'some first class material'; from Sir Edward Buck, a senior Civilian, he heard 'many curious yarns' about the machinery of government; from an official in the Finance Department he expected to be supplied with 'goodish material', and from Mrs Burton, the effervescent Simla lady who inspired the fictional Mrs Hauksbee, he gained 'half a hundred ideas and some stories'.[11] When Lieutenant Beames of the 19th Bengal Infantry confessed he was in love, Kipling scented a story, took him to the Club, 'filled him up with Beaune for [my] own base ends', then sat back with his pipe and listened. A close confidante could not understand why he was the recipient of so many confessions because 'he made use of every item for his work that he could glean'. But often he did not need to extract information: he simply had to listen, look and memorize. Mere observation sufficed with a woman like Lady Edge, the wife of the Chief Justice, who 'was inclined to be naughty / Though *much* over forty' and gave 'herself away in double handfuls'.[12]

Kipling soon abandoned his facile parodies and began to concentrate on political satire. His targets included ICS officers engaged in a vendetta in Madras, their Governor (Grant Duff) for his smug complacency in the matter, General Roberts for nepotism in military appointments, and 'Pagett', an imaginary Liberal MP prone to pontificating about Indian affairs. The most successful was 'The Rupaiyat of Omar Kal'vin', a brilliant pastiche of Fitzgerald's translation of the 'Rubaiyat' directed at the policies of Sir Auckland Colvin, the Financial Member of the Viceroy's Council.

> Whether at Boileaugunge* or Babylon,
> I know not how the wretched Thing is done,
> The Items of Receipt grow surely small;
> The Items of Expense mount one by one.

The verses, which appeared in the *Gazette* at the beginning of 1886, prompted a generous response from Colvin, who told the author 'it was a joy to find that the days of wit and delicate humour are not yet dead in the land'. Kipling was surprised by the compliment and wondered how long he would have had to wait in England before the Chancellor of the Exchequer congratulated him on an attack on his financial policy.[13]

Political satire was soon eclipsed by its social equivalent as he began to explore the possibilities of Anglo-India as a subject. In *Departmental Ditties and Other Verses*, Kipling's first real book, he concentrated on a new theme, adultery and other forms of unfaithfulness. He had touched on the subject in *Echoes*, and he later published an amusing skit suggesting that Cupid ran the largest and most important department in Simla. But in the 'Ditties' section of the new volume it was allowed to dominate half the material: in the second poem ('Army Headquarters') a woman persuades her husband to transfer her lover from his regiment so that she can keep him in Simla; in the third ('Study of an Elevation in Indian Ink') a dullard, Potiphar Gubbins C.E., is promoted beyond his talents as a result (it is implied) of his wife's charms; the fourth ('Delilah') portrays a wife confiding state secrets to her journalist lover; the sixth ('The Story of Uriah') tells how a wife and her lover arrange for her husband to be transferred to Quetta (where he dies) so that they can be together in Simla; in the seventh ('The Post that Fitted') a man uses his prospective father-in-law to procure him a good job before jilting the daughter; in the eighth ('A Code of Morals') a junior officer warns his wife about a general who is both amorous and predatory; and the twelfth ('Pink Dominoes') recounts a mix-up at a fancy dress

---

*A suburb of Simla close to Viceregal Lodge.

ball after which a wife, either from a sense of gratitude or under a threat of blackmail, persuades her husband to promote the man she had mistaken for her lover.* Later in the volume, in 'Certain Maxims of Hafiz', Kipling produced a particularly cynical couplet:

> The temper of chums, the love of your wife, and a new piano's tune —
> Which of the three will you trust at the end of an Indian June?

These poems, together with the Mrs Hauksbee stories, made Kipling's early reputation and also left an enduring image of Anglo-India at play. All but one of the ditties are comic in tone but serious in undertone, making piquant points not so much about infidelity as about the official corruption which (in these cases) it engendered. Kipling wrote them, he said, 'with a purpose and for a moral end arrived at in a rather odd way'.[14] The very unhumorous exception, 'The Story of Uriah', indicates that, while light-hearted or fairly harmless adultery attracted his indulgence, he could be ferocious about affairs with painful consequences. Cuckolding an elderly Civilian, secure and self-satisfied at his desk in Simla, was one thing; it was quite different to betray one's husband and conspire to send him to the appalling climate of Baluchistan. In the poem Jack Barrett is ordered to Quetta at the worst time of the year, leaving his wife in Simla to enjoy three quarters of his income; without understanding the reason for his transfer, he soon dies, 'attempting two men's duty' in the heat, and, like Uriah the Hittite, is briefly 'mourned' by his Bathsheba. After recounting the tale, the poet then dwells on the possibility of divine retribution, speculating that by now Jack's 'spirit knows / The reason of his transfer / From the Himalayan snows', and concluding that on the Day of Judgement when

> . . . Quetta graveyards give again
> Their victims to the air,
> I shouldn't like to be the man
> Who sent Jack Barrett there.

As the episode was a real one, the final stanzas were no doubt intended to discomfort the guilty couple. Years later Robinson wrote

---

*The enumeration is taken from the first British edition (1890). 'Delilah' did not appear in the original Indian publication.

that 'those who had known the real "Jack Barrett", good fellow that he was, and the vile superior and faithless wife who sent him "on duty" to his death, felt the heat of the spirit which inspired Kipling's verse in a way that gave those few lines an imperishable force'.[15]

Departmental Ditties appeared in May 1886 masquerading as a government envelope in brown paper, bound with wire, tied with red tape, and facetiously addressed to 'All Heads of Departments and all Anglo-Indians'. The first edition of 500 copies, which Kipling published himself at the *Gazette*, sold out immediately, prompting him to make the semi-accurate observation that Anglo-Indians liked reading about themselves, and persuading the Calcutta publisher, Thacker, Spink & Co, to bring out a second edition the same year, a third in 1888 and a fourth in 1890 (by then garbed in a hard cover). Delighted to find strangers reading it in trains and hotels, Kipling was also amused by the diversity of critical opinion, reviewers being on the whole complimentary but divided over questions of authorial intentions and the moral lessons of the verses.

The most perceptive review came from Sir William Hunter, a retired Civilian and historian of Bengal who published his judgement in September 1888 in the London magazine, the *Academy*. Hunter praised Kipling for his wit, malice and lightness of touch, observed that his characters were silly but real, and predicted that he would become a 'literary star of no mean magnitude' with better things to do than break 'those poor pretty Simla butterflies on the wheel'. The review was a kind one, especially as it was written only weeks after Hunter himself had become a victim of the poet's satire. Earlier in the summer Kipling had become irritated by Hunter's sympathy for the Indian National Congress, which had been expressed in articles in *The Times*, and decided to hurt him with 'a little *bandillero* [*sic*]' to dissuade people from taking him too seriously. Stung by the subsequent barbed poem, which accused him of aspiring to fame through journalism and of bluffing the British public with 'this demos – demonstration stuff', Hunter sent him a dry note about his 'little pasquinade', regretting that Kipling devoted his talents to 'clever trifles of this sort' and adding that they practically fixed his standard at the level of 'the gymkhana and the mess-room'. The younger writer was unabashed. He admired Hunter's scholarship, was grateful for the review, and recommended his books to people ignorant of India. But warned by an official at the India Office that Hunter was 'in earnest' and should not be 'flouted', Kipling became 'as cross as a bear with a sore head' and resolved to counter any further 'pretence of earnestness' on his part with 'yet more lampoons'.[16]

During his twentieth year Kipling's main literary project was a novel he called 'Mother Maturin', a story about an old Irishwoman who kept an opium den in Lahore. Admitting it was 'not one bit nice or proper', he thought it carried 'a grim sort of a moral' and tried to 'deal with the unutterable horrors of lower class Eurasian and native life as they exist outside reports and reports and reports'. Although Trix said it was 'awfully horrid' and Alice considered it 'nasty but powerful', the work was an 'unfailing delight' to its creator, especially when he found his characters living permanently with him. By the summer of 1885 he had written 237 pages and was predicting publication in at least two volumes; a couple of years later, after completing *Plain Tales from the Hills*, he announced that he was returning to a 'certain never ending novel'.[17] And in fact it never did end. Some of the descriptions later appeared in *Kim*, but the project itself was abandoned, and the manuscript disappeared.

Plain Tales, which gave Oscar Wilde the feeling that he was sitting 'under a palm-tree reading life by superb flashes of vulgarity',[18] was a prose companion of *Departmental Ditties*. Appearing in 1887, it was followed the next year by six shorter collections of stories, published under the generic title 'The Indian Railway Library', which each went on sale at the price of one rupee (a little over a shilling): *Soldiers Three*, *The Story of the Gadsbys*, *In Black and White*, *Under the Deodars*, *The Phantom Rickshaw* and *Wee Willie Winkie*. The thirty-nine 'plain tales' and the thirty-seven rather longer ones of the Railway volumes – an astonishing level of productivity for a part-time writer – can be broadly divided into five groups of subjects: Anglo-Indians in Simla, Anglo-Indians in the plains, native Indian life, the British Army in India and – the least successful – sentimental tales about children.

One story, 'The Man Who Would Be King', resists classification. Widely regarded as one of Kipling's most brilliant works, it was inspired by the author's meeting with an unknown freemason, who persuaded him to deliver a mysterious message to another unknown freemason at a railway junction on the edge of the Great Indian Desert. Kipling transformed the masons into swashbuckling adventurers who carve out a kingdom in the mountains of Kafiristan before over-ambition costs them their conquests, their plunder and their lives. It has plausibly been argued that the story, an adventure in its own right worthy of Stevenson, is an allegory of imperialism.[19] The exploits of Daniel Dravot and Peachy Carnehan, who train tribesmen to defeat their enemies and then unite them all in a Pax Dravotica, are a replication on a small scale of the feats of the British in India from Clive to Arthur Wellesley; and their fall, provoked by Dravot's decision to take a native woman as his queen, may be seen as a warning that empires can be overthrown when the customs of subject peoples are too greatly violated.

The tone of the Simla tales is set by the notorious Mrs Hauksbee, a witty, cynical and 'honestly mischievous' woman whose intrigues in the hills are generally beneficial – at any rate for such as Pluffles, the 'callow' subaltern she rescues from the predatory Mrs Reiver (who was 'bad from her hair – which started life on a Brittany girl's head – to her boot-heels, which were two and three-eighth inches high').[20] Mrs Hauksbee inhabits a world heavily populated by people who gossip, go to parties and itch for illicit liaisons. Marital infidelity is a recurring topic, as it was in *Departmental Ditties* and as it continued to be in *The Story of the Gadsbys* and *Under the Deodars*. And as with the verses, the subject is judged not as a moral absolute but according to the circumstances of each affair. In one story Kipling declares that this is also Simla's 'eccentric' way of treating adulterous relationships: 'Certain attachments which have set and crystallised through half-a-dozen seasons acquire almost the sanctity of the marriage bond, and are revered as such.' But others equally old never win 'recognised official status'. Some people have the gift that secures them 'infinite toleration', and some have not. One couple who enjoy no one's toleration, least of all Kipling's, are the adulterous lovers in 'At the Pit's Mouth': the Tertium Quid laughs over his lover's shoulder as she writes letters to her husband, 'stewing in the plains' on two hundred rupees a month; they both laugh at one of her husband's replies; they cavort publicly around Simla and frolic on a horse blanket in the cemetery; and on one of their rides the Tertium Quid and his horse fall 900 feet down a precipice.[21]* As with 'The Story of Uriah',

---

*Not such an improbable death as it may seem. Murray's *Handbook to the Punjab* warned travellers that before 1875 'at least 22 ladies and gentlemen were killed by falling over precipices at Simla'. In 1884 Kipling's horse Joe broke out of his stable one night at Dalhousie and fell to his death down a hillside.

Kipling's position is clear: he is not condemning adulterers as a group but only those who are insensitive, blatant and cruel.

Another theme lurking among these tales is the power of women not simply to manipulate men but also to destroy their work. The worst example of this is the case of Wressley who writes a scholarly history of Central India, presents it to the silly girl he is in love with and, on her admission that she doesn't understand it (all 'those howwid wajahs'), sinks the entire edition in a hill lake.[22] But even women who are not stupid or wicked can obstruct a man's work. Before Captain Gadsby's wedding his friend Mafflin 'strolls off, singing absently:

> You may carve it on his tombstone, you may cut it on his card,
> That a young man married is a young man marred!'

And in case the reader misses the point, the 'Envoi' to *The Story of the Gadsbys* is a poem containing the moral:

> Down to Gehenna or up to the Throne,
> He travels the fastest who travels alone.

A great deal that Kipling said and wrote can be contradicted by other things he said and wrote. Similarly, the apparent misogyny of certain stories is belied by the sympathy and understanding he could show women in other stories written at the same time. In 'The Bronckhorst Divorce Case', one of the 'plain tales', the author is entirely on the side of a maligned wife who has a brutish husband; and in 'The Hill of Illusion', a dialogue between a couple planning to elope, his handling of the woman's hesitations about her future as an outcast is sensitive and astute.

The tales of the plains are less frivolous than those of Simla because they generally deal either with the British-Indian relationship or with Anglo-Indians at work. During his middle years on the Subcontinent Kipling began to appreciate the qualities of the Indian Civil Service. At the beginning he had been overawed – insofar as he ever could be overawed – by the Civilians at the Punjab Club; certainly he later met enough mediocre ones at Simla and Lahore to write disparagingly about them in verse and in fiction. But by the end of 1885 he had come to recognize that the ICS was an impressive and hard-working body of men devoting their lives to the welfare of the native population.[23] In 'On the City Wall', a remarkable story in which Kipling managed to display perception and an appreciation of Indian life at the same time as he mocked the idea of Indian self-government, he included a long passage extolling the work of the ICS:

> Year by year England sends out fresh drafts for the first fighting-line which is officially called the Indian Civil Service. These die, or kill themselves by overwork, or are worried to death or broken in health and hope in order that the land may be protected from death and sickness, famine and war, and may eventually become capable of standing alone. It will never stand alone, but the idea is a pretty one and men are willing to die for it, and yearly the work of pushing and coaxing and scolding and petting the country into good living goes forward. If an advance be made all credit is given to the native while the Englishmen stand back and wipe their foreheads. If a failure occurs the Englishmen step forward and take the blame.

As Kipling came to admire the work of the district officers, he was also able to empathize with them, to understand the conditions in which they lived and worked, the loneliness, the vulnerability, the threat of sudden death, the physical and emotional strain suffered by a tiny minority always being moved about, separated from wives in summer and from children for years, people who felt they were living on the edge of a volcano in an alien and potentially hostile world. He sympathized with men and women in remote 'stations' trying to retain their self-respect and even their sanity. The image of Victorians in the tropics dressing for their solitary dinners invariably provokes mirth, but Kipling saw the importance of such rituals in the struggle against cracking up or 'going to seed'. In one of his stories a forestry official, living by himself in a bungalow among the trees, puts on a stiff white shirt each night to 'preserve his self-respect in his isolation'. Kipling did the same in the house in Lahore, even when his family were away, because 'one knew if one broke the ritual of dressing for the last meal one was parting with a sheet-anchor'.[24]

Social rituals were also indispensable even when the neighbours were scarce, distant and unattractive. If sanity were to be preserved, people had to meet even if they did not like each other and had nothing to talk about; whist was a vital part of Anglo-Indian life because it enabled a man to spend several hours in the company of three others with whom he might not have anything else in common. The four whist players in 'At the End of the Passage' are an assistant engineer at a remote railway station, a surveyor who has 'ridden thirty and railed one hundred miles from his lonely post in the desert', a Civilian who has 'come as far to escape for an instant the miserable intrigues of an impoverished native state', and a doctor who has left 'a cholera-stricken camp of coolies to look after itself for forty-eight hours while he associated with white men once more'. They do not have any particular regard for one another and in fact squabble whenever they meet; nor is the whist enjoyable because it is played 'crossly, with wranglings as to leads and returns'. But they play regularly, even in the hot weather when the 'Great Indian Empire ... turns herself for six months into a house of torment', because they need to meet, 'as men without water desire to drink. They were lonely folk who understood the dread meaning of loneliness.'

Another hazard of life in a small station is illustrated by 'A Wayside Comedy', a story written with an 'economy of implication' of which Kipling was justly proud. Kashima, caged in by the scrub and rocks of the Dosehri hills, has a British population of two couples and a bachelor officer: all three men love the same woman (who only loves her husband) so that two men and the other woman are miserable, drained by bitterness and hatred for each other. Yet none of them can escape: they are trapped in their cage and tortured by their relationships while they try to follow the rules of a conventional middle-class existence.

In an article for the *Gazette* published shortly before he left India, Kipling wrote of the man who returns to the 'Old Station' after a season or so away only to find that his closest friend has recently died: 'You are behind the times!' he is told. 'Dicky went out three weeks ago with something or other ... I've forgotten what it was, but it was rather sudden ... Poor old Dicky!'[25] Everyone who went to India knew about the risk of sudden death — the evidence is still there on the gravestones and memorials that reveal how many Anglo-Indians died young. Death from heatstroke, from disease, from overindulgence, death from working in plague districts or famine areas — they were all so familiar that Anglo-Indians had to accept them as events too natural and frequent for them to waste time in prolonged grief. When a man died, he was buried, briefly mourned and forgotten. As Kipling put it in *Departmental Ditties*:

> Ay, lay him 'neath the Simla pine –
> A fortnight fully to be missed,
> Behold, we lose our fourth at whist,
> A chair is vacant where we dine.
>
> ('Possibilities')

A few years after his return to Britain, Kipling sent the *Gazette* 'The Exiles' Line', a poem portraying 'the soul of our sad East' as it is carried back and forth between Britain and India in the ships of the P & O Company. Written again with the metre (though without the zest) of Fitzgerald's 'Rubaiyat', the poem presents the boat as a microcosm of Anglo-India:

> The tragedy of all our East is laid
> On those white decks beneath the awning shade –
> Birth, absence, longing, laughter, love and tears,
> And death unmaking ere the land is made.

The voyage is joyless, dutiful and inescapable for Anglo-Indians, 'gypsies of the East', people with no real home at either end of the journey:

> Bound on the wheel of Empire, one by one,
> The chain-gangs of the East from sire to son,
> The Exiles' Line takes out the exiles' line
> And ships them homeward when their work is done.[26]

Kipling's great sorrow, a friend believed, was that his poor eyesight prevented him from joining the Army. When he heard of the exploits of Westward Ho! 'old boys' now living as subalterns in India, he used to sigh and regret that he had not been able to go to Sandhurst. Perhaps the sorrow and the sigh were rather artificial because it is difficult to imagine that even with perfect eyes he would have traded his pen for a rifle. In Lahore he joined the 1st Punjab Volunteers but failed to turn up for parade duty and was asked to resign. Even so, he became fascinated by the military, and his interest and concern for the British soldier were among the most enduring of his life. In India he came to know men from all ranks of the British Army,* from Sir Frederick Roberts to the NCOs and privates, whom he immortalized as Tommy Atkins, Danny Deever and his 'three musketeers', Mulvaney, Ortheris and Learoyd.

Kipling tried to keep in touch with the careers of the 'old boys', of Cunliffe of the 9th Lancers and 'Dolly' Stockwell, the adjutant of a Highland regiment, of 'Poodle' Townsend and 'Tuppeny' Edwardes who won promotion and a medal respectively for their roles in a military expedition in the hills. The fate of Lieutenant Dury, a 'good fellow' killed in Burma in 1885, moved him to verse:

> A scrimmage in a Border Station –
>   A canter down some dark defile –
> Two thousand pounds of education
>   Drops to a ten-rupee *jezail* –
> The Crammer's boast, the Squadron's pride,
> Shot like a rabbit in a ride.

> ('Arithmetic on the Frontier')

Later he described the death of an 'old boy' in a passage in *Stalky & Co*, a powerful illustration of emotional repression cultivated by the clichéd ethos of the stiff upper lip. Duncan is lying wounded under a cart, 'propped up on one arm, blazing away with a revolver' at Afridi tribesmen on the North-West Frontier, when an old schoolfriend, who has not seen him for years, dashes out from a nearby fort and reaches the cart. Later the would-be rescuer revisits their school and describes the scene to the enraptured boys:

He'd been shot through the lungs, poor old man, and he was pretty thirsty. I gave him a drink and sat down beside him, and – funny thing, too – he said, 'Hullo, Toffee!' and I said, 'Hullo, Fat-Sow! hope you aren't hurt,' or

---

*In 1885 the British Army in India had 59,000 troops, while the Indian Army consisted of 124,000 native soldiers; 5,000 British officers commanded the two forces. A large majority of the British troops were stationed on the Frontier and in the cities of the north; southern Indians outside Bangalore and Madras seldom saw a white soldier. As the population of the Indian Empire (which included modern Burma, Pakistan and Bangladesh – but not Sri Lanka) was 270 million in 1885, the ratio of British soldiers to native inhabitants was 1 to 4,219.

something of the kind. But he died in a minute or two – never lifted his head off my knees.[27]

Kipling had many acquaintances among the officer class and a few friends such as Dunsterville, whom he extolled in the last chapter of *Stalky* as a frontier officer with initiative who performs heroic feats without paying much attention to his distant and slow-moving superiors. But he does not seem to have liked officers very much – his fictional captains such as Gadsby are generally not appealing – and they do not seem to have cared for him. No doubt the main problem was that he admired their profession while they had little regard for his. As one officer on the staff of the Quartermaster-General remarked, Kipling was 'looked upon with great disfavour by Staff officers as being bumptious and above his station'.[28]

Private soldiers and NCOs might also be suspicious of the inquisitive journalist, but they were unlikely to look upon him with 'disfavour'. Kipling visited their barracks at Mian Mir, questioning, listening and, according to Robinson, coming to know 'the undercurrent of the soldier's thoughts ... better than sergeant or chaplain'.[29] His first friends were in the Northumberland Fusiliers, known as 'the Fighting Fifth'. Lieutenant Hill, a Westward Ho! 'old boy', introduced him to the regimental sergeant-major with the explanation that Kipling had 'an idea for turning out something new in writing about military life by getting into direct touch with Tommy Atkins himself'. The NCO duly presented him to Corporal Macnamara, whose group of 'boozing chums' were in charge of the rifle range, and friendship, encouraged by a round of beer, soon followed. The corporal, who appreciated his visitor for being 'free wid his beer and talkin' loike one of ourselves bedad', was shortly immortalized as Private Mulvaney.[30]

Subsequently managing to pick up his 'canteen talk' at the shooting range, Kipling came to learn army slang 'down to the ground' and enjoyed seeking out the men who made the battalion's songs.[31] His knowledge of barracks life was such that one day in Simla the Commander-in-Chief asked the proud young journalist what the soldiers 'thought about their accommodation, entertainment-rooms and the like'. A few years later Private George Housman read Kipling's soldier ballads (sent to him in Burma by his poet brother 'A.E.') and wrote, 'There never was such a man, and I should think never will be again, who understands "Tommy Atkins" in the rough, as he does.'[32]

His sympathy for the soldiers went even deeper than it did for the ICS. At least the Civilians had some idea of what they had applied for, their work was absorbing, and they had an annual opportunity to stay in a hill station. But 'Tommy Atkins' knew nothing about India before his arrival, his work there was boring and took up little time, and he was not welcome at Simla. Bewildered by his new environment, he was naturally prone to homesickness. As Private Ortheris confesses in one of the 'plain tales':

> I'm sick for London again; sick for the sounds of 'er, and the sights of 'er, an' the stinks of 'er; orange-peel and hasphalte an' gas comin' in over Vaux'all Bridge. Sick for the rail goin' down to Box 'ill, with your gal on your knee an' a new clay pipe in your face. That, an' the Stran' lights when you knows ev'ry one ...[33]

Homesickness was soon joined by boredom, the monotony of marching in the cold weather down the Grand Trunk Road from Umballa to Cawnpore. ('Boots-boots-boots-boots – movin' up and down again', as Kipling wrote of infantry columns in Africa.) But the hot weather was far worse. Apart from the threats of malaria, typhoid, cholera, heatstroke and venereal disease, soldiers had to contend with the sheer tedium of an existence in a sweltering barracks. Once early morning drill was over, there was little to do except sweat and smoke and drink too much beer, swear at the coolies, fight occasionally with each other, and contemplate an evening with drink and prostitutes. They could afford both, for the cost of living was low, and they had little else to do with their wages.

The combined pursuit of sex and alcohol led to frequent trouble in the bazaars. In most clashes between British and Indians, Curzon observed, 'the cause of the mischief is that the English soldiers are either after a woman or are drunk'.[34] Realizing that basic instincts could not be suppressed by preaching or the Temperance Movement, the military authorities had tried to reduce the risk of violence and venereal disease by permitting the existence of cantonment brothels where prostitutes were reserved for white soldiers and subjected to medical inspection. The system, however, enraged the 'purity' watchdogs in Britain who organized a crusade, championed in India by

Lady Roberts, which persuaded her husband to close the brothels. A parliamentary Bill instigated, a colonel complained, 'by morbid moral faddists and sexless unprofessional sisters', consolidated their victory and led directly, in the words of one viceroy, 'to even more deplorable evils ... an increase in unnatural crimes' and, for those tempted to the bazaars, a great deal more venereal disease. By 1895 more than a quarter of the British Army in India was being treated for syphilis, a figure that fell only when the cantonment brothels were discreetly reopened after Roberts and his wife had gone home.[35]

Kipling understood soldiers much better than Roberts, who urged them to join the Army Temperance Association, or a later Commander-in-Chief, Lord Kitchener, who advocated exercise and self-control to avoid a disease that would not only mortify their mothers but also cause their noses to rot and fall off.[36] The youthful expert on barrack-room life knew that boredom and discomfort could not be alleviated by visits to a 'coffee palace' or the temperance room with its out-of-date newspapers. The soldiers' existence was hard enough without the removal of the main sources of solace. As he recalled in his memoirs:

> I came to realise the bare horrors of the private's life, and the unnecessary torments he endured on account of the Christian doctrine which lays down that 'the wages of sin is death'. It was counted impious that bazaar prostitutes should be inspected; or that the men should be taught elementary precautions in their dealings with them. This official virtue cost our Army in India nine thousand expensive white men a year always laid up from venereal disease. Visits to Lock Hospitals [for the treatment of the disease] made me desire, as earnestly as I do today, that I might have six hundred priests – Bishops of the Establishment for choice* – to handle for six months precisely as the soldiers of my youth were handled.

Kipling's views on the issue of prostitution were unusual for the period. Though the vast number of prostitutes in late Victorian Britain testifies to a very much larger number of customers, very few people apart from contributors to underground journals, openly wrote about the subject with such understanding and lack of pruri-

---

*The Anglican bishops of India and Ceylon had declared that 'the discouragement and repression of vice are of far higher importance than the diminution of suffering or other evils resulting from vice . . .'[37]

ence as Kipling. In 'On the City Wall', a tale about an Indian prostitute called Lalun, he favourably contrasts the Eastern attitude to her work with that of the West, where 'people say rude things of Lalun's profession, and write lectures about it and distribute the lectures to young persons in order that Morality may be preserved'. In another Indian story, 'Love o' Women', Kipling shows compassion for both the white woman who becomes a prostitute and the philandering soldier who has reduced her to this condition. And his poem, 'The Ladies', recounting a soldier's affairs with Burmese, half-caste, Indian and English women, is entirely free of moral messages. On sexual matters its author was a great deal more liberal than most Liberal Victorians.

As Kipling never saw a battle in India, he had to conjure the fighting in his stories from incidents he had read or heard about. In January 1887 he reported in the *Gazette* that five men and a bugler of the 2nd Queen's Regiment had stripped naked, swum across a Burmese river and burned a village on the opposite bank. A few weeks later he published 'The Taking of Lungtungpen' in which Mulvaney gives a fictional account of the same incident somewhat enlarged: the number of soldiers is quadrupled and the village is upgraded to a town.

Kipling has been accused of having a 'romantic attitude to war' which led him 'into the error that soldiers enjoy fighting'.[38] But whatever other soldiers in other places and in other times may have felt, British troops in India did enjoy fighting – as their diaries and letters invariably show; apart from anything else, it was a relief from the monotony of the barracks routine. Each time a frontier expedition was planned, Lieutenant Dowdall reported in a string of letters to his mother, 'every single man' in the Yorkshire Light Infantry was in 'tearing spirits', 'keen as blazes', 'keen as ginger' and in the 'wildest state of excitement'. Two colour-sergeants about to return to England re-enlisted for the Zhob Valley Expedition even though as a result they were obliged to do another five years' service in a country they disliked. The whole regiment wanted action and medals, and its one anxiety was that the tribesmen might surrender before there was any fighting.[39]

The charge that Kipling's view of war was romantic can be judged by comparing him with figures such as Macaulay, Tennyson or

Chesterton, poets who romanticized fighting men because they did not know them. Mulvaney and his friends are not heroes; they do not fight Homeric encounters against great odds. In Kipling's work there is no Roman leaping into the Tiber after holding a bridge against an entire army, no undismayed man riding into 'the jaws of death' without reasoning why, no lunatic 'at Flores in the Azores' taking on fifty-three Spanish ships with his solitary vessel – not even a 'last and lingering troubadour' buckling on his sword and confounding the Turks at Lepanto. Kipling's soldiers have human proportions – they parade, drink, tell stories and fall in love; sometimes they loot ('Loot'), sometimes they steal dogs ('Private Learoyd's Story'), sometimes they kill each other in fits of jealousy or heat hysteria ('Danny Deever', 'Love o' Women', 'The Story of Tommy', 'In the Matter of a Private'), sometimes they fight bravely because they are drunk, and sometimes they run from the battlefield, 'shammin' wounded', chucking away their rifles and ''idin under bedsteads' ('That Day', 'The Drums of the Fore and Aft'). Even at their best they are not usually better fighting men than their foes. A verse in 'Fuzzy Wuzzy' suggests they can be worse:

> We took our chanst among the Kyber 'ills,
> The Boers knocked us silly at a mile,
> The Burman gave us Irriwaddy chills,
> An' a Zulu *impi* dished us up in style:
> But all we ever got from such as they
> Was pop to what the Fuzzy made us swaller;
> We 'eld our bloomin' own, the papers say,
> But man for man the Fuzzy knocked us 'oller.

Yet whatever their defects they are always human, from 'that very strong man, T. Atkins' (to whom *Soldiers Three* is dedicated), to Mulvaney, that 'grizzled, tender and very wise Ulysses'. Kipling understood them and wrote about them in a way that no one had done since Shakespeare. As his official biographer pointed out, English literature has 'no adequate account of the British soldier, what he thought of his officers, and what he talked about the night before the battle', between *Henry V* and Kipling.[40]

The Army had long possessed a bad name in Britain: Wellington made several laudatory remarks about private soldiers and their fighting qualities, but the only one remembered is his observation that they were 'the very scum of the earth' who had enlisted 'from having got bastard children … for minor offences [and] many more for drink'.[41] Kipling thought their reputation so unfair that he resolved to do something about it. 'The mischief', he told a friendly corporal, 'is that if you have ten blackguards in a regiment, the whole regiment has to take the blame for what those fellows do and civilians go about and say: – "That's the army" when it's only half-a-dozen file of drunken sweeps that ought to be in Chokee.'[42] In *Soldiers Three* he announced that, while Tommy 'ought to be supplied with a new Adjective to help him to express his opinions', he was not a 'brute' but a 'great man' bewildered to hear himself described one day as 'the heroic defender of the national honour' and the next as belonging to 'a brutal and licentious soldiery'. In the poem 'Tommy' he memorably reinforced the point:

> Yes, makin' mock o' uniforms that guard you while you sleep,
> Is cheaper than them uniforms, an' they're starvation cheap;
> An hustlin' drunken soldiers when they're goin' large a bit
> Is five times better business than paradin' in full kit.

> > Then it's Tommy this, an' Tommy that,
> > an' 'Tommy, 'ow's yer soul?'
> > But it's 'Thin red line of 'eroes' when the
> > drums begin to roll,
> > The drums begin to roll, my boys, the drums
> > begin to roll,
> > O it's 'Thin red line of 'eroes' when the
> > drums begin to roll.

Kipling's picture of Anglo-India is by far the fullest, broadest and most vivid that was ever done. For decades it dominated people's views on the subject, though its image of the British in India was partially superseded by the narrower and more one-sided depiction in Forster's *A Passage to India*, published in 1924. Yet even in its heyday the authenticity was disputed. Was it a genuine likeness? Were the characters real? Men with military experience differed in their opinions, some complaining that Kipling's soldiers were more old-fashioned and worse educated than the troops of the period, while others praised the 'literally photographic' accuracy of Tommy's portraits in verse.[43] The sergeant-major of the 5th Northumberland Fusiliers, who enjoyed first-hand knowledge of author and subject, believed Kipling 'knew more of the psychology of the private soldier of his day than any civilian ever had, or could have known ...'[44] Private Housman held a similar view.

An ingenious theory suggests that officers who read Kipling somehow managed to mould their men so that they became like his soldiers. General Sir George Younghusband had served in India for many years without hearing the words or expressions used by the fictional men; puzzled, he asked his brother officers, who confessed that they too were ignorant of the diction. But a few years later he discovered that 'the soldiers thought, and talked, and expressed themselves exactly like Rudyard Kipling had taught them in his stories ... Kipling made the modern soldier.'[45]*

The civilian portraits invite a comparable confusion. While serving in Ceylon in 1907, Leonard Woolf observed that the British there were 'astonishingly like characters in a Kipling story'. But he could never make up his mind 'whether Kipling had moulded his characters accurately in the image of Anglo-Indian society or whether we were moulding our characters accurately in the image of a Kipling story'. Sometimes he wondered whether he was a real person with a real job or simply living a story from *Under the Deodars*.[47]

Wider questions also suggest themselves about the Empire's effect on Kipling and his effect on it. How much did he incarnate the late Victorian sense of Empire and how far did he create it? The answer to this and to the puzzles pondered by Woolf and Younghusband, is surely 'a bit of both'.

It is often said that Anglo-Indians universally disliked their portrait. Doubtless many did, especially earnest Civilians and memsahibs brimming with rectitude who resented the implication that they were frivolous and adulterous. One 'loon', who sent Kipling an anonymous letter complaining of the 'flagrant immorality' of the 'plain tales', asked where he thought he would go after his death.

---

*In similar fashion, according to Proust, Renoir made the modern French girl, who increasingly came to resemble his paintings.[46]

Some of the British at home were also shocked. Maud Diver wrote *The Englishwoman in India* (1909) with the purpose of refuting the idea that Anglo-Indian ladies misbehaved; and Lord Curzon, while he was assuring Queen Victoria that Calcutta society was not 'frivolous, or immoral, or particularly dull', felt the need to correct 'the unfair and rather malevolent impressions that have gone abroad and have received some colour from the too cynical stories of Rudyard Kipling'. In his book, *British Social Life in India* (1938), Dennis Kincaid relied on the testimony of his grandmother to record that in Simla the writer was considered a cad, a bounder and 'a subversive pamphleteer given to criticise his betters'.[48]

In Kipling's defence it must be said that he never aspired to paint a comprehensive portrait of Anglo-India. For all his success in penetrating the different layers of civilian and military rank, he knew he had a restricted view, that because of his circumstances he had to concentrate on a relatively small province only recently incorporated into the Empire. Had he been living in Madras, a city created by the British with two hundred years of colonial history and a negligible military presence, his view would have been very different. As for the accusations of 'flagrant immorality', Kipling never suggested that life in Simla was wholly frivolous or improper. In his preface to *Under the Deodars* he tried 'to assure the ill-informed that India is not entirely inhabited by men and women playing tennis and breaking the Seventh Commandment' – an assurance the ill-informed might have queried when they found that most of the volume's stories were about precisely such people. But writing in his newspaper Kipling described Anglo-Indian women as nice, worthy and not very attractive ('the climate kills good looks'). It was 'utter rubbish' to think they were 'fast', because most of them were 'a good deal steadier than women at home'; only some of the older ones, 'the Lillie Langtrys of India', tended to be a little 'fast'.[49] Later, in his novel *The Naulahka*, Kipling portrayed a Civilian's wife who is not at all like Mrs Reiver or Mrs Hauksbee: she is tired, dutiful and in need of a holiday, 'her thoughts ... bounded by the thought of going home' to a 'little house near Surbiton, close to the Crystal Palace, where her three-year-old boy was waiting for her'.

Lord Hailey, who had been a young Civilian in the 1890s, recalled that Simla had then been 'intellectually a serious place' and that Kipling's tales were 'misleadingly derogatory'.[50] But the existence of a frivolous side to its character is surely proved by the frequent complaints that serious people made about it. When he was not writing to Queen Victoria, Curzon could admit to feeling annually more afflicted by its 'garish setting of inane frivolity' and 'its atmosphere of petty gossip and pettier scandal'. A member of his Council was amazed by the vulgarity and silliness of English people trying to amuse themselves.[51] And Sir William Hunter, in his review of *Departmental Ditties*, admitted Simla's dual nature when he pointed out that beside the 'silly little world' which disported itself in the verses, there was 'another Anglo-Indian world which for high aims, and a certain steadfastness in effort after the personal interest in effort is well nigh dead, has never had an equal in history'.[52] Kipling would not have argued with that.

Simla's frivolous reputation preceded Kipling and seems to have originated under the regime of Lord Lytton, Ripon's very flirtatious predecessor. The town was sometimes compared to Capua, and in 1885, a year before the 'plain tales' began to appear, a young artillery officer was reluctant to visit the place because he had heard that its 'main occupations' were 'gambling, drinking and breaking the 7th Commandment'. No doubt Simla had many faithful and high-minded women whom Kipling considered inappropriate as models for his light-hearted tales and verses in the *Gazette*. But there were other types as well. Sir George Macmunn believed that Mrs Hauksbee was a 'well drawn specimen' and recalled that he had known half a dozen women in Simla who resembled her. Another retired officer, General Pearse, remembered 'a few frisky young Dames, and a few young fellows full of mischief and devilment'. Most women dressed their jampannies* in light costumes to be 'discernible even in a darkish night. But those who were given to tender meetings by moonlight midst those dark umbrageous, pine-lined roads, chose the darkest of liveries for their menials'.[53†]

The best evidence for the authenticity of Kipling's India comes

---

*Women in hill stations were transported by a type of sedan chair called a jampan, which was carried by two pairs of native jampannies. The jampan was superseded by the rickshaw around 1880.

†In Kipling's poem, 'The Tale of Two Suits', a drunken lover, unaware that two Simla ladies have similar costumes for their rickshaw carriers, talks ardently in the dark to the wrong woman.

not from the autobiographies of men writing decades afterwards or the remembered reminiscences of Dennis Kincaid's grandmother, but from the papers of people writing at the time without a view to publication. The Reverend Lancelot Phelps, a Fellow and Tutor of Oriel College, corresponded with large numbers of ICS officers after they had left Oxford in the 1880s and 1890s. Their preserved replies reveal a good deal about Anglo-Indian life, including the fact that many young Civilians read Kipling's books, found them 'capital' and 'excellent' and urged their former tutor to read them as well. The letters also suggest that the works were regarded as an accurate representation of Anglo-India. One correspondent reported that Englishwomen in the Subcontinent did nothing all day and seemed to go rapidly to pieces: 'The amount of malicious scandal talked is fairly amazing, and Kipling is much more true to the life in his women-kind than most Anglo-Indians would allow.'[54] Another, pleased that his old tutor had enjoyed *Plain Tales*, said he had heard no one object to the book in India and was surprised by Phelps's judgement that some of the stories made the book 'unfit for ladies'. Anglo-Indian society, he wrote, was 'a very remarkable puzzle': things were 'done and said out here, and not resented, which would create the wildest scandal in England'. Sometimes ladies said things which 'almost petrified' him with surprise. As an illustration of Anglo-Indian attitudes to scandal, he pointed to the case of Arthur Crawford, a Civilian in the Bombay presidency for thirty-five years, who

> has certainly run away with two women, has been separated from his own wife, and during one Poona season lived with two actresses whom he imported from America. Yet thereafter he was received into social circles as if nothing had happened ... Everyone seems to take [such behaviour] as a matter of course. Perhaps it's the climate which produces a sort of native-like apathy.[55]

4

Cities of Dreadful Night

As the epigraph to a chapter in *Kim*, Kipling used two verses of his poem, 'The Two-sided Man':

> Something I owe to the soil that grew –
>   More to the life that fed –
> But most to Allah Who gave me two
>   Separate sides to my head.

> I would go without shirts or shoes,
>   Friends, tobacco or bread
> Sooner than for an instant lose
>   Either side of my head.

No doubt most people have two sides to their heads, but few keep them quite as separate and inimical as Kipling managed to do. One side stayed with him in the office and the Club, mocking Indians for their political pretensions and their 'orientally unclean ... habits.'[1] And the other, intensely receptive to sights, smells and sounds, roamed the bazaars and the native states, absorbing the experience without feeling the need to censure.

In the *Plain Tales* Kipling created a police officer called Strickland, who spends his leave disguised as a native, 'swallowed up for a while' by India. He knows the Lizzard-Song of the Sansis and the Halli-Hukk dance, and when he is married and settled in Anglo-India, he hears the sounds of the bazaars beseeching him to return and take up his wanderings and his discoveries.[2] Plainly a case of partial self-projection by Kipling, Strickland owes something to the figure of Sir Richard Burton, the great explorer and pioneering anthropologist who could speak twenty-nine languages and twelve dialects. Like the police officer, Burton was a master of disguise, able to pass himself off on the way to Mecca as a Persian, a dervish and a Pathan; but his earlier career in India had languished after army colleagues decided that his investigations into the homosexual brothels of Karachi had been too eagerly carried out.

Kipling could not closely resemble Burton or Strickland because he was not a great linguist: much as he came to love France and admire French literature, he never spoke the language well. In India he took lessons in Urdu and could speak a fair amount of Hindustani, but it is unlikely that he was able to read the Perso-Arabic or Devanagari scripts. Linguistic shortcomings did not, however, prevent him from penetrating the native life of Lahore nor from making remarkable translations of Indian speech in the dialogues of his works.

'Memory depends on smell,' Kipling wrote after a visit to an Indian coalfield. 'A noseless man is devoid of sentiment, just as a noseless woman [whose husband has disfigured her for infidelity], must be devoid of honour.'[3]* All his life he associated places with smells, which he allowed to define his nostalgia:

> Smells are surer than sounds or sights
> To make your heart-strings crack –
> They start those awful voices o' nights
> That whisper, 'Old man, come back.'
> That must be why the big things pass
> And the little things remain,
> Like the smell of wattle by Lichtenberg,
> Riding in, in the rain.

('Lichtenberg')

In London the British soldier of 'Mandalay' yearns for Burma's 'spicy garlic smells', while in India Private Ortheris pines for the

---

*The origins of this punishment, which has a long history, appear to lie in the ancient Hindu epic the *Ramayana*. After the giantess Surpanakha fails to seduce Rama and tries to swallow his wife Sita, her nose is cut off by Rama's half-brother, Lakshman.

'stinks' of London, the smells of gas and asphalt and orange-peel over Vauxhall Bridge. When Kipling visited Egypt in 1913, more than twenty years after he had last been in an oriental country, he found Cairo brought back the East to him in pungent gusts, 'above all, in the mixed delicious smells of frying butter, Mohammedan bread, kababs, leather, cooking-smoke, assafetida, peppers and turmeric'. The 'right-minded man' loved the smell of burning turmeric because it represented the nightfall that 'brings all home, the evening meal, the dipping of friendly hands in the dish, the one face, the dropped veil, and the big guttering pipe afterward'.[4]

Kipling also used smells in combination with sights to describe the essential characteristics of a moment in a landscape: the hot night blast at Lahore's Delhi Gate, 'a compound of all evil savours ... that a walled city can breed in a day and a night';* the 'Great Indian Empire' in the heat, combining 'the foul smell of badly-trimmed kerosene lamps' and the stench of 'native tobacco, baked brick, and dried earth'; dusk on the Grand Trunk Road when

> Swiftly the light gathered itself together, painted for an instant the faces and the cart-wheels and the bullocks' horns as red as blood. Then the night fell, changing the touch of the air, drawing a low, even haze, like a gossamer veil of blue, across the face of the country, and bringing out, keen and distinct, the smell of wood-smoke and cattle and the good scent of wheaten cakes cooked on ashes.

The sensory receptiveness of Kipling's second side, its capacity to watch and listen and not condemn, its pleasure in simply absorbing impressions from the Grand Trunk Road, that 'broad smiling river of life', allowed him to experience much more of native India than most British people managed to do. He had the 'quaintest details', Robinson recalled, about local habits, language and ways of thought, so that Indians regarded him as different from other sahibs. Even 'the most suspected and suspicious of classes, the religious mendicants', talked freely to him, while 'one long-limbed Pathan, indescribably filthy, but with magnificent mien and features', used to terminate his wanderings in Afghanistan by turning up 'for confidential colloquy

---

*From 'The City of Dreadful Night', a title Kipling gave to his sketch of Lahore in *Life's Handicap* and which he used again for a collection of articles on Calcutta in 1888. The phrase was taken from James Thomson's poem of the same title.

with Kuppeleen Sabib'.[5] When Kipling moved in 1887 to Allahabad, his closest friend there remembered, his knowledge of 'native folk' gained him invitations to places where foreigners were seldom asked. At one sumptuous evening with fireworks, singing and dancing by nautch girls, 'nose rings set in diamonds, anklets of massive gold', she watched 'the young weaver of tales taking it all in and knew that he was adding to his characters and settings'.[6]

Kipling's knowledge of castes and creeds impressed his friends. Like his father, he preferred 'Mussalmans' to Hindus and did not disguise his preference. Every Englishman, he believed, leaned towards one community or the other, depending on where he began his work in India. Like many of his compatriots, Kipling considered Muslims as more straightforward than Hindus and found it easier to sympathize with their monotheistic religion than with a jumble of human and animal gods. In later life he claimed never to have met an Englishman who hated Islam and its peoples although he knew Englishmen who hated other faiths: 'where there are Muslims,' he quoted from an Urdu saying, 'there is a comprehensible civilisation'.[7]

The Pathan tribesman from the Frontier was his favourite image of a Muslim, and consequently nearly all the Muslims in his works are warlike men of action.[8] By contrast he associated Hindus not with the equally redoubtable warriors of Rajputana but with sedentary Bengali babus who talked too much and achieved too little. He studied the tenets of Hinduism, learning about gods and rites and practices, and he created some delightful Hindu characters such as Purun Dass in *The Second Jungle Book* and Hurree Chunder Mookerjee in *Kim*. But he despised Hindu mythology: most of the *Ramayana*, he decided at the age of 20, was an 'infinity of trivialities', while the *Mahabharata* was a 'monstrous midden', a lump of 'hopeless, aimless, diffuse drivel (tempered with puerile obscenity)'.[9] While Islam had been an active, conquering faith, Hinduism seemed to encourage fatalism, apathy and a fundamental escapism. Besides, Kipling held it responsible for most of India's social problems, not simply the dirt and squalor of Benares and Calcutta, but others intrinsic to the systems of caste and social custom which discriminated against all women as well as those men who were not Brahmins.

Yet while he felt little respect for Hinduism as a religion, Kipling was adamant that respect should be shown to those who practised it. His explorations of old Lahore made him realize that the British could not hope to understand native life and therefore should not attempt to regulate it. India's peoples lived in worlds largely untouched and unaffected by their foreign rulers and – so long as 'no one steals too flagrantly or murders too openly' – ought to be left undisturbed.[10] They should be allowed to enjoy the practical benefits of the Raj peace and justice, quinine and canals, railways and vaccinations – without having to submit to Western notions on education and religion. Kipling shared the ICS distrust of missionaries, who complicated Civilians' work by provoking native unrest and who did not 'understand why you should save bodies and leave souls alone'.[11] In his story, 'The Judgment of Dungara', the author sides with a sensible assistant collector who finds 'one creed as good as another', and mocks a fatuous missionary who manages to lose all his converts. Throughout his life he remained remarkably broad-minded in his views on religion, and in 'Hymn before Action' he called on the Christian God to protect the conquered people of other faiths who were preparing to fight for the Empire:

> For those who kneel beside us
>   At altars not Thine own,
> Who lack the lights that guide us,
>   Lord, let their faith atone.
> If wrong we did to call them,
>   By honour bound they came;
> Let not Thy Wrath befall them,
>   But deal to us the blame.

In general Kipling liked Indians as individuals and got on well with those he met: servants and print-workers, men from the bazaars, colourful characters he encountered on his journeys to the native states. His attitudes and his behaviour towards them are well illustrated by a long letter written at the age of 20 to a cousin in England. To gain their confidence, he told her, Indians had 'to be handled like children or young horses'. His own workers at the *Gazette*, for example, were 'touchy as children; obstinate as men; patient as the High Gods themselves; vicious as Devils but always loveable' if handled well. And 'the proper way to handle 'em [was] not by looking on 'em as "excitable masses of barbarism ... [or] ... down-trodden millions ... groaning under the heel of an alien and unsympathetic despotism", but as men' with their own language, proverbs, allusions and feelings, which it was the Englishman's business to understand, quote, sympathize with and master. But the letter, written over a period of six weeks by both sides of his head, also explained why almost all Englishmen, however much they learned to 'handle 'em', failed to understand Indians. In fact they could only do so by discarding much of what they had been taught at home. Without shelving their education and upbringing, they would inevitably despise men who took bribes, did not wash, maltreated their women, thought of nothing except intrigue and seduction, and possessed an 'absolute incapacity for speaking the truth'.[12]

Kipling regarded the Indian treatment of women as the main obstacle to closer relations between the natives and their rulers, for how could the British understand India when they were unable to see through the purdah and the latticed windows to that half of the population living beyond them? Yet he also considered the situation of women, chained by custom and domestic tyranny while their men demanded Western freedoms for themselves, as responsible for the worst social evils of the Subcontinent. His 'pet subjects', he told his former schoolmaster Crofts, were infant marriage and enforced widowhood. The partiality of elderly Brahmins for child-brides led naturally to a proliferation of young widows who, neglected by their families and prevented from remarrying, were often forced into prostitution. Claiming an 'extensive and peculiar' experience of this problem, he estimated that the widows became prostitutes in seventy-five cases out of a hundred.[13]

One instance of male tyranny particularly enraged him. An articulate and educated Hindu woman called Rukhmabai refused to live with her husband Dadaji, an indolent and dissipated individual to whom she had been married at the age of 11. She had remained, however, in her mother's house, experiencing a growing aversion to her husband and a determination never to live with him. At the age of 22, when Dadaji went to court to obtain his conjugal rights, she defended her case by claiming that he was diseased, impecunious and immoral. But Rukhmabai was not merely interested in justice for herself. As she showed in two letters published pseudonymously in *The Times of India*, she was determined to make her case a matter of principle, to become if necessary a martyr for the cause of Hindu women, hoping by example to improve the wretched existence imposed on them by infant marriage, drudgery, compulsory widow-hood and lack of education.

The judge in the Bombay High Court, Justice Pinhey, found in favour of Rukhmabai, declaring that it would be a 'barbarous', 'cruel', and 'revolting' thing to compel her to live with Dadaji who, he added, should not have attempted 'to recover her person, as if she had been a horse or a bullock'.[14] A few months later, in April 1886, the verdict was overturned, the Court of Appeal deciding that, according to Hindu law, Rukhmabai was obliged to reside with her husband. The following year, when another judge ordered her to go to Dadaji's house, Rukhmabai declared that she would prefer to suffer the maximum legal penalty, six months in prison.*

The case caused uproar in the Indian and Anglo-Indian press. While Hindu traditionalists feared that Pinhey's verdict was an attack on their culture and presaged an upset of their social order, British journalists tended to use it as a way of demonstrating the moral superiority of their national values. The British had previously been reluctant to interfere with native practices, making exceptions only where those practices, such as suttee (widow-burning) and female infanticide, were a form of murder. Kipling usually supported that reluctance, but on the sufferings of Indian women he refused to compromise. After learning the verdict on Rukhmabai's appeal case, he wrote a strong editorial article for the *Gazette* condemning the 'utter rottenness' of Hindu law and declaring that the society which tolerated its 'cowardly cruelty' placed itself 'below all civilisations'. When Rukhmabai was sentenced to prison for refusing to join her husband, he demanded reform of the Hindu marriage laws, arguing that the Hindu millions would be grateful to any power that struck a blow at the 'ghastly tyranny' of the Brahmins and regretting that the Government was 'unreasonably frightened by a portentous Hindu bogy, which only needs to be faced with steadfastness to collapse and shrink into nothingness'.[16]

In January 1887, in the middle of the saga of Rukhmabai, Kipling observed in the *Gazette* that, although the British had educated

---

*The case eventually ended with a compromise reached out of court. Realizing that her example would not lead to the emancipation of Indian women, Rukhmabai succumbed, renouncing her martyrdom by agreeing to give Dadaji 2,000 rupees on condition that he dropped his demands.[15]

'Young India' a good deal, 'we have not yet educated him up to the level of recognising his wife as his equal'.[17] The occasion was an article in support of Lady Dufferin's Fund which had been set up to provide medical aid (supplied mainly by female doctors from England) to Indian women who were denied access to male doctors and consequently suffered appalling levels of mortality during childbirth. Three weeks later, after the foundation stone had been laid for a women's hospital in Lahore, he published 'For the Women', simultaneously a bitter attack on Hindu men, 'Servants of the Cow', and a plea that they, beneficiaries of the West in so many ways, should allow their women to enjoy the benefit of medical aid. After describing the 'foul horrors' of childbirth, and the dirt, danger and superstition attending it, he made his entreaty:

> Help here – and not for us the boon and not to us the gain;
> Make room to save the babe from death, the mother from her pain.
> Is it so great a thing we ask? Is there no road to find
> When women of our people seek to help your womankind?

> No word to sap their faith, no talk of Christ or creed need be,
> But woman's help in woman's need and woman's ministry.
> Such healing as the West can give, that healing may they win.
> Draw back the *purdah* for their sakes, and pass our women in!

The following year, on Lady Dufferin's departure from India, a group of Bengali women sent her a farewell message of gratitude that Kipling transformed into 'The Song of the Women', a mawkish though powerful poem about the blessings her work had started to bring. But his most incisive comments on the issue of Indian women appeared in an article deriding the 'very pitiful' judgement of the *Indian Mirror*, a native paper in English, on the case of Rukhmabai:

'Anomalies, however outrageous, must be for a time tolerated, if only for the sake of social traditions which are after all the backbone of a nation.' And so the article runs on, showing behind every line of fluent English, the bound and crippled spirit of the ultra-orthodox Hindu, very careful that the 'sacredness' of the marriage tie shall shackle women only. Then our contemporary, having done its duty, launches into its usual clamour for 'representative institutions', its proofs that the Hindu is intellectually equal to the Englishman, and the supreme necessity of giving salaried appointments to the Bengali. It is time that this double-faced policy were abandoned. A class cannot claim all the advantages of Western civilization, and avoid all the responsibilities which that civilization entails, on the plea that it is a very venerable race, highly sensitive, and bound hand and foot by the traditions of the priests. English instinct revolts at this; recognising the race that babbles of High University Education one moment, and the sacredness of wedding babes to babes at the next, as a hybrid, and therefore a lower people. Honest paganism, naked and unashamed before the sun, men can understand and respect; but the shifty, crafty composite creed that cries: – 'Are we not all brothers, and are not my women-folk cattle as the law directs?' is worthy of nothing but scorn. For his own sake, if ever he wishes to be taken seriously, the 'enlightened' native must look to it that the progress he is so proud of reaches his family, and is not merely a weapon to use in the struggle for appointments.[18]

Kipling's other 'pet subject' was sanitation in the cities. Indians, he told readers of the *Gazette*, were 'undeveloped on the sanitary side, children in their inability to understand the dangers of dirt, and fatalists in their apathetic indifference to those dangers'.[19] The old city of Lahore, he believed (until he saw Calcutta), was as filthy as any place could be, and its municipality, composed exclusively of native members, was a slothful, negligent, stupid and 'irreclaimably perverse body' of men. Its equivalent in Calcutta was no more distinguished, boasting that its city was a metropolis when in fact it was a midden crying out for a bucket and broom. The appointment of a British health officer to the city in 1886 provoked outrage in the Indian press which argued that a native should have been selected for the post. Kipling was brusquely dismissive of the fuss. 'Sympathy with native wants etc' was a 'pretty sentiment', but in sanitary matters it was a dangerous delusion. It might be a 'great and desirable virtue' to sympathize with the 'teeming millions', but the less an Englishman sympathized with their views on sanitation, 'the better it is for the "teeming millions". They live longer.'[20]

He returned often to the subject, urging municipalities to spend more money on sanitation and less on education. A single 'decent primer on Sanitary Engineering and sewage disposal', he said privately, would be worth more than 'all the tomes of sacred smut ever produced'.[21] But he never expected the municipalities to instigate the improvements themselves: indeed they were so lazy and incompetent that he hoped, one day in the distant future, that their 'futile bickerings' would be replaced by a 'large and enlightened city despotism'. Educated Indians, especially Bengalis, irritated him by proclaiming their readiness for self-rule while appealing to the Government for help on 'every conceivable trifle' and demonstrating their inability to 'perform the simplest duties of corporate life'. He was convinced that Indians needed – and would continue for a long time to need – British supervision; as soon as that disappeared, 'the old, old, racial ineptitude' would reassert itself. In troubled times the 'childish pride', the 'slackness of brain' and the love of authority for its own sake would give way to 'dazed bewilderment'. At moments he came close to suggesting that Indians were congenitally useless and inferior. The theory (which he did not truly hold) would at least have explained the fact that three decades of peace and British effort had bred no artists or engineers, or that 'of all the disabilities under which the land lay, not one had been lifted by its own endeavours'.[22] But it never seems to have occurred to him that permanent subordinates treated as perpetual children are unlikely to develop qualities of leadership and initiative.

Kipling associated indigenous shortcomings with the Indians he least liked: Bengalis, of whom there were 69 million in 1881; well educated natives, estimated at about 50,000 at this time, and the 73 founding delegates of the Indian National Congress, who held their inaugural conference in 1885. But he knew hardly anyone belonging to these groups; he seldom met middle-class Indians even in Lahore. Mistrust of Bengali babus was of course an old British tradition. Viceroys in India and secretaries of state in Whitehall alternated dismissive comments about their loquacity with anxieties that the encouragement of native ambitions might lead to 'the supremacy of Baboodom'.[23] On the ground district officers regarded them as 'the curse of the country', compared them to snakes and Pharisees, and wished they were dealing with more manly peoples such as Sikhs, Rajputs and Pathans.[24] Among the most senior British figures in India at that time, only Ripon seems to have realized that the future governing élite would come not from the princely families but from the growing, Bengali-dominated class of educated natives.

Contempt for babus was one of the few Anglo-Indian prejudices that Kipling adopted without examination. Long before he visited Bengal he mocked them in the pages of the *Gazette* as smooth, seditious, garrulous and ineffectual: to the 'obstinacy of men', they added the 'unreasoning petulance of small children, always morbidly afraid that someone is laughing at them'.[25] When he finally saw them in their own province 'among ledgers', he admitted they made excellent accountants – and that was what they should remain. In crises they were useless, running to the British for help or running away altogether.[26] Their problem, according to Kipling, was their hybrid nature, an unsuccessful product of superficial Western education grafted on to the obscurantism of the Subcontinent. This type of grafting had been precisely the objective of earlier British administrators such as Lord William Bentinck and Thomas Babington Macaulay. Kipling disagreed with it entirely. Indians should study subjects useful for their country and themselves, not alien writers such as Wordsworth; they should remain Indians rather than become brown Englishmen.

Given all this, Kipling's antipathy to the Indian National Congress is not difficult to understand. At first a small, urban-based organization dominated by Hindu lawyers, Congress began its existence in the 1880s, proclaiming an 'unswerving loyalty' to the British Crown and declaring that the continued affiliation of India to Great Britain was 'absolutely essential' to the interests of national development. In the early years it pressed for the admission of more Indians to the ICS and for greater Indian representation on the legislative councils – aims so modest that the movement gained a certain amount of sympathy from Dufferin and Lansdowne, the viceroys in office during its first decade. But the initial British view that Congress was a loyal and harmless body slowly altered as its demands for representative institutions became stronger, and as officials gradually suspected it of becoming detrimental to Muslim interests.

At the age of 20 Kipling had no doubts about the nature and purpose of Congress – and he remained undoubting for the rest of his life. When he was in India he insisted that the organization did not represent anybody except a small group of university-trained hybrids, while later it devoted itself entirely to the interests of the Brahmins. From first to last, he declared in 1930, it had been a Brahmin plot, 'Brahminee . . . plus Balliol', a movement injurious to all other castes because Brahmins were bound to misrule people they regarded as inferior, damned for their sins in past lives and working out their sentences in this one. [27]* When reporting the Congress conference in Allahabad at the end of 1888, he pilloried the delegates for demanding liberties for themselves but not for their women:

> Of the twelve hundred men who, later, would claim what one of their most eloquent speakers called 'the Freedom', not twenty had looked upon the civilisation whose rights they demanded, whose duties they would not discharge; not fifty would suffer their wives to 'see the corn grow', not a hundred would allow their maidens to wait for girlhood ere they were wedded; and not one had, with hand or head, struck out an original thought for the betterment of his fellows. [28]

His report also contained a dismissive reference to Andrew Hearsey, a former army officer and now a supporter of Congress, who went straight to the newspaper offices with a horsewhip and tried to thrash the editor. But Kipling continued to ridicule nationalists. Two years later, with the collaboration of Lockwood, he published 'The Enlightenments of Pagett MP', a story in which Orde, an ICS officer, debates with Pagett, their creator's archetypal Liberal ignoramus. Pagett is an enthusiast for Congress and believes that it represents 'the natural aspirations and wishes of the people at large'. But he becomes perturbed when Orde introduces him to Indians who either scoff at the movement or have never heard of it. Next he is disillusioned about educated 'Young India', who turns out to be 'callow', and slowly it dawns on him that Congress is wrong or muddle-headed on a great many issues; in short, Pagett is enlightened. [29] The 'story' was an exercise in propaganda rather than fiction, and Kipling had the sense not to include it in any of his books.

Some ICS officers believed that their duty was to prepare India for the day of their departure, but very few expected that moment to occur in the foreseeable future. Most officials found their Indian colleagues in the ICS were poor district officers: while they made 'fair

---

*Although Lord Curzon and Lord Milner, two proconsuls who shared most of his views on imperialism, were graduates of Balliol, Kipling used the Oxford college, as his friend Cecil Rhodes had done, as a metaphor for radical intellectuals eager to subvert the Empire by encouraging native opposition. Lockwood had similar views, blaming Balliol for breeding 'Radicals and kidgloved socialists'.

though weak judges', they proved to be 'hopeless failures' in executive positions.[30] When Sir William Wedderburn, an early President of Congress, urged Curzon to employ more Indians in the senior ranks of the ICS, the Viceroy replied that in his experience highly placed natives were unequal to emergencies and inclined to abdicate their responsibilities or run away.[31] Kipling stated his beliefs in 'On the City Wall': 'overmuch tenderness' had encouraged natives to think they were capable of running the country, and 'many devout Englishmen believe[d] this also, because the theory [was] stated in beautiful English with all the latest political garnish'. But it was not true: India could 'never stand alone'.

Kipling found evidence for his view in the case of Rajendra Chanda Ghose, a deputy collector in Bengal, who explained to the Government that he had not made an adequate tour of his subdivision because part of it had been 'disturbed'. It was difficult, commented Kipling in the *Gazette*, to 'conceive the frame of mind of a man who could put down on paper such a humiliating avowal of cowardice'. Ordinary shame, he thought, should have counselled 'a fabrication in some way less injurious to the Babu's character as an official'.[32] Subsequently, in the story 'The Head of the District', Chanda Ghose was transformed into Grish Chunder Dé, a Bengali appointed to succeed the dying Orde (no longer dealing with Pagett) in a district on the North-West Frontier. Orde is a model Civilian, devoted to his duty, remembering on his death bed by the Indus that four villages within the border need a remittance because their crops have been poor. By contrast, Grish Chunder Dé knows nothing of the frontier (it was unfair and unrealistic of Kipling to appoint a Bengali to the Punjab) because he is a hybrid with 'much curious book-knowledge of bump-suppers, cricket-matches, hunting-runs, and other unholy sports of the alien' but little knowledge of India outside Bengal. As soon as there is trouble with the tribes, he takes flight – his brother, mistaken for him, is decapitated – and the situation is only brought under control by the skill of Tallantine, the British official who had been passed over as Orde's successor.

Readers of the *Gazette* and stories such as this would have concluded that the author had only one side to his head – its nature given to telling Indians what was good for them, its style directed by a somewhat grudging and sarcastic paternalism. But out of the office, on his travels or writing his stories, the other side prevailed and the broad-mindedness returned. Purun Dass, a former prime minister of a native state, is a natural leader, 'a man accustomed to command'; the physical stamina of the Babu in *Kim* 'would astonish folk who mock at his race'; and even Grish Chunder Dé, however inadequate on the frontier, 'had wisely and ... sympathetically ruled a crowded district in South-Eastern Bengal'.

A rather brash and know-all tone pervades Kipling's teenage articles on Indian subjects. But this was soon discarded in favour of receptive and unprejudiced reporting of spectacles such as the Mohurrum Festival in Lahore or the Festival of Lamps in the Shalimar Gardens. Travelling in new regions was too absorbing to allow him the time or inclination to sneer. He was so exhilarated by a visit to Rajputana – sleeping in kings' palaces or on cotton bales under the stars, hearing the roar of tigers in the hills, listening to 'all sorts and conditions of men' as they told him the stories of their lives – that he 'clean forgot ... there was a newspapery telegraphic world without'.[33] In the articles accompanying this journey, which began appearing in the *Pioneer* at the end of 1887, he wrote enthusiastically about native qualities that he had previously disparaged. Hindu rulers were extolled – admittedly they were maharajas rather than babus – and their public works applauded. Jeypore (Jaipur) had a fine hospital, a good water supply and the best gardens and museum in all India. Udaipur might be the opposite, 'as backward as Jeypore is advanced', but this too deserved praise: backwardness was 'eminently suited to a place like Udaipur'. Its Maharana had been 'wise in his determination to have no railroad to his capital', because he had thus preserved it from 'the tourist who would have scratched his name on the Temple of Garuda and laughed horse-laughs upon the lake'.[34]

Yet it is in the Indian stories of *Plain Tales* and the subsequent collections that Kipling most clearly displayed his essential sympathy for the peoples among whom he lived. Four of the stories are about love between Englishmen and native women, and all end in grief and tragedy for the women. In two ('Beyond the Pale' and 'Without Benefit of Clergy') the misery is caused by fever, disease and the risk of attempting to cross the racial divide; in the others ('Lispeth' and 'Georgie-Porgie') it results from the heartless behaviour of superficial Englishmen. When Georgie-Porgie and his English bride go out on to the veranda after dinner, they hear a distant wailing sound. 'I suppose', says Georgie-Porgie, 'some brute of a Hillman has been beating his wife.' In fact it is his abandoned Burmese mistress, who has travelled hundreds of miles to find him, 'crying, all by herself, down the hillside, among the stones of the watercourse where the washermen wash the clothes'.

A different and much wider kind of sympathy infuses *Kim*, the greatest of all Kipling's Indian work, a novel that took him eight years to complete and which he did not publish until 1901. Critics have detected blemishes of 'orientalism' in the text, reprehensible stereotyping in phrases such as 'the huckster instinct of the East', 'the immemorial commission of Asia', 'the Oriental's indifference to mere noise'.[35] But Kipling was only recording what he – and a lot of other people – had noticed on their travels in India. In any case it is a minor defect beside the book's overall achievement: the panorama of the north, its peoples and religions, its landscapes of plains and mountains, its description of the Grand Trunk Road (which Forster considered the greatest thing any Englishman had written about India)[36] and, above all, its four great Indian figures (the Lama, the Babu, the Pathan horse-dealer, the dowager Sahiba from Saharunpore) and its vivid host of minor characters. It is a beautiful book that could only have been written by someone who, whatever else he may have felt, loved India deeply.

Kim has justly been described as 'the answer to nine-tenths of the charges levelled against Kipling and the refutation of most of the generalisations about him'.[37] Yet it does not quite answer the charge of racism, unless racial disparagement (which was almost universal at the time) is withdrawn from the sheet and the charge is restricted to feelings of perpetual racial superiority. Kipling certainly regarded Indians as inferior in various ways, especially in running an administration, and few contemporaries in Britain or elsewhere would have disagreed with him. Yet that in itself does not demonstrate a claim to racial superiority, as Ruskin did when he called the English 'a race mingled of the best northern blood', or Tennyson when he wrote, 'the noblest men methinks are bred/Of ours the Saxon-Norman race ...'[38] Rather it reflects the much less contentious view that at that time the British were more capable of performing certain tasks than the Indians. And that seemed entirely natural: after all, they possessed the experience and self-confidence innate in citizens of a prosperous country with a large empire and a long and relatively peaceful history of political development.

Certainly the British in Kipling's stories seldom exhibit any moral superiority. For each hard-working and incorruptible official, there are a number of frivolous and less reputable figures whose deficiencies are displayed. An army captain is criticized for referring to natives as 'niggers', and an Anglican chaplain looks at Kim's Lama 'with the triple-ringed uninterest of the creed that lumps nine-tenths of the world under the title of "heathen"'. No one could accuse Kipling of being uninterested in 'heathen' – or of referring seriously to non-Christians as such. He loved the intercommunal brotherhood of his Masonic lodge in Lahore where 'there aint such things as infidels' among the 'Brethren black an' brown'.[39]

The charge of racism is commonly accompanied by the quotation of lines from 'The Ballad of East and West', which imply that the peoples on opposite sides of the globe are so different that they will never understand each other until the Day of Judgement:

> *Oh, East is East and West is West, and never the twain shall meet,*
> *Till Earth and Sky stand presently at God's great Judgment seat;*

Yet the apparent message of these lines in contradicted by the rest of the verse, which asserts that two men of similar courage and ability can be equals despite multitudinous differences of class, race, nation and continent.

> *But there is neither East nor West, Border, nor Breed, nor Birth,*
> *When two strong men stand face to face, tho' they come from the ends of the earth.*

5

A Sense of Empire

AT THE END of 1887 Kipling left Lahore to work on the *Pioneer*, the *Gazette*'s more eminent sister paper in Allahabad. The chief proprietor had suggested the move three years earlier, but the young journalist had not felt ready to leave the Family Square and settle eight hundred miles away. Only after five years in the Punjab, during which he became a contributor to the *Pioneer*, did he feel it was time to go. He was offered a rise in salary from £500 to £540, a job less immured in an office, and a chance to work for one of the Subcontinent's major newspapers, a publication which, though founded to reflect the Government's views, had fumed against the Liberalism of Lord Ripon and was now an abusive critic of the Indian National Congress.

Unlike Lahore, Allahabad was not in any sense a frontier city. Once a provincial capital of the Mughal Empire and still one of Hinduism's sacred sites – the vast Kumbh Mela pilgrimage festival takes place every twelve years at the confluence of the Ganges and Yamuna rivers – it was ceded to Britain in 1801 and later became the capital of the United Provinces.* Of similar size to Lahore (over 150,000 inhabitants) but with an inverse ratio of Hindus to Muslims

---

*These were still called the North-Western Provinces in Kipling's day (an anomaly by then, because they lie to the south-east of the Punjab). They were renamed when the North-West Frontier Province was formed in 1901.

(these formed less than a third of the population), Allahabad also had more than 5,000 British, Eurasian and other European residents, many of them living in the spacious and exclusive civil lines to the north of the main bazaars.

Deprived of his family haven, Kipling stayed at the Allahabad Club, which he found a dreary place where men gambled seriously and women found such 'twaddle' to read in the library that they 'cackled and shrieked' behind the baize doors. But in the summer of 1888 he moved into 'Belvedere', the home of two new friends, Alec Hill, a professor of science at Muir College (the kernel of Allahabad University), and his American wife Edmonia (known as 'Ted'). A tall and attractive woman whom Kipling claimed to be in love with, Mrs Hill soon filled the role of confidante and adviser (but not lover) to the young writer. She read his stories, which she did not approve of, and supplied him with details to use for female characters and their conversation. When she went away, he grumbled that he had no 'sympathetic soul' with whom to discuss his ideas and outlines.[1]

Although he was only 22, Kipling's incipient baldness made him look about forty. He might have been regarded as fine looking, conceded Mrs Hill, had it not been for his bristling eyebrows, his large moustache and his disfiguring, thick-lensed spectacles. He was short (five foot six) and sallow-skinned, but he looked good on a horse, and in hot weather she thought him very smart in his white mess jacket and yellow cummerbund. An entertaining if rather exhausting lodger, he loved limericks, word games and clever repartee; he was 'animation itself' and 'fairly scintillated' with guests, making them laugh with his story-telling. He was also popular with servants, especially his 'devoted man', Kadir Baksh, who looked after him and was 'more attentive than a parent to a child'.[2]

Allahabad never appealed to him as Lahore and Simla had done. He was an 'old hand' now, jaundiced, a little intolerant – and his 'stamping grounds' were far away to the north-west. A few years earlier he would have wanted to explore the city's bazaars, befriend the Muslim merchants and artisans, test the truth of a police claim that Allahabad had a 'very bad character' and was 'full of the most turbulent and notorious ruffians of the worst description'.[3] Yet his curiosity had diminished. Mrs Hill recalled that he went to grand Indian parties to celebrate Hindu festivals, but he had become 'too respectable', he admitted, 'to mix among the lower-class natives' as he had once done. Too respectable, and perhaps too irritable as well: he recounted to Mrs Hill how he had been 'plagued by natives' on a train, especially by a couple who chewed *paan* and spat betel juice in his compartment, and he sent her a derisive description of 'fat Eurasian and slatternly half caste girls tramping' up and down the platform at Allahabad station.[4]

Kipling's curiosity revived when he left the city, as he proved with his reports from Rajputana at the end of 1887, and as he demonstrated with his vigorous criticisms of Calcutta and Benares early the following year. The proprietors of the *Pioneer* wisely felt it would be better for both their employee and their business if he wrote about his travels instead of sitting in an office aiming barbs at the Government. But they also gave him more responsibility – and a less laborious routine – on his returns to Allahabad. At the beginning of 1888 he was appointed editor of *The Week's News*, a supplement of the *Pioneer*, in which he gave the public its first sight of his best Indian and Anglo-Indian stories.

In May 1888 Kipling was recalled to Lahore to edit the *Gazette* while Kay Robinson was absent. Mrs Hill noted in her diary how he did 'love those wild men of the north', whom he called his 'own folk'; after living among the 'frog-like' easterners of Allahabad, he was happy to be back among the 'savage, boastful, arrogant, hot-headed men' of the Punjab.[5] But little else pleased the acting editor on his return to Lahore in the hot weather. He found himself 'gummed' into an office chair from eight in the morning until six in the evening, followed by post-dinner visits to the inferno at the printing press. Moreover, as his family was in Simla, he had to return to the 'wearying, Godless futile life' at the Club – 'same men, same talk, same billiards'.[6]

His last visit to Simla in the summer failed to improve his temper. One dinner party (with the Lieutenant-Governor) was a 'portentous dull affair', while another, 'adorned with music and recitations', was so 'mournful and grotesque' that it failed to provide him with even a sentence for his work. Soon he was cancelling dinners and dances, assuring Mrs Hill that he was not 'gallivanting' about, and confessing that Simla had become an 'abomination' to him. After denouncing the behaviour of one middle-aged coquette, he asked his confidante's forgiveness for being 'brutal', explaining that Simla always made him 'savage' – and that season more than ever.[7]

These experiences reinforced his eagerness to pursue his 'scheme', a plan to return to Britain and earn his living as a writer in London. He was already disenchanted with India and his two newspapers, and the weeks in Simla increased his determination to quit the *Pioneer*, leave journalism and eventually become a novelist. Like Ulysses he had already seen 'cities and men', but now he needed to see more and experience more – and to write about it. He also needed a newer and larger readership than Anglo-India could provide. It was no longer enough to write for 'Men 'neath an Indian sky/Cynical, seedy and dry' – even if his opinion of them had improved. He still wanted to write about India, but now for a British audience, to tell his fellow countrymen what was going on in their greatest imperial possession. India, he maintained, had been so maligned by 'Globe-trotters', who wrote of the place with 'the unbridled arrogance of five weeks on a Cook's ticket', that he wanted to avenge her by writing the reality.[8] But mingled with these motives were more personal inducements. After six years in India he was bored of a life where work was an editorial desk and pleasure consisted largely of 'dolorous dissipations of gymkhanas where everyone knows everyone else, [and] the chastened intoxication of dances where all engagements are booked ... ten days ahead'. As he admitted in the *Pioneer*, he dreamed of London's music, its girls, its theatres. It was pathetic, Mrs Hill recorded, to hear him proclaiming his ambition to have enough money and time to go to every theatre in the British capital.[9]

Kipling's last months in India were busy, productive and controversial. Apart from his journalism, he indulged his flair for annoying both friends and enemies, and he oversaw the publication of the six Railway Library volumes of Indian and Anglo-Indian stories written since *Plain Tales*. Two of his targets in verse were Lord Dufferin, the subject of the brilliant but unfair satire in 'One Viceroy Resigns', and General Roberts, a 'pocket-Wellin'ton' whom Kipling generally admired but on this occasion decided to arraign for nepotism. The barb at Roberts angered the *Pioneer*'s chief proprietor, who was also upset by his employee's coverage of the Congress meeting in Allahabad at Christmas 1888. Given Kipling's hostility to Congress and the *Pioneer*'s sneering contempt for nationalism, it was surely provocative to let him loose at such a meeting in his own town. Andrew Hearsey's attempt to horsewhip the editor might have been foreseen.

Certainly the manager of the newspaper 'did not heave any sigh of regret' when his subordinate announced his departure: he even advised Kipling, whom he regarded as overpaid, that he would never make his fortune with a pen[10] – an opinion echoed in the same year by the proprietor of the *Daily Telegraph*, who thought his work 'hardly reache[d] the standard required of a position' on his paper's staff, and the American publishers, Harper Brothers, who allegedly rebuffed him with the words, 'Young man, this house is devoted to the production of literature.'[11] Despite the manager's reservations, however, the *Pioneer* asked him to send regular contributions from abroad.

In February 1889 Kipling returned to Lahore to say goodbye to his parents. Although he was perplexed to find that Punjabi schoolboys had been infected with cricket 'mania', he was once again glad to be in his 'own land' with the horse-dealers, carpenters and clerks ('we don't keep babus in these parts') who came to pay their respects.[12] On 9 March he sailed from Calcutta for San Francisco with Alec and Edmonia Hill. He had not left the Subcontinent for six and a half years.

Kipling's last sight of British India was Burma, although he instantly realized from its smell that it was foreign and should not have belonged to an administration based in Calcutta. He liked the place immediately, noting how its architects had cleverly copied nature, the shapes of the pagodas looking like toddy-palm trees, their tinkling bells resembling the rustling of leaves. Although notoriously energetic himself, he enjoyed the enervating aura of this 'delightfully lazy land full of pretty girls and very bad cheroots'. What was the point of working, he asked the readers of the *Pioneer*, if one could spend one's time with 'grinning good-humoured little maidens' and fall 'deeply and irrevocably in love' with a girl in the old Moulmein pagoda?[13]

His brief visit to Burma had no effect on Kipling's love life or his view of the British Empire, but it was responsible for some of his most magical verses. 'Mandalay' is simultaneously a celebration of Burmese charms, a lament for a lost love, and an iteration of one of his favourite themes – the homesickness and nostalgia of people who have lived in Britain and India and pine for the one they have most recently abandoned ('If you've heard the East a-callin', you won't never 'eed naught else'). In his articles for the *Pioneer* he assembled all the ingredients – girls and cheroots, ricefields and palm trees,

Buddha and pagodas, elephants and teak logs – before evoking Burma in a handful of nouns and half a dozen verses.

> For the wind is in the palm-trees, and the temple-bells they say:
> 'Come you back, you British soldier; come you back to Mandalay!'

When the poem was published in *Barrack Room Ballads*, 'old Burmese hands' could see that its author had been a tourist and not a resident. As one of them pointed out in a letter to the *Gazette*, Burmese girls did not wear petticoats or caps or yellow clothes (which were reserved for monks); nor did they kiss their idol's feet or call him Buddha or 'the great Gawd Budd, (in Burma he was referred to as 'the Gautama'); and in addition the author had taken 'a very great stretch of poetical licence' in making the dawn come up 'like thunder outer China 'crost the Bay!'[14]

At sea between Burma and Singapore Mrs Hill claimed to witness the inception of the barrack room ballads. Kipling was standing by the deck rail, humming (as he often did when composing verse) and shaking the ash from his pipe overboard, when suddenly he exclaimed, 'I have it. I'll write some Tommy Atkins ballads.'[15] This seems not in fact to have been the conception – he had referred some weeks earlier to his 'barrack room ballads' but it may have been a compelling moment, a luminous comprehension of the genre that later made his reputation in England. And at the same time – in or on the way to Singapore – his imagination began to conceive a wider vision of the British Empire. He had come to know India, as he told a cousin, 'from the barrack room and the brothel, to the Ballroom and the Viceroy's Council', but the knowledge was restricted to an Indian or Anglo-Indian context. Now, as he embarked on those voyages that led him so many times across the world, he began to understand India's role in the imperial scheme and, beyond that, to sense the range and possibilities of the Empire. In an almost delirious mood in Singapore he envisaged a future in which the still weak and immature colonies would come together forged 'in one great iron band girdling the earth'. 'Within that limit Free Trade. Without, rancorous protection' – but the band itself would be impregnable – 'too vast a hornet's nest for any combination of Powers to disturb'.[16]

His departure from India gave Kipling the chance to experience the rest of the Empire, especially the large settler colonies of Canada and the southern hemisphere that dominated his imperial thinking for the next twenty years. But it also gave him the opportunity to view India from a more distant perspective, to discover a coherence in Britain's role that clarified his imperialism at a certain cost to his art.

During his years in India he had treated the administration impartially, as prepared to praise as he was ready to criticize. In spite of its qualities, he knew it was sometimes misguided, always cumbersome and occasionally absurd – a reasonable target, therefore, for sporadic censure and ridicule. He savaged the policies of Ripon and the record of Grant Duff, he teased Colvin for manipulating the figures in the budget, and in the story 'Tod's Amendment' he gave a 6-year-old boy more understanding of agricultural tenancies than the Legal Member of the Viceroy's Council, whose 'knowledge of natives was limited to English-speaking Durbaris, and his own red *chaprassis* [messengers]'. During the Simla season of 1885 Kipling had suggested in the *Gazette* that Lord Dufferin's Councillors – the Cabinet of India – transmigrated after death into 'the bodies of the great grey Langurs'. On seeing their 'grey, hairy monkeyish faces' three years later, he described them in private as '*very* like apes',[17] though in verse he was more polite and more accurate, portraying them in 'One Viceroy Resigns' as 'earnest, narrow men,/But chiefly earnest, and they'll do your work,/And end by writing letters to the *Times*'.

His attitude towards the ICS was no more deferential. Some of his fictitious officers were admirable, but others were pedantic bureaucrats, impractical theorists ('over-engined for the beam') or social hazards ('like unto a blandishing gorilla'). In his newspaper articles he denounced officers who appeared to have fallen below the Service's high ethical standards through involvement in business transactions forbidden by the 'covenant' they had to sign on joining the ICS: Mr H.E.Sullivan, a senior Civilian in Madras who had allegedly bought a tea plantation, was thus able to learn from the *Gazette* that he was a 'man of deft excuses' who 'for the honour of [the] service' should sue for libel or resign; if he stayed in Madras and became acting governor, 'every moment of [his] rule' would be 'an insult to the land'.[18]

When writing about the ICS as a body, Kipling was more appreciative, but even then he detected inherent weaknesses, a regrettable naïvety, a credulousness when dealing with aspirations and capabilities. For thirty years, he wrote in the *Gazette*,

> desperately earnest and energetic Englishmen have been devoting the flower of their lives to the leverage of a certain section of the community under their care, in one particular and well-defined direction. By help on all sides; by propping and pushing, by praise and threats; by ever ready watchfulness to guide the weak hand and to encourage the faint heart; by bearing themselves the blame of failure, and giving away freely the credit of success due to their own care and efforts, these Englishmen have come to believe – and their zeal must be their excuse – that the helped hand can execute, and the nursed brain plan, in time of stress, for itself . . .[19]

But this was a delusion, Kipling argued, as Anglo-Indian businessmen understood. The non officials were more hard-headed than the Civilians and knew that natives could not be trusted to run things by themselves. 'European supervision', he quoted from the Bengal Chamber of Commerce, was 'an essential element in this country', and he praised Bombay for possessing 'a strong enough non-official element to break the dead weight of the laziest local government'.[20]

While in India Kipling preferred to write stories about men and women sent out by the military and the India Office in London. Afterwards the emphasis changed, a new tendency emerged, his stories became less interested in Anglo-Indian lives and characters than in the work they did and the cause of the Empire they served.[21] There was no clear break, no radical alteration of mood, but a subtle change of ratio between criticism and tribute, between satire and panegyric.

His first major endorsement of the Empire had come at the end of 1885, half-way through his Indian years, in two long letters to his cousin Margaret Burne-Jones. In the first he explained that, living in a country where people starved from 'purely preventable causes' or were 'in native states hideously misgoverned from their rulers' own folly', a journalist could do a worthwhile job by alerting the public – and the administration – to the problems of a particular district and hammering away at them until something was done. 'There's no finer feeling in life', he told her, 'than the knowledge that a year's work has really done some living good, besides amusing and interesting people, for a Province that you are generally interested in and love.'

Margaret's reply has been lost, but a sentence which he flung back at her in his second letter – 'Do the English as a rule feel the welfare of the natives at heart?' – provoked a passionate response.

If you had met some of the men I know you would cross out that sentence and weep. What else are we working in the country for [?] For what else do the best men of the Commission die from overwork, and disease, if not to keep the people alive in the first place and healthy in the second [?] We spend our best men on the country like water and if ever a foreign country was made better through 'the blood of the martyrs' India is that country. I couldn't tell you now what the men one knows are doing but you can read for yourself if you will how Englishmen have laboured and died for the peoples of the country ... have you ever heard of a 'demoral-ized district'; when tens of thousands of people are panic stricken say, with an invasion of cholera – or dying from famine? Do you know how Englishmen, Oxford men expensively educated, are turned off to 'do' that district – to make their own arrangements for the cholera camps; for the prevention of disorder; or for famine relief, to pull the business through or die – whichever God wills. Then another man, or may be boy takes his place. Yes the English in India do do a little for the benefit of the natives and small thanks they get.[22]

In the Indian tales Kipling wrote in Britain and America, the imperial accent is placed on service not dominion. In two stories he daydreamed of colonizing Kashmir with British and Eurasian set-tlers,[23] but his major works of the period make it plain that conquest and annexation were no longer part of his imperial scheme. The British were in India now for a moral purpose, for the good of the native inhabitants, whom it was their duty to lead through example to a safer and more prosperous future. From Vermont in 1896 he even felt able to claim that there had been 'no civilising experiment in the world's history, at all comparable to British rule in India'.[24]

Almost uncritical admiration for the administrative services was displayed in a series of post-India stories such as 'The Head of the District', 'The Tomb of his Ancestors', 'The Bridge-Builders', and 'William the Conqueror'. All paid tribute to their protagonist as a model of courage and responsibility, but 'The Tomb of his Ancestors' also celebrated those families that served 'India genera-tion after generation as dolphins follow in line across the open sea'.

The Chinn family knew exactly what it had to do: 'A clever Chinn passes for the Bombay Civil Service', while a 'dull Chinn enters the Police Department or the Woods and Forests'. As he demonstrated in his poignant poem, 'The Exiles' Line', Kipling recognized the degree of self-sacrifice required of such families. An official knew he would spend most of his career in India while his children were at school or in the care of governesses in England, and his parents had retired to Eastbourne or somewhere else on the south coast.

Late Victorian imperialists liked to stress the importance of 'the strong man ruling alone'. Now that the framework of empire was in place, they believed that the great civilizing experiment would succeed if carried out by men possessing the ancestral virtues – what Sir James Stephen, a former legal member of the Viceroy's Council, called 'the masterful will, the stout heart, the active brain, the calm nerves, the strong body'.[25] Kipling also believed in 'the strong man' with energy and initiative, governing in his twenties half a million people and 4,000 square miles, a man bound to the laws of civilization but unfettered by codes and regulations and orders received through a telegraph wire. Several men in his later Indian stories exhibit Stephen's requisite qualities, living solitary lives, receiving little praise for their work, often falling sick and sometimes dying from disease and overwork. They are well-drawn and fairly accurate portraits of ICS officers, but the very similarity of the characters, their work and their sense of duty, tends to diminish the quality of the fiction. By 1895 Kipling had so lost the scepticism with which he used to describe Anglo-India that he could not only produce Scott, the indefatigable famine worker in 'William the Conqueror', but also describe a meeting with his future wife in a gush of sentimentality.

> He had no desire to make any dramatic entry, but an accident of the sunset ordered it that, when he had taken off his helmet to get the evening breeze, the low light should fall across his forehead, and he could not see what was before him; while one waiting at the tent door beheld, with new eyes, a young man, beautiful as Paris, a god in a halo of golden dust, walking slowly at the head of his flocks, while at his knee ran small naked Cupids.

ICS rule was essentially paternalist which, as Kipling recognized and accepted, meant treating the Indians as children. Young officials, each responsible for hundreds of thousands of people, had to assume a moral authority which their subjects had to respect – an authority which patted the good children who were obedient and deferential and punished the naughty ones who rebelled. Kipling also regarded Indians as people going through a 'childish' phase of their history who would continue to benefit from adult tutelage: if Findlayson in 'The Bridge-Builders' carried on building bridges with Indian labour, then one day – perhaps not very soon – they would learn to build bridges by themselves. The paternalists were so few in number that Kipling knew they could not achieve much for 270 million people beyond building roads, canals and a system of justice. But they were able to provide peace and security, especially for minorities. 'If we didn't hold the land,' he told Margaret Burne-Jones, 'in six months it would be one big cock pit of conflicting princelets.'[26] At the age of 19 Kipling identified a truth which the next century largely failed to recognize: that, when all appropriate qualifications are made, minorities usually fare better within imperial or multinational systems than in nations dominated by the ethos and ethnicity of a majority.

He also identified a number of threats, both external and internal, to the imperial project, and decided to warn readers about them in his stories. Much has been made of his place in the 'Great Game'* played by British and Tsarist officers as their empires jostled for position before a clash that was often predicted but in fact never took place. Yet although he feared the Russians across the frontier in central Asia because of their talent 'only second to ours of turning all sorts of clans and races into loyal supporters', the 'Game' occupies little space in his work: a story about a cavalry officer imprisoned by the Russians ('The Man Who Was'), a poem about Russian duplicity ('The Truce of the Bear'), and an improbable and unconvincing subplot in *Kim*, when a Russian agent is foiled and humiliated by Kim and the Babu. In Kipling's eyes the real enemies of British India were British: zealous and misguided missionaries (secular as well as religious) and interfering politicians in England.

Kipling wanted to reform India by removing the things he could

---

*The phrase was first used by one of the 'Game's' earliest victims, Captain Conolly, who was executed in 1842 by the Emir of Bokhara, but it was not widely known until Kipling publicized it in *Kim*.

not stomach, the abuses such as child marriage, the squalor and danger of life in the urban slums. But he did not want to stop Indians being Indians or to transform them into something else. Privately he might agree with Macaulay's notorious dictum – 'that a single shelf of a good European library was worth the whole native literature of India and Arabia' – but he saw no point in teaching Indians about Chaucer or Milton (as happened at the Punjab College): they should learn about their own culture or useful subjects such as railway work.[27] After the opening of Mayo College in Ajmer in 1885, Kipling had publicly proclaimed the 'infinite good' that would be achieved by bringing together 'the sons of princelings' as 'schoolboys under direct English influence, and in the healthy moral atmosphere that springs from intelligent and sympathetic English supervision ...'[28] But he did not really manage to convince even himself. It was all very well creating Indian Etons for Rajput noblemen, but what, apart from a reduction in bloodshed, could they achieve? Some years earlier Sir Alfred Lyall had admitted that 'we do not altogether improve the nobles by keeping them from fighting';[29] and Kipling agreed that the vitality of a warlike people could not be preserved indefinitely without allowing them to wage war. The Sikh Sirdars, he reported during his tour of Rajputana, were known to be 'rotting on their lands', the Rajput Thakurs confessed they were 'growing rusty', and the noble warrior with his horse and sabre had become 'an anachronism in a blue turban'.[30] Indian neo-Etonians had no obvious role in India.

Kipling was less ambivalent in his attitudes to religious missionaries. As with many of his views on political and social issues, these had been inspired by Lockwood, who used to scoff at 'warm evangelical gush' and 'the pernicious nonsense purveyed by the ecclesiastical wind-baggeries'.[31] During his Indian years Kipling opposed missionary activities and he continued to do so, in fiction and in journalism, long afterwards. The imposition of Christianity on reluctant and defenceless subject peoples seemed to him utterly wrong, as he explained to a leading American Presbyterian in 1895.

> It is my fortune to have been born and to a large extent brought up among those whom white men call 'heathen'; and while I recognize the paramount duty of every white man to follow the teachings of his creed and conscience as 'a debtor to do the whole law', it seems to me cruel that

white men, whose governments are armed with the most murderous weapons known to science, should amaze and confound their fellow creatures with a doctrine of salvation imperfectly understood by themselves and a code of ethics foreign to the climate and instincts of those races whose most cherished customs they outrage and whose gods they insult.[32]

The West, he felt, should not interfere with non-Christian creeds because they were vital to their believers' cultures and social systems. But he also thought that Christianity did not possess so untainted a history that it was justified in giving lessons to other religions. In his dark story 'The Mark of the Beast', he inflicts a horrifying punishment on a drunken Englishman who insults a Hindu idol. And in 'They' the narrator reflects silently on 'the more than inherited (since it is also carefully taught) brutality of the Christian peoples, beside which the mere heathendom of the West Coast nigger is clean and unrestrained'.

Yet for Kipling the most insidious foes of the British Empire (at least until he identified the German threat) were the Radical and Liberal politicians in London. He loathed 'gentlemen ... from England' who 'spend a few weeks in India, walk round this great Sphinx of the Plains, and write books upon its ways and its works, denouncing or praising it as their ignorance prompts'.[33] And he hated them even more if they returned to Westminster and pontificated about places they had 'done' in a few days from the comfort of Government House and a first-class railway carriage. This was not a view restricted to Kipling but one widely held by Anglo-India. As a contemporary ICS officer complained in private, MPs invaded them in 'the cold weather and having shot our game, drunk our wine and generally done well unto themselves at our expense abuse us to the [British public] when they get home and cut us when we meet them in Piccadilly'.[34]

Kipling could not understand why anyone should pay more attention to the views of political tourists than to those of men who had dedicated their careers to India. One group produced theories formulated in a state of ignorance while the other spent their careers trying in practical ways to alleviate famine and disease. As one perceptive critic has written, Kipling had 'little time for visionaries who forget about present hells to build future Utopias'[35] – and in his work he frequently caricatured them at the same time as he extolled their opponents. In an imaginary dialogue published in the *St James's Gazette*,[36] a Civilian chatting to a soldier (both of whom have been deriding MPs) is asked what he has done for Indians. 'Nothing much,' he replies. 'I've built some canals to irrigate their crops, so that they shouldn't absolutely die of starvation; put down railroads to carry 'em grain, tried to prevent 'em from dying in their own dirt, and given 'em the rudiments of law.'

By contrast, the 'Member for Lower Tooting', while 'wandering about India in top-hat and frock-coat, talked largely of the benefits of British rule, and suggested as the one thing needful the establishment of a duly qualified electoral system and a general bestowal of the franchise'.[37] But in private Kipling could be vicious. In 1893, on hearing of the death of an MP in Allahabad (who was probably 'telling us how to govern the native'), he expressed the hope that, as the man was a 'Liberal Home ruler', he had been struck down by cholera.[38]

Part Two

Imperial Apostle

6

The Long Trail Home

───────────◆───────────

I N 1889, AT the age of 23, Kipling left India and discovered the seas. Their call summoned him for the rest of his life – 'You have heard the beat of the off-shore wind,/And the thresh of the deep-sea rain'. Annually for the next twenty years he traversed one ocean or another, except in 1890 when he sailed only as far as Naples in the Mediterranean. These voyages also inspired a large and varied body of work: numerous tales of seas and sailors, a novel about Massachusetts fishermen, propaganda articles on the Royal Navy, and a collection of poems, *The Seven Seas*, which contains the two great Browning monologues that Browning did not write – 'McAndrew's Hymn' and 'The Mary Gloster'.

The voyage home was one of discovery and imperial possibility but also of less pleasing things. He did not like the appearance of the Chinese or the smell of Canton, which he found more over-powering even than Benares. Hong Kong may have been superior to Calcutta, and its British businessmen were certainly more suc-cessful than their kinsmen in India, but he was as disgusted at encountering English prostitutes in a brothel – which he investi-gated with characteristic thoroughness – as he had been on board ship by the sight of a European stewardess serving ill-mannered 'half-breeds'. It was a relief to sail to Japan with its pretty girls and cleanliness. But he made some magnificently naïve judgements about the country, claiming that its people lacked firmness and excoriating the Westernization of its politics, clothing and architecture.[1]

Kipling contrived to dislike America and Americans before he had crossed the Pacific. On discovering a pirated American edition of one of his books in Yokohama, he stormed out of the shop and threatened to write a furious article concentrating on the 'slovenly way' Americans spoke English. On steaming through the Golden Gate, he noted with pleasure that the blockhouse guarding San Francisco harbour could easily be silenced by two gunboats from Hong Kong. And immediately on arrival in America, he set upon its citizens in a flurry of articles and indiscreet remarks about their violence, greed, corruption, table manners, their ways of speaking and spitting, the vulgarity of their women and the way their girls 'kicked up and carried on with young men'.[2]

Yet there was always an ambivalence in his views towards the United States. Beside his disgust at certain local habits sat his admiration for the scale and enterprise, his love of the landscape and his veneration of American writers: he regarded Mark Twain, whom he visited on this journey, as 'about as big a man as ever lived', and a few years later he sent $50 to help preserve Edgar Allen Poe's cottage because, despite his disapproval of 'buying dead men's camps', he wanted to acknowledge his heavy literary debt to Poe.[3] In addition, as America was as good a place as any to acquire copy, he zealously asked questions and heard answers, 'swapping stories' in the 'smoker' of the train to Oregon, listening to 'the blasphemies of miners and stockmen till far into the night', and interrogating an army officer who had worked with Colonel Custer about Red Indian customs in Arizona and New Mexico.

After crossing the continent by himself, Kipling rejoined the Hills in Pennsylvania and stayed near them in Beaver, where he was evidently a less congenial companion than he had been in India or the Far East. He became very angry when made to sit next to the driver in a cab, which surprised Mrs Hill, 'accustomed as he was to hobnobbing with natives of India'. But there, she reflected, he had been a superior, whereas now the driver was his equal. Her family's servants were also puzzled by him, especially when he insisted that a barber shave him in bed.[4] As in his encounters with the ship's stewardess and the prostitutes in Hong Kong, Kipling was discovering that, in the world outside India, race and class relations were not as straightforward as they had seemed to the young sahib.

Another curious episode of the season was his tentative courtship of Mrs Hill's younger sister, Caroline Taylor, followed by their brief and unconvincing engagement. Nearly sixty years later Mrs Hill stated that the marriage had been prevented by her father, who 'said he had given one daughter to an Englishman [and] would not give another',[5] a claim that has not been corroborated by anyone else or by anything the fiancé ever wrote. Doubtless Kipling's gallantry was inspired by his feelings for the elder sister, but even these were by now diminishing. When Alec Hill died the following year, Kipling made no attempt to revive the intense friendship with his hostess from Allahabad. A chance meeting in London with his old love, Flo Garrard, followed in May 1890 by a disappointing visit to her in Paris, where she was studying at art school, had brought on a brief and angry bout of misogyny.

Arriving in England in October, he announced that he had come to London to start 'that queer experience known as a literary career'. Rooms were quickly found in Villiers Street, just off Charing Cross between the Strand and the River Thames. It was as central and as representative a location as he could have wished, the London of hansom cabs and theatres and the Café Royal, yet also the centre of music-halls, prostitution and crime. Kipling recognized and appreciated the contrasts as he took his 'nightly prowl' through 'four packed miles of seething vice': the area, he recalled later, was 'primitive and passionate in its habits and population', but 'through all this shifting, shouting brotheldom the pious British householder and his family bored their way back from the theatres, eyes-front and fixed, as though not seeing'.[6]

The chief pleasure of the place was the music-halls. From his desk he could see the entrance to Gatti's, which he loved to visit after dinner for 'the smoke, the roar, and the good-fellowship of relaxed humanity'. The place 'opened a new world' to him and filled him with new ambitions: surely, he told Mrs Hill, 'the people of London require a poet of the Music Halls'.[7] His ambition was quickly fulfilled. Much of his ballad-writing was inspired by the songs, rhythms and voices of the Bessies and Bellas and their male counterparts on the stage. He passionately believed in the music-halls' contribution to English culture, 'a necessary part of our civilisation', and many years later urged a correspondent to write their history: such a book, he hoped, would promote 'a revival of "national" street songs which will help to defeat the imported stuff we've suffered under so long'.[8]

From Villiers Street Kipling confessed that he had never felt 'so utterly isolated and yet so immediately in touch with all the world'. But the isolation and the climate depressed him. Hating the rain and the yellow fogs, he yearned for sunshine. By Christmas he felt 'more heartsick' and 'thoroughly wretched' than anyone in London who was not actually starving. The following month he had a nervous breakdown, finding it impossible to work or think or even read.

Within weeks of his arrival in England, Kipling had become a celebrity, lionized in London after his Indian Railway Library stories had been published there. He soon realized, however, that he did not care for a role which caused him to be 'much persecuted with dinners', and he was uneasy when aristocrats backed him into corners and poured 'melted compliments' down his throat: it made him feel like a purple monkey on a yellow stick with instructions to amuse. Public praise, conferred by reviews and crowned by a leading article in *The Times* in March 1890, was matched by private awe and admiration. Sidney Low, the editor of the *St James's Gazette*, wondered aloud if Kipling might become 'greater than Dickens', while Mowbray Morris, the editor of *Macmillan's Magazine*, rejoiced that this 'wondrous smart young fellow with his pen' was providing him with 'very spirited stuff indeed' – what a relief, he said, from Stevenson's 'tiresome' literary dexterity and the 'silly little verses' that Tennyson was then writing.[9]

Kipling was fortunate with his early critics, especially the Scottish literary pundits such as J.M.Barrie and Andrew Lang, and the Editor of the *Scots Observer*, W.E.Henley. But the first wave of admirers consisted largely of solid and conservative Victorian men of letters, not a literary avant-garde heralding a new epoch: only Henry James, who in 1892 described Kipling as 'the most complete man of genius' he had ever known, was a writer of the first rank.[10] The 'smart young fellow' was grateful for the applause and joined the Savile Club, where the sponsors of his election included Thomas Hardy, Rider Haggard, Henley, Lang and James (whose almost simultaneous sponsorship of Oscar Wilde was unsuccessful). Yet that inherent pugnacity that had intensified since his return to London could be directed even at his admirers. After embroiling himself in an angry dispute with Harper

Brothers at the end of 1890, he was incensed when the integrity of the American publishers was publicly defended by Hardy, William Black and another of his new friends, Sir Walter Besant. The satirical pencil was quickly sharpened and out rolled 'The Rhyme of the Three Captains', a clever though protracted ballad in which the targets are punned together – 'the bezant is hard, ay and black'. Kipling seldom felt remorse for anything he said or wrote, but he regretted this poem. As he admitted to Edmund Gosse, an admiring critic who believed the young writer should become 'another Waring' and 'go back to the Far East', the attack should have been concentrated on 'the Yank yahoo across the water'. He was relieved to learn that Hardy was not angry, promised 'it shall not occur again', and told Gosse he did not want to hurt 'one of these three good men' by reprinting the rhyme.[11] Two years later, however, it appeared among the 'other verses' in the *Barrack Room Ballads*.

Kipling's most important champion was Henley, a model for Long John Silver and a poet whose head rests immortally 'bloody but unbowed'. A forceful but generally benevolent character who enthusiastically collected young writers, Henley appealed to Kipling as a Tory Imperialist who hated Gladstone. His protégé once had the temerity to compare Henley's free verse to 'fishing with barbless hooks', but the master's 'volcanic' reaction to such impertinence did not affect his enthusiasm for his new discovery.[12] After allegedly dancing on his wooden leg on reading 'Danny Deever', Henley published that and the most memorable of the other barrack room ballads ('Tommy', 'Fuzzy-Wuzzy', 'Gunga Din' and 'Mandalay') in his paper in the first half of 1890.

If, as the writer Philip Guedalla observed, the exoticism of the Indian works astonished a 'generation which regarded stories of Scottish life as travellers' tales from the far North',[13] the impact of the ballads was even greater. Utterly unlike anything coming from the Decadents' school of absinthe drinkers, almost entirely breaking with the subjects and styles of Tennyson or the Pre-Raphaelites, the ballads were original both in language and in content. No wonder Henley and his circle were enchanted. Here was a poet not writing about impossible love, improbable valour, wine and roses, or the Middle Ages, but a bard using the dialect of the London working class in traditional ballad form to depict the personal and much neglected feelings of the British soldier.

Kipling was as prolific in London as he had been during his last years in India. Several of his finest and most moving Indian stories (such as 'The Courting of Dinah Shadd', 'Without Benefit of Clergy' and 'At the End of the Passage') were published in various magazines and collected in 1891 in the volume *Life's Handicap*. Others (such as 'In the Rukh' and 'Love o' Women') were written over the following two years and appeared in *Many Inventions*, a collection which included 'The Record of Badalia Herodsfoot', his solitary (but successful) attempt to write a story of the London slums and one of several tales that should have diluted the charge of misogyny. The inspiration for the heroine beaten to death by her drunken husband was found in the area he lived in: Villiers Street, he recorded many years later, had been 'intensely, shall we say, human, and alive with Badalias'.[14]

The productivity was remarkable, but the quality was more than usually uneven. *Life's Handicap* may contain some of the best Indian tales but it also includes some of the most boring ('The Lang Men o' Larut'), least funny ('Reingelder and the German Flag') and most repellent ('Bertran and Bimi') stories that Kipling ever wrote. And at the same time that he was producing all these ballads and stories, he made a disastrous attempt to write a novel. *The Light that Failed*, kindly described by Henry James as 'the most youthfully infirm of his productions',[15] is philistine and misogynist and leaves the reader wholly unconvinced – a feeling reinforced by the decision to produce a short version with a happy ending for *Lippincott's Magazine* and a longer one with an unhappy ending when the novel was published in book form. Maisie may be the first portrait of a feminist in British literature, but she is a two-dimensional figure too obviously inspired by her creator's personal unhappiness over Flo Garrard. The 'hero', Dick Heldar, exhibits Kipling's most hairy-chested sentiments, 'yearning for some man-talk and tobacco' after spending a day with a woman, and sharing with his friend Torpenhow 'the austere love that springs up between men who have tugged at the same oar together and are yoked by custom and use and the intimacies of toil'.

Despite his successes and the affection of the Savile's literary men, Kipling was curiously aggressive towards the London literary world from the beginning. In his memoirs he recalled that Besant had advised him to 'keep out of the dog-fight' – and he did so in the sense that he neither reviewed nor criticized 'any fellow-craftsman's output'. But the belligerence was startling, even if it was not directed at individual targets. Later he recalled that he had experienced 'a feeling of great strength' on going to London and meeting 'the men he was pitted against'.[16]

Although no one in 1889 was pitted against him, Kipling was already obsessed by long hair and its decadent implications. While staying in Lahore at the beginning of the year, he had been irritated by a 'long-haired aesthete' preaching to him on the ethics of art; and as soon as he reached London, he was complaining about 'long-haired literati'.[17] Scarcely a month after his arrival Kipling felt able to describe London's literary world to readers of the *Gazette*.

> But I consort with long-haired things
>   In velvet collar-rolls,
> Who talk about the Aims of Art,
>   And 'theories' and 'goals',
> And moo and coo with womenfolk
>   About their blessed souls.

Appalled by their views and appearances, the poet had no difficulty in deciding that he preferred soldiers.

> It's Oh to meet an Army man,
>   Set up and trimmed and taut,
> Who does not spout hashed libraries
>   Or think the next man's thought,
> And walks as though he owned himself,
>   And hogs his bristles short.

('In Partibus')

The assault was continued in the 'other verses' of *Barrack Room Ballads*, especially in 'Tomlinson', an arid figure who dies in Berkeley Square without any apparent experience of life beyond books. At Heaven's Gate, when St Peter asks him what good he has done for the sake of men, Tomlinson finds it difficult to reply.

'This I have read in a book,' he said, 'and that was told to me,
And this I have thought that another man thought of a Prince in Muscovy.'

Similar jibes appear in *The Light that Failed,* with Heldar, who had been in the Sudan campaign, complaining he has been told 'all about art' by 'half-a-dozen epicene young pagans' and a man who has been 'as far as Brighton beach'. But Kipling did not become personal in print until in his memoirs he referred to 'the suburban Toilet-Club school favoured by the late Mr Oscar Wilde'.[18]

It would of course be impossible to place Kipling among the diehard opponents of the creed, 'art for art's sake': the bulk of his own work, especially the prose, was written for no sake but its own. Yet he conceived a violent dislike for the men preaching and practising the creed in London in the 1890s, especially Walter Pater, a crucial influence on Oscar Wilde, who at one 'awful dinner . . . moaned and frothed and yammered over Blake's poems'.[19]

Kipling's return to England coincided with the triumph of Wilde: *The Picture of Dorian Gray,* the literary apogee of the Aesthetic Movement, was published in *Lippincott's* in the summer of 1890. Wilde represented 'the Nineties' — at any rate the first half of them — in a way that automatically excluded Kipling. The young Anglo-Indian was not at that stage interested in definitions of art or the function of criticism. His own sense of humour inclining towards farce, he could not appreciate Wilde's epigrams and paradoxes. And he could never have created — nor wanted to create — a character like Lord Henry Wotton, who is repeatedly described as speaking 'languidly' and 'languorously' in *Dorian Gray.*

It might not have mattered if Wilde had been a solitary figure, as he became in 1895 after his conviction for sodomy, abandoned even by the Pre-Raphaelites, even by Burne-Jones, Kipling's uncle, who was disappointed that he did not shoot himself. But Wilde represented an arrogant and ostentatious movement that repelled Kipling, a *fin de siècle* world of velvet collars and self-preening aestheticism, of absinthe and Paris garrets and the Domino Room of the Café Royal, of Decadent poets imitating Baudelaire and knowing nothing of the living culture of the London streets. Apart from sharing their profession, Kipling had nothing in common with Arthur Symons or poor Ernest Dowson, pining for both the innocence of Cynara and that more earthly oblivion where 'absinthe makes the tart grow fonder'. Nor could he ever have felt comprehension or sympathy for Max Beerbohm, that fastidious and dandified figure who later became his most persistent scourge.

It is true that some of the Decadents also liked the music-halls, but not for the same reasons as Kipling. Concerned by the spreading gap between 'high' and popular culture – a gap he spent most of his life trying to shrink – Kipling loved the halls for what they were, a vital and creative expression of working-class life. The Decadents had neither such love nor such interest. They went, as Beerbohm admitted, so that they could 'bask in the glow of [their] own superiority', despising the 'guffawing clowns' as they discussed Fra Angelico and Marcus Aurelius in the 'joyous vulgarity' of their environment.[20]

Kipling found it difficult to understand writers who wrote mainly about their own passions and torments. He wanted to write about people he had met all over the globe, about the places they lived in and the work they did. On several occasions he publicly stressed the writer's humble role in the scheme of things. As he told the Royal Academy in 1906, writers 'must recognise the gulf that separates even the least of those who do things worthy to be written about from even the best of those who have written things worthy of being talked about'. And as he had written earlier in praise of his old school, it was surely better 'to turn out men who do real work than men who write about what they think about what other people have done or ought to do'.[21]

If his profession prevented him from doing 'real work' himself, at least he could become, in the phrase of C.S.Lewis, 'the poet of work' – or rather of work well done, of the skills and application of the men he had met and watched and admired. The keynote of Kipling's 'teachings', one critic recognized, was 'the sacredness, the imperativeness, to each man, of his own day's work'. Most of the stories in the volume, *The Day's Work* (1898), deal with work and responsibility, and one of his favourite maxims, though frequently rephrased, was, 'If you give a man more than he can do he will do it. If you only give him what he *can* do he'll do nothing.'[22]

Long hair and aestheticism formed only a part of Kipling's disenchantment with England on his return in 1889. Politics provided a more enduring distaste. For seven years he had listened to the conservative views of his father and other members of the Punjab Club, and he had come to share most of them, especially his elders' identification of the internal enemies of the Empire, socialists, Irish nationalists, Gladstonian Liberals. The first two categories quickly joined the third in the list of the poet's targets. At the end of *Barrack*

Room Ballads 'An Imperial Rescript' takes a tilt at socialism while 'Cleared' opens his polemics against the Irish. Having decided on a very casual acquaintance that 'the Irish MP appears to be an awful rotter',[23] he produced his diatribe – 'We are not ruled by murderers, but only – by their friends' – on learning that the nationalist leader, Charles Stewart Parnell, had been exonerated of condoning the Phoenix Park murders in Dublin in 1882.

Yet nothing upset Kipling more than his perception of a widespread lack of interest in the health of the Empire. Perhaps he exaggerated this: the fact that J.R.Seeley's great imperialist tract, *The Expansion of England*, sold half a million copies in the 1880s suggests that imperial sentiment was very much on the increase.[24] But many of the people he met in 'society' derided his 'poor little Gods of the East, and asserted that the British in India spent violent lives "oppressing" the Native'.[25] In any case the imperialist spirit of the population was usually aroused only by news of military campaigns, especially calamities such as the Boer victory of Majuba Hill in 1881 or the death of General Gordon at Khartoum. Few people seemed interested in the management of the imperial domains. The Decadents in the Café Royal cared nothing for their contemporaries in the ICS sweltering to manage districts of half a million people.

So appalled was Kipling by the apparent ignorance and lack of awareness of imperial issues that he resolved to tackle them, 'to tell to the English something of the world outside England'. The notion grew, he recalled later, into 'a vast, vague conspectus … of the whole sweep and meaning of things and effort and origins throughout the Empire'.[26] The first blast of this crusade, 'The English Flag'(1891),* hit the imperial note so well that the aged Tennyson instructed his son to congratulate Kipling on his 'fine and patriotic poem'.[27] The theme is memorably encapsulated in the second line (suggested by his mother), 'And what should they know of England who only England know?' – and the 'they' are identified in the third and fourth.

> The poor little street-bred people that vapour and fume and brag,
> They are lifting their heads in the stillness to yelp at the English flag!

---

* He was actually writing about the British flag, the Union Jack. And he was not always so respectful. In 'The Widow at Windsor', one of the barrack room ballads written in 1890, he records Tommy referring to 'the bloomin' old rag over'ead'.

As a contrast to these insular, ignorant, 'whimpering' Little Englanders, Kipling paints an epic canvas of the duties, opportunities and self-sacrifice of the imperialist idea.

'Never the lotos closes, never the wild-fowl wake,
'But a soul goes out on the East Wind that died for England's sake –
'Man or woman or suckling, mother or bride or maid –
'Because on the bones of the English the English Flag is stayed.

If Kipling found his imperial voice with 'The English Flag', he assumed the portentous robes of the infallible prophet two years later in 'A Song of the English', an inferior successor and a second-rate anticipation of 'The White Man's Burden'. The poem opens with a verse of uncustomary pomposity.

Fair is our lot – O goodly is our heritage!
(Humble ye, my people, and be fearful in your mirth!)
For the Lord our God Most High
He hath made the deep as dry,
He hath smote for us a pathway to the ends of all the Earth!

But in the rambling sections that follow, the message comes through with vigour.

We were dreamers, dreaming greatly, in the man-stifled town;
We yearned beyond the sky-line where the strange roads go down.
Came the Whisper, came the Vision, came the Power with the Need,
Till the Soul that is not man's soul was lent us to lead.

The poet's role as imperial visionary had begun.

7

The American Years

Kipling's second most unsuccessful novel was published in London and New York in 1892. Subtitled 'A Story of West and East', *The Naulahka* has little of the verve and brilliance of its verse relation, 'The Ballad of East and West'. There are fine descriptions of Indian ambience and several familiar themes: the importance of duty and work, the problem of Rajput nobles 'rolling in idleness' because they are not allowed to fight each other, the absurdity of British MPs in India who 'sat their horses like sacks, and talked interminably of good government'. But the characterization is weak and the story, though readable, is little more than an adventure yarn, replete with bullets, poison and other stock paraphernalia of late Victorian melodrama. The novel lacks the precision, economy and control of the short stories.

The chief problem of the book, however, stems from the fact that it is the work of two authors. Wolcott Balestier was the agent of an American publisher who had recently come to London where his charm, enthusiasm and hard work won him many friends in literary circles. Kipling was mesmerized and enthralled and, while a recent writer's attempt to convert their friendship into a homosexual affair is unconvincing,[1] they became close companions. Even so, it was untypical of Kipling to collaborate with another man, particularly an amateur. A fastidious and possessive stylist, he seldom accepted non-factual amendments to his stories except from dramatists and script writers. Not until 1916, when he allowed Baden-Powell to rewrite the *Jungle Books* as morality lessons for the *Wolf Cubs' Handbook*, did he again compromise the integrity of his written work.

Kipling soon became acquainted with Balestier's American family, especially his sister Caroline, a rather plain, dark-haired, masculine-looking woman who lacked her brother's charm. Three years older than Rudyard, whom she found 'refreshingly unEnglish', 'Carrie' was efficient, strong and capable. Despite these and other qualities, however, she did not make an appealing impression on Lockwood and Alice, who met her while on leave from India. 'That woman is going to marry our Ruddy,' Mrs Kipling quickly perceived, while her husband pronounced the laconically withering verdict, 'a good man spoiled'.[2]

In his tentative and desultory fashion, reminiscent of his behaviour towards Caroline Taylor a year earlier, Kipling began to court Carrie at the end of 1890. By the following summer they seem to have been semi-engaged, secretly engaged or perhaps – after a short break-up – re-engaged. Then the effects of ill-health, overwork and anxiety over the relationship overwhelmed him, and his doctors recommended a sea voyage.

The obedient patient duly embarked for Cape Town in August, and from there sailed to New Zealand, which he regarded as the 'loveliest land in the world', and Australia, which delighted him less, mainly because it seemed 'second hand American'. Although he claimed to have picked up a 'stack of yarns' in both places,[3] the dominions always managed to inspire his spirit more than his work. New Zealand gave him one important though enigmatic character, the eponymous Mrs Bathurst, but he did not create her until ten years after he had left Auckland. British Columbia, the second 'love-liest land', gave him virtually nothing – like the rest of Canada. And southern Africa, which later became his favourite landscape of all, inspired only mediocre stories even if its politics and warfare prompted some of his sternest and most trenchant political poetry.

Defeated by uncooperative steamship schedules, Kipling abandoned his intention of visiting Robert Louis Stevenson, now marooned on Samoa for the rest of his life, and sailed to Ceylon instead. He then crossed over to India and travelled up through the Hindu south, a region quite unlike any he had known in the north, 'the flat, red India of palm-tree, Palmyra-palm, and rice', before reaching Lahore and his parents in December. During his travels he had 'crossed the trails' of many 'old boys' from Westward Ho! and in Lahore he ran across Dunsterville. At Christmas he suddenly left India and, in spite of various plans, never returned.

The abrupt departure was caused by a telegram from Carrie announcing the death of her brother Wolcott from typhoid. What happened next is not certain but Rudyard seems impulsively to have proposed to her by telegram. Arriving in London on 10 January, he took out a special licence on the 11th and arranged the wedding for the 18th. Perhaps it required Wolcott's death to force him to make up his mind and a brisk schedule to prevent him from changing it. In any case, after what he described as 'months of delay and tribulation', he and Carrie were 'launched on the threshold of things' from All Souls Church in Langham Place.

The ceremony was a rapid and, according to Henry James, 'dreary little' affair. All the couple's close relations were ill or abroad, except for Rudyard's cousin Ambrose Poynter who was best man, and the congregation consisted of James, who gave the bride away, the publisher William Heinemann, and Edmund Gosse with his family. Afterwards James described his temporary daughter as 'a hard devoted capable little person' whom he didn't 'in the least understand [Kipling's] marrying'.[4] The failure to comprehend was shared and sometimes expressed among others of Kipling's friends and relations. Time has failed to enhance understanding. Carrie's loyalty, stoicism and business efficiency were attested and admitted, but these qualities were increasingly accompanied by bossiness and parsimony. Her attractiveness, such as it was, soon declined: six years after her wedding, a fellow passenger on a vessel sailing to South Africa described her as a fat and dowdy woman who gobbled her food.[5]

The relationship was not the 'dark marriage' suggested by one biographer, and no time need be wasted on the theory that, in 'doing his marital duty', Kipling was effectively 'sodomising ... Wolcott'.[6] But neither was it a joyful or romantic union. Within two years of his marriage Kipling was giving sombre and unenthusiastic advice about the institution to a friend who had just become engaged: marriage's principal merit was the teaching of 'the tougher virtues – such as humility, restraint, order, and forethought'.[7] Carrie looked after him well yet so protectively that he became too dependent and consequently too obedient. References to her as the 'Commandress in Chief' and to himself as her ADC may have been jocular, but they were not inaccurate. Even their younger daughter, Elsie, no dainty or easy-going woman herself, admitted that Carrie dominated her father's life, exhausting him with her 'difficult temperament' and 'her possessive and rather jealous nature'.[8]

Carrie's matronliness also affected the writing – not the skill with which it was done but the method by which it was approached and the tone and contents which it possessed. Some of the stylistic changes can be ascribed to maturity and middle age, but after his marriage Kipling worked more and more through his imagination, less and less through his ears and eyes and nostrils. By the turn of the century he was seldom finding his characters in the taverns or on the wayside or in army barracks. Nor did his subject matter often include married people with extra-marital aspirations; light-hearted accounts of infidelity had vanished from both the poetry and the prose. Under the stern stare of their new superintendent, Kipling's narrators were gradually transformed, seldom carefree '*chroniqueurs*' now – or even happy husbands – but solitary men, widowers and bachelors.[9]

The honeymoon was supposed to consist of a fortnight in London, followed by a voyage to the United States (including a visit to the Balestier family base in Vermont) and a holiday in the Far East. Kipling hoped that his 'little tour round the world' would enable him to 'pick up new tales', but instead he concentrated on writing a series of acerbic articles for *The Times*. 'Rud has liver,' Carrie noted in her diary in April, 'sweet to live with – slanders my native home.'[10] Certainly he was not prepared to make concessions to Americans just because he had married one of them: New York was swiftly dismissed in print as 'the shiftless outcome of squalid barbarism and reckless extravagance'. Kipling could admit that the American was a 'hundred years ahead of the English in design, comfort and economy, and . . . labour-saving appliances in his house'. But that didn't make him civilized. '*Au fond*', the critic declared privately a few months later, America was 'barbarism – barbarism plus telephone, electric light, rail and suffrage'. The 'moral dry rot of it all' was evident everywhere, in bad construction and slovenly workmanship. The problem with American society, he explained later, was that it was too bored and too well fed to make the effort to become civilized.[11]

The Japanese stage of the honeymoon was truncated in Yokohama when the couple learned that the New Oriental Banking Corporation (in which Kipling had invested most of his savings) had suspended payment. They reacted stoically to the reverse, recrossed the Pacific and North America, and rented a cottage in Vermont to live in during Carrie's first pregnancy. Captivated by the new landscape, Kipling bought land from Beatty Balestier, his boisterous, hotheaded and heavy-drinking brother-in-law, and decided to build a house. After less than two years in England, he had become an expatriate.

He settled in a nation rapidly transformed by industry, railways and massive immigration, a nation of huge cities and giant monopolies plunging into its capitalist future. But the process, which was then enabling America to overtake Britain as the world's leading industrial power, had brought few benefits to Vermont and the rural areas of New England, whose condition was worsening in the current economic depression. The landscape was depopulated and reverting to forest; the elderly remained, but most of the young had departed for the Middle West or for the towns of Massachusetts and Rhode Island. There were plenty of abandoned farmhouses, white, clap-boarded and beautiful, which Kipling could have bought and renovated. But all his life he veered between veneration of the past and enthusiasm for the modern, and at that stage he wanted to build his own dwelling.

Even today his home, Naulakha,* seems to be one of the few ugly houses in Vermont. Looking eastwards across the valley of the Connecticut River, its exterior is stark, grey-green and uninviting. Charm is also absent from the interior, although Carrie's lack of decorative skills is no longer so obvious. Kipling's admiration for American 'labour-saving appliances' is well displayed, and the house is free of Victorian fuss and mustiness. The most important room, the study, was placed at the southern end of the building, defended by an anteroom where Carrie had her desk.

Kipling loved the idea of an open-air life, building, planting, working with animals. But he was not adept at practical work. Heaven, he admitted, hadn't made him 'to put up bedsteads', and he regretted his inability to construct a wigwam for Josephine, the

---

*Named in honour of Wolcott, it is the Hindi word for 9 lakhs (900,000), though in the novel it was misspelt. Kipling put the k and h in the correct order for his house.

daughter who was born a few months before the completion of Naulakha in the summer of 1893. He claimed to be a 'bit of a maniac about horses', but he was unable to drive a buggy or handle an ox-cart properly.

Nevertheless, he was happy to be living 'a sane clean life', writing without distractions but with 'sunshine and a mind at ease'. He had never felt healthier than in the 'diamond clear weather' where there was no 'dust nor smoke nor defilement of any kind'. The snows and icicles of the first winter made him feel he was living in a fairy-tale – 'one sings and shouts for joy of being alive'. At other times of the year he tried to identify local plants and birds, and he lamented the fact that compulsive shooting had made the countryside 'very silent and unalive'. No pen, he wrote after two years, could describe the turning of the leaves, but his own managed very well to depict

the insurrection of the tree-people against the waning year. A little maple began it, flaming blood-red of a sudden where he stood against the dark green of a pine-belt. Next morning there was an answering signal from the swamp where the sumacs grow. Three days later, the hill-sides as far as the eye could range were afire, and the roads paved, with crimson and gold. Then a wet wind blew, and ruined all the uniforms of that gorgeous army; and the oaks, who had held themselves in reserve, buckled on their dull and bronzed cuirasses and stood it out stiffly to the last blown leaf, till nothing remained but pencil-shading of bare boughs, and one could see into the most private heart of the woods.[12]

Naulakha, a few miles outside the town of Brattleboro, was private, isolated and 'wondrous self-contained'. Kipling made few friends in the neighbourhood and was only seldom involved in local issues: on one occasion he tried and failed to prevent the construction of a tram line in Brattleboro, and on another he succeeded in persuading the Government to allow a post office to be set up near his house. He claimed to be 'excellent friends' with the inhabitants of the place but admitted that they were perplexed by his failure to attend their 'chicken suppers and church sociables and turkey sprees'. They, however, did not regard the Kiplings as such excellent friends and considered them stand-offish, an impression reinforced by the curious formality of life at Naulakha, where the two of them dined by themselves in evening dress, apparently so as to retain the respect of their English servants – a breed hitherto scarcely known to Kipling. Even so the couple were not always successful in dealing with employees: one day both the cook and the serving-maid left together, the latter because she refused to wear a cap with lace frills.[13]

A few visitors trekked out to see them in rural Vermont. Arthur Conan Doyle, on the eve of creating the incomparable Brigadier Gerard, tried to teach Kipling golf and later sent him a pair of Swedish skis. Rural sports were an acceptable diversion from work, but public life was not: invitations to read and lecture and make speeches were relentlessly turned down with the excuse that Kipling could 'only write stories'. One of the most travelled men in literary history even temporarily lost his appetite for travel. After settling in Vermont he never went west of his home town. Occasionally he visited American friends, who tended to belong to political and literary circles in Boston, Washington and New York. But he preferred to be in his house or with animals. A British diplomat recorded that he was much happier looking at bears and elephants in the Washington zoo than attending a disorderly session of Congress.[14]

In Vermont Kipling was able to play several of his favourite and most endearing roles: devoted son, loyal husband, adoring father and inventive playmate for other people's children. Josephine, pretty, clever and touchingly affectionate, was an incessant source of pride and delight. Forgiving her for having 'had the bad taste to be born on Gladstone's birthday', her father devoted long periods to playing games, telling stories and reciting Indian rhymes. Yet captivation by his young family (Elsie was born in February 1896, John in August 1897) did not lessen his attachment to the Family Square, even though the institution had been buffeted by distance and two marriages. While his parents had been on leave from India in 1890–1, Rudyard had lived with them for most of the time in London's Earl's Court; and on his retirement in 1893, Lockwood immediately set off for Vermont, where he picked up his son and took him on a trip to Canada. Rudyard, he reported, was a 'hoary old sceptic with regard to everything American and continually snubs my enthusiasms and admirations'.[15]

The Kipling parents were also visited during the summers of 1894 and 1895 at their retirement home in Wiltshire. Rudyard liked the landscape, 'fat and fleecy and green', but complained unceasingly that the 'infernal' English climate was 'only fit for marine monsters';

soon he was looking forward to returning to Vermont where the sun did 'more than look like a badly poached egg at the bottom of a bowl of thick soup'. As yet England had little appeal for him; his affection was largely restricted to its position as 'the Head Quarters of the Empire'.[16] It was the idea of England rather than the reality, the sense of its capacity and potential, that attracted him.

The solitudes of Vermont made Kipling healthy, energetic and productive. Four years in New England generated a flow of poems, stories and a novel that was barely interrupted except by a brief depression caused by news of the death of Stevenson. Yet little of his American writing has anything to do with America. In 1897, after leaving the United States, he rejected a request to write articles about American 'manners and customs' because he would be able to say 'ten times more' in a short story than in an essay.[17] But he did not want to say much anyway. Although he claimed to know New England's farmers, small manufacturers and country town life, he did not write about them. His only story set in Vermont, 'A Walking Delegate', is a boring satire on socialism in which the characters are horses.

During his last year in the United States Kipling wrote *Captains Courageous*, his sole 'all-through American story'. Increasingly fascinated by ships and seas, he decided to write a novel about fishermen and went to stay in the Massachusetts port of Gloucester. Although upset by his failure to preserve anonymity – newspapers discovered him and told their readers about his quest for 'local colour' – he enjoyed his studies of the trade and habits of the town's mariners. Revelling in a 'profligate abundance of detail', he visited the Fishermen's Institute, bought fishing books in the local store, ate in sailors' eating houses and was 'immortally sick' on a pollock-fisher. It was the type of research he had loved in India – and which he seldom managed to do again.

The novel is predictably strong in its seascapes and its depiction of the ambience on board a fishing vessel. But everything else is weak, especially the moralistic and hortatory message. A spoilt little rich boy on an ocean liner is washed overboard and rescued by a fishing schooner. In spite of his demands to be put ashore, he is forced to work as a member of the crew for three months – and of course he is redeemed by the experience of humble hard work.

Captains Courageous was Kipling's third unsuccessful novel in a row. Yet still he yearned 'wildly to write a real novel – not a one volume or a two volume but a really decent three-decker' of 900 pages. Whatever people might say about the short story, he believed that the novel was 'the *real* vehicle. Independent firing by marksmen is a pretty thing but it's the volley-firing of a full battalion that clears the front.'[18] Kipling wrote a great piece of fiction in *Kim*, but that magical, picaresque half-novel had only a solitary deck. He toyed with the idea of writing a sequel and even of resurrecting 'Mother Maturin', but nothing came of it. Never again did he attempt to assemble a full battalion.

The most frequent location for his American work was India. He had written nostalgically about the Subcontinent a month after arriving in England in 1889 and experiencing London's 'greasy souptureen' of a sky.

> It's Oh to see the morn ablaze
>   Above the mango-tope,
> When homeward through the dewy cane
>   The little jackals lope,
> And half Bengal heaves into view,
>   New-washed – with sunlight soap.

> ('In Partibus')

And his nostalgia persisted so that he used to yearn to revisit 'Pindi racecourse or the elephant lines at Mian Mir. But although his plans to return to India with Carrie never materialized, his imagination remained there, encouraging him to write some of his most serious stories about Anglo-India and the imperial mission.*

The most imaginative exercise of Kipling's life was the writing of the *Jungle Books*, which he began at the end of 1892. Not only did he create a cast of anthropomorphized animals; he also put them in a place, the Seonee Jungle, which he had never visited. His experience of India was largely confined to the mountains and farmlands of the Punjab, the courtly cities of the Rajputs, and the Gangetic Plain. As he had never seen anything like the Seonee on the banks of the Waingunga in the Central Provinces, he had to rely on conversations,

---

*See above, pp. 78–80.

photographs, a book (Sterndale's *Mammalia of India*) and his own innate sense of place. While in India he had talked to forest officers, local shikaris and Anglo-Indians who went to the jungle to shoot tigers; and although he did not keep a diary, he learned and remembered enough to create an enchanting landscape for two volumes of stories. As he admitted, he put in nearly everything he knew or 'heard or dreamed about the Indian jungle'.[19]

He loved writing the books and enjoyed replying to children's letters about them. But of course he was not simply writing animal stories to amuse children. The tales are also fables with a moral, allegories with a message. The verses of 'The Law of the Jungle', recited by the wise bear Baloo, lay down rules for the safety of individuals, families and communities. Individualism must be tempered by loyalty to the tribe – 'For the strength of the Pack is the Wolf, and the strength of the Wolf is the Pack' – while survival depends on respect for the rules. The wolf pack is strong and successful so long as it retains order, discipline and obedience to the Law. The monkey-folk, by contrast, are feckless and irresponsible outcasts who are 'the people without a Law – the eaters of everything'. In their garrulous ineffectualness they resemble some of Kipling's least favourite categories – democrats, Bengali babus and intellectuals who talk too much.

The creatures of the *Jungle Books* are plainly not animals although they possess some animal characteristics. Another group of stories contains animals that are entirely humanized: the polo ponies in 'The Maltese Cat', the horse agitator in 'A Walking Delegate', the socialist wax-moth in 'The Mother Hive'. Yet despite the Aesop precedent, the genre – beyond the *Jungle Books* – was not a successful one for Kipling.

Even more unfortunate was the humanization of machines and bits of engines. Stories such as 'The Bridge-Builders' or 'The Devil and the Deep Sea' contain such a mass of technical detail that they are not only irritating but often incomprehensible to readers who are less fascinated than the author by bridge construction and marine engineering. More off-putting still are tales like '.007', when a new railway engine talks to other railway engines, or 'The Ship that Found Herself', a parable about team spirit in which the discordant parts of a new vessel learn to harmonize with each other and thus endow the ship with a soul. Henry James exaggerated and also oversimplified the chronology when he deplored his friend's descent from 'the simple in subject to the more simple – from the Anglo-Indians to the natives, from the natives to the Tommies, from the Tommies to the quadrupeds, from the quadrupeds to the fish, and from the fish to the engines and screws'.[20] But he had a point.

During his American years Kipling also compiled *The Seven Seas*, a book of poems displaying the broad range of style and subject matter that he now possessed.* The volume shows that *The Day's Work* and the *Jungle Books* had not exhausted his interest in India and the British Army: a third of the book is devoted to another series of 'barrack-room ballads', poems such as 'The 'eathen' and 'Back to the Army' revealing once again a close understanding of military life and an uncanny empathy with Tommy Atkins. But by consigning the ballads to the end of the book, Kipling accentuated a change of emphasis. Mulvaney was giving way to McAndrew. The barracks were ceding priority to the shipyards. India as the focus of his imperialism was losing out to an older vision of empire, expansion by sea and by ruling the waves, a process begun by Elizabethan buccaneers and still very much alive.

The volume's human and geographical range is suggested in the humorous verses of 'In the Neolithic Age'.

> Still the world is wondrous large, – seven seas from marge to marge, –
>   And it holds a vast of various kinds of man;
> And the wildest dreams of Kew are the facts of Khatmandhu,
>   And the crimes of Clapham chaste in Martaban.

But the tone of the seamen's dramatic monologues, recalling Browning at his best, is relentlessly serious. 'The Mary Gloster' and 'McAndrew's Hymn' are tributes to hard work, duty, self-sacrifice and resilience. On his deathbed Anthony Gloster, a coarse, self-made, millionaire shipowner, summons his son and harangues him on the contrast of their lives. He has worked at his trade for fifty years, taken risks, made money (not always scrupulously) and now regrets that, instead of sending Dickie to sea, he stood his son an

*Kipling's title refers to the North and South Atlantic, the North and South Pacific, the Arctic and Indian Oceans, and the Mediterranean Sea. The book was published in London by Methuen, but the prose works were now in the hands of Macmillan. In New York, Kipling used a variety of publishers until 1899, when he entrusted his work to his friend Frank Doubleday at Doubleday and McClure.

education at Harrow and Trinity College. Dickie is berated for mud-
dling 'with books and pictures, an' china an' etchin's an' fans', for
having rooms at Cambridge which were 'beastly – more like a
whore's than a man's', and for marrying 'that thin-flanked woman, as
white and stale as a bone', who gave him his 'social nonsense' but
never a 'kid' of his own. The reference to Harrow and Trinity is
revealing because these were the places where his first cousin,
Stanley Baldwin, was also educated. Kipling's feelings for Baldwin
were perfectly friendly, but the connection between the Glosters and
the cousins is unmistakable. As his parents were too poor to send
him to university, Kipling had left school at the age of 16 to learn an
unprestigious trade in a harsh environment. Yet his close relation
had the wealth to enjoy leisurely years at a major public school and a
great Cambridge college. Kipling was envious and afterwards sceptical of the value of such privilege. Although he admired scholarship
and later enjoyed collecting honorary doctorates, he was never convinced that an education like Baldwin's was a great asset. Education
as apprenticeship, training for a specific craft, appealed to him far
more.

McAndrew is very different from Anthony Gloster. The dour,
God-fearing Scots engineer has a rigid creed: 'Law, Orrder, Duty an'
restraint, Obedience, Discipline!' His work is unglamorous, he is
paid less and thanked less than the officers on the upper deck, yet he
is the crucial figure in the ship, the man who knows how it works, the
man ultimately responsible for the safety of the passengers and the
crew. Like Gloster and Kipling, he scoffs at social pretensions, deriding some 'Viscount loon', dressed in tennis shoes and yachting cap, a
'damned ijjit' who asks, 'Mister McAndrew, don't you think steam
spoils romance at sea?' He also assails the Romantic poets and their
successors.

> I'm sick of all their quirks an' turns – the loves an' doves they dream –
> Lord, send a man like Robbie Burns to sing the Song o' Steam!

Kipling was naturally pleased that no writer before him had seen
'the romance and heroism' of the engineer's life. And he was also
pleased with his poem, which Conan Doyle heard him recite with
dramatic power and a sustained Glaswegian accent. He was particularly flattered by a letter from the American Admiral Melville, Chief

of the Navy Bureau of Steam Engineering, who rejoiced that at least one passenger in the world saw beyond the brass buttons of the upper deck to 'the real man' upon whose hand and brain the ship's safety depended. Kipling replied, asking Melville to check the poem for technical errors, and was delighted to be told that there were none.[21]

For Henry James *The Seven Seas* was 'all prose trumpets and castanets and such – with never a touch of the fiddle-string or a note of the nightingale'. But he admitted that it was 'magnificent and masterly in its way, and full of the most insidious art'.[22] A distinguished American reviewer regarded the book's dominant tone as that of 'the new patriotism, that of imperial England' which bound all parts of its wide-stretched empire 'in the indissoluble bond of common motherhood and [with] the ties of common convictions, principles and aims, derived from the teachings and traditions of the motherland'.[23] This might be a more accurate description of the tone of Kipling's two subsequent volumes of verse, but it is also apparent in 'The English Flag', already mentioned, and in 'The Native-Born', where the narrator asks his readers to charge their glasses and drink to 'the men of the Four New Nations' (Canada, Australia, New Zealand and South Africa) and to all the places and peoples (even their uncomprehending English brothers) who form 'the last and the largest Empire'.

The four new nations were added to Britain to produce the title of the next book of poems, *The Five Nations*. At times Kipling dreamed of adding a sixth, the United States, and had playfully suggested that someone should combine 'The British Grenadiers', 'Marching through Georgia' and other songs to create 'the greatest song of all – The Saga of the Anglo-Saxon all round the earth'.[24] American politics and personalities, however, combined to destroy his dream of an Anglo-American condominium over half the world. The same combination destroyed his American idyll.

From the beginning of his time in the United States he had known or been in touch with members of Washington's intellectual élite, men such as John Hay, the future Secretary of State, and the historian Henry Adams. In 1895 he met Theodore Roosevelt, then in his last period of comparative anonymity, and was so impressed that he soon added him to his pantheon of political men of action, a special temple of the later 1890s whose heroes included Cecil Rhodes,

Joseph Chamberlain and Alfred Milner. But in the same year he also met the President of the United States, Grover Cleveland, the stolid, uncompromising and very conservative Democrat who was nearing the end of his second term of office. Cleveland did not enter the pantheon. Kipling privately dismissed him and his entourage as 'a colossal agglomeration of reeking bounders',[25] as extraordinary a description of the honest and plainspoken President as it was of the generally courteous and high-minded men who formed his administration. But had Kipling been moved to relent – and relenting was not one of his strong points – the impulse would have been strangled by the Venezuelan boundary dispute.

For half a century Britain and Venezuela had been in dispute over the frontier demarcation between the South American republic and British Guiana. But the matter had not become an issue until the discovery of gold in the disputed area prompted insistent offers of arbitration from the United States; and it did not become a crisis until the summer of 1895 when Richard Olney, the pugnacious new American Secretary of State, brought his country and Britain to the edge of a ludicrous war. In a boorish reassertion of the Monroe Doctrine, Olney ordered his ambassador in London to tell the British Government that the United States was 'practically sovereign on this continent' (which must have been news to Canadians, Mexicans and others), that political union between European and American states was 'unnatural and inexpedient' (news again to citizens of Canada and Newfoundland), and that the Latin American republics were 'the friends and allies' of the United States for reasons of 'geographical proximity', 'natural sympathy' and 'similarity of governmental institutions' (news for atlas readers who could measure the distance between Chile and the United States, for Latin Americans who naturally sympathized with their relations and co-religionists in Portugal, Spain and Italy, and for anyone who could appreciate the difference between dictatorship and democracy even when both types of regime called themselves a republic).[26]

Lord Salisbury, Prime Minister now for the third time, could not resist a condescending and ironic reply. Wise and cynical, a statesman whose successes owed much to his refusal to proclaim them, he found Olney's message so brash – even after Cleveland had 'softened' the 'verbiage' – that he failed to restrain his natural causticity. The Monroe Doctrine, he declared, was theoretically sound, but it was not in the code of international law and it could not be applied to the present situation; indeed the United States had no legitimate concern in the delimitation of the 'frontier of a British possession which belonged to the Throne of England long before the Republic of Venezuela came into existence'. Cleveland, exhilarated by a duck-shooting expedition to North Carolina, went 'mad clean through' on reading the message and threatened to use force if Britain did not accept the American offer of arbitration. His action led to a frenzy of bellicose Anglophobia among press, politicians and people (especially Irish-Americans who offered 100,000 troops) so desperate to fight that they were unable to reflect how the Monroe Doctrine might be defended with their solitary modern battleship against the might of the Royal Navy.* Roosevelt, Kipling's new friend, at least realized that American coastal cities would be bombarded but he felt war would be worthwhile because the United States could seize Canada. It took the collapse of the stock market, mainly caused by the withdrawal of British investment, to sober the warmongers.

In any case, British ministers, distracted by events in South Africa, were in no mood to fight: they also realized they would have difficulty in explaining to their voters and even their colleagues what the contest was about. They backed down, agreed to arbitration, and were rewarded three years later when a commission, which included the American Chief Justice, accepted most of the British argument.

Kipling was astonished that there had been any question of war: it was the 'futilest piffle' he had ever heard of, and he wished he could have written 'a set of verses chaffing the thing dead'. Nor could he understand the anti-British hostility that had suddenly been uncorked. He was bewildered and upset; it was like being 'aimed at with a decanter across a friendly dinner table'.[27] As the vilification in the press continued, he wondered whether he could go on living in a place where most of the inhabitants wanted a war with his own country. He wished to write his tales in peace, he told a friendly American magnate, but how could he do so when the President 'out of sheer duck-shooting excitement fires left and right into the face of a friendly power?' In January 1896 he decided that 'this folly' had put

---

*The United States Navy grew very quickly after the crisis: by 1914 only Britain and Germany had more battleships.

an end to the family's 'good wholesome life' in America and they would have to begin again somewhere else.[28]

The Kiplings' life in Vermont would have become less good, less wholesome and probably less safe even without Cleveland and Venezuela. There had long been friction between Carrie and Beatty, her younger brother and neighbour. He was dependent on her and their mother for various matters, including the mortgage on his farm, and he resented the bossy and patronizing manner with which Carrie both helped and lectured him about his insolvency and his drinking. The dispute exploded in May 1896 when a drunken Beatty came across Kipling, who had just fallen off his bicycle, on the road to Brattleboro. He accused his brother-in-law of telling lies about him and his finances and, when told to refer to Kipling's lawyer, threatened to blow out his brains. Rudyard asked for confirmation of the threat, received it, and the following day filed a complaint, which led to Beatty's arrest. At the subsequent hearing in Brattleboro, Kipling's much guarded privacy was swept away as lawyers forced him to spend a humiliating afternoon answering questions about the feud in front of a crowd of journalists.

The dispute left Kipling, in the words of Carrie's diary, 'a total wreck': over the following days his wife described him as 'dull', 'listless', 'dreary' and 'very miserable'. The local newspaper, *The Phoenix*, assured him that 'Brattleboro folk' hoped he would stay in Naulakha and that 'the mature fruit of his genius' would ripen in Vermont.[29] But he had had enough. In June he went salmon fishing in Canada, where Carrie hoped he would regain 'some of the nerve and strength ... frittered away in so unworthy a cause'.[30] On his return he packed up Naulakha and left America a week before the hearing was scheduled to resume. President Cleveland and brother-in-law Beatty had ended his expatriate existence.

8

The Prophet's Burden

TORQUAY, A MYSTERIOUS choice for the Kiplings' first home in England, was not an improvement on Vermont. The town was so 'smugly British' that it made Kipling want to 'dance naked through it with pink feathers' in his stern. Local society was 'ponderous', 'fat old ladies' living in villas with clipped hedges and shaved lawns. And although it was good to be back in the 'beautiful fatted and washed English scenery', he wished the place hadn't been 'quite so infernally respectable'.[1]

He tried to like Devon, bicycling on a tandem with Carrie along country lanes and fly-fishing in its trout streams. He tried to like his new home, Rock House, though he admitted it was built in 'the vilest sort of 1860 architecture'. Perched on a hillside above cliffs, it had views of the sea that enabled him to glance up from his writing on to the decks of fishing craft below. But the countryside was marred by the 'eternal' rain just as the house was blighted by its 'Feng-Shui – the Spirit of the House', which engendered depression. After eight months of damp, mildew and raw sea fog, the family set off for London in May 1897 and a few months later settled in Rottingdean, between the sea and the Sussex Downs, where they lived for five years in a house called 'The Elms'.

While in Devon Kipling met naval officers at Dartmouth and thus initiated his long and faithful relationship with the Royal Navy. From London he went to Chatham Dockyard and spent three hours of 'unmitigated hell' in a torpedo boat destroyer careering at thirty 'smitten knots' around the mouth of the Thames. The following month he was invited to watch the manoeuvres of the Channel Squadron off the north coast of Ireland, an experience he very much enjoyed; although he considered the new admiral 'rather an ass', he greatly admired the squadron. A year later he went out again on manoeuvres and was so impressed with the fleet that he wrote a series of articles in the *Morning Post* with the aim of making the public 'take an interest'. On this occasion he recited some poems at a ship's concert and was carried in triumph around the quarterdeck.

'McAndrew's Hymn' and other nautical verses brought him the same admiration from sailors as *Barrack Room Ballads* had brought him from soldiers. Kipling loved ships and sailing talk and was justly regarded as the poet of the engine-rooms: the Lord had granted McAndrew's wish to 'send a man like Robbie Burns to sing the Song o' Steam'. But he had gone to the barracks outside Lahore as a teenage reporter; he cruised with the Royal Navy as a distinguished guest, fêted by officers not only because he knew about boats but because by 1897, the year of the Queen's Diamond Jubilee, he was a famous writer and was widely regarded as the new apostle of the Empire. The first experience gave him Mulvaney, Danny Deever and Tommy Atkins; the second produced articles and letters of support for the Navy. Fame had blocked Kipling's descent to the lower decks. He wrote great verses about the sea but he never wrote a good story about the Navy.

Two events over the winter of 1895–6 had focused Kipling's attention on the Empire, alerting him to the dangers it suddenly had to confront. The Venezuelan crisis produced a potentially lethal and very unexpected foe in the United States; the Jameson Raid, the chief component of a British conspiracy to overthrow the Boer republic of the Transvaal, conjured up a more frightening enemy in Germany.

Dr Jameson's invasion of Boer territory had the backing of Cecil Rhodes, the Prime Minister of Cape Colony, and the complicity of Joseph Chamberlain at the Colonial Office in London. But it provoked outrage in Germany, which had recently acquired colonies in East Africa and South-West Africa and which was now developing close ties with the Boers. Kipling as yet knew little about South Africa and was not greatly concerned by the regional implications of the absurd incursion.* But he was terrified by the possibility of a German-American alliance, two of the world's great industrial powers lining up against the third. And he was outraged by the intervention of Kaiser Wilhelm who, after proclaiming on New Year's Day that Germany was now a world empire, sent a public telegram congratulating the Transvaal president, Paul Kruger, for overcoming the 'armed bands' and 'disturbers of the peace' and for 'defending the independence of the country'.

Kipling did not know that Wilhelm had sent the telegram to avenge an unintended snub by Lord Salisbury the previous summer at Cowes where he had gone to visit his grandmother Queen Victoria on his yacht. He did not know that the German monarch was gleefully baiting the British military attaché in Berlin about Britain's isolation or telling his ambassador in London to come home if it became apparent that Whitehall had supported Jameson. And perhaps he did not know that Kruger had celebrated the Kaiser's birthday with an appeal for Germany's 'friendship to be more firmly established than ever'. But he was certain from that moment that Germany would become Britain's principal enemy in the twentieth century.

Jan Smuts, the future South African Prime Minister, rightly regarded the Jameson Raid as 'the real declaration of war in the great Anglo-Boer conflict'.[2] Kipling wrongly considered it 'the first battle in the war of '14–'18 – a little before its time but necessary to clear the ground'.[3] His warnings about both world wars were astonishingly prophetic, but his biased history does not help explain the origins of the first. The Jameson Raid marked not the countdown to 1914 but the beginning of Kipling's obsession with Germany. He had mildly mocked the Kaiser's social programme in 'An Imperial Rescript' in 1890, and the following year he had sworn never again to travel in a German ship because 'hot boiled pigs' feet and sauerkraut' were not his 'ideal of grub'. Yet in 1893 he had published 'In the Rukh', a story containing a highly sympathetic portrait of a German official in the Indian Forest Department. It was the Kaiser's telegram that converted him to relentless Germanophobia. By the summer of 1897 he was predicting a 'big smash' with the Germans, whether over South Africa or elsewhere, and, fortified by his recent voyages with the

---

*See below, pp. 133–6.

Navy, he believed they could be easily 'kicked'.[4] The following year Germany decided to become less kickable by accelerating its programme of naval construction.

Confidence in his own judgement was not dented by the Anglo-German Agreement of 1898. British ministers had long been worried by the prospect of German dominance in the Transvaal, by now the world's largest gold producer and the key region in the area. Their fears may have been exaggerated – Kruger playing the German 'card' did not mean he wished to become part of the Second Reich – but they persuaded Salisbury to make an agreement in which Germany effectively accepted British paramountcy in southern Africa. Chamberlain grumbled that, by making concessions over the future of Portugal's African colonies, Britain was paying blackmail to the Germans to induce them not to interfere where they had 'no right of interference'.[5] But he admitted it was sometimes worthwhile paying blackmail – as indeed it turned out to be in this case. Despite the anti-British feelings of its press and public opinion, Germany remained neutral in the Boer War, with the Kaiser even giving advice to his uncle, the Prince of Wales, on how it should be fought.

None of this mellowed Kipling, who had noted the growth of the German Navy. Nor did the Kaiser's personal telegram of sympathy during a nearly fatal bout of pneumonia in New York in 1899. That same year the poet predicted 'the Great War', accurately foretelling the name by which it would be known and the period during which it would begin. Three years after that he damned Germany in public. Incensed by a proposal from Berlin that the Royal Navy be used to collect debts that Venezuela owed Britain and Germany, he published a vitriolic poem, 'The Rowers', whose final two lines caused an uproar – 'With a cheated crew, to league anew / With the Goth and the shameless Hun!'* 'The Goth', 'the Hun' and 'the Teuton' soon became his habitual terms for describing German citizens. During the Great War he urged a newspaper editor not to capitalize the word 'Hun' and to refer to him as 'it'.[6]

The Kruger Telegram and the earlier Venezuelan crisis had prompted a more sombre and almost humble response in 'Hymn Before Action' (1896).

---

*See below, p. 206.

The earth is full of anger,
    The seas are dark with wrath,
The Nations in their harness
    Go up against our path . . .

. . . E'en now their vanguard gathers,
    E'en now we face the fray —
As Thou didst help our fathers,
    Help Thou our host to-day!

The British may be undeserving of God's protection, they may be fools and sinners with deaf ears and uncaring souls, but the appeal is still made: 'Jehovah of the Thunders, Lord God of Battles, aid!' The alarmist message, the vision of enemy hordes in harness, proved too much for Moberly Bell, the assistant manager of *The Times*, who felt it was the wrong time to publish it. Yet within a few years others were giving the same warnings in similar tones. In a valedictory of apocalyptic pessimism Salisbury warned Curzon in 1902 of enemies gathering, of 'large aggregations of human forces' assuming a 'more and more aggressive aspect', of them merging 'in menacing and dangerous masses' to threaten the Empire.[7]

'Hymn Before Action' was the first of the imperial anthems, anticipating 'Recessional' in content and expression and humility before God. Kipling usually published his anthems in *The Times* and refused payment because they were of a 'national character', a gesture that indicates a conscious assumption of the role of a prophet whose purpose is to warn his people of coming dangers. The poems may sound like rhymed editorials full of Old Testament sonorities and incantations. But they are much more than that. The biblical language and allusions appealed to people who had been educated not only through the Classics but through the Gospels, the Epistles and the Hebrew prophets as well. They understood the message and they accepted it. Concurrently Kipling was producing cruder work, celebrating the English talent for being polite and violent at the same time ('Et Dona Ferentes'), and boasting of England's ability to turn Egyptians into soldiers and scholars ('Pharaoh and the Sergeant' and 'Kitchener's School'). But the anthems are the poems that resonated then — and still do, however unfamiliar the Bible has become and however much the message now grates. The series of them that lasted the six years from 'Hymn Before Action' to 'The Islanders' (1902) demonstrates Kipling's extraordinary gift for persuading people that what they were reading was how they felt.

In 1892 Tennyson had died after forty years as Poet Laureate. He had succeeded Wordsworth who in turn had succeeded Southey. If these standards were to be maintained, then the post should have been offered to Swinburne: as the Queen informed Gladstone, in his fourth stint as Prime Minister, Swinburne was 'the best poet in my dominions' – or so she had been told.[8] But neither Gladstone nor his successor, Lord Rosebery, filled the vacancy, and it was left to the Conservatives to find a new laureate when they came to power in 1895. Arthur Balfour, who was Salisbury's nephew and political heir, recommended the expatriate in Vermont, who was duly 'sounded out'. When Kipling refused, Salisbury selected Alfred Austin, an incredible choice that may have been made simply to annoy the literary establishment: the Prime Minister was proud of his philistinism (which in fact he exaggerated – he liked to relax with volumes of Goethe and Sophocles) and referred to his house, Hatfield, as 'Gaza, the capital of Philistia'.[9]

Kipling refused the post partly because he disdained official honours and partly because he was reluctant to write on request. As he explained to an editor wanting to alter a story, 'writing to order means loss of power, loss of belief in the actuality of the tale and ultimately loss of self-respect to the writer'.[10] Unwillingness was accompanied by a simple inability to compose something he did not want to write for an occasion he did not wish to commemorate. During the first half of 1897, when he was being badgered to write a Jubilee ode, he complained that writing about the Queen was outside his 'beat', that it was Austin's job in any case, and that London was full of loyal poets scribbling away.[11] Only when the Jubilee was nearly over did he write the ode that many had been waiting for.

In June 1897 work began on two of the most famous poems in the English language. At the time neither pleased its author, who regarded them with diffidence: 'The White Man's Burden' was soon put aside while a draft of 'Recessional' (originally called 'After') was abandoned when Kipling went off with the Navy and allegedly consigned to the waste-paper basket on his return. The composition of 'Recessional' has become legendary and confused, its message and sentiments have provoked passion and controversy, and its language, form and contents appear to have been borrowed from the Bible and other sources: there are clear references to two books of the Old Testament (Job and Deuteronomy), two psalms (51 and 90) and the Epistle to the Romans, while, as Lord Birkenhead suggested, Kipling's debt to the works of Emerson, Newman and Francis Quarles strays close to the borders of plagiarism.[12] It is nevertheless one of those rare poems that articulates a mood and a moment in a nation's history.

RECESSIONAL*

God of our fathers, known of old,
    Lord of our far-flung battle-line,
Beneath whose awful Hand we hold
    Dominion over palm and pine —
Lord God of Hosts, be with us yet,
Lest we forget — lest we forget!

The tumult and the shouting dies;
    The captains and the kings depart:
Still stands Thine ancient sacrifice,
    An humble and a contrite heart.
Lord God of Hosts, be with us yet,
Lest we forget — lest we forget!

Far-called, our navies melt away;
    On dune and headland sinks the fire:
Lo, all our pomp of yesterday
    Is one with Nineveh and Tyre!
Judge of the Nations, spare us yet,
Lest we forget — lest we forget!

If, drunk with sight of power, we loose
    Wild tongues that have not Thee in awe,

---

*The *Shorter OED* defines recessional as a hymn sung during 'the recession or retirement of the clergy and choir ... at the close of a service'. The title was presumably chosen because the poem appeared at the end of the Jubilee ceremonies. Since it was written as the Empire approached its apogee, 'Recessional', with its suggestion of withdrawal and imperial decline, was not an obviously appropriate heading even for a pessimist. But applied to Kipling and the trajectory of the Empire during his lifetime, it becomes more suitable.

Such boastings as the Gentiles use,
    Or lesser breeds without the Law –
Lord God of Hosts, be with us yet,
Lest we forget – lest we forget!

For heathen heart that puts her trust
    In reeking tube and iron shard,
All valiant dust that builds on dust,
    And guarding, calls not Thee to guard,
For frantic boast and foolish word –
Thy Mercy on Thy People, Lord!

The poem was composed, according to Kipling, to 'the simple jog-trot' of 'Eternal Father strong to save',[13] a model of appropriate solemnity containing an apposite refrain ('O hear us when we cry to Thee / For those in peril on the sea'). But the spirit comes from the Old Testament, specifically from the 'jealous God' of Deuteronomy.

> Then beware lest thou forget the Lord, which brought thee out of the land of Egypt, from the house of bondage. Thou shalt fear the Lord thy God, and serve him, and shalt swear by his name. Ye shall not go after other gods, of the gods of the people which are round about you; (For the Lord thy God is a jealous God among you) lest the anger of the Lord thy God be kindled against thee, and destroy thee from off the face of the earth. (6:12–15)

Kipling's 'Lord God of Hosts' is the same deity as 'Jehovah of the Thunders' in 'Hymn Before Action': the God who has made a covenant with a favoured people and, as Judge of the Nations, has granted them 'dominion over palm and pine'.* But the modern prophet fears that his people, like the ancient Israelites, no longer hold Him 'in awe'. They have become boastful, arrogant and blasphemous, and unless they reform, unless they reveal 'an humble and a contrite heart', they will go the way of Nineveh and Tyre. Appeals are thus simultaneously made to God for his mercy and to his people for repentance.

---

*Although the line is hardly more than an abbreviation of Emerson's couplet, 'And grant to dwellers with the pine / Dominion o'er the palm and vine', its five words manage to evoke the range of an empire that can encompass both Canada and Ceylon.

This particular prophet did not believe in the Old Testament or its God. He was not indeed a 'churchman' in a physical or spiritual sense. But he thought lessons could be learned from the Hebrew prophets and decided that the Authorized Version was the right language in which to teach them.

Kipling returned to the *Jungle Books* for one of his main themes: the superior civilization of those obeying the Law over those who live 'without the Law'. But he invited trouble by turning these into human categories instead of restricting them to the wolf pack and the monkey-folk. In his inimitable way Orwell observed that the phrase, 'lesser breeds without the law', was 'always good for a snigger in pansy-left circles', where it was taken to refer to 'natives' or 'coolies' being kicked about by a 'pukka sahib in a pith helmet'.[14] This view is still found in India and elsewhere; and in 1964 the Methodist hymnal dropped 'Recessional' because black Methodists believed the words carried an 'unmistakable racial slur'.[15]

It was an unfortunate and perhaps tasteless choice of phrase, but no reading of the poem or its precursor justifies the interpretation. 'Hymn Before Action' contains a plea for God's mercy on the colonial peoples* and uses the adjective 'lawless' to describe the Empire's enemies. The relevant biblical text is Paul's Epistle to the Romans where the apostle writes:

> For as many have sinned without law shall also perish without law: and as many have sinned in the law shall be judged by the law … For when the Gentiles, which have not the law, do by nature the things contained in the law, these, having not the law, are a law unto themselves. (2: 12, 14)

As the epistle's context makes clear, the Gentiles are the Roman rulers who, being without the Law of Christ, act as they please.[16] Kipling transformed the Gentiles into their modern equivalents, the Kaiser and his henchmen, and the 'lesser breeds' into the German people and anyone else, especially the Americans and perhaps also the Boers, whom he considered guilty of boastful lawlessness.

On 16 July Kipling sent 'Recessional' to *The Times* with the explanation that 'we've been blowing the Trumpets of the New Moon a little too much for White Men, and it's about time we sobered

---

*Quoted above, p. 58.

down'.[17] Coupled with the poem, this suggests that he was in an unusual mood of humility and contrition. But the evidence of other writings at the time indicates that it can have been only one of several moods. 'The White Man's Burden', begun a week before he started 'Recessional', promotes a dedicated but much less humble approach to imperial responsibility. 'Premiers at Play', an anonymous article inspired by the presence of the eleven colonial premiers at a conference with Chamberlain in London, is an optimistic picture of imperial collaboration at the time of the Jubilee. A letter to Rider Haggard reveals that in 'Recessional' Kipling had meant to say, 'Don't gas but be ready to give people snuff' – yet had 'only covered the first part of the notion'. And a letter written to Moberly Bell only four days after the poem's publication admitted that, when thinking of his 'pious hymn', he was (like Lord Clive), 'astounded at [his] own moderation'.[18]

'Recessional' was published in *The Times* of 17 July on the same page as a message from Queen Victoria expressing her gratitude for the spontaneous outburst of loyalty and affection that had greeted her sixty years on the throne. The two effusions were jointly awarded a leading article in which the newspaper commended the note of 'moral responsibility' ringing out 'as clearly in the simple grandeur of the Queen's message as in Mr Kipling's soul-stirring verses'. The reaction to the work was astounding, surprising even the author, who remarked that 'the idea must have been in the air or men would not have taken to the rhymed expression of it so kindly'.[19] The poem was hailed as moving and opportune, one that struck the 'right note', 'went home to all our hearts', 'touched the solemn organ-stops' in a way that brought out the 'deepest response of our race'. Its author's status was quickly elevated. He had assumed the mantle of Tennyson; he had combined Shakespeare's 'glowing patriotism' with Milton's 'solemn piety' and Dryden's 'measured stateliness'. The despised Austin may have been Poet Laureate through a whim of Lord Salisbury, but Kipling was now widely acclaimed as the 'Laureate of the Empire', the 'laureate by divine right of English peoples' and the 'laureate of that larger England whose wreath it is not for any prime minister to bestow': ten years later, on receiving an honorary doctorate from Cambridge, he was hailed by the Public Orator in Latin as the 'poet laureate of our Navy, our soldiers, and the whole British Empire'.[20] The impact of 'Recessional' and some of its successors was such that, as Mark Twain observed, Kipling was 'the only living person not head of a nation, whose voice is heard around the world the moment it drops a remark, the only such voice in existence that does not go by slow ship and rail but always travels first-class by cable'.[21]

With 'Recessional' Kipling came to be regarded as a national symbol, a one-man embodiment of the Empire with a talent for anticipating a public sentiment (as well as encouraging and perhaps moulding it) just before it became apparent. But unlike Tennyson he was not a reverential songsmith of national valour: what a character of H.G.Wells called his 'lyric delight in the sounds and colours, in the very odours of empire',[22] enabled him to evoke the scale of the imperial experience, the sweep of an enterprise which, as he himself had witnessed, stretched from the Viceroy's Council in Simla to the Mounties of western Canada. This panoramic view of the Empire was closely followed by a realization of the perils that threatened it, so that in the mid-1890s Kipling added the role of national prophet to that of imperial laureate. The acquisition of his new position made people accept his authority to preach as he did, blatantly in his poems, more obliquely in his stories. He was, proclaimed the novelist Rider Haggard, the 'true watchman of our Empire'. What Seeley had taught scholars, observed Besant, the watchman had taught the 'multitude'. 'I want to convert you to Imperialism,' Kipling told Andrew Carnegie, the philanthropic steel magnate.[23] But he wanted to convert the rest of the Anglo-Saxon world as well.

An opportunity was provided by expansionist stirrings in the United States. Deprived of a war against Britain over Venezuela, the more bellicose segment of American public opinion had been looking for another target and now demanded a fight over the remnants of Spain's American empire. Roosevelt articulated a widespread view when he said America needed a war and privately called President McKinley a 'white-livered cur' for hesitating to attack Spanish forces struggling to suppress the Cuban separatist revolt of 1895. The civilized McKinley wanted neither a war nor, at least initially, Cuban independence, and his polite negotiations with Madrid, during which he demanded an armistice and autonomy for the island, were going well. But after the mysterious sinking of the *Maine* battleship in Havana harbour, and under pressure from a public noisily incited by the Hearst and Pulitzer press, he gave Congress the choice of war or peace. Despite the President's reminder that Spain had conceded every important point, Congress opted for war. Within weeks of its declaration in April 1898, American forces had overwhelmed the Spanish in Cuba and the Philippines, and in July they occupied Puerto Rico. In the consequent peace treaty Spain relinquished Cuba, which became nominally independent though effectively a one-crop economic colony of the Manhattan banks. It also ceded Puerto Rico and Guam as well as the Philippines (for which the United States paid $20 million to Spain and a great deal more to suppress Filipino rebels who saw no advantage in exchanging Spanish colonists for Americans). As the new century approached, the United States became a world power ready for imperialist instruction from Rudyard Kipling.*

The uncrowned laureate cheered as he watched American developments. 'My sympathies are with you', he told a railroad magnate on realizing that America was 'going to walk into Cuba ... There is no place in the world today for worn-out nations.'[25] As the American triumph unfolded, he rhapsodized at the prospect of the nation across the Atlantic at last deciding to share the burden of civilizing the backward regions of the globe. Since it was 'the fate of our breed to do these things,' he told a correspondent in Connecticut, it was 'a joy and gratification beyond words' for him to see the Americans 'swinging into line on [their] side of the world and getting to business instead of heaving rocks at one another and turning out the militia for railroad strikes'. By August he realized that 1898 had been 'a grand year for the White Man'. The Americans had stopped regarding British imperialists as robbers and hypocrites. They were taking up the same task themselves and in consequence some of them received highly patronizing advice from a man who claimed to know all about it. Colonies were 'like babies', he informed another correspondent as

---

*Kipling's American friends were divided over the Spanish-American conflict. John Hay, now Ambassador to the Court of St James, thought it a 'splendid little war', and Roosevelt resigned as Assistant Secretary of the Navy to lead the 'Rough Riders' in battle. But Andrew Carnegie belonged to the Anti-Imperialist League, and so did Mark Twain, who parodied the 'Battle Hymn of the Republic' in a manner worthy of Kipling.

> Mine eyes have seen the orgy of the launching of the Sword;
> He is searching out the hoardings where the strangers' wealth is stored;
> He has loosed his fateful lightning, and with woe and death has scored;
> His lust is marching on.[24]

the Filipinos launched their ferocious three-year revolt in February 1899. 'They are all very aggravating at first but they are worth it.'[26] Yet the instructor was unaware of his condescension. After all, the Americans were now 'worth talking to'. They were 'equals', they could 'understand things', they were – 'thank God' – on 'the threshold of … the White Man's work, the business of introducing a sane and orderly administration into the dark places of the earth' that lay in their sphere. Speaking as the embodiment of Britain, 'rather more than eight hundred years old' and 'bred and trained for imperial labour', he declared to a professor who had enlisted with the 50th Iowa Volunteers at Camp Cuba Libre in Florida:

> I have only this spring called in 60,000 [troops] from an eight months old war amid the underheaps [sic] of the Indian frontier: and 22,000 men are now going in to arrange matters with a merry barbarian down in the south of Egypt. Behind all these men, who die or will die of fever, sun, cholera, the sword and syphilis, stand all my administrators who without hope of reward or public favour or any expressed approval will go out and die in strange places for the good of the various races they have taken under their wing. I have suppressed much evil in many lands; I have made two blades grow where but one grew before: I have brought peace where there was only war; I have abated famine and sent my picked men to fight pestilence. And this I have done, O Theophilus, not once in a year, but yearly for fifty years.[27]

In February 1899 'The White Man's Burden' was published in *The Times* in Britain and in *McClure's Magazine* in the United States. Specifically addressed to the American people (and indirectly exhorting them to annex the Philippines), it appeared on the day the Filipino revolt broke out and a day before the American Senate voted as Kipling had urged.

> Take up the White Man's burden –
>   Send forth the best ye breed –
> Go bind your sons to exile
>   To serve your captives' need;
> To wait in heavy harness,
>   On fluttered folk and wild –
> Your new-caught, sullen peoples,
>   Half-devil and half-child.

The Prophet's Burden

Take up the White Man's burden –
  In patience to abide,
To veil the threat of terror
  And check the show of pride;
By open speech and simple,
  An hundred times make plain,
To seek another's profit,
  And work another's gain.

Take up the White Man's burden –
  The savage wars of peace –
Fill full the mouth of Famine
  And bid the sickness cease;
And when your goal is nearest
  The end of others sought,
Watch Sloth and heathen Folly
  Bring all your hope to nought.

Take up the White Man's burden –
  No tawdry rule of kings,
But toil of serf and sweeper –
  The tale of common things.
The ports ye shall not enter,
  The roads ye shall not tread,
Go mark them with your living,
  And mark them with your dead.

Take up the White Man's burden –
  And reap his old reward:
The blame of those ye better,
  The hate of those ye guard –
The cry of hosts ye humour
  (Ah, slowly!) toward the light: –
'Why brought ye us from bondage,
  Our loved Egyptian night?'

Take up the White Man's burden
  Ye dare not stoop to less –
Nor call too loud on Freedom
  To cloak your weariness;
By all ye cry or whisper,
  By all ye leave or do,

> The silent, sullen peoples
> Shall weigh your Gods and you.
>
> Take up the White Man's burden –
> Have done with childish days –
> The lightly proffered laurel,
> The easy, ungrudged praise.
> Comes now, to search your manhood
> Through all the thankless years,
> Cold, edged with dear-bought wisdom,
> The judgment of your peers!

The Iowan Volunteer admired the poem and was gratified to have been sent the prose version six months earlier. Other addressees of the message were less appreciative, even Roosevelt, that breezy and energetic expansionist who agreed with his friend Kipling on most things except the Venezuelan boundary dispute.* 'Rather poor poetry,' he remarked to Henry Cabot Lodge, grudgingly adding that it made 'good sense from the expansionist standpoint'. 'Better poetry than you say', replied the Anglophobic senator, 'apart from the sense of the verses'.[28] The sense was also resisted in the American press, newspapers from the *Buffalo Express* to the *Iowa State Register* competing to publish parodies with titles such as 'The Black Man's Burden', 'The Poor Man's Burden', 'The White Woman's Burden' and even 'The Old Maid's Burden'. One assiduous collector of Kiplingiana pasted over eighty such parodies into his scrapbook.[29]

The title of the poem was as controversial and as easily misunderstood as the 'lesser breeds' phrase in 'Recessional'. Again it is an unfortunate and perhaps tasteless form of words – and looks trebly so a hundred years later. But 'white' here plainly refers to civilization and character more than to the colour of men's skins. The 'white men' are those who conduct themselves within the Law for the good of others: Gunga Din may have a 'dirty' hide, but he is 'white, clear white, inside'. As in the Bible, whiteness represents goodness and purity: bleached

---

*And the fate of the American Indians. In his autobiography Kipling admitted he 'never got over the wonder of a people who, having extirpated the aboriginals of their continent more completely than any modern race had ever done, honestly believed they were a godly little New England community, setting examples to brutal mankind. This wonder I used to explain to Theodore Roosevelt, who made the glass cases of Indian relics [in the Smithsonian Institution] shake with his rebuttals.'

angels countering the darkness of evil – what Victor Hugo meant when he used to say, 'before God, all Souls are white',[30] or what Blake's eponymous 'Little Black Boy' expresses when he insists, 'but O! my soul is white'. When the Israelites 'learn to do well', Isaiah's God tells them, though their 'sins be as scarlet, they shall be as white as snow' (1: 18). More recently, Bertie Wooster is not referring to his valet's pigment when he praises Jeeves for being 'very white'.

Even so, as one estimable critic has judged, the poem is 'profoundly racist in sentiment'.[31] The Filipinos – and by implication many other non-European natives in the world – are wild, sullen, slothful and heathen. Childish and diabolical in equal measure, they will obstruct all efforts to 'improve' them, clinging to the familiar bondage under Pharaoh rather than striking out with Moses towards the Promised Land.

The message to the Americans (who cannot have much appreciated the reference to their 'childish days') was close to the justification Kipling habitually gave for British rule in India. After the rulers have taken possession, they remain to toil and to serve, to prevent famine and to cure sickness, to dedicate their lives and even to die for the sake of the 'new-caught, sullen peoples'. It is literally a thankless task: no pomp, no material reward, 'no tawdry rule of kings' – just the blame and hate of the people 'ye better'. As in the great bulk of Kipling's work, there are no trumpetings here, no references to honour and glory, no smug reminders of military heroics. Whatever his reputation then and later, that was never his style.

In spite of the prejudice and the violence of expression, the message of 'The White Man's Burden' is idealistic. Like Canning, the Foreign Secretary who had championed South American independence in the 1820s, Kipling was calling 'the New World into existence to redress the balance of the Old'.[32] But his appeal had less to do with international politics. It was a question of duty, the world's two most advanced nations taking up the burden of dragging the most backward regions 'towards the light'.* Commending the poem, the *Spectator* declared that 'the duty of the white man is to conquer

---

*As Ambassador to Britain, Hay voiced similar views on the nature of the Anglo-American partnership: 'We are joint ministers of the same sacred mission of liberty and progress, charged with duties we cannot evade by the imposition of irresistible hands ... for all nations of the world will profit more or less directly by any extension of British commerce and the enterprise and enlightenment that go with it.'[33]

and control, probably for a couple of centuries, all the dark people of the world, not for his own good but for theirs'.[34] This is blunter, uglier and goes further than Kipling intended. But it comes to a similar conclusion. In a world without Oxfam and the United Nations, it was the responsibility of the richest and most civilized nations to help the poorest, not for reasons of vanity or self-aggrandizement, but because it was their duty to keep the peace, to bring justice and education, to protect minorities, to prevent people from dying of disease and starvation. Their officials would not be thanked and their work might not endure, but it was their duty to try, to do their best to alleviate suffering where they found it. Whatever economic considerations were also concerned – and these (which Kipling understood little about) have sometimes been exaggerated – the aim itself was not ignoble. And in expressing it as he did, the poet provided a plausible moral justification for imperial rule.

It was a habit of Kipling's to work concurrently on projects that were very different not only in content but also in style, tone and quality. This puzzled admirers who, however uplifted they may have felt on reading 'Recessional' or 'The White Man's Burden', did not experience similar feelings on reading the schoolboy stories written at the same time. Kipling loved writing *Stalky & Co*, inflicting noisy readings on his cousins and roaring with laughter at his own jokes. He had been happy at Westward Ho! and he was happy to recreate and embellish incidents from his schooldays, practical jokes, tricks on masters, japes in dormitories and schoolrooms culminating in scenes of 'side-splitting' mirth.

Yet for all its coarseness and modest barbarism, *Stalky* does not endorse the usual Victorian ethics. The Empire is of course present in the background – most of the boys are being trained for the Army – but there are no imperial lessons. Nor do the ethics of the public school and the cricket pitch receive approbation. The gang of Stalky, M'Turk and Beetle are mild subversives with an ambivalent attitude towards authority. They certainly do not play the game, worry about fair play or even watch cricket matches; one master accuses them of taking no interest in the 'honour' of their house. Furthermore, they exhibit none of the jingoism of which their creator was then being accused. One day a real jingoist does visit the school, an 'impeccable Conservative', an MP who tells them 'they would not always be boys', that one day 'the fair fame of their glorious native land' would depend on them, and that some of them no doubt 'anxiously looked forward to leading their men against the bullets of England's foes'. Unaware of the 'sour disgust' felt by his audience, he launches into his peroration, shaking a Union Jack at the boys and telling them that no one should look at it unless they are determined to add to its 'imperishable lustre'. The schoolboys listen with embarrassment and disbelief at the vulgarity of the performance, shuffling off to their dormitories to denounce the 'Jelly-bellied Flag-flapper'. Kipling thought the flag worth following – and told people so – but he was not a flapper.

Hostile criticism of Kipling had been negligible until near the end of the 1890s when *Stalky* and the imperial anthems presented irresistible targets for Liberals, Radicals and aesthetes. Robert Buchanan claimed that *Stalky* could only have been written by the 'spoiled child of an utterly brutalised public', adding that Kipling adumbrated all that was most deplorable, all that was 'most retrograde and savage, in the restless and uninstructed Hooliganism of the time'.[35] But political scribes aimed more naturally at 'The White Man's Burden'. Wilfrid Scawen Blunt, the champion of Irish and Egyptian nationalism who modelled himself as a poet and lover on Byron (his wife's grandfather), mocked the burden which the white man 'yearns to take / On his white Saxon back for his white conscience sake', and brought in Satan to reveal the truth, that the white man's burden was simply 'the burden of his cash'.[36] A more direct parody came from Henry Labouchere, the radical journalist and parliamentary scourge of imperialism and the House of Lords.

> Pile on the brown man's burden,
> And if ye rouse his hate
> Meet his old-fashioned reasons
> With Maxims up-to-date;
> With shells and dum dum bullets
> A hundred times make plain
> The brown man's loss must ever
> Imply the white man's gain.[37]

Wilde's coterie was also prominent among the critics. Richard Le Gallienne, the poet whom Wilde compared to the angel Gabriel, admired Kipling's skills, his 'wonderful transmuting of the commonest material', his ability to make magic in 'Mandalay' out of the 'very refuse of language'. But he was appalled by his exploitation of Christian terminology to justify the unChristian proceeding of conquering countries for 'the purely selfish and natural purpose of extending out trade'. 'Recessional' and 'The White Man's Burden' were 'political catch-words imbedded in rather spirited hymns': they were the writings not of Kipling the poet but of Kipling the 'unofficial M.P. for British possessions'. Taken as a whole, the work was a vindication of 'the Englishman as brute' and philistine. Kipling taught a series of noble lessons, 'to do one's duty, to live stoically, to live cleanly, to live cheerfully', yet at the same time the 'old-fashioned vices of [his] prejudiced Toryism' made him a very dangerous influence on 'progressive thought', an enemy of 'all that our best poets, philosophers, and social economists have been working for'.[38]*

Le Gallienne at least thought about his subject and wrote a serious study. Max Beerbohm, a Wildean disciple who referred to his master as 'the Divinity', merely felt. And his feelings for Kipling were strangely out of character. This sophisticated, heavy-lidded, rather preposterous and very unproductive Spirit of Oxford went berserk at the thought of Kipling: his modest oeuvre was expanded in consequence by critical articles, a parody and at least nine caricatures aimed at a man who refused to hit back. He mocked him as an 'idol of the market place', despised him as a poet and seer – 'all the ye-ing and the Lord-God-ing and the law-ing side of him' – and hated 'the smell of blood, beer and "baccy"' which, he claimed, exhaled from his pages. Beerbohm himself was not the type to allow such smells to come 'betwixt the wind and his nobility'. On the title-page of one of Kipling's books he wrote

By R.K. the
Apocalyptic Bounder
who
can do such fine things
but
Mostly prefers to stand
(on tip-toe and stridently)
for all that is
cheap
and nasty.[39]

---

*By 1919 Le Gallienne had come to regard Kipling as 'a deep and serious poet', a realist and prophet with a crucial moral influence on their generation.

9

Rhodes and Milner

K IPLING GAVE HIS heart and sometimes his head to a lengthy list
of political causes: British rule in India, Imperial Federation,
Tariff Reform, the survival of France, compulsory military service,
the preservation of Ulster from home-ruled Ireland, the protection
of Britain from the dangers of Germany, trade unionism, suffra-
gettes, Free Trade and the Liberal Party. Yet he spent more time and
passion promoting the cause of British supremacy in southern Africa
than on any other issue.

In the late 1830s and 1840s Dutch settlers, who called themselves
Afrikaners or Boers (farmers), had crossed the Vaal River to avoid
British rule and set up their own republic south of the Limpopo. In
1877 the area, known as the Transvaal, had been annexed by Britain,
but three years later a revolt, culminating in the Boer victory at
Majuba Hill, recovered most of its independence. By conventions in
Pretoria (1881) and London (1884), the Transvaal regained internal
self-government while the imperial power reserved control over its
foreign policy. Britain also claimed suzerainty – which the Boers disputed and eventually rejected – but curiously it did not regard the
Transvaal as a colony or a part of the Empire.

Since the 1870s the British had aimed for strategic reasons to unite
South Africa as an imperial dominion, though they showed little
interest in the interior until the discovery of diamonds and gold. The
subsequent emergence of the Transvaal as the world's leading gold

producer – and potentially the political as well as the economic centre of South Africa – made them less neglectful. Outnumbered by Afrikaners in the Cape as well as in the Transvaal and in the Boers' other republic, the Orange Free State, the British soon felt they were losing control of a region whose future seemed likely to be decided by a tussle between two equally obstinate leaders, Cecil Rhodes, the 'Colossus of the Cape', and Paul Kruger, the doughty, bible-booted patriarch who dominated the Transvaal. As Lord Selborne, Chamberlain's deputy at the Colonial Office, wondered, would South Africa emerge as another, possibly hostile, United States, or would it become a safe, self-governing dominion such as Canada? Kruger and his God-fearing burghers would not accept an answer that threatened their survival as a chosen people. After Jameson had revealed the aggressive nature of British intentions, they bought large quantities of European weapons, including 37,000 Mauser rifles from Germany.

Kipling had stayed in Cape Town during his voyage to the Antipodes in 1891, but his enthusiasm dates from his second visit at the beginning of 1898, when tension between the Boers and the British was running high. In India he had known a viceroy and a commander-in-chief, but his age had precluded anything more than acquaintanceship with senior administrators. In South Africa he embraced the friendship (which on his side bordered on hero-worship) as well as the imperial vision of the two most powerful Englishmen in the Cape, Cecil Rhodes and Sir Alfred Milner. He also courted and received the more aloof amity of Joseph Chamberlain, the equally powerful Colonial Secretary, and enjoyed a warmer congeniality with the lesser figure of Leander Starr Jameson, Rhodes's lieutenant and leader of the notorious Raid. Kipling succumbed to Jameson's charm and admitted that he 'loved' as well as admired 'the doctor'. In 1905, during Jameson's premiership of the Cape, he exclaimed: 'Fancy a man, with no personal ambition whatever, playing the game because it ought to be played!' A few years later he referred to him as 'the noblest Roman of them all' and claimed to have based the poem 'If' on his character.[1] This last assertion is puzzling because, whatever individual qualities Jameson and the poem may have had, it is difficult to see how they overlap: 'If you can keep your head when all about you / Are losing theirs and blaming it on you', 'If you can wait and not be tired of waiting', 'If you can dream and not make dreams your master' – it was eccentric to apply these lines to the man who blundered impatiently into the Transvaal, surrendered rather quickly when surrounded by armed Boers, and was led weeping into captivity.

In 1898 Kipling sailed to South Africa with his family, thereby inaugurating a tradition that lasted for a decade, giving the children two summers a year and enabling him to indulge his current political passion while travelling ecstatically through the veld or writing in a little white house in the shadow of Table Mountain. They were having 'a truly monumental time', he reported in April, witnessing 'nothing less than a new nation in the throes of birth'. For a month he travelled by himself in the north, finding 'a new people growing up by Bulawayo', before going via Kimberley to Johannesburg. On his return to London, he made a speech lauding the men who were bringing civilization to South Africa. Their principal obstacle, he told the Anglo-African Writers' Club, was the Dutch in Cape Colony, an unhygienic people who objected to railways, education, inoculation and other 'elementary rudiments of civilization'. But the British, he added, must be patient with them: they must 'try by example and precept to coax them along the road to material development of the land'.[2]

Kipling was now exhaling the spirit of Cecil Rhodes. The two men had met in 1891, they had recently dined together with Milner on the poet's election to the Athenaeum Club, and the 'Colossus' had once been dignified by some unpublished verses. But it was only now that the two were able to talk long and often. The Kiplings lunched with Rhodes the day after their arrival in South Africa, and several 'memorable' days followed. Rudyard was soon mesmerized by the sense of power emanating from the other man. 'What's your dream?' Rhodes asked him, provoking the response that the questioner 'was part of it'. After a month in the region, Kipling told a correspondent that 'Rhodes alone was worth the voyage'.[3]

The career of the 'Colossus' was in decline even though he was still only 45. He had already made a fortune in diamonds, and he had already expended most of his political power. For five years he had ruled Cape Colony as Prime Minister and his eponymous country Rhodesia as Chairman of the British South Africa Company under Crown charter. In the Cape he had formed an alliance with the Bond, the Afrikaners' political party, supporting it against more lenient British parliamentarians on a bill intended to permit white men to flog their servants. Further north he had sent Jameson to charm the African chief Lobengula, persuade him to give up much of his territory and then deal with the consequent Matabele rebellion. But the Raid, which he had plotted and then tried to abort on realizing it was premature, was a disaster. His irresponsibility cost him both posts and lost the colonial power the support of the Cape Dutch. As the Bond broke with him, politicizing the communities in the Cape, the Transvaal united behind Kruger, who also received the backing of the Orange Free State. The laager mentality had been reactivated – by Rhodes.

As a young man of 24 Rhodes wrote that Britain's duty was to 'seize every opportunity of acquiring more territory' because 'we are the finest race in the world and ... the more of the world we inhabit the better it is for the human race'. Later he visited Windsor and told Queen Victoria he was doing his 'best to enlarge Your Majesty's dominions'. The primary aim was comprehensible enough: to establish a political federation of southern Africa within the Empire and under British control. It was the extravagances beyond that thrilled Kipling and his other followers: the scale of the man and his dream, the way he liked to 'think in continents'; the way he talked about splashing red paint across Africa, building a railway from the Cape to Cairo; the way he talked about his ambition, wishing he could annex the planets, expecting to be remembered for 4,000 years; and the way he was going to achieve it all by himself.[4]

Kipling accepted Rhodes at his own estimate. 'He isn't a politician,' he told St Loe Strachey, the Editor of the *Spectator*. 'He's the political arena itself ... You must go to Africa and get the measure of the size of the man.' After Rhodes's death he went further: 'Rhodes was Africa.'[5] In a letter written thirty years later he even awarded the 'Colossus' the capital letters normally reserved for God: 'I don't think that anyone who did not actually come across Him with some intimacy of detail can ever realise what He was. It was His Presence that had the Power.'[6]

Behind the lumbering façade, Kipling perceived a character with 'feminine intuition' that was in some ways 'childlike in its simplicity'. Rhodes was curiously inarticulate, 'he implied and filled in by gestures', he appealed to Kipling (as 'a purveyor of words') to tell him

what he was 'trying to express'.[7] This may not have been very difficult because the two shared both dreams and prejudices. They
divided men into those who worked and those who 'loafed'; they disliked the 'Balliol prig', Rhodes regarding this specimen as 'about the
worst style of man the world produces';[8] and they had similar views
on the limitations of the democratic process. 'Rhodes is not exactly
what you call a Liberal,' Sir Edward Grey (the future Foreign
Secretary and a notably unpriggish product of Balliol) said after
meeting him in 1892. 'He has a new version of "one man, one vote"
for South Africa, viz. that he, Rhodes, should have a vote, but
nobody else should.'[9]

The relationship was inevitably unequal. Rhodes was the master,
Kipling the pupil learning lessons that he would pass on after the
other's death. But Rhodes valued the companionship of the man he
believed had 'done more than any other since Disraeli to show the
world that the British race is sound at core and that rust or dry rot are
strangers to it'.[10] He was also hospitable and concerned, inviting
Kipling to dinner with the assurance that there would be no one
there to bore him. At his estate at Groote Schuur, an old Dutch
granary restored by Herbert Baker, he even built him a house, The
Woolsack, a single-storeyed construction with a veranda surrounded
by pines and oaks and a garden with a distant view of mountains.

Milner was equally appreciative of 'the Ruddi-Kipple's' company
during the visit of 1898. Kipling, he reported, was not only a great
poet but also the 'most companionable creature and not the least
spoiled, which is wonderful'. Milner was sad not to have spent more
time with him but delighted that the writer has seen 'through that
utter imposture, the simple-minded Boer patriot, dear to the imagination of British radicals'.[11]

The new High Commissioner's career had included law, journalism, a fellowship at Oxford and stints as an official in the Treasury
and in the Egyptian administration of Sir Evelyn Baring, the future
Lord Cromer. A man of outstanding intellect, Milner appealed to
Kipling as a scholar-administrator, a leader with much conviction
and little vanity who did the 'real work' of empire while others talked
about it – in fact a much more suitable exemplar of the 'If' creed
than Jameson. Observing his work during the Boer War, Kipling
admired 'this silent capable man worrying out his path alone ... in
the face of all conceivable discouragements'. As an administrator

Milner was 'detestable to a certain type of politician' – an additional qualification in Kipling's eyes because it was as easy to agree with Milner about the shortcomings of politicians as it was with Rhodes.[12]* Although he had been a Liberal candidate in 1885, Milner came to despise Parliament ('that mob at Westminster') and, in words that might have been penned by Kipling, he called it a 'fool's trick' to 'waste the energy and devotion' of a small number of imperial administrators 'trying to do the impossible ... to keep an Empire for people who are dead set on chucking it away'.[14]

Milner had been sent to South Africa in 1897 to repair the damage caused by the Jameson fiasco. He was appalled by the idiocy of the Raid and the unscrupulous manner in which it had been carried out. But he agreed with its objective, the absorption of the Transvaal into the British Empire. And in singlemindedness and inflexibility, he was a match for Kruger and Rhodes.

It is often difficult to reconcile Milner's Dr Jekyll side (brilliant, courteous, high-minded and urbane) with his Mr Hyde contrasts (racist, bigoted and almost fanatic). As High Commissioner he played both roles in equal measure. He regarded South Africa as 'the weakest link in the Imperial chain' and was determined to weld it, under the Union Jack, into a 'self-governing white Community supported by well-treated and justly governed black labour from Cape Town to the Zambesi'.[15] The theory that he and the British Government went to war to grab the goldfields, a capitalist conspiracy manipulated by Julius Wernher and Sir Alfred Beit, has been discarded by modern historians. So has the view that they fought for the rights of the 'uitlanders', the largely British immigrants living in the Rand, the gold-mining area of the Transvaal. They fought for a future union between unequal partners under the British flag, a union in which the Afrikaners would be gradually denationalized and

---

*The three men would have disagreed, however, on the merits of Balliol. Another unpriggish graduate of the Oxford college, Milner used the Balliol connection to good effect in South Africa. Although naturally drawn to Balliol Unionists such as Curzon, he retained the support of the college's Liberal Imperialists, H.H.Asquith and Sir Edward Grey, during the Boer War. Sir Henry Campbell-Bannerman, the Cambridge-educated Liberal leader trying to keep a divided party together, was irritated by what he called the *religio milneriana*, the loyalty of Balliol Liberals to Milner during the war: according to his official biographer, he regarded 'this blind belief in the Balliol hero ... as a psychological infirmity of the Oxford mind'.[13]

swamped by British immigrants. Milner insisted that denationalization was a prerequisite for the future of the country. Without it the rural Afrikaner community would never assimilate with the British, and Kruger's 'medieval race oligarchy' would continue to keep the uitlanders in a state of 'permanent inferiority'.[16]

Lord Salisbury, the Prime Minister, privately admitted that 'of course the real point to be made good to South Africa is that we not the Dutch are boss'.[17] But as this was not an attractive or an easily marketable policy, the Government had to come up with something else. Milner, whose professed aim was to precipitate a crisis with the Transvaal, decided that the best issue on which to arouse British public opinion was Kruger's denial of the franchise for recent uitlander settlers. His subsequent encouragement of their grievances was rewarded in March 1899 when 22,000 British uitlanders petitioned the Crown for the restitution of their rights. In an incendiary dispatch to London, Milner claimed that the petitioners had been placed in the intolerable position of 'helots'.

The cause was superficially plausible. Although the uitlanders paid most of the taxes and produced the bulk of the Transvaal's wealth, they were excluded from political power and subjected to a corrupt and inefficient government led by an uncouth primitive who believed that the earth was flat. But since they were there voluntarily in order to enrich themselves by digging for gold, they were hardly in the position of helots. Moreover, as Salisbury had admitted some years earlier, 'universal suffrage mainly exercised by a floating population of mining adventurers' could not be an 'ideal form of government'.[18] The Boers' civilization may have been obscurantist and crude, but it was after all their own: if they were obliged to respect other people's rights, it should have been those of the black African tribes who were there before them. Kruger believed that the enfranchisement of the uitlanders would have meant suicide for the volk. No doubt he exaggerated, but the Calvinist Afrikaners of the veld were genuinely horrified by the new 'Sodom and Gomorrah' they believed the uitlanders were erecting on the Rand. Even Rhodes admitted publicly that, if he had been Kruger, he might not have given the franchise to the uitlanders because it would have meant the end of his power. In any case the British argument, advanced by such anti-democrats as Milner and Kipling, was not especially convincing. It was strange to argue for the enfranchisement of 'floating ... adventurers' in the Transvaal when

Britain itself was still far from universal male suffrage (however many centuries its citizens may have lived there), and the female half of its population was still excluded on principle.

Milner's chief backers in the Cabinet, Salisbury and Chamberlain, agreed that a crisis should be precipitated in the Transvaal. But whereas they wanted one to force a Boer climb-down and a compromise settlement, Milner wanted a climacteric that would culminate in either a war or a complete capitulation by Kruger. The subsequent conflict was known at the time as 'Joe's War', after Chamberlain. It wasn't: if it was anyone's, it belonged to Milner. At the famous confrontation between Kruger and the High Commissioner at Bloemfontein in June 1899, the Transvaal leader offered to compromise by halving the years of residence required before uitlanders were given the franchise. Milner remained intransigent before the man he privately referred to as 'a frock-coated Neanderthal', provoking Kruger to tell him accurately that 'it is our country that you want'. In August, under pressure from the Afrikaners in the Cape, Kruger made further concessions, offering to reduce the residence qualification to five years and to award ten seats in the Volksraad (the parliament in Pretoria) to the Rand. A relieved Chamberlain believed that war had been averted, but Salisbury noted ominously that Milner, who had been 'spoiling for the fight with some glee ... does not like putting his clothes on again'.[19]

The British Prime Minister complained that Milner was dragging his country into a war, but the charge was not quite fair.[20] Without Milner there would have been no war; but even with him in Africa, Salisbury and Chamberlain, who were after all his superiors, could have prevented one. At the end of August the gap between Chamberlain and Kruger could easily have been bridged. But by then the two strongest men in the Cabinet had become imbued with the obduracy of the Milner spirit. Although Salisbury and Chamberlain accepted the Boer concessions, they did so churlishly in a Note of such haughtiness – even threatening to dispatch troops unless the Transvaal's response was 'prompt and satisfactory' – that Kruger withdrew his offers.

During the summer the Afrikaner premier had behaved as a sensible and honourable statesman; if anyone had been guilty of Neanderthal behaviour, it was Milner. But in September an exasperated Kruger returned to the laager, remaining there for the rest of his life, and the following month he sent Britain an ultimatum which no power could have accepted: war within forty-eight hours unless the imperial government agreed to withdraw its troops from the Transvaal borders, to remove all units disembarked during the last three months, and to prevent those reinforcements still on the high seas from landing at any South African port. Relieved that the ultimatum had 'liberated [me] from the necessity of explaining to the people of England why we are at war', Salisbury revealed the real reason for the conflict when he informed the House of Lords that the moment had 'arrived for deciding whether the future of South Africa is to be a growing and increasing Dutch supremacy or a safe, perfectly established supremacy of the English Queen'.[21] In October, aiming for a rapid victory while they still outnumbered British troops by four to one, the Boers of the Transvaal, supported by those of the Free State, invaded the British colonies of Natal and the Cape.

That year, 1899, was the only year before 1909 in which the Kiplings did not visit South Africa. They went instead to the United States to see Carrie's mother as well as Roosevelt, the recently elected Governor of New York, and to exchange grey skies and boiled potatoes for sunshine and cheap oysters. The plan proved a disaster. All three children became ill on the January voyage, and their parents succumbed after arriving in New York. Kipling caught pneumonia and was delirious for days before nearly dying on the last night of February. His recovery was very slow and he was too weak to be told that Josephine, his loveliest and favourite child, had died in early March at the age of 6. Carrie displayed remarkable fortitude in nursing him without revealing the tragedy, the first of those that were to eviscerate their family.

Kipling spent three months convalescing in America before recrossing the Atlantic in midsummer. He never returned to the United States. His chief joys and sorrows, he later explained, had come out of that land, and he could not bear to revisit the place where his 'little maiden' had died. His young cousin Angela Mackail recalled that after Josephine's death she never saw him as 'a real person' again. He seldom talked about his daughter and did not mention her in his autobiography, but he commemorated her in one poem ('Merrow Down') and three magical tales. In 'The First Letter' and 'How the Alphabet was Made', two of the *Just So Stories* written at

The Woolsack and told to his surviving children, Kipling portrayed a father and daughter relationship transparently inspired by Josephine and himself. And in *They*, a story of a blind woman in a house populated by the ghosts of children, he drew on a treasured ritual when the narrator, sitting in a chair, feels his

> relaxed hand taken and turned softly between the soft hands of a child . . . The little brushing kiss fell on the centre of my palm – as a gift on which the fingers were, once, expected to close: as the all-faithful half-reproachful signal of a waiting child not used to neglect even when grown-ups were busiest – a fragment of the mute code devised very long ago.

His doctor in America had advised him to rest and not work until the end of the year. But the excitement provided by the Boer War was probably more therapeutic than a long and dreary convalescence. Kipling's first work on the conflict was 'The Old Issue', an obscure poem whose meaning might have remained impenetrable to readers of *The Times* had it not been for a leading article explaining that, 'as Mr Rudyard Kipling bids the world mark, in the spirited poem we publish this morning', the Boers were seeking safety in the 'discredited devices of despotism' which had been 'resisted and overthrown by our fathers at home centuries ago'.[22] A more substantial contribution to the war effort appeared in the *Daily Mail* on 31 October under the title 'The Absent-Minded Beggar'.

> When you've shouted 'Rule Britannia,' when you've sung 'God save
> the Queen,'
>   When you've finished killing Kruger with your mouth,
> Will you kindly drop a shilling in my little tambourine
>   For a gentleman in *kharki* ordered South?
> He's an absent-minded beggar, and his weaknesses are great –
>   But we and Paul must take him as we find him –
> He is out on active service, wiping something off a slate –
>   And he's left a lot of little things behind him!
> Duke's son – cook's son – son of a hundred kings –
>   (Fifty thousand horse and foot going to Table Bay!)
> Each of 'em doing his country's work
>   (and who's to look after their things?)
> Pass the hat for your credit's sake,
>   And pay – pay – pay!

This and the subsequent verses are not of high quality, as Kipling himself knew. He was a little embarrassed about them, admitting to Sir Arthur Sullivan (who set them to music) that they were a 'disgrace', but he was also touchy, as he demonstrated much later by dispatching an angry remonstrance to Lord Newton who had deplored the work in the House of Lords.[23] Yet it was not as if he had been attempting to write another anthem of spiritual uplift. In form, sentiment and language, he was deliberately returning to the barrack room ballads for the purposes of charity and propaganda. In language that everyone would understand, he managed to convey not just the plight of Tommy Atkins but also the condition of those he left behind, the girl 'he married secret', the 'kiddies' around her, the 'gas and coals and vittles, and the house-rent falling due'. This 'ain't the time for sermons with the winter coming on': the girl must be helped, she and her children cannot be sent to the workhouse while Tommy is away hammering Kruger and saving the Empire. The humanity of the poem and its simple message had an astonishing impact: accompanied by a drawing of the wounded but undaunted Tommy, the verses soon cluttered tables and mantelpieces throughout Britain, stamped on mugs, ashtrays, tobacco jars, plates, biscuit tins and other souvenirs. The sale of such items – and the poet's waiving of copyright – enabled a fund for soldiers' families to raise the immense sum of £300,000.

British public opinion had caught imperial fever at the time of the Jubilee in 1897 and again the following year when Kitchener 'avenged' Gordon at Omdurman and then browbeat the French at Fashoda to achieve Salisbury's aim of excluding France from the Upper Nile. But it had not become greatly excited by the tribulations of the uitlanders and it displayed little inclination to fight for them. Public feeling was stimulated by the dispatch of troops and, in a smaller, more sentimental way, by 'The Absent-Minded Beggar', but the fervour was not ignited until, in very British fashion, the Army lost the opening battles of the war. In December, after it had been beaten three times in 'Black Week', Queen Victoria declared that she was 'not interested in the possibilities of defeat', a view that seemed to represent a national mood. It certainly reverberated within Kipling, who was able to discern such moods even more accurately than his sovereign. Although depressed by the war news and sleepless with anxiety over the troops, he remained confident of victory.

South Africa, he predicted at New Year, would emerge from the war as 'a nation among the nations – one of the free white peoples', its citizens developing their country as the Canadians had dealt with their land and the Australians were dealing with theirs.[24]

Kipling had no difficulty in accepting the British Government's justifications for the war. He embraced the real reason – Salisbury's 'who's boss' rationale – as easily as he did the cause of the uitlanders' rights. The conflict, he told American friends, had 'the merit of being the one war that had been directly fought on the plain issue of elementary political freedom for all white men'. Even the American War of Independence, he added, hadn't been 'a tithe as justified as this row'.[25] How incredulously the friends across the Atlantic read this letter is not recorded. It would certainly have been beyond the comprehension of Joseph Conrad whom the *Spectator* had described a few years earlier as 'the Kipling of the Malay Archipelago'. While the novelist realized that the Boers were 'struggling in good faith for their independence', his other views on South Africa were similar to those of the Conrad of India: that the Boers had 'no idea of liberty' but were '*un peuple essentiellement despotique*, like by the way all the Dutch'; that liberty could 'only be found under the English flag all over the world'; and that the war was not 'so much against the Transvaal as a struggle against the doings of German influence. It is the Germans who have forced the issue.' But Kipling's poem 'The Old Issue' – with its oblique message claiming a parallel between the Anglo-Boer conflict and the English struggle for liberties against King Charles I – made Conrad 'die laughing'. 'If I am to believe Kipling this is a war undertaken for the cause of democracy. *C'est à crever de rire.*'[26]

Kipling did not accept that the Transvaal was 'merely fighting for its independence': Afrikaner objectives, he believed, embraced the whole region – as did those of the British. In an ugly but prescient prediction during the war, he accused Boers of wanting 'to sweep the English into the sea, to lick their own nigger and to govern South Africa with a gun instead of a ballot box'.[27] Kipling was no more concerned about the political rights of native Africans than he had been about Indian constitutional rights in the Subcontinent. But he shared Milner's paternalist regard for their welfare and would have condemned the enforcement of racial segregation. In 'The Old Issue' he had written of 'Watchers 'neath our window' and the 'hirelings of his pay' who 'shall deal our justice ...':

Hate and all division; hosts of hurrying spies;
Money poured in secret, carrion breeding flies ...

Cruel in the shadow, crafty in the sun,
Far beyond his borders shall his teachings run.

After predicting Dr Verwoerd's police state, Kipling anticipated the apartheid regime of Dr Malan. 'We put them', he wrote of the Boers after the war, 'into a position to uphold and expand their primitive lust for racial domination.'[28]

While he regarded Afrikaners as backward and disliked the way they treated the 'Kaffirs', Kipling respected the 'burghers' of the Transvaal and the Orange Free State. They may have been uncouth but they were pioneers, they fought for what they believed in, and they fought cleanly and well. His admiration did not extend to their Dutch brethren in the Cape who, he claimed, had held the British 'as a subject race for twenty years' and were now 'saturated with disloyalty'.[29] This primitive view was inspired by Milner, who was rancorously obsessed by this alleged disloyalty and described them as 'fellow-citizens' with the Transvaalers. How two such intelligent men could have failed to understand the case of the Cape Afrikaners remains a puzzle. Unlike the uitlanders, the Dutch were not gold-digging immigrants in a foreign country: their ancestors had been there before the British occupied the Cape during the Napoleonic Wars. In any case Jan Hofmeyr and his colleagues in the Afrikaner Bond had remained allies of Rhodes until Jameson and his buccaneers destroyed their trust in 1895. But even the Raid did not transform them into rebels. Three years after, the Chairman of the Bond thanked the Lord that he was a British subject, while Hofmeyr declared that he had been born under the British flag and would have 'no difficulty dying under it'. If the Afrikaners of Cape Colony combined 'local patriotism' – ties with the northern Boers – with loyalty to the Empire, these did not need to be incompatible affiliations: similar blends could be found in Scotland and Ireland. But Milner resisted such complexity of feeling, and so did Kipling. The poet was not one of nature's parrots but occasionally, under the influence of a powerful politician – Milner, Rhodes and, to a lesser extent, Chamberlain – he repeated the master's incantations. For him the Cape Dutch remained dirty, idle, garrulous and disloyal.[30]

Kipling was no more a warmonger than he was a jingoist. He had none of those romantic notions that induced the young Winston Churchill to scamper about India and South Africa in quests for glory. But he welcomed the war for the benefits it would bring South Africa, Britain, the Empire and the Army. A federated South Africa under the British flag would be a new nation, another Canada. Britain at war would be transformed, tougher, more realistic and less arrogant. The Empire at large, its colonies rushing to send troops to help the 'mother country', would be united as never before. And best of all, the war would do 'untold good' to the Army, making it larger, more efficient and better prepared to face the coming 'Armageddon' with Germany.[31]

10

Lessons from the Boers

———◆———

Two hospitable requests for Kipling's company during the coming winter arrived in the summer of 1899. Curzon's invitation to stay with him in Calcutta was turned down because viceroys were 'not exactly my line'. But a summons to visit Cape Town from the almost equally viceregal figure of Rhodes had a more stimulating effect. The autumn's events in South Africa were 'so exciting' that Kipling could not resist the opportunity of seeing what was happening there. Within days of the outbreak of fighting, he was writing of his desire to witness the reconstruction of the country after the inevitable Boer defeat. Black Week slightly dented his optimism, but a fortnight later he was telling the Duchess of Sutherland that it was 'possible to take too black a view of the war': if the defeats had punctured the 'national vanity', that in itself would do Britain 'all the good in the world in the long run'. Perhaps his confidence was strengthened by his longing to exchange England, where the entire family and the nanny had caught influenza over Christmas, for a restful voyage followed by the sunshine and blue skies of the Cape.[1]

The Kiplings arrived in Cape Town in early February, just after the Boer victory at Spion Kop and just before the British counter-offensive started to achieve momentum. After two weeks at a hotel on the slopes of Table Mountain, Kipling set off on his travels, taking a hospital train to the Modder River, where the British had won a costly victory in November. In March he visited the main base camp at Stellenbosch with Rhodes, who had been besieged for four months in Kimberley, where he had made a nuisance of himself: arrogant, defeatist and sometimes hysterical, the 'Colossus' had frequently harangued the competent British commander on military matters he knew nothing about. If the officer had been anyone other than the patient Colonel Kekewich, Chamberlain observed later, Rhodes would have been put in gaol.[2]

But nothing diluted Kipling's euphoria as he travelled across the newly conquered areas of the Free State. He was having 'the greatest of times', Carrie noted in her diary, and had 'joined up all his ideas with the others of many years ago'.[3] In the middle of March he was asked by Lord Roberts, the new Commander-in-Chief, to help set up a newspaper for the troops in Bloemfontein, the Free State's capital, which had just been captured. The *Friend* welcomed Kipling on to the staff with a leading article praising him for having 'contributed more than anyone perhaps towards the consolidation of the British Empire' and for his unique ability to 'translate to the world the true inwardness of Tommy's character'.[4]

Kipling cared less for the eulogy than for his return to a newspaper office where the smells and bustle and companionship made it seem 'like old times in India'. He stayed at the post for only a fortnight but much appreciated the experience, urging his colleagues to publish soldiers' poems in 'Tommy's vernacular' instead of the 'Queen's English'.[5] A few of his own verses were also printed, including a generous elegy on the death of a Boer commander, General Piet Joubert. But his most interesting contribution was his co-authorship of a declaration of 'British principles' that included 'the absolute independence of the individual', 'prompt and equal justice ... to all men', 'antipathy to anything savouring of military despotism', and 'religious toleration and freedom of belief for all peoples'.[6] They did not include 'elementary political freedom for all white men', the privilege he claimed for the uitlanders but which, if translated to mean universal male suffrage, he did not recommend even for Britain.

At the end of March the resurrected journalist made a speech at a dinner for Roberts and Milner at Bloemfontein. In an unwonted mood of triumphalism, he proposed

the health of the man who has taught the British Empire its responsibilities, and the rest of the world its power, who has filled the seas with transports, and the earth with the tramp of armed men, who has made Cape Town see in Table Bay such a sight as she never saw before, and please God will never see again; who has turned the loafer of the London streets into a man, and called out him who led our forces to Kandahar, and knew not what he did; who has made the Uitlander of South Africa stand shoulder to shoulder with the boundary rider of New Zealand, and taught the man of New South Wales to pick up the wounded men who wear the maple-leaf – and all in support of the Mother Country. Gentlemen, I give you the name of the Empire-builder – Stephanus Paulus Kruger.[7]

In the same week the creator of Mulvaney was driven in a cart with a fellow journalist to watch his first battle, an inconclusive skirmish at Karee Siding a few miles north of Bloemfontein. Although hoping for a reasonably quiet picnic, they came under fire when British cavalry drifted in their direction and attracted the enemy's attention. Some years later he claimed he had been 'very nearly shot' because a subaltern of engineers had inaccurately told him that an area of scrubland in front of them was 'all clear': as it turned out to be 'anything but cleared', he was forced to lie on his stomach 'in great bodily and mental stress for some hours'.[8] 'Hours' would have been an exaggeration even in the singular.

But it was not an exaggeration to claim that in South Africa his 'position among the rank and file came to be unofficially above that of most Generals'.[9] The author of 'Tommy' and 'The Absent Minded Beggar' was enthusiastically greeted when he visited army encampments in the Free State. In Cape Town he paid almost daily visits to hospitals and was much moved by the affection of the wounded. He was full of caustic remarks about the officers, an observer recalled, but had only praise for the 'patience and fine feeling' of the men.[10] Julian Ralph, a fellow journalist in Bloemfontein, accompanied Kipling to an army hospital and heard men say as he left, 'God bless him; he's the soldier's friend'. He was like 'a comrade', recalled Ralph, 'when he talked to a private, and talk to them he did. Jack tar, Colonial, regular, and Pathan, he talked to all alike.'[11]

Nothing delighted Kipling more than the sight of colonial troops in South Africa: the 'spectacle of the three Free Nations' hurrying to 'secure moderately decent Government for a sister people' was 'most wonderful'.[12] All Britain's colonies except the Cape unanimously sided with the 'mother country', and a 'competition in patriotism' emerged between New Zealand and the Australian colonies, all eager to send troops to South Africa. When the first five volunteers set out from the Queensland mining town of Charters Towers, a major observed that 'though the numerical strength of the contingent was not great, it still showed the world that every portion of the Empire would be represented'.[13] Kipling was ecstatic, particularly at the discovery of 'a new nation – Australia', which he had not appreciated properly during his brief visit in 1891. He saw a lot of the Australian troops in Africa and declared that he had never come across a 'cleaner, simpler, saner, more adequate gang of men'.[14] In lyrical mood he wrote of the Australian soldier riding into Lichtenberg and finding that the smell of rain-soaked wattle brought all his native country back to him. And in 'The Parting of the Columns' Tommy recalls the comradeship of the campfire and the hospital train.

> Our blood 'as truly mixed with yours – all down the Red Cross train.
> We've bit the same thermometer in Bloemingtyphoidtein ...
>
> Think o' the stories round the fire, the tales along the trek –
> O' Calgary an' Wellington, an' Sydney and Quebec ...

After thanking the colonial troops for having 'learned us how to camp and cook an' steal a horse and scout', he realizes he has also learned that 'the world's no bigger than a Kraal'. Closer colonial ties were now happily inevitable.

The contribution of the 'three Free Nations' was not numerically large: fewer than 30,000 men (more than half of them Australians) or less than 10 per cent of the British troops involved. But the significance, as Kipling recognized, was in the participation and the enthusiasm with which it was offered. Critics claimed that the Empire was being weakened and humiliated; in fact it became stronger and more cohesive – only its image was damaged by the Boer victories. The Australian colonies, which federated in the course of the war, began to find a new national identity within the Empire. As a result of the conflict, New Zealand developed its own nationalism in competition with Australia, and both they and Canada became more self-assertive, though within an imperial context; all three made enormous contributions to the Empire in the two world wars. And even if Britain did not, as Kipling hoped, dispense with snobbery, 'material luxury and over much ease', the mother country also changed.[15] The war may not have been waged with great skill, but it was fought with determination and to the end; afterwards the issue of army reform was taken seriously by the Government even if the battlefields of Flanders later showed that insufficient tactical lessons had been learned in South Africa.

Despite the adulation and the exhilaration of being in South Africa, Kipling believed he could do more useful work in England, where he returned in mid-April. The evidence suggests he could not. He wrote letters and cajoled; he published a protest in the *Spectator* about the appointment of certain generals; he sometimes dined with the war's overseer, Chamberlain, whom he regarded as 'a mighty interesting man', the 'only man in the Cabinet', and 'worth his weight in diamonds' because he understood business.[16] But he spent more time playing the part of the patriotic squire, forming a volunteer company, building a drill-hall in the village and establishing a rifle-range on the Downs which he liked to visit and where he observed the men's improving marksmanship.

In October 1900 he made his first party political speech, declaiming in support of the Unionist candidate in his parents' constituency during the 'Khaki' election. There had been no doubt about his political loyalty before: he had frequently criticized Gladstone in the 1880s and he had welcomed the victory of Salisbury's Conservatives and their Liberal Unionist allies in 1895. But this was his first vocal effort on behalf of a party he both supported and harangued for the rest of his life.

Salisbury was much vilified, especially by a fiery young Liberal, David Lloyd George, for going to the country at such an opportunistic moment. In fact he had resisted his colleagues' clamour to dissolve Parliament at the supreme moment of jingoistic euphoria, the relief of Mafeking in May after a seven-month siege; and it may be added that Lloyd George called an election in similar circumstances for almost identical reasons at the end of 1918. Certainly Kipling had no problem either with the tactics or with Chamberlain's message that 'Every seat lost to the government was a seat gained by the Boers', a slogan that seemed even more provocative when a telegraphic mistake altered 'gained' to 'sold'.[17]

Kipling was far less tolerant of British military preparations. 'I knew for sure we were fools,' he told a correspondent, 'but I didn't know how thick and wide and consistent our folly was.' The Government was 'stiff-necked and slow', and its ministers were about as 'slack-backed and muddleheaded as they make 'em', especially the War Secretary, the 'limp and luckless Lansdowne'.[18] These were easy targets and were hit by others too. Lord Lansdowne was a distinguished public servant in several fields, but his inertia and complacency while in charge of the British Army mark the low point of his career.

Before the conflict the War Office had plans neither for a campaign in South Africa nor for the defence of Cape Colony and Natal; and the deficiencies of the Royal Medical Corps, obvious to anyone at the time, were later demonstrated by the statistic that only a quarter of the British dead (5,774 out of 21,942) died in battle. At a time when Milner was making war almost inevitable at his Bloemfontein meeting with Kruger in June 1899, Lansdowne seemed unworried by the fact that Britain had only 10,000 troops in South Africa to defend its colonies against an estimated 54,000 Boer fighting men, or by the realization that an army corps from Britain could not be placed on the Transvaal's border in less than four months. His Under-Secretary, George Wyndham (whom Kipling had lectured on foreign policy the year before), was equally unperturbed, assuring Curzon that it would be unnecessary to send British units from India. In September Curzon sent them anyway, and they arrived just in time to prevent the capture of Natal by Joubert. Had it not been for the Viceroy, Milner wrote later, Boer flags would have been floating over Durban and Pietermaritzburg by the end of October.[19]

Generalship in South Africa was an even easier target. Salisbury was so puzzled by the ineptitude of the officers that he wondered whether Britain might not have done better with an army of 'Red Indians'. Curzon attributed the problem to lack of brains, dolefully comparing the conflict to the American Civil War in which the North had been consistently defeated until it had 'weeded out all the rotten generals who had made their way, in the long period of peace, to the top'.[20] The chief target of Kipling's pen (though mainly restricted to private letters) was the bulky figure of the Commander-in-Chief, Sir Redvers Buller, whose early defeats were soon rewarded with the nickname, 'Sir Reverse': the ''eavy-sterned amateur old men' in the poem 'Stellenbosch', the general taking no chances but 'markin' time' to earn decorations, were clearly inspired by Buller. But Kipling was equally dismissive of the officer corps, the 'excessively incompetent amateurs', the aristocrats who did 'not take the trouble to learn their job'. Sickened by their performance, he raged against the 'bullock-stupidity' of this 'bum-headed army'. But it was not just the fault of Buller: it was 'us – England. Our own face in a foul mirror but our own face.'[21]

After Black Week Lord Roberts was appointed Commander-in-Chief, although Buller remained in command of the army in Natal. 'As a Roberts man', Kipling was delighted by the change: despite his satire on the general's nepotism in India, he had remained an admirer of the diminutive 'Pocket-Wellin'ton' of his poem 'Bobs'. Perhaps his partisanship made him exaggerate the skill with which 'the Little Man' and his Chief of Staff, Kitchener, sorted out the muddle they found in South Africa.[22] The rehabilitation of Buller would be an arduous and perhaps unfruitful exercise. But the propaganda aimed at him by partisans of Roberts in the press and in the Army has obscured some of his wiser moments. Buller had been right to warn Lansdowne that more troops were needed to defend Natal, right to warn General White not to go north of the River Tugela and thus risk entrapment in Ladysmith, right also to resist Milner's request to concentrate his army in the Cape and effectively abandon the eastern colony altogether. Moreover his advance through Natal in 1900 was successful as well as economical with casualties. Kipling's assertion that he had been 'practically booted into Ladysmith' is an ill-informed assessment of both the military situation and Buller's role in the town's relief.[23]

Under Roberts and Kitchener the Army's march towards the Transvaal and the extinction of independent Afrikanerdom seemed impressive and inexorable. Kimberley and Ladysmith were relieved in February, Bloemfontein was occupied in March, while May saw the relief of Mafeking rapidly followed by the capture of Johannesburg and Pretoria. Possession of Kruger's capital soon persuaded Roberts that the war was 'practically over': he applied to go home and was succeeded by Kitchener in November.

But the performance of his army, so reinforced now that it far outnumbered its opponents, was not as convincing as it appeared. By abolishing the regimental system of transport in the middle of a war, Roberts and Kitchener created a confusion beyond anything that

Buller could achieve – a muddle that, among other things, led to the Boers' capture of two hundred wagons at Waterval Drift. The evolution of Kitchener of Khartoum into 'K of Chaos' was an epithet at least as deserved as 'Sir Reverse Buller'. The two men also made a large number of tactical blunders, especially Kitchener's crass frontal attack at Paardeberg, which caused the highest British casualties of any day of the war. But Roberts's worst misjudgement was his naïve belief that he was fighting a traditional war, that he had only to capture Bloemfontein to subdue the Free State, that he had only to take Pretoria to win the war. In March 1900 Buller warned him that guerrilla warfare would break out in the districts left behind during the rapid advance. Roberts paid no attention and so bequeathed Kitchener a frustrating irregular war that lasted twice as long as the conventional campaign.

In the course of 1900 Kipling switched his anger from the incompetence of Buller to the gentleness of the British war effort and the leniency accorded to the enemy. The Boers were hitting their opponents as hard and as often as they liked, while the British were being typically 'polite, generous and lofty', advancing 'against 'em as if they were street-fighters that we didn't want to hurt'.[24] On returning with his family the following Christmas, he was flabbergasted by Britain's 'silly sentimental methods' of conducting war. Whereas America's General Sherman 'would have wound it up in six months', the British seemed to 'delight in stopping to caress the enemy'. Cape Town was without martial law even though it was full of active rebels who received minuscule sentences for their treacheries.[25]

Burning the enemy's farms was not a conspicuously caressing policy, and Kitchener realized that something must be done for Boer families who would otherwise die of starvation among the ruin of their crops. At the end of 1900 the Commander-in-Chief decided to bring them into specially constructed relief camps, a policy which shocked conservatives and radicals in contrary ways. Kipling was incredulous that the guerrillas should be allowed to behave like 'Apaches ... having the time of their lives' while the British were 'looking after their wives and kids so they have nothing to worry about'. The English working classes, he reported, were 'simply furious at the idea of feeding the women at all while their husbands are in the field against us'.[26]

The establishment of the camps, and the conditions inside them, were a godsend for British opponents of the war, enabling the Liberal leader, Campbell-Bannerman, to inveigh against 'methods of barbarism' and prompting Lloyd George to denounce the Government's 'deliberate and settled policy' of 'extermination'. Termed 'concentration camps' by two radical MPs, they were later used as anti-British propaganda by the Nazis who claimed that Britain had invented the concept. In fact the term comes from the *campos de reconcentración* into which Spanish forces had swept Cuban civilians in the war of 1895–8; but neither in Cuba nor in South Africa were they intended to be sites of extermination. The mortality rate in Kitchener's camps was high as a result of negligence, poor medical facilities and the disruption of supplies by guerrilla action. But it does not compare very badly with the death rate in the British Army encampments or among the children of the Boer republics even in peacetime. Just before the end of the war the most brilliant of the Boer generals, Louis Botha, admitted, 'one is only too thankful nowadays to know that our wives are under English protection'.[27]

Peace negotiations opened in the spring of 1902, a week before Kipling returned to England after his third successive winter in the Cape. The Treaty of Vereeniging was signed on the last day of May, and the following week Kipling was delighted to hear that 'Recessional' was being sung at peace services in South Africa. In Rottingdean his widowed and irrepressible aunt, Georgy Burne-Jones, expressed her view of the conflict and its outcome by hanging a blue banner outside her house proclaiming, 'We have killed and also taken possession'. A noisy and indignant crowd gathered in order to pull it down, and her nephew was required to come over from The Elms to quieten things.

Kipling's relief at the termination of the war was marred both by the death of Cecil Rhodes and by his own misgivings about the quality of the peace. Rhodes had long suffered from a bad heart, and his return from England to the Cape in February, at the height of the South African summer, hastened his death. Although his doctors had warned him not to travel, he insisted on obeying a summons to appear in the Supreme Court at the hearing of a case against Princess Catherine Radziwill, a Polish adventuress who had attempted blackmail and forgery to extract some of his money. Shortly after giving evidence at the hearing, which the Princess failed to attend, his condition worsened: he rambled around Groote Schuur trying to find enough air to breathe; in the evenings he was driven to a cottage on the coast in the hope that the cooler air would help him sleep. Kipling visited Rhodes almost daily at one place or the other until he died at the end of March. The body lay in state in the Parliament in Cape Town and was then taken in procession to the cathedral. Kipling marched with the coffin and described the funeral as the 'most superb pageant and impressive spectacle' one could dream of: 'a whole city of 60,000 moved as one man with a common grief and reverence'.[28] The day before he had read his own deep-felt memorial for his hero at a private service at Groote Schuur.

> Dreamer devout, by vision led
>   Beyond our guess or reach,
> The travail of his spirit bred
>   Cities in place of speech.
> So huge the all-mastering thought that drove –
>   So brief the term allowed –
> Nations not words, he linked to prove
>   His faith before the crowd.
>
> It is his will that he look forth
>   Across the world he won –
> The granite of the ancient North –
>   Great spaces washed with sun.
> There shall he patient make his seat
>   (As when the Death he dared),
> And there await a people's feet
>   In the paths that he prepared.
>
> There, till the vision he foresaw
>   Splendid and whole arise,
> And unimagined Empires draw
>   To council 'neath the skies,
> The immense and brooding spirit still
>   Shall quicken and control.
> Living he was the land, and dead,
>   His soul shall be her soul!
>
> (Verses 2, 3 and 4 of 'The Burial')

The poem was also read out at Rhodes's burial in the Matopo Hills in Rhodesia, the site he had chosen overlooking 'great places washed with sun'. Kipling did not travel north for the burial but he remained loyal to Rhodes and his dream for the rest of his life; only Milner received a comparable fealty. A few years later he wrote further verses extolling the 'alert, devouring' eyes and the 'imperious hand ordaining matters', lines which, like some of those quoted above, appeared on the memorial designed by Herbert Baker. Uncharacteristically, Kipling welcomed the idea of a memorial of pharaonic grandeur with a temple and a gigantic statue, approached by avenues with bronze lions and sculpted sphinxes. But he appreciated the 'austerity and weight' of Baker's more classical conception (also with lions) and watched its development with devout interest. After some hesitation he became an enthusiast for Rhodes's scholarships – which he came to recognize as the 'greatest of all his works' – and for several years he served as a trustee of the Rhodes Trust.[29]

Depressed and bereft in Cape Town in April 1902, Kipling dispatched gloomy letters about the situation in South Africa. The loss of Rhodes, he told his old friend Mrs Hill, was a 'great public calamity'; no words could give her an idea of 'that great spirit's power or the extent to which the country worshipped him'. Without him the political situation was already deteriorating. Like Milner, Kipling was convinced that the Cape's constitution should be suspended so that the colony could have 'decent and orderly Crown rule till the people have sobered down and got their breath'. Had he lived, Rhodes might have arranged it. But the current Prime Minister, a 'dry and glittering old ass' called Sir John Gordon Sprigg, was now 'prancing round full of beans under the delusion that he can run, and incidentally [govern] Cape Colony under the forms of constitutional government'.[30]

The magnanimity of the peace terms at Vereeniging disgusted Kipling as much as they depressed Milner (who had hoped for an unconditional surrender). Neither wanted an amnesty for the Cape rebels any more than a pledge that the Boer republics would eventually achieve self-government under the Union Jack. Kipling does not seem to have been worried by the infamous concession that the question of extending the franchise to native Africans would not be considered until after the introduction of Afrikaner self-government – a clause demanded by Milner that excluded them for ninety-two years and ridiculed Chamberlain's effort not 'to purchase a shameful peace by leaving the Coloured population in the position in which they stood before the war'. But he was horrified by the generosity of the financial clauses, the offer of loans to the burghers and the payment of £3 million to cover the Boers' war debts and losses (a figure which increased with time and which outstripped compensation paid to British colonists and the uitlanders of the Transvaal).[31] The clauses were not only 'insulting' to the loyalists but stupid as well because the Boers, Kipling predicted, would not spend the money on widows and orphans but merely use it to re-arm and fight again with Cape Colony as a base.[32]

Kipling's pessimism suppurated for the rest of the year. In September he refused an invitation from Curzon to attend the Delhi Durbar because, 'instead of seeing India consolidated', he felt obliged to return to the Cape to enjoy 'the felicity of watching South Africa being slowly but scientifically wrecked by "the strongest government of modern times"'.[33] Returning to The Woolsack in January, he briefly allowed himself the optimism to believe that the country was 'going ahead by leaps and bounds', and he even thought of building a house in the northern Cape. But a conciliatory post-war visit by Chamberlain, his favourite Unionist politician, caused a relapse. 'He has come,' he reported to Milner, who was now administering the former Boer republics from Johannesburg: 'he has seen: he has been spoofed'; and the villain of the day was Sir Walter Hely-Hutchinson, the Governor of Cape Colony, who had convinced him that Hofmeyr and the Afrikaner Bond were as loyal as the loyalists. Kipling was repelled by Hely-Hutchinson and his wife because they believed the Dutch were the 'natural aristocrats of the land' and therefore more appropriate allies than British 'traders'. As for Chamberlain, he simply despaired that the 'only man in the Cabinet', the politician to whose 'chariot wheels' he was bound, should have been deceived by the lying protestations of Hofmeyr and the Bond. Out of 'gratitude for the past', however, he wrote a 'peaceful and reconciliatory poem of the situation as it ought to be' – and sent it to the Colonial Secretary.

> Here, in a large and a sunlit land,
>   Where no wrong bites to the bone,
> I will lay my hand in my neighbour's hand,
>   And together we will atone

For the set folly and the red breach
And the black waste of it all;
Giving and taking counsel each
Over the cattle-kraal.

('The Settler')

In a letter accompanying the verses Kipling queried Hofmeyr's sincerity and doubted that even he could 'dam up or divert the waters of strife that he has led in channels of his own crooked digging since 1881'. Chamberlain thanked him for the poem, which he observed was more cheerful than the letter, suggested that the devil was not 'so black as he is painted', and admitted that he had a higher opinion of Hofmeyr's 'sagacity as well as of his sincerity than some of our English friends at home and in South Africa'.[34]

Kipling might have been expected to catch in fiction the spirit of British South Africa as he had once grasped the character of Anglo-India. In fact he made little effort to do so. Such creative energy as he possessed after Josephine's death was channelled into *Kim*, which was completed at the end of 1900, and a play based on the *Jungle Books*.* After that he became too involved, too desperately partisan, to write good fiction. The solitudes of the veld are brightly conveyed in 'The Way That He Took'; the snobbery and rigidity of the officer class are mocked in 'The Outsider'; and Cape Town and Rhodesia form the backdrop of his powerful and most enigmatic story, 'Mrs Bathurst'. But overall the standard is mediocre. For most of his life Kipling simultaneously produced prose and poetry of comparable quality, although his great later stories were not matched by equivalent verse. Only during the South African period did the poems consistently outshine the fiction.

The Poet Laureate, Alfred Austin, wrote some memorably awful verses about soldiers dying for England but sleeping with God (and lying ''neath some green southern sod').[36] But Kipling as usual renounced bombast and vulgar patriotism; he avoided any note of

---

*Kipling wrote *The Jungle Play* between the end of 1900 and midsummer 1901. Although he expected it to be performed, the work was subsequently buried among his papers and was only discovered and identified by Professor Thomas Pinney in 1998.[35]

national self-congratulation; and he resisted the temptation to pleasure rejoicing crowds with odes celebrating the reliefs of Ladysmith, Kimberley and Mafeking. In spite of his political beliefs, much of the poetry was compassionate and sympathetic to participants on both sides, from the sharing of Australian nostalgia in 'Lichtenberg' to the onomatopoeic empathy of 'Boots', the tribute to nurses who died in South Africa ('Dirge of Dead Sisters'), and the poems that suggested reconciliation ('The Settler') or appreciated the qualities of the Boer soldier ('Piet') and his commanders ('General Joubert'). The only people rigorously excluded from his sympathy are the British upper and upper-middle classes dominating the War Office and the officer corps, or else playing cricket and shooting pheasants rather than helping the war effort at home.

None of the South African political poems celebrate imperial success. Nearly all of them, especially those printed in *The Times*, are about 'lessons' – lessons taught by the war that must be learned if the Empire is to survive. The lesson of 'Stellenbosch' is that idle, elderly generals should not command; of an obscure poem, 'The Reformers', that the British should abandon some of their comforts and 'ensnaring ritual' and adopt 'the cleaner life, the sterner code'; and of the savage and also obscure 'Rimmon', that the War Office is aged and useless, a 'gilt, swag-bellied idol' surrounded by howling eunuchs. There is no obscurity, however, in 'The Lesson'. The early disasters were 'our fault, and our very great fault, and *not* the judgment of Heaven'. But now that we realize this, we must learn the lesson, get rid of 'all the obese, unchallenged old things that stifle and overlie us'. It is a time for optimism, for gratitude for what the war has taught us: 'We have had no end of a lesson, it will do us no end of good! . . . We have had an imperial lesson; it may make us an Empire yet!'

But the sternest of all the sermons, the most scolding, intemperate and brilliant of all the prophet's rebukes, was 'The Islanders', a poem prompted by Lord Roberts, who in December 1901 suggested that Kipling should write 'some stirring lines' to warn the public of the need for compulsory military service.[37] The work opens in familiar Old Testament vein, this time from Job 12, 'No doubt but ye are the People', though the rest of the verse, 'and wisdom shall die with you', is omitted. Then Kipling launches into his theme, that the peace and security built up by their ancestors are being jeopardized by the frivolity and slothfulness of the contemporary British. Fenced

MEN of different trades and sizes
Here you see before your eyeses;
Lanky sword and stumpy pen,
Doing useful things for men;
When the Empire wants a stitch in her
Send for Kipling and for Kitchener.

1. Imperial icons from the *Struwwelpeter Alphabet*

2. Alice Kipling, Rudyard's mother, 'all Celt and three-parts fire'

3. 'Sage Yorkshire outlook':
Lockwood Kipling with his son

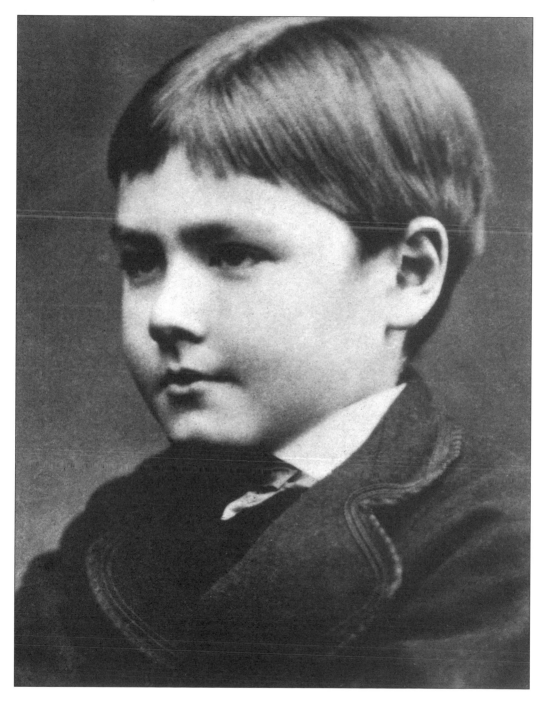

4. Rudyard at the beginning of his exile from India

5. The Anglo-Indian chronicler

6. Lahore, 'that wonderful, dirty, mysterious ant hill'

7. Confidante and 'sympathetic soul': Edmonia Hill in Allahabad

8. Social centre of the summer Raj: The Mall at Simla

William Nicholson.

9. Haggard's 'true watchman of our Empire': Kipling by William Nicholson, *c.* 1899

10. Exemplifying the modern: Naulakha in Vermont

11. 'The Commandress-in–Chief': Caroline Kipling by Philip Burne-Jones, 1899

12. Quintessential England: Bateman's in Sussex

13. Milner's 'frock-coated Neanderthal': Paul Kruger, Prime Minister of the Transvaal

14. Friends in the Press: Perceval Landon, H.A. 'Taffy' Gwynne (*standing*), RK and Julian Ralph in Bloemfontein

15. Cecil Rhodes, 'dreamer devout' and 'Colossus' of the Cape

16. Alfred Milner, 'one of the sanest of men' and chief architect of the Boer War

17. Leander Starr Jameson, doctor, raider and improbable inspiration for 'If'

W. Strang.

Rudyard Kipling
his profile

18. Poet and Prophet: Kipling by William Strang

19. Joseph Chamberlain: 'The statesman
. . . who stepped aside from the sheep
tracks of little politicians'

20. 'A machine of necessary industry':
George Curzon on his appointment as
Viceroy of India

21. Lord Salisbury, the Prime Minister
determined to prove that 'we not the
Dutch are boss' in South Africa

22. Not 'so damn necessary' to the Tories:
Arthur Balfour, Salisbury's successor,
a 'strange evasive undulating man'

23. 'Pedantry set on the throne':
Lord Ripon, Viceroy of India, RK's first
Liberal target

24. H.H. Asquith, the Prime Minister
whose drinking RK noticed but whose
merits he refused to acknowledge

25. RK's least
favourite politicians:
Winston Churchill,
whom he accused of
'political whoring',
with David Lloyd
George, the 'Welsh
thief' who increased
his tax bill

26. Lord Beaverbrook: after years of friendship RK decided that 'it don't pay to build dams with the Beaver'

27. H. Rider Haggard, most loyal and congenial of fellow reactionaries

28. Stanley Baldwin, cousin, Prime Minister and 'Socialist at heart'

29. Prophesying civil war:
RK at Tunbridge Wells,
May 1913

30. '. . . he did not shame his kind':
Lieutenant John Kipling of the Irish
Guards, 1897–1915

31. 'Pocket-Wellin'ton': Field Marshal
Lord Roberts, C–in–C in India, South
Africa and Britain

32. 'The King's Pilgrimage': Kipling and George V visiting war graves

33. 'I love [Law] because he hates': the Kiplings with Andrew Bonar Law in France

34. Rudyard and Carrie Kipling

by their 'careful fathers' and ringed by their 'leaden seas', the people have grown too accustomed to a life of quiet and ease.

> Ancient, effortless, ordered, cycle on cycle set,
> Life so long untroubled, that ye who inherit forget
> It was not made with the mountains, it is not one with the deep.
> Men, not gods, devised it. Men, not gods, must keep.

Absorbed by the demands of their leisure, their 'witless learning' and their 'beasts of warren and chase', the upper classes neglected their islands' defences – and have paid the price for their negligence.

> Then were the judgments loosened; then was your shame revealed,
> At the hands of a little people, few but apt in the field.

Since they preferred to train dogs and horses for sport instead of men for soldiering, they responded to the Boers' assault by sacrificing striplings.

> Sons of the sheltered city – unmade, unhandled, unmeet –
> Ye pushed them raw to the battle as ye picked them raw from the street.

Turning in desperation to the colonies, they then 'fawned on the Younger Nations for the men who could shoot and ride!' Yet as soon as victory was assured, they went back to their old ways.

> Then ye returned to your trinkets; then ye contented your souls
> With the flannelled fools at the wicket or the muddied oafs at the goals.

It was difficult to get more offensive than this, but Kipling tried. To those who rejected spending money on defence because it would 'mar' their comfort and diminish their trade, he asks if they will

> … wait for the spattered shrapnel ere ye learn how a gun is laid?
> For the low, red glare to southward when the raided coast-towns burn?

And if they wait supinely for invasion, what will happen next?

> Will ye pitch some white pavilion, and lustily even the odds,
> With nets and hoops and mallets, with rackets and bats and rods?

Will the rabbit war with your foemen – the red deer horn them for hire?
Your kept cock-pheasant keep you? – he is master of many a shire.

Having alienated squires, sportsmen, shooting-men, soldiers, businessmen and politicians, he then proceeds to mock intellectuals, churchmen, democrats and trade unionists.

Arid, aloof, incurious, unthinking, unthanking, gelt,
Will ye loose your schools to flout them till their brow-beat columns melt?
Will ye pray them or preach them, or print them, or ballot them back from
your shore?
Will your workmen issue a mandate to bid them strike no more?

'The Islanders' was accompanied by a *Times* leader reproaching an educational system that encouraged 'an abnormal reverence for athletic prowess' and sent 'so many young men of the governing classes out into life with no higher ideals than those of the cricket ground or football field'. The combination of press and poet caused apoplexy among readers. One correspondent was particularly insulted by the phrase, 'flannelled fools', which he dismissed as 'vulgar abuse', while another complained that the poem would 'only furnish the unmanly envy and immoral calumnies of Continental slanderers with fresh material for their insidious and cowardly campaign of aspersion of England and the British Empire'. Incensed by the reference to 'muddied oafs', the Headmaster of the Scottish school Loretto pointed out that three-quarters of his 'old boys' serving as volunteers in South Africa had been in the rugger Fifteen. Like 'hunting men [and] stalkers', footballers were joining up out of all proportion to their numbers; and the nation should be grateful that their sport cultivated, 'more than any other pursuit, except perhaps hunting ... the quality of which our Army has stood in greatest need – viz., initiative'.[38]

Lockwood Kipling was surprised that the reaction was not stronger. As his son offered 'so easy and open a mark', it was curious how 'very lightly let off [he was] considering the provocation' he gave. Rudyard was unrepentant. Cricket bored him, but he did not loathe the game, despite Beresford's recollection that he shuddered at 'the mention of the name of W.G.Grace'. Besides, the cricket pitch provided useful analogies for other fields of life, and team spirit was always to be revered. [39] Even in 'The Islanders' Kipling admired the thoughtfulness and preparation the game required and suggested it as a model for military training.

> Soberly and by custom taken and trained for the same;
> Each man born in the Island entered at youth to the game –
> As it were almost cricket, not to be mastered in haste,
> But after trial and labour, by temperance, living chaste.
> As it were almost cricket – as it were even your play,
> Weighed and pondered and worshipped, and practised day and day.
> So ye shall bide sure guarded when the restless lightnings wake
> In the womb of the blotting war-cloud, and the pallid nations quake.

Cricket itself might be all right, but its commercialism and self-importance were absurd. As *The Times* pointed out, the results of test matches with Australia were being treated as if they were as 'vital to our race' as issues 'decided at Trafalgar and Waterloo'. In private Kipling scoffed at critics who pointed out that certain cricketers had died in the fighting: they were merely using some 'good men, who happened to be cricketers', to justify the activities of professionals who were still earning money in wartime. 'I ought to have written *hired* fools,' he told his friend Rider Haggard, 'instead of flannelled.'[40]

He was not of course the only Victorian writer to disparage the 'games ethic'. Improving the countryside, Ruskin argued, would be a more useful activity than 'fruitless slashing of the river'. Wilde, observed on the tennis court as 'a great wobbly blancmange trying to serve underhand', did not pursue his tennis career: questioned later about his favourite sports, he confessed that he played no outdoor games at all except dominoes, which he sometimes played outside French cafés.[41] Such sentiments, however, could be dismissed as typical of eccentric aesthetes. But Kipling had sinned against the very people who had made him their idol. 'In the stupid early years' of the twentieth century, Orwell wrote, 'the Blimps, having at last discovered someone who could be called a poet and was on their side, set Kipling on a pedestal' and gave poems such as 'If' an 'almost biblical status'.[42] And now there he was, mocking from his pedestal all the Blimps' idols.

Late Victorian Britain regarded the 'games ethic' (and its relation 'muscular Christianity') as an essential part of the expansion and consolidation of the Empire. Sports were seen as vital for training the soldiers and administrators of the imperial future. They developed character, they inculcated virtues that Kipling himself had often endorsed: courage, loyalty, obedience, self-control, leadership and endurance. After the relief of Chitral, that classic example of Victorian pluck on the North-West Frontier in 1895, J.E.C.Welldon, the Headmaster of Harrow and future Bishop of Calcutta, argued that the qualities displayed by the little garrison and the relief column were acquired on the sports grounds of the great public schools. 'In the history of the British Empire,' he claimed, 'it is written that England has owed her sovereignty to her sports'. Welldon, who may not have been aware that Kipling had satirized him as the 'Jelly-bellied Flag-flapper' of *Stalky*, ascribed Britain's special aptitude for 'taking up the White Man's Burden' to 'the spirit of organised games'.[43]

Orwell argued that, although the Battle of Waterloo may have been won on the playing fields of Eton, 'the opening battles of all subsequent wars have been lost there'.[44] In 'The Islanders', written forty years earlier, Kipling was accurately predicting the outcome of those battles if public school attitudes persisted in the military. Even if he didn't know that Wellington never said anything so silly (apart from anything else, the 'fields' were not used for organized sports when he was a pupil), Kipling's knowledge of the Army and the officer corps in South Africa would have made him realize that the claim was untrue. In 'The Islanders' he was berating the 'people' and their governors for the Boer victories and warning them that the consequences of military unpreparedness would be far worse in future. He was right, of course. But after the war in South Africa, and especially after the advent of a Liberal Government, Kipling's role changed. No longer the apostle whom everyone wanted to hear, he was consigned to the role of Cassandra, condemned to utter prophecies that no one would heed.

Part Three

Cassandra's Dominions

11

The Discovery of England

———◆———

THE KIPLINGS HAD not intended Rottingdean to be a permanent home but a staging post between the escape from Devon and the finding of the ideal English house in the quintessential rural setting. Even as they were settling into The Elms on the village green, they went looking for houses in Dorset with Thomas Hardy and his wife.

Yet Kipling liked the house he had rented and tried to buy it from an exacting owner. He liked the village, where his Burne Jones relations had one house on the green and the family of Stanley Baldwin's wife had another. And he loved the 'blunt, bow-headed, whale-backed Downs' that he commemorated in 'Sussex', a poem proclaiming that the county was his most beloved spot on earth. But Rottingdean, he soon complained, was becoming over-populated; trippers from Brighton peered over his ivy-draped wall in the hope of seeing the great man tending his garden. The coast had not yet become 'the almost fully developed suburb, of great horror', which later appalled him. But he wanted somewhere quieter. And he wanted a place where Josephine had never played.

Kipling's house-hunting coincided with his discovery of the motor car, and the combination resulted in the revelation of England, the 'most wonderful foreign land' he had ever been in. The 'real joy of motoring' was the exploration of the country and its history, for the car was a 'time-machine' in which one could 'slide from one century to another at no more trouble than the pushing forward of a lever'; in six hours he could experience landscapes of the Romans, the Normans, the Barons' War and the Regency. His enthusiasm had been replicated a few years earlier by the discovery of London taxicabs and 'the joy of seeing an impersonal machine recording one's progress in four penny spasms'. Cutting the journey from Harrods to Charing Cross by eighteen minutes was too exciting to permit nostalgia for hansom cabs.[1]

There was no room either for equine sentimentalism in the country. Abolishing the horse allowed him to dispense with the 'whole tribe of coachmen, saddlers, corn-dealers, smiths, and vets'. This was a strange satisfaction for a man who was simultaneously discovering rural England and celebrating its history and survival in his work. Kipling had strong intuitive feelings about the land and its past; he respected the inherited wisdom of its people; and he talked about the need for rural regeneration. At the same time he exulted in the mechanical progress that could only result in the destruction of traditional rural occupations. The two sides of his head were once again in contraposition.

The Kiplings first saw Bateman's, their future home, in August 1900, but their hesitations lasted long enough for someone else to intervene to rent it. Two summers later they paid £9,300 for the property with thirty-three acres of land, a holding which they later much multiplied. Kipling was enraptured by the solid Jacobean house in a valley of the Weald down the hill from Burwash village. It was 'beamed, panelled, with old oak staircase all untouched and unfaked'; no Victorian 'improvers' had been anywhere near it. He was especially proud of its antiquity, claiming with some exaggeration that the 'new' end had been built before the *Mayflower* sailed to America and that the water-mill had been paying taxes in Domesday Book.[2] Henry James thought it a 'delicious old house, an absolute intact treasure from Charles I's time'. If it seemed 'an oddly discordant setting for its owner's furious modernism and journalism', Kipling's 'excellent appreciation and affection for it' – and the couple's 'intelligent way of living' there – 'pleasantly bridge[d] the hiatus'.[3]

The least socially pretentious of men, Kipling insisted that Bateman's was not a manor-house but the home of a successful Sussex ironmaster of the seventeenth century. Delighted by its gardens, its oasthouses and its dovecot, he was thankful there was no park or lodge 'or any nonsense of that kind'; certainly there was no nonsense about possessing a long drive, for the cart road ran fifty yards from the front door. Neither did the ownership of riverbanks seem a social encumbrance because the River Dudwell appeared only on maps and had to be hunted with a pole through alder bushes. Or so he thought. In fact after heavy rains the invisible 'brook' ripped its banks, flooding his garden and 'playing skittles with the lawns and the roses'.[4] The dampness of the place was a primary cause of the Kiplings' persistent colds.

The new squire was selective about his squirearchical duties: not an attender at church services or village fêtes, yet an assiduous cultivator of his land. He spent the morning in his study, crouched at his desk or pacing up and down the room, and after lunch he tramped with Carrie across their fields. His physique had barely changed over the years: less hair on the top of his head and more bristling to his eyebrows and drooping to his moustache – but little alteration in his weight. In the country he dressed in 'plus-fours' and a Trilby or shabby cap, adding leather gaiters in wet weather. On his excursions around his domain, he slashed at nettles and other weeds, he fished for trout in his unpredictable river, and he discussed (or rather let Carrie discuss) crops, ditches and barn repairs with the foreman.

Kipling tried hard to become an active agriculturalist. He planted larches, nursed ailing apple trees, made attempts at bee-keeping that initially resulted in swollen hands and inedible honey.[5] Eager to learn the arts of cultivation, he asked Rider Haggard for advice and unsuccessfully urged *The Times* to produce an agricultural supplement. But his real contribution to the English countryside was his appreciation of its lore and its inhabitants.

One aged 'rustic', he told Carrie's sister Josephine, was a 'mine of wisdom about trees, hedges, plants and the Earth generally'. His movements were scarcely faster than the hour hand of a watch, but he worked continuously and he was 'serenely indifferent to any weather'. Watching him cut down and grub out an old hedge gave one a 'new respect for mankind'. The hedger may have been Mr Isted, whom Kipling lauded in his autobiography as 'a poacher by heredity and instinct' who was 'more "one with Nature" than whole parlours full of poets'. He became the 'special stay and counsellor' of this particular poet and was transformed by him into Master

Hobden, the eternal repository of rural wisdom.[6] In his delightful poem 'The Land', Kipling charts the history of his Lower River-field from the Roman era through the Danish and Norman conquests to himself. All the occupiers have problems with the quirky little brook and rely on Hobden for advice, a situation which leads to the conclusion that 'whoever pays the taxes old Mus' Hobden owns the land'. In one of the numerous cases where Kipling the authoritarian yields to Kipling the champion of the vagrant and the underdog, the squire refuses to summons the old man to judgement.

> His dead are in the churchyard – thirty generations laid.
> Their names went down in Domesday Book when Domesday Book
> was made.
>
> And the passion and the piety and prowess of his line
> Have seeded, rooted, fruited in some land the Law calls mine.
>
> Not for any beast that burrows, not for any bird that flies,
> Would I lose his large sound council, miss his keen amending eyes.
> He is bailiff, woodman, wheelwright, field-surveyor, engineer,
> And if flagrantly a poacher – 'tain't for me to interfere.

His sympathy with contemporary Hobdens was genuine. It was a 'crying scandal', he told the Editor of the *Spectator*, that in villages all over Sussex 'these blessed "weekenders"' were buying cottages, 'whitewashing them, decorating them, naming them "The Crib" etc and ousting the eighteen bob labourer who has *no* weekend'.[7] But for once Kipling did not have an answer to a social problem. He was so enthralled by the internal combustion engine that he seemed not to realize it would destroy the labourers' livelihoods as well as enable many more weekenders to invade the countryside.

Kipling appreciated the contrasts of Sussex, the marshes at Rye and Romney, the chalk of the South Downs, the woods and meadows of the Weald. Apart from India it was the only landscape that inspired a substantial body of work both in fiction and in verse. The stories often revert to the Hobden themes, that the land belongs to the people who work it, that newcomers must submit to the environment if they are to appreciate it and become accepted. In 'Friendly Brook' the eponymous stream obligingly drowns a blackmailer from London. In 'My Son's Wife' a member of the 'Immoderate Left' is redeemed by inheriting a house in the country and preferring good-hearted hunting folk to the company of his radical intellectual friends. And the rich Americans of 'An Habitation Enforced' settle happily in Sussex because they understand their role: 'It's *not* our land. We've only paid for it. We belong to it, and it belongs to the people ...'

Kipling knew very well that rural life was not idyllic and never had been. He also knew that it had to change: continuity not timelessness was its essence. Hoping that the Boer War would regenerate Britain and the Empire, he naturally did not believe – or hope – that the countryside and its social structure would remain exempt from the process. One couldn't expect men who had fought in South Africa to return eager to mow the squire's lawns.

> Me that 'ave been what I've been –
> Me that 'ave gone where I've gone –
> Me that 'ave seen what I've seen –
>   'Ow can I ever take on
> With awful old England again,
> An' 'ouses both sides of the street,
> And 'edges two sides of the lane,
> And the parson an' gentry between,
> An' touchin' my hat when we meet –
> Me that 'ave been what I've been?
>
> ('Chant-Pagan')

For all his passion for his country, Kipling sometimes doubted its value and its virtue. 'England is a stuffy little place,' he told Rhodes near the end of the war, 'mentally, morally and physically.'[8] And sometimes he even wondered whether it was quite real.

> *If England was what England seems,*
> *An' not the England of our dreams,*
> *But only putty, brass, an' paint,*
> *'Ow quick we'd drop her! But she ain't!*
>
> ('The Return')

The Sussex tales were not an interlude in Kipling's career, a pastoral sabbatical from haranguing his countrymen about their responsibilities. The stories and poems of *Puck of Pook's Hill*, which he began writing in 1904, and its sequel *Rewards and Fairies* do not simply reflect the other, non-imperial side of his head. However unlike 'The Islanders' or 'The White Man's Burden', they belong to different parts of the same essentially didactic design. 'And what should they know of England,' he had once asked, 'who only England know?' If the British were to be persuaded to defend the Empire, they had to be taught about it first. But they also had to be taught about their own country, to learn to value and appreciate it and to understand why it was worth protecting. The defence of England was not an insular concern but an imperial one, because without the islands the Empire would not exist.

In Sussex Kipling acquired a deep sense of history as well as of place. Stimulated by the discovery on his land of relics ranging from the Neolithic to the Cromwellian, he was able to envisage the connecting layers of a continuous past. People and their landscapes change from layer to layer, but they are moulded by previous layers and they remain in touch with them. Woods are cut down for pasture, replanted centuries later and cut down for timber – but it is the same plot of land. The countryside renews itself generation after generation.

Urged to make speeches about England and the Empire, Kipling replied that Providence had so arranged it that he could only 'afflict' his neighbours by writing. His correspondent was 'perfectly right' in her belief that 'England needs being taught about the Empire', but tempted though he was 'to wade in and "jaw"', he would have to do his 'whack of it in stories and rhymes'.[9] At the time of this letter, he was embarking on his 'whack' with the first of the Puck stories. Intended to make the history of 'our wonderful land a little pleasing to children', these tales revolve around Dan and Una (alias John and Elsie Kipling) who are introduced by Puck, the ancient fairy, to figures and situations of the past. The teaching is not forced. Dates and battles do not matter. Nor does chronology: the Norman stories are placed before the tales of the Roman centurions. But they give a marvellous sense of a multi-layered past that any intelligent child can love and understand. Learning history by rote, memorizing the order of kings and queens, has now mercifully been abolished, but its replacement, teaching history on an unstructured basis of unconnected themes, leaves contemporary children recognizing only two epochs divided by the railway age, their own and the 'olden days'.

They would *understand* more by reading *Puck*. Rosemary Sutcliff, one of the best of all children's writers and Kipling's only real literary disciple, pointed out that

> Children are prone to grow up seeing history as a series of small static pictures, all belonging to Then and having nothing to do with Now. The two *Puck* books, stories and songs alike, with their linking of past and present in one corner of England, must help them to feel it as a living and continuous process of which they themselves are a part, must help them to be at least a little aware of their own living roots behind them, and to see their own times in better perspective ...[10]

She published those words in 1960 when, as she sadly admitted, the Puck stories were 'in almost total eclipse'. Forty years later, the 'almost' can be omitted.

The unchronological sequence of the Puck stories is deliberate. The Norman tales come first because the real birth of England and the subsequent national continuity are ascribed to the Conquest and its aftermath. The reconciliation of conquerors and conquered, the blending of the Norman and Anglo-Saxon 'races', did not happen quite as Kipling suggests. But the idea of England as a consequence of this fusion makes a good point and a good start. So does Sir Richard's enthralment to his new home.

> I followed my Duke ere I was a lover,
>   To take from England fief and fee;
> But now this game is the other way over –
>   But now England hath taken me!

(Sir Richard's Song')

The Roman stories are not so much histories about Britain as parables about empire and civilization. Kipling claimed he did not intend to write parables, 'but when situations are so ludicrously, or terribly, parallel,' he remarked to George Wyndham, 'what can one do?'[11] Hadrian's Wall may not be quite the North-West Frontier. The Picts may not be quite Pathans in disguise. The centurions may not be exactly British officers in India, though they share certain renowned characteristics of the ICS: the paternalism, the self-sacrifice, the almost invincible incorruptibility. 'And you on the Wall,' says the general with ambitions to wear the Purple, you 'among the heather, will weep because your notion of justice was more to you than the favour of the Emperor of Rome.' But the parallels are transparent and proved irresistible to Kipling because the defence of civilization against barbarism requires timeless qualities. The defenders must be like the Roman centurion who pleads with the Legate not to send him to Rome 'where laurel crowns are won'.

> Let me work here for Britain's sake – at any task you will –
> A marsh to drain, a road to make or native troops to drill.
> Some Western camp (I know the Pict) or granite Border keep,
> Mid seas of heather derelict, where our old mess-mates sleep!

('The Roman Centurion's Song')

If the defenders retain the centurion's qualities of character, discipline and self-sacrifice, their civilization will be safe. But if they become soft and rich and complacent, they will inevitably be overcome. When an 'armed and agile nation' (like the Kaiser's Germany) threatens a neighbour, it must be resisted with steel, not bribed to go away.

> It is always a temptation to a rich and lazy nation,
>   To puff and look important and to say: –
> 'Though we know we should defeat you, we have not the time to meet
>   you,
> We will therefore pay you cash to go away.'
>
> And that is called paying the Dane-geld;
>   But we've proved it again and again,
> That if once you have paid him the Dane-geld
>   You never get rid of the Dane.

('Danegeld')

The subsequent stories in the Puck volumes range from the Bronze Age to George Washington, ending with 'The Tree of Justice', an emotive tale of reconciliation in which King Harold, forty years after his supposed death at Hastings, appears before the Norman monarch and is given King Henry's wine cup to drink from. As with Rosemary Sutcliff, Kipling's most successful historical stories are those written about the twelfth century and before.

He much enjoyed writing these 'yarns' and tried to make them straightforward and direct. Not wishing people to notice his style and to be diverted by the 'gloss', he aimed to make the 'medium as little insistent as possible'. As usual in his more mature work, he obsessively excised superfluous words – and quite often words that would have made the sense rather clearer. 'Wordiness is effeminacy and unforgivable,' he told poor Edmund Gosse, who had sinned: unnecessary words were the 'enemy of vigour' and weakened the 'instrument of language'. He had learned to prune them from writing telegrams at the *Gazette* and claimed his style was not indebted to anything or anybody but the telegraph system.[12]

Wielding a camelhair brush dipped in Indian ink, he read his work and blacked out the superfluities. Before re-reading, he let it 'drain' and then blacked out some more – and still more. Craftsmanship, he called it, and he never regarded himself as anything other than a craftsman. But then all true artists were craftsmen, even Shakespeare, who was 'first and foremost a good workman with his eye on his actors'. The Elizabethan bard was a craftsman, not an 'irresponsible demi-god'; his 'soul-development' was not important.[13] True artists were men who went soberly each morning to their desk, their easel or their keyboard. They did not see the world through an opium haze or the 'green hour' of absinthe and sugar and cracked ice.

The poems sprinkled among the pages of *Puck* and *Rewards and Fairies* include some of the gentlest and most delightful that he ever wrote. Without being instructive, they manage to convey lessons and images of history that, if taken young, remain with the reader forever. No child can read 'A St Helena Lullaby' without realizing the connection between nemesis and unlimited ambition. No one can hear 'The Harp Song of the Dane Women', a Nordic lament devoid of Latinate words, without seeing the Vikings' wives on the shore-line as their men's long-boats set out across the North Sea.

> What is a woman that you forsake her,
> And the hearth-fire and the home-acre,
> To go with the old grey Widow-maker?

And no one can read 'Cities and Thrones and Powers' without understanding, as Kipling did, the transience of all human institu-tions, even the Roman and British empires.

Cities and Thrones and Powers
   Stand in Time's eye,
Almost as long as flowers,
   Which daily die:
But, as new buds put forth,
   To glad new men,
Out of the spent and unconsidered Earth
   The Cities rise again.

Only occasional notes of bossiness and exhortation intrude. In 'The Children's Song', God is invoked in Victorian housemaster style to 'Teach us to rule ourselves alway, / Controlled and cleanly night and day.' And in 'If', that brilliant but unintended parody of public school reverence for the stiff upper lip, we are urged to perform all sorts of impossible tasks.

If you can bear to hear the truth you've spoken
   Twisted by knaves to make a trap for fools,
Or watch the things you gave your life to, broken,
   And stoop and build 'em up with worn-out tools;

If you can make one heap of all your winnings
   And risk it on one turn of pitch-and-toss,
And lose, and start again at your beginnings
   And never breathe a word about your loss;

If you really can put up with these and many other trials, you will become, as everyone knows, 'a Man, my son!' – like Dr Jameson and Lord Milner. Or you may become inhuman.

The Puck volumes did not quite satisfy Kipling's urge to encourage the historical inquisitiveness of children. As they neared completion, he began collaborating with a professional historian, C.R.L.Fletcher, on *A History of England*, published by the Oxford University Press in 1911. He knew he could not write history himself: incapable of impartiality, he would 'more than likely ... go off theorising and making' his facts fit his theories. But he was eager to write poems for a children's history by an Oxford don who shared his politics and loved making dubious historical comparisons. In the current atmosphere of corrupting Liberalism, he believed 'the Work was needed ... extremely urgently'.[14]

The result of the collaboration is an embarrassment. Kipling regarded Fletcher as a serious historian who had written a 'very good' text. Perhaps he read it in careless or dyspeptic mood because the text is in fact lamentable: racist, bigoted, anti-Irish, anti-Catholic, anti-Parliament and proudly propagandist. Besides being 'as nearly worthless as a book can be', the *Manchester Guardian* regarded it as the 'most pernicious' volume 'designed to influence the minds of children' that the newspaper had ever seen.[15] Even if Kipling was already, as Kingsley Amis observed of a later period, 'falling off the right wing of the Conservative Party',[16] the association is incomprehensible.

The volume has the lonely merit of being the vehicle for the publication of several of Kipling's finest poems on England and on national themes: 'The Roman Centurion', 'Danegeld', 'The Dutch in the Medway', a warning about the dangers of neglecting naval defence, and 'The Glory of the Garden' which closes the book with its sermon that England's strength and health can only be preserved by unglamorous hard work.

> Our England is a garden that is full of stately views,
> Of borders, beds and shrubberies and lawns and avenues,
> With statues on the terraces and peacocks strutting by;
> But the Glory of the Garden lies in more than meets the eye ...
>
> Our England is a garden, and such gardens are not made
> By singing: – 'Oh, how beautiful,' and sitting in the shade,
> While better men than we go out, and start their working lives
> At grubbing weeds from gravel-paths with broken dinner-knives.

I 2

The Colonial Sisterhood

'INDIA'S FULL OF Stalkies – Cheltenham and Haileybury and Marlborough chaps – that we don't know anything about, and the surprises will begin when there is really a big row on.' Asked who will be surprised, the speaker replies: 'The other side. The gentlemen who go to the front in first-class carriages. Just imagine Stalky let loose on the south side of Europe with a sufficiency of Sikhs and a reasonable prospect of loot. Consider it quietly.'

Kipling gave these words to the narrator of 'Slaves of the Lamp' in 1897, the year of the Jubilee, a year and a half before the opening of the Boer War. Never again did he allow himself – or a character speaking on his behalf – to express such sentiments. Never again did he assume that public schoolboys commanding Indian troops would defeat a European army, however luxuriously it travelled. The war in South Africa exhausted his frugal store of bravado and complacency. Gentlemen amateurs, whatever spirit they had imbibed at public school, must now give way to well-trained professionals.

His advocacy of military service predated 'The Islanders' (published early in 1902) and was inspired by acquaintanceship with the Army. 'All the chaps who've done their whack' in the war, he reported in December 1901, seemed 'pretty red-hot on the subject of conscription'. More than 200,000 trained men would soon return from South Africa 'clamouring for it', men who were now an important national asset and who must, on their return, carry over their training into Britain's 'soft slack civil life'. It was an issue he was determined to tackle, 'going into the mess', as he put it, because he believed the 'common people' were ripe for it. In fact most of the people he met seemed ripe for it. 'What would you have given,' he asked one officer in South Africa, 'for a sound working knowledge of rifle-shooting and extended order drill put into you from your twelfth to your fifteenth years, instead of a hasty and inadequate team run through in a month?'[1]

Friendly journalists were peppered with suggestions. If Strachey of the *Spectator* wanted 'some interest and a row', he should inaugurate a demand for conscription. H.A. 'Taffy' Gwynne, the Editor of the *Standard* and a future mouthpiece for Kipling in the British press, was exhorted to tackle 'boldly' the subject of national service and to demand a referendum on the issue. And Sir Clinton Dawkins received, for publication in the *National Service Journal*, a letter pointing out that a 'highly efficient system of conscription' already existed in the public schools – for games. Under that system the 'conscript' was compelled to 'drill' for several thousand teenage hours at cricket and football; annually nearly 10,000 boys emerged from their schools well trained in these sports. Yet if just 10 per cent of the 'hours devoted to cricket and footer drills could be taken up for military drill and target work', in five or six years the boys would become trained potential officers as well. The confusing relationship between games and warfare, complementary and dialectical as they alternately seemed to Kipling, continued. When giving advice on a campaign for compulsory drill, he told the organizers not to start 'agitating' in winter but to 'catch the public in the spring between cricket and footer'.[2]

Kipling's technical virtuosity allowed him to make his point in abundant styles. Sometimes, as in 'The Army of a Dream', it appears as boring political propaganda masquerading as a short story. Sometimes it is made with hortatory metrical passion, as in 'The Islanders'. Occasionally, as in 'The Reformers', the point is almost lost in the obscurity of a recondite and allusive mood. But at his best Kipling often borrowed from other places and other eras to create a powerful and apposite image. He did not much like the Dutch at the time, because of their kinsmen in South Africa, and he did not much like them in the future, because of their neutrality in the First World War. But he admired them for the resilience and hard work that had made them an independent nation. Their dykes provided both a practical defence against the sea and a historical metaphor for national defiance. If the dykes were neglected, the sea came in and overwhelmed; if a nation's defences were unmanned, the enemy could walk through them. In both cases the negligent were betraying their fathers and their sons.

Now we can only wait till the day, wait and apportion our shame,
These are the dykes our fathers left, but we would not look to the same.
Time and again were we warned of the dykes, time and again we delayed:
Now, it may fall, we have slain our sons, as our fathers we have betrayed.

('The Dykes')

Until the Boer War, Kipling's politics had been international, imperial and sometimes visionary. Now they became national as well, a development that led to his increasing identification with the Conservative Party:* if he wanted his crusades to succeed, he needed to work with the least bad of the parties. But he refused to become a politician, despite several offers from winnable constituencies. In 1904 he declined to stand for Edinburgh South on the grounds that Westminster was not his 'beat'.[3]

Unfortunately, the only member of the Government whom Kipling admired was not a Tory. With his stiff accoutrements of orchid and monocle, Chamberlain may have looked like a pillar of unbending conservatism. In fact he was a radical, firstly in the municipal politics of Birmingham, later in the imperial arena. After Salisbury's retirement in 1902 he was the only member of the Cabinet with a sense of leadership. But he was a Liberal Unionist and, although he received support from *The Times*, the Conservatives wanted a prime minister of their own.

Arthur James Balfour was the temperamental opposite of both Chamberlain and Kipling. He was charming, witty and exasperatingly indolent: as his War Secretary observed, he was 'always far too clever to know the facts'. Once, when forced to choose between lunch with the Kaiser and the Eton and Harrow match, he chose the

---

*The Conservatives were the dominant partners in the Government. Their coalition with the Liberal Unionists was usually referred to as the Unionist Party for the first two decades of the twentieth century.

cricket.[4]* After feigning indifference as to whether he succeeded his uncle (Salisbury), he nonchalantly assembled a Cabinet consisting largely of aristocratic friends and relations: they included a brother, a first cousin, a first cousin's husband, his fag at Eton, his fagmaster at the same institution, and a man for whom he had recently acted as best man.

Kipling liked Balfour personally – almost everyone did – but he was allergic to effete aristocrats in politics. He was a Conservative with a capital C but he was not a Blimpish reactionary. He preferred Tory policies to Liberal ones on questions of empire, defence and taxation, but he was not a squire lamenting the passing of the eighteenth century: he remained a devotee of scientific endeavour and technological advance. His Conservatism had nothing to do with Balfour's lounging world of grouse moors, country house parties and that well-born, mildly intellectual coterie known as the 'Souls'. He quickly saw through the new Prime Minister's intelligence to the inherent levity beyond. Angus Wilson may be wrong to think that a line of 'The Islanders' is personally directed at Balfour: 'Arid, aloof, incurious, unthinking, unthanking, gelt' – whatever the applicability of the other adjectives, he was not 'unthinking'. But there is no problem identifying the prototype of the Grey Cat in 'Below the Mill Dam', a story published two months after the Prime Minister took office. Balfour's characteristics are brilliantly reflected in the cat's elegance and languor, her innate conservatism that fears change and 'damnable inventions', her reverence for the past, her defence of privilege and her enjoyment of the 'dim delicious half-tones' of Life. A single sentence from the cat encapsulates the manner.

---

*Kipling was not aware of this dilemma – and for once, given the identity of the guest, he would have approved of the man who put sport before business – but he understood Balfour very well. Sitting next to him at a formal lunch in 1925, he inscribed on the back of A.J.B.'s programme at the Worshipful Company of Stationers:

The Foundations of Philosophic Doubt
Are based on this single premiss:
'Shall I be able to get out
To Wimbledon in time for tennis?'[5]

In 1892 Balfour had been happy to lose the General Election so that he could spend a long holiday preparing a new edition of his book, *In Defence of Philosophic Doubt*, a publishing event for which he made the world wait another twenty-eight years.

'Your assumptions are deliciously sweeping, but may I point out that a decent and – the dear old Abbot of Wilton would have put it in his resonant monkish Latin much better than I can – a scholarly reserve does not necessarily connote blank vacuity of mind on all subjects.'

Chamberlain remained inside the Cabinet (but outside its social cabal) for the first year of Balfour's premiership. Despite his alleged weakness in South Africa and his earlier attempt to promote a German alliance, he was still regarded by Kipling as the 'only man in the Cabinet', the one person in British politics with a mission to inspire. More even than Rhodes and Milner, he embodied the best qualities of a murky profession. He got things done; he persuaded people to do them. He cleared Birmingham's slums; he broke the Liberals over Home Rule; he envisaged an imperial future and tried to make it happen. Instead of waffling in the House of Commons, he toured the country, preaching his crusades.

Chamberlain had accepted the Colonial Office in 1895 because he wanted to undertake the 'great work of controlling and civilising the tropics'. He enjoyed some success in West Africa over boundaries and tropical disease, but he devoted most of his attention to the large settler colonies. This naturally appealed to Kipling, whose mental trajectory from India had also reached the dominions. So did the aim of creating a popular imperialism, of making the British understand what their Empire was and what it stood for. The colonies were not just an agglomeration of scattered territories, fortuitously acquired: they formed an entity ready to be bound together.

At the Colonial Conference of 1897 Chamberlain had observed that the colonies were 'still children, but rapidly approaching manhood', and that the time had come to transform their relationship into a 'true partnership', one of privilege and responsibility, especially as far as defence expenditure was concerned. At the next conference in 1902 he used Matthew Arnold's image of England as a 'weary Titan' struggling beneath 'the too vast orb of her fate' and desperately needing her 'children's' assistance. The British Empire, he told a Birmingham audience three years later, had altered: the colonies were no longer the colonies of the past. 'We are sister States in which the mother country . . . by virtue of all that has been done in the past, may claim to be first, but only first among equals.'[6]

Partnership between Britain and the dominions (Kipling's 'Five

Free Nations') was an idea that had been long supported by his admirer. For about twenty years, the poet claimed in Canada in 1907, he had done his best to make the people of the 'sister nations' interested in each other. Thanks to the Boer War, in which the 'Five' had gone through the same 'fuss' together, that had now been achieved. Applauding Chamberlain's statement towards the end of the conflict that the Government was not entitled to make a South African settlement unacceptable to the dominions, he urged quicker and closer imperial co-operation.[7] Like Chamberlain, he relished the image of female consanguinity to illustrate the new relationships. In 'The Young Queen', composed for the inauguration of the Australian Commonwealth in 1900, he has the 'Old Queen' (Britain) rather confusingly addressing Australia as 'Daughter no more but Sister, and doubly Daughter so ...' Yet in 1897, before the war began, he had restricted Canada to the role of daughter in 'Our Lady of the Snows', a poem criticized across the Atlantic because its title suggested Canada might be too cold a destination for emigrants.

> A Nation spoke to a Nation,
>   A Queen sent word to a Throne:
> 'Daughter am I in my mother's house,
>   But mistress in my own.
> The gates are mine to open,
>   As the gates are mine to close,
> And I set my house in order,'
>   Said our Lady of the Snows.

Chamberlain had been inspired by his 1887 visit to Canada – which he regarded as the flagship of the Empire – to turn the idea of Imperial Federation into a cause. For much of his life he had believed that the Empire could jog along on its traditional diet of Free Trade. But he noticed sooner than most of his contemporaries the economic challenges of the United States and Germany. Improving Britain's ability to compete through better education was one answer to these challenges; binding the Empire by economic interest, as well as by ties of culture and sentiment, was another. Appalled by his country's educational inferiority to Germany and America, he made a remarkable personal contribution in founding Birmingham University with its faculty of commerce and its emphasis on applied science. Perhaps he would have been better employed as President of the Board of Education than as Secretary of State for the Colonies. Certainly his last great crusade, the economic binding of the Empire by granting its components preferential trading terms, proved to be as unsuccessful and as damaging to his party as his earlier stand against Gladstone over Ireland. By dividing the Liberals over Home Rule in 1886, he had given two decades of dominance to the Conservatives and their new Liberal Unionist allies; now, by splitting the Unionists over Tariff Reform, he helped give the country seventeen years of Liberal prime ministers. No other politician has had such a negative electoral influence on the fortunes of his two political parties.

The contest between Free Trade and Protection rivals Ireland and the franchise as the longest political saga of the nineteenth and early twentieth centuries. At the time of Chamberlain's campaign the question could be simply phrased. Now that the Empire was more closely bound by transport, migration and shared experience, should it continue its policy of Free Trade, with which it had flourished for half a century, or should it establish a protectionist colonial bloc to defend itself against the growing power of Germany and the United States? Kipling referred to Free Trade as a 'heresy',[8] but by then it had become an orthodoxy, embraced by almost all the Liberal Party and by many Unionists as well. The 'little Englander' view that Britain would become more prosperous without colonies was virtually extinct; even John Morley, its wizened embodiment, was about to become Secretary of State for India. Yet if the Free Trade successors of Cobden and Bright now wanted the colonies, they also wished to expand the country's trade with the rest of the world. They wanted what later historians have called the 'imperialism of Free Trade', a kind of 'informal empire' whereby Britain could enjoy the benefits of commerce in such places as China and Latin America without sending great navies and garrisons.[9]

The aristocratic leaders of the Unionist Party backed Free Trade, Lord Salisbury observing that the idea of Imperial Federation lent itself more to 'peroration than argument'.[10] The commercial statistics, revealing that Britain's trade with the rest of the world was growing faster than imperial commerce, sustained his case. But Free Trade also possessed a moral dimension, the belief that it was a necessary colleague of capitalism, democracy and liberalism, a force for the advancement of progress and civilization in the world.

Imperial Preference was also more than an economic argument. While it was plainly intended to assist colonial economies, its essential aim, as Chamberlain explained, was to 'consolidate the British race', to create a bloc whose survival would be safeguarded by the economic and military interdependence of the Five Nations and the other colonies. Sounding, as he sometimes did, like Kipling on a plinth, the Colonial Secretary proclaimed that the Empire did not 'mean mere pettifogging considerations of profit and loss'. It meant a 'spirit infused into the whole race which raises and elevates us above the petty and sordid considerations of ordinary life'. The Empire was 'based upon a community of sacrifice'.[11]

Fiscal policy was not of course determined by the Colonial Secretary but by the Chancellor of the Exchequer, Charles Ritchie, an ardent Free Trader. In his budget of April 1903 Ritchie infuriated Chamberlain by scrapping duty on all imported corn. Chamberlain, who had been urging the introduction of Imperial Preference for colonial wheat, was not a conciliatory man, and he retaliated the following month by launching his crusade among his constituents in Birmingham. The British people had an opportunity, he told them, which would not recur, to show that they had it 'in their hearts' to do all that was necessary to consolidate their Empire.[12]

Shortly afterwards Kipling visited the House of Commons and saw Chamberlain, who was 'very full of his preferential tariff' and believed that the issue would split the parties in new directions. Satisfying himself that the scheme was 'more or less workable', Kipling complained of the Free Traders' insistence that it was a moral issue, instead of 'a simple matter of business – to be tried wholly, in part, or not at all, precisely as circumstances may warrant'.[13] But later he became as doctrinaire as the opposition. Construing Free Trade in private notes for the benefit of Unionist politicians, he defined the 'fundamental law of British trade' at that time.

> 'Be it enacted that where and when any conceivable article can, for any reason, be produced one tenth of a penny cheaper by any foreigner than it can be so produced by any Englishman the said article shall be imported into England without any duty let or hindrance, and the resulting displacement of labour shall be called benefiting the consumer.'
>
> Under this beneficent law it is further enacted that any Englishman

who finds himself unable to compete with any State-aided or subventioned European or any partially dressed and casually housed Asiatic shall be at perfect liberty to change his employment and at his own expense discover some trade or occupation in which he shall be able to compete ...

If you allow a man to be chased from trade to trade long enough, he will eventually fetch up on the street corner. *And that is where the Socialist is waiting for him* ...

Free Trade was thus the 'direct parent' of socialism because 'the workman cannot live on the wage which his European and Asiatic protected fellow workers – *not* the capitalist – allow him'.[14]

In the autumn of 1903 Chamberlain resigned and took his case to the country. Balfour re-balanced his Cabinet by disposing of three Free Trade ministers and remaining, as he often did, perched elegantly on the fence. With most of the press and Westminster against him, Chamberlain and the Tariff Reform League were faced with an enormous task of persuasion. But they soon acquired the support of the *Standard* and the *Daily Express*, edited respectively by Gwynne and R.D.Blumenfeld, an American expatriate and inventor of the unmemorable slogan, 'Tariff Reform Means Work for All'.

Both men were friends of Kipling and both were among the great survivors of Fleet Street – Blumenfeld editing the *Express* until 1929, Gwynne in charge of the *Standard* and then the intrepidly reactionary *Morning Post* until 1939. Much of their time at their desks was spent reading and reacting to exhortations from Bateman's: whom to employ, where to send him, what to write about, what line to take, what to emphasize and what to leave out altogether. Gwynne relished the treatment, frequently travelling to Sussex for more personal urgings. Kipling thought him 'as straight and as honest as they make them' – a curious description of one of Fleet Street's most notorious intriguers – and Carrie also approved. 'Such a nice man,' she noted in her diary, 'and very keen for the game of Empire'.[15]

While he incited support for Tariff Reform, Kipling was naturally more interested in the human aspect of imperial consolidation. He helped The Children of the Empire, an association aimed at fostering 'awareness' among the youth of the Five Nations. He urged colonies to advertise themselves better in Britain, to establish shops in London in which to display their produce, because the British had not 'even begun to scratch the Empire from a commercial point of view'.[16] But his main pursuit was the encouragement of emigration to the dominions.

British emigrants, as the Liberal politician Sir Charles Dilke had pointed out, cared little as a body whether they went to lands flying the Union Jack: they crossed the seas 'at the prompting not of sentiment but of interest'.[17] The statistics provide confirmation: during the last four decades of the Victorian Empire, well over half the people leaving Britain settled in the United States. Much disturbed by the trend, Kipling castigated the mismanagement that had allowed America to drain from the Empire 'a many million good, competent and law-fearing men' and change them into mere 'citoyens'.[18] Particularly alarmed by the situation in South Africa, where the defeated Boers still outnumbered the British, he urged schemes of emigration to the Transvaal and the currently named Orange River Colony. Although landowners might be reluctant to lose their best yeoman farmers, counties should be encouraged to select men and collect subscriptions so that they could begin a new life in South Africa.[19]

Convinced that the Boers would, unless thwarted, soon acquire overall control of the country, he could not understand why so few people realized the urgency of British settlement. He was a 'bit annoyed', he told two brothers, that they should have emigrated to the Argentine when they were needed in South Africa where they could have made as good a living breeding horses as in South America. Far more annoying was the short-sighted attitude of the Rand magnates who should have been spending 'some of their millions' on settling English farmers instead of leaving everything to 'the mercy of the Dutch'. 'Wake up the Rand millionaire,' he instructed Gwynne, and tell him to 'develop the country. He let us down in the Raid and he'll let us down now if he isn't kicked.'[20]

After the Liberal Party came to power following Balfour's resignation at the end of 1905, Kipling predicted that South Africa would be 'betrayed' and handed over to the Afrikaners. He therefore transferred his feelings to Rhodesia and urged emigrants to go there, 'the last loyal white colony' in the region. It had 'no end of a future', he assured a friend while imploring him to 'steer' any 'good young whites' towards Rhodes's creation. He was even thinking of buying a farm there himself and employing a man 'just to hold it down and fly a flag above it'.[21]

The situation was more encouraging in Canada, which received almost as many British emigrants as the United States in the first decade of the twentieth century, and twice as many in the second. But Kipling remained dissatisfied. 'Canada's weakness is lack of men. England's is an excess of voters who propose to live at the expense of the State'. As it was thus plainly in the Empire's interest to distribute citizens of a small and over-populated island to vast, largely uninhabited colonies, he could not understand why the Government refused to promote such a distribution. The consequence of inertia was that 'the races which work and do not form committees'* were now pouring men into the country: it made him 'jealous and afraid to watch aliens taking, and taking honestly, much of this treasure of good fortune and sane living'.[22]

Kipling's grumbling chauvinism disguised a valid point. William Booth, the founder of the Salvation Army whom he had met and admired in New Zealand in 1891, was another strong advocate of settling 'surplus' British stock in the colonies; and his organization's policy of assisted emigration succeeded in settling 200,000 working-class men and women in Canada before 1930. Government promotion of such schemes would no doubt have infringed the principles of Free Trade and *laissez-faire*, but it would certainly have helped commerce. As Britain was above all a trading nation, it would have been sensible to encourage the growth of colonial populations and thereby increase the market for its industrial goods.

Kipling's interest in Canada, and his belief in its future, were among the most enduring and reassuring of all his enthusiasms. He had not visited British North America since 1896 when he had gone there on holiday to escape from Grover Cleveland and Beatty Balestier. But in 1897 he had composed 'Our Lady of the Snows', a reverential expression of gratitude for Canada's willingness to grant preferential tariffs for British products. Many years later he still claimed that the decision was 'one of the most significant things that had happened' in the contemporary Empire.[23]

Canada also inspired the solitary speech-making tour of his life. In the autumn of 1907 the Kiplings crossed the Atlantic so that Carrie could see her mother and he could give a speech at McGill University, which had awarded him an honorary degree in 1899. A

---

* Presumably Germans and Scandinavians.

third reason, which he gave in a newspaper, was to escape the 'canker and blight that [had] settled in England for the last couple of years' (since the advent of the Liberals); a fourth was the desire to see 'what our Eldest Sister' (recently promoted from daughterhood) was doing. The main feature of the journey, however, was unplanned. During the voyage he accepted an invitation to deliver a series of speeches at branches of the Canadian Club right across the continent. From Vancouver to Ottawa, travelling in a private railroad car, he duly preached the imperial message, lauding Canada for its loyalty, its vision and its pioneering spirit, warning of the dangers of socialism and military weakness, and urging the Government to attract 'good men' and capital to the dominion. The oratory was widely reported and greatly cheered, even from afar by his mother, who wondered why he, the descendant of so many preachers, had not developed this talent sooner. Kipling described the trip as a 'lark but very like hard work'.[24] He did not repeat the experience.

Tactile acquaintance with Canada was not always so agreeable as sisterly appreciation from across the Atlantic. Crowds may have hailed him wherever his train halted, but they were 'young, callous, curious and godlessly egotistic' multitudes who took 'everything out of you and put little back'. Then there was the problem of the French Canadians, most of them Québécois, who had opposed participation in the Boer War and were 'au fond ... very, *very* like Brother Boer'. Even the Government, under the Liberal Prime Minister Wilfrid Laurier, was not quite the model of sibling co-operation that Kipling expected. While Australia and New Zealand favoured the establishment of some imperial structure of military collaboration, the Canadians objected that this would contradict the principle of colonial self-government. At the Imperial Conference of 1907 they were again obstructive, causing Kipling to shake his head and wonder why Canada, 'of all of us', should choose to 'brigade herself' with the Boers and 'block the forward rush'.[25]

Still, it was a 'marvellous land', redeemed by optimism, material progress and a profound faith in the Empire. The hope of developing post-war South Africa was being 'murdered' by the Liberals in London, but not even an Imperial Government could kill the hopes of Canada. There was too much potential in the growing cities and in the pioneering task of opening up vast tracts of the continent. Kipling relished the 'clean smell' of the place, the 'mixed odours of sawn lumber, virgin earth, and wood-smoke'. And he relished – and always exaggerated – the contrast between Canada and its almost overwhelming southern neighbour: 'on one side of an imaginary line ... Safety, Law, Honour, and Obedience, and on the other frank, brutal decivilisation'.[26]

Canada might easily have become the Scotland of a North American Union. Geography, the proliferation of north-south axes of communication across the continent, favoured such a development. So did the growth of American investment which, negligible before 1900, had overtaken Britain's by 1922. Kipling monitored the United States' efforts to make seductive trade agreements with Canada, and friendly editors were duly warned of these iniquities. But his trust in Canadian loyalty and good sense kept him generally optimistic. There was no need, he told Gwynne on his return in 1907, to worry about annexation because the Canadians 'don't love the Yanks'.[27]

Four years later his optimism evaporated when Laurier's Liberals campaigned for a reciprocal trade agreement with the United States, whose President Taft was claiming that reciprocity would make Canada an American 'adjunct'. Fearing that the dominion might be tempted by the prospect of instant financial gain, Kipling accepted a request from the *Montreal Star* to air his views on the subject. At his most solemn and portentous, he told the newspaper's readers that nine million people could not enter such an arrangement with ninety million strangers on an open frontier of 4,000 miles without losing their national integrity. At odds of ten to one they would be compelled to accept American standards on all things and might even find themselves sharing the same murder rate. Reciprocity doubtless had advantages for the United States, but Canada would gain little and suffer 'a very long repentance'.[28]

Against the predictions, Laurier was defeated in the election of September 1911 by Robert Borden's Conservatives campaigning on the slogan 'No truck nor trade with the Yankees'.[29] The Kiplings rejoiced at an outcome that 'settled' Canada's position in the Empire and gave an example to Australia and South Africa. Carrie noted exultantly that it was 'the first black eye' her country had ever received, while her husband confessed to Milner that he had not been so happy for seven or eight years. Max Aitken, a Canadian businessman who had recently become a British MP, later assured

Kipling that his letter in the *Montreal Star* had much influenced the result.[30]

Such optimistic developments had not taken place in British politics for a long time. In fact everything, as far as Kipling was concerned, had been drifting downhill since Salisbury's retirement and Chamberlain's resignation. Two decades of Unionist predominance were limping to their end, and the surviving giants of the poet's pantheon were moving towards political eclipse or physical prostration. After Milner's return from South Africa in 1905, Kipling wrote 'The Pro-Consuls', a curiously plural title to an encomium of a single white man's burden, of a man whose strength, hard work and self-sacrifice should have prepared the foundations of a great South African future.*

> Through the night when hirelings rest,
>   Sleepless they arise, alone,
> The unsleeping arch to test
>   And the o'er-trusted corner-stone,

---

*Kipling was worried that the plural of the title might imply that he was also praising the Empire's more flamboyant proconsul, Lord Curzon, who was on the verge of resigning the Indian viceroyalty. He therefore headed his verses with a quotation from a leading article in *The Times* of 6 July praising Milner for the 'strong and firm' foundations he had laid in South Africa.

Kitchener, who was now Commander-in-Chief in India, had been intriguing against Curzon in an attempt to abolish the Indian Government's Military Department and thus bring all areas of the Army under his control. Kipling does not seem to have known much about the issue but he sympathized with Kitchener because he believed it was more important that India 'should be defended than that it should be ever so "strenuously" administered'. Doubtless he was influenced by Gwynne, one of Kitchener's most effective allies in Britain, who bizarrely claimed in the *Standard* that the nation wanted the hero of Omdurman to be 'a kind of military dictator' in India.[31] Kitchener's system of dictatorship was the chief cause of the military fiasco in Mesopotamia in the First World War (see below pp. 267–8).

Kipling instinctively supported the military against the civilian administration in the Subcontinent. When soldiers of the West Kent Regiment were accused of raping an elderly Burmese woman in Rangoon in 1899, his 'own notion of the fuss' was that the woman, who went out of her mind and died soon afterwards, had invited the outrage because she belonged to 'that breed which invited casual attention with appropriate gestures'.[32] This Sussex-based notion was not shared in India, even by the military authorities. Since the West Kent officers tried to protect the culprits, Curzon – with the agreement of the C-in-C (a predecessor of Kitchener's) – punished the entire regiment by sending it to Aden for two years without leave.

'Gainst the need, they know, that lies
Hid beneath the centuries.

Milner's most controversial South African policy contributed to the Unionists' electoral disaster in January 1906. At the request of the Rand magnates, he agreed that indentured Chinese coolies should be brought in to hasten the revival of the gold mines. Although reasonably well housed and fed, the Chinese lived in compounds in a state of semi-servitude without access to the law courts. Their condition prompted the cry of 'Chinese slavery', an even more emotive and influential phrase than Campbell-Bannerman's 'methods of barbarism'. The slogan gave the Liberals another moral cause and enabled trade unionists to unite for the first time to condemn the Government's South African policy. But Kipling was disgusted by the row. On visiting a compound early in 1906, he found no bars or padlocks and declared that food and sanitation compared favourably with English cottages: the coolies, whom he observed buying corned beef, wheaten bread and vinegar, lived on 'rather better grub' than the Army.[33]

Balfour blamed Milner for a defeat which cost the Unionists 60 per cent of their seats and reduced them to a rump of 157 MPs. The scheme of allowing overseers to inflict corporal punishment on the Chinese was an 'amazing blunder' that violated 'every canon of international morality, of law, and of policy'.[34] But the débâcle had other causes attributable to the Prime Minister's languid leadership and the party split over Tariff Reform. Above all, the electorate was simply bored with the Unionists, who had mismanaged the war and been in power for too long.

Although the result was widely seen as a defeat for Tariff Reform, Kipling disagreed from afar. Wintering in Cape Town, he told Gwynne the issue had not been Free Trade but 'Chinese slavery' – or rather, the Liberals' exploitation of the issue. He also blamed the 'infernal and eternal slackness' of the Government since Chamberlain had left it. As he had been criticizing the Unionists for many years, he found it a 'very cheering point' that so many ministers had been defeated. He certainly did not regret the departure of Balfour, who was easily beaten in East Manchester, and hoped he would never come back as Prime Minister. But however much he despised the Tories, he knew that the Liberals would be worse. In South Africa, he noted, the Boers were already crowing and assuming that Campbell-Bannerman's new Government would return to Gladstone's policies of weakness and concession. 'The work of years' was going to be 'chucked away for a whim of the English electorate'.[35]

The chief anomaly of the election was Chamberlain's success in Birmingham, where he and his adherents won all of the city's seven seats. It was the last triumph of his career. Six months later he suffered a paralytic stroke that ended his political life. He died in 1914.

Chamberlain's campaign for Tariff Reform had been a brilliant if quixotic enterprise. Yet it was too hastily done and too inadequately researched. no solution was found then – or later – to the electoral unpopularity of food taxes. In retrospect Imperial Federation was probably a chimera, anxiously embraced by Edwardian imperialists who bellowed 'Land of Hope and Glory' to abate their pessimism and numb their suspicion that the trend of history was against them. Yet it was a serious attempt to confront the problem of national decline and it did receive an after-life during the Great Depression, when the Ottawa Agreements of 1932 endorsed Imperial Preference as a means of bolstering dominion economies; the principle was not wholly abandoned until Britain joined the European Economic Union in 1972. Meanwhile the belief in imperial co-operation lingered long enough to inspire the idea of the British Commonwealth.

For Kipling, Chamberlain remained 'the statesman who in the evening of his days, crowned with years and honour, beheld what our Empire might be made, who stepped aside from the sheep-tracks of little politicians, who put from him ease, comfort, friendship and lost even health itself that he might inspire and lead a young generation to follow him along the new path'.[36] As with Rhodes and Milner, he was commemorated in moving sonorities of verse.

> The peace of shocked Foundations flew
>   Before his ribald questionings.
> He broke the Oracles in two,
>   And bared the paltry wires and strings.
> He headed desert wanderings;
>   He led his soul, his cause, his clan
> A little from the ruck of Things.
>   *'Once on a time there was a Man.'*
>
> ('Things and the Man')

13

Liberal Treacheries

———————————

BENEFIT OF THE DOUBT was not a verdict that Kipling found easy to give. Certainly he wasted little time examining the policies of the new Liberal Government before denouncing them as socialistic, inept, unpatriotic and extortionate. Inaugurating his most strident decade of political aggressiveness, he pronounced the most talented single-party ministry of the century to be incapable: 'every form of unfitness' had 'combined in one big trust – a majority of all the minorities – to play the game of Government'.[1]

British politicians were a 'macaroni-backed crew' whose talents and principles remained invisible to Kipling. In all his correspondence there is scarcely a favourable word for any of them except Rhodes, Milner, Chamberlain and later Andrew Bonar Law, the melancholy, teetotal iron dealer who succeeded Balfour as leader of the Unionists. Political vices, by contrast, were always luminous to Kipling, even on those occasions when they happened to be absent. Hardly a Liberal measure was condemned without a slur against its author and its supporters. Kipling's own principles were now enmeshed in the politics of personality.

The Prime Minister himself received comparative leniency. After the 'methods of barbarism' speech, Kipling light-heartedly referred to Campbell-Bannerman as this 'Mildly nefarious / Wildly barbarious / Beggar that kept the cordite down'.[2]* It was difficult to dislike such a large, wise and imperturbable gastronome, as idle a Scot as

Balfour though with a more soporific manner: even as Prime Minister he admitted he was an 'immense believer in bed, in constantly keeping horizontal'.[3] Yet after his heart attack in November 1907, Kipling noted 'with joy' that 'C B' was 'violently unwell'. The nastiness is slightly ameliorated by the subsequent sentence – 'As a premier he is better extinct' – which implies that he did not actually wish him to die.[4] And in any case Kipling's nastiness was essentially impersonal. He seldom hated people he knew; he hated people as representatives of causes and ideas that he detested. And then he found personal reasons for disliking them as well.

Campbell-Bannerman's successor, H.H. Asquith, was the third indolent premier in a row. A friend of Balfour, he shared the Unionist leader's love of wine, golf, bridge and smart society, to which his second wife, the exhaustingly malicious Margot, had introduced him. But his serious side was more serious than Balfour's: he had a political agenda to accompany the parliamentary skills and the powerful intellect. Kipling refused to acknowledge it: Asquith was simply a drunk in need of an income to pay for an expensive wife. In a question typifying his blend of broad- and narrow-mindedness, he asked a parliamentary friend why, when the country had a 'sot' as Prime Minister, people made such a 'fuss about a little simple fornication or adultery out of office hours?' A man could not 'attend debates with his concubine, whereas he can and does try to legislate with a quart and a half of mixed liquors inside him'. He was, he added, 'all for the lady as against the liquor'.[5]

Perceived ministerial transgressions were often followed by querulous instructions from Bateman's to Fleet Street. In one letter Blumenfeld was urged to deal with both 'Honest' John Burns, the President of the Local Government Board, and John Seely, the War Office minister who had defended the decision to 'betray the Somalis to the Mad Mullah' (in other words, to abandon some untenable positions in the interior of Somaliland). Seely's principal crimes were that he had deserted the Unionists over Protection and,

---

*On a Friday night in June 1895 the Unionist opposition had sprung a successful censure motion on Campbell-Bannerman, the War Secretary, for his alleged failure to supply the Army with sufficient cordite. Lord Rosebery, the Prime Minister, could have reversed the vote and continued in power, but his cabinet was so fractious and divided (Campbell-Bannerman was the only member on speaking terms with all his colleagues) that he grabbed the opportunity to resign.

as Liberal Under-Secretary at the Colonial Office, had presented the Government's South African policy in the House of Commons – iniquities identical to those of Winston Churchill, who received even rougher treatment: 'you can cure a woman of being a personal prostitute', Kipling believed, but it was 'impossible to cure a political prostitute from whoring'.[6]* Yet the poet's most consistent charge, intensifying over the years of Asquith's Government, was corruption. Believing that all the Liberal ministers (except Grey, the Foreign Secretary) were 'desperately dependent on their salaries',[†] he automatically assumed that they clung to office for that reason – especially the 'extravagant' Asquith. They were an 'agile and mendacious gang of picaroons', reminding him of a 'race-day knot of pickpockets being chivvied up and down the various platforms of Waterloo by a phalanx of heavy-footed bobbies'. Implying that only landowners and industrialists were naturally loyal, Kipling suggested that J.L.Garvin, the Editor of the *Observer*, should 'point out the extremely limited stake anyone in the ministry' had in the country outside his monthly pay. And as ministers doubtless did little work, Garvin might also produce a 'plain weekly diary setting out in strictly non-political language, exactly what they have done each week'.[7]

Soon after taking office the Liberals alarmed Kipling over three of his most ardent enthusiasms – South Africa, the Army and the Royal Navy – and then gave him two further anxieties, an increase in his tax bill and debate over the future of the House of Lords.

His involvement with South Africa remained his chief political passion until 1910 when, as he believed, the Liberals destroyed its future by creating the Union. He had been appalled by Chamberlain's

---

*Churchill seems to have been unaware of this hostility. He loved Kipling's poetry, which he used to recite lolling in his bath or sitting in a wicker chair at Chartwell gazing at the Weald. Some of the prose stayed with him also: Churchill's great Dunkirk speech ('we shall fight on the beaches, we shall fight on the landing grounds, we shall fight in the fields and in the streets . . .') owes sense and resonance to the seals of *The Jungle Book* who 'fought in the breakers, they fought in the sand, and they fought in the smooth-worn basalt rocks of the nurseries'.

†Most Cabinet ministers have been dependent on their salaries since the end of the Salibury-Balfour era of predominantly aristocratic ministries. The salary at the beginning of the twentieth century (£5,000) was much higher in real terms than it was a hundred years later.

refusal to suspend the constitution of the Cape, which left the gains of the war to the whim of the colony's electorate in 1904. But the Progressive Party, assisted by some speeches from Kipling, was victorious at the polls, and Dr Jameson was installed as Prime Minister. Kipling's optimism returned with the appointment of his old friend, but the mood did not survive the Liberal victory in Britain. He seemed to have difficulty in remembering that the Liberal Imperialists had supported Milner, preferring instead to think that Liberal sentiment was represented by mavericks such as Sir Wilfrid Lawson, who had referred to supporters of the war as 'Union Jackasses', or Lloyd George, who had referred to the Boers as 'the Liberal Forwards'[8] – a view that would have earned the enmity of Kipling long before he was required to pay super tax. Boer rejoicing at Campbell-Bannerman's triumph enabled Kipling to see 'clearly' what he had known all along, 'how close and intimate were the relations between the rebs [*sic*] and the Liberals'.[9] Consequently, ignorance and malice would dominate the new Government's policy in South Africa; and the wrecking of Milner's work of reconstruction would follow.

The Liberals' opening announcement – that full self-government would soon be granted to the Transvaal and the Orange River Colony – confirmed this opinion. Predicting that the move would lead to a South Africa 'permanently & constitutionally handed over to the Dutch', Kipling remarked that it was 'rather sickening to be shelled by one's own side!'[10] Milner, who knew that his work was being dismantled, agreed. He attacked the decision in his maiden speech in the House of Lords in February 1906, arguing later that he could not have remained silent about a policy that would lead to the economic ruin of South Africa and the political alienation of its people from Britain.[11]

The following month a Liberal backbencher moved a resolution in the House of Commons censuring Milner for illegally authorizing the flogging of Chinese labourers. Radical hostility to Milner was so great that such a move could have been foreseen; so perhaps could the hypocritical indignation of a party that was returning power in the former Boer republics to men who habitually beat native Africans with a sjambok. Less predictable was the reply of the Government's spokesman, Churchill, who had been an admirer of Milner during the Boer War and had been elected as such as a

Unionist MP in the 'Khaki' election of 1900.* Moving an amendment that condemned the floggings but asked the House to 'refrain from passing censure on individuals', the junior minister adopted a bumptious and patronizing manner towards a man regarded so highly as an administrator that Balfour had recently offered him both the Colonial Office and the viceroyalty of India. After convicting Milner of 'a grave dereliction of public duty', Churchill suggested there was no point in further pursuing a man who had become a nobody, someone who now had no authority, no employment, no influence and not even a pension.[13] Milner never forgave him. Nor did Kipling, who deplored his 'paltry exhibition'. Although Churchill and his favourite poet came to agree on almost every issue from India to Nazi Germany, the statesman remained permanently unpardoned. Even after he had rejoined the Tories, combated the General Strike and become personally 'very ingratiating', he was regarded with distrust. The only point where he would draw a political line, Kipling said as late as 1935, 'would be in following Mr W. Churchill'.[14]

Milner retired from public life and accepted directorships in the City. When wintering at the Cape, Kipling supplied him with information about South Africa, and in England they continued to meet, spending Empire Day (24 May) alternately in each other's houses until the First World War. Milner remained first among the heroes of the poet's pantheon, 'a scholar and an administrator and one of the sanest of men'. Kipling always admired the manner, the work and the vision of a public servant who believed that imperialism had 'all the depth and significance of a religious faith', a significance that was 'moral more than material'. He tried to persuade him to return to politics and sometimes believed that 'the noise of the trumpets' would call him back.[15] Milner resisted the call until Ulster's trumpets were blaring in 1914. Two years later Lloyd George had the sense to employ his administrative skills in the War Cabinet and afterwards at the Colonial Office.

In January 1907 the Afrikaners won a majority in the Transvaal; in July they were victorious in the Orange River Colony (thence the Orange Free State); and six months later Jameson was defeated in

---

*His election propaganda at Oldham had surpassed that of Chamberlain. 'Be it known', his poster proclaimed, 'that every vote given to the radicals means 2 pats on the back to Kruger and 2 smacks in the face for our country.'[12]

the Cape. With Louis Botha, the Boers' ablest general, now Prime Minister in Pretoria, Kipling concluded that the war had been absolutely futile. The Afrikaners had lost little during the struggle (and anyway they had been lavishly compensated) and now they were being rewarded with the peace. The situation was practically the same as before the fighting: 'a dominant and divinely anointed Dutch Race sitting on the heads of the Uitlander who pays the taxes'. Four years after its surrender, the enemy had been given control of the revenues and administration of 'the conquered country! And all because a few men in England told lies about "slavery"'.[16] Worse still, the handover of South Africa to the Boers entailed the subjection of the loyalists to the rebels. In one of his bitterest poems Kipling compared the South African British to liberated slaves being resold into slavery.

> What is their sin that they are made
> Rebellion's lawful prey?
> This is their sin: that oft betrayed
> They did not oft betray.

Published in Gwynne's *Standard*,[17] the poem appealed to the British to wake up.

> At a great price you loosed the yoke
> 'Neath which our brethren lay
> (Your dead that perished ere 'twas broke
> Are scarcely dust to-day).
> Think you ye freed them at that price?
> Wake, or your toil is vain!
> Our rulers jugglingly devise
> To sell them back again ...

> ('South Africa')

But the British public was bored by South Africa; and its juggling rulers enjoyed a huge majority in the House of Commons.

The Kiplings returned to Cape Town in January 1908 'just to watch the corpse being (in)decently buried' at the elections that ended Jameson's premiership. 'The funeral', he reported sarcastically to Milner, had been 'managed with great decency and silence befitting the occasion.'[18] He and Jameson played golf on the Wynberg links to take their minds off the political situation, but he knew the time had come to leave South Africa for good. He hated the thought of going, for ten winters had made him 'put out roots in this queer and stubborn soil'. He loved the sunlight, the spaces, the view from Table Mountain that made the Bay of Naples look like a faded print.* But his friends had gone or were going, and the cause for which he had followed Rhodes and Milner was in permanent eclipse.

Lord Selborne, Salisbury's son-in-law who succeeded Milner as High Commissioner, invited Kipling to Johannesburg to try to convince him that the situation was not as bleak as he thought. Kipling did not go and was unconvinced by Selborne's assertion that, while 'many of the details of Milner's work' had been disturbed, the work itself was 'indestructible'. The High Commissioner deplored the way that 'Milner's friends at home' were revelling in 'dismal pessimism' because the new South Africa, built by Milner with the assistance of Roberts and Chamberlain, would survive. Kipling privately objected to being treated as a 'thrice-panoplied ass' and combatively replied. He quite agreed with Selborne that South Africa would remain within the Empire: why should the Boers want to leave when they could live happily, protected by the Royal Navy, on taxes raised from the uitlanders? But the fact that Botha was more co-operative than Kruger did not attenuate the betrayal. Milner had been sent out to South Africa 'to do certain work, on certain lines, in furtherance of certain principles' – in other words to maintain British supremacy in South Africa by binding together, under the Crown, the Cape, the Transvaal, Natal and the Orange Free State. Later the British Government had 'abandoned those principles, obliterated the main lines' of Milner's work and 'handed over absolute control of the details to another race'.[20]

Kipling's correspondence over the 'betrayal' was more virulent and obsessive than ever. Over and over again he reverted to his twin themes: the 'scientific elimination of the Imperial factor' in South Africa and the handing over of a 'higher civilisation to a lower one'. The Liberals had wrecked an empire out of 'sheer petty spite' ('their leading motive') by returning a backward and now hopeless land to

---

*Kipling's nostalgia for South Africa was stronger and more enduring than for any other place on the planet. 'That d—d country', he reflected in 1925, 'is too like a woman. One can't help loving her more for her badnesses which are many; and as I lost my heart to her a quarter of a century ago, I'm now an old and impenitent lover.'[19]

its former 'sullen barbarism'. It was an 'unspeakably revolting' process: until then he had not realized that 'the English of the Island were so genuinely vindictive against the English of the Empire'. The Boers were a 'semi-civilised people of primitive tastes' who lacked history, arts, crafts, cookery and architecture. Worse still was their 'hopeless abject incompetence and conceit'. And most galling of all, as one tirade concluded, was the fact that in England he had to pay a shilling in the pound 'to keep up the Navy to guard these swine from having the stuffing knocked out of 'em by the Germans'.[21]

In 1910 the Union of South Africa was created, replete with what Kipling called the 'strongest purely Dutch Government' that had ever been seen on the continent. But there was now nothing one could do about it beyond trying to annoy the Boers by referring to the union as British South Africa.[22] His views and predictions, like Milner's, had been unattractive in tone and assumption, but as so often they turned out to be accurate. The two men shared the belief that South Africa would eventually be lost to the Empire if the Transvaal were granted self-government before British colonists had become a majority there.[23] This was not quite true: Smuts, Botha and many other Boers found the imperial stage a congenial one on which to play. But South Africa never became like Canada or Australia; it was never really one of the 'Five Free Nations'.

Neither Milner nor Kipling championed the cause of coloured or black Africans. But they were concerned that they should be ruled justly, and they knew that a Boer-dominated Union would mean – in Milner's words – 'the abandonment of the black races' and – in Kipling's – permission for the Boers to 'uphold and expand their primitive lust for racial domination'.[24] In 1908 white delegates from the four South African colonies had discussed the terms of union at a National Convention and produced a draft constitution, which black leaders rejected for its colour-bar clauses and its racially discriminatory franchise. A black delegation then went to London to urge Parliament to reject the South Africa Bill, but the Government refused. 'Solving' the region's constitutional future was a higher priority for the Liberals than worrying about 'rights'. The road to apartheid was now open.

Kipling was eternally vigilant about the state of the armed forces. The seas and their vessels continued to enthral him but now they also inspired anger and disputatiousness. Even minor naval issues could provoke a barrage of letters. On learning in South Africa that the strength of the Simonstown base was to be reduced, he urged Gwynne to start a campaign against the Admiralty. And on hearing that there had been some 'monkeying about with the loadline and deck loads' of the merchant marine (for which he managed to blame Lloyd George), he dispatched urgent letters to naval experts and called for another campaign from Gwynne.[25]

He was even more vociferous on larger issues, thus emerging as an antagonist of the Government's chief reforming figures in military affairs, Richard Burdon Haldane, the War Secretary, and Admiral Sir 'Jacky' Fisher, the First Sea Lord. To them and to everyone else, Kipling repeatedly stressed his point: that Britain depended for its survival on armed forces that were no longer adequate to protect the islands. By way of illustration he published 'The Dutch in the Medway', a poem pointing to the lesson of 1667 when Charles II and his ministers economized by laying up the fleet and sending away its seamen, thereby encouraging the Dutch Admiral de Ruyter to sail up the Medway and burn some of the Navy's best ships in Chatham Docks. The relevance of the message two and a half centuries later was heavily underlined: look what had happened when a previous government had squandered money that should have been spent on feeding its sailors, repairing its ships and buying weapons.

> Mere powder, guns, and bullets,
>   We scarce can get at all,
> Their price was spent in merriment
>   And revel at Whitehall,
> While we in tattered doublets
>   From ship to ship must row,
> Beseeching friends for odds and ends –
>   *And this the Dutchmen know!*

On naval as well as army matters Kipling had decided not to emulate Tennyson: no jingoist glorifications of naval heroism but a sober and admonitory description of the Navy's most humiliating moment in the most dismal period of its existence.

Fisher believed that 'five strategic keys lock up the world', all of them British or under British control: Singapore, the Cape,

Alexandria, Gibraltar and Dover. But there was no point in having them without command of the oceans in between. Britain's long unchallenged naval supremacy was responsible for the Victorians' sense of imperial security: since the Indian Mutiny there had been no real threat to British rule anywhere except in South Africa, where the Navy, by deterring interference and supplying a war effort 6,000 miles away, could claim some share of the victory. But by the turn of the century that supremacy was being challenged by Germany and the other Powers. If Britain's industrial strength was in relative decline, then its naval preponderance was also bound to suffer – especially as improvements in arms and technology now made battle-ships much more expensive to build. Gunboat diplomacy was obsolete because gunboats were no longer effective. Although the British continued to possess by far the largest fleet in the world, they could not hope to patrol the oceans as in earlier times. Agreements were therefore made with Japan (1902), France (1904) and Russia (1907) that, together with the Anglo-American 'great rapprochement', effectively entailed sharing the Atlantic, the Pacific and the Mediterranean. Britain needed to keep its main force ready for the Germans in the North Sea.

The German naval programme had in British eyes only two purposes: to enable the Kaiser to attack Britain and to expand the Reich's colonial possessions. Churchill, who became First Lord of the Admiralty in 1911, argued that, while Britain's navy was a necessity, Germany's was a 'luxury' unnecessary for anything except expansionism. Although German admirals talked about a 'great overseas policy' for the Kaiser (at the expense of the British Empire), their fleet had defensive purposes as well. They needed to be able to resist a British naval blockade that, as the Admiralty believed, might be the decisive factor in a European struggle; and they were determined to avoid any repetition of the Napoleonic Wars when (by twice destroying the Danish fleet) British ships had gained control of the Baltic as well as the North Sea.[26]

Berlin never aspired to naval parity with Britain. However powerful their economy now was, the Germans could not afford to match the Royal Navy at the same time that they were building an army capable of fighting France and Russia simultaneously. And indeed, in spite of its construction programme, Germany's tonnage of warships in 1914 was only half the size of Britain's. Even so the threat was real. The Royal Navy could not concentrate its entire strength in home waters: it had global commitments and had to be prepared for unexpected challenges – such as hunting down enterprising German cruisers causing havoc in the South Seas in 1914–15. Furthermore the British could not risk maintaining an advantage in the North Sea so slender that it could be wiped out by bad weather or bad luck. There may have been no serious danger of an invasion, as there was in 1804 and 1940, but without local superiority there was a danger that the Kaiser's ships might break out into the Atlantic and decide the outcome of a future conflict.[27]

Realizing that the country, the Empire and Free Trade were all menaced, the Admiralty reacted with pugnacity. Fisher planned and executed the British response with a policy of modernization, concentration and reorganization. Obsolete ships were scrapped and replaced by fewer and more efficient 'Dreadnought' battleships and 'Invincible' battle-cruisers; at the same time destroyers and submarines were introduced. A powerful Navy, argued Fisher, obviated the need for a large standing army: in the event of war, the Navy 'could have the German fleet, the Kiel Canal and Schleswig-Holstein within a fortnight'.[28]

Critics within the Navy complained that the construction of the new vessels would cancel out Britain's advantage in existing ships – a curious argument implying that it would have been better for Germany to take a technological lead. More logically they expressed doubts about a policy that would reduce the size of the Navy and leave its conventional cruisers unmodernized. But while it may have been natural for naval officers to hold these views, it was strange of Rudyard Kipling to agree with them.

There was much about Fisher that Kipling should have liked. A gritty individualist and technological radical, he had entered the Navy at the age of 13 and had served as a midshipman in the Crimean War. Apart from the modernization of ships and engines, his reforms included improving conditions on the lower deck and reducing caste discrepancies between executive officers and engineers. In July 1904 this English cousin of 'McAndrew' invited Kipling on to a submarine and was adjudged a 'good man' by his guest; five years later he was pronounced a 'thorough going knave' and, another five years on, a 'wily scoundrel not troubled with scrupulosity'.[29] The change of opinion was caused by Kipling's admiration for Fisher's chief new antagonist, Lord Charles Beresford, the Admiral of the Channel Fleet (until 1909) who believed the First Sea Lord's reforms were weakening the Navy's capacity to counter the German threat.

A socialite and intermittent Tory MP who dismissed submarines as 'Fisher's toys', Beresford was an unlikely figure for Kipling to champion, even if he did begin each day with the Kiplingesque greeting, 'Good morning, one day nearer the German war.'[30] The creator of Gloster and McAndrew now found aristocratic charm more alluring than in the past – as the rows over the House of Lords soon showed. But that does not explain his stance any more than do the demotion of Simonstown or Beresford's justified demands for a naval general staff.

Kipling hated the changes because in the discarding of outdated ships he saw a fulfilment of 'Recessional': 'Far-called, our navies melt away; / On dune and headland sinks the fire'. Fisher was closing down the imperial dockyards in Jamaica, Nova Scotia and elsewhere; he was recalling 155 superannuated warships from around the globe and having most of them scrapped. By doing so he 'signalled', as Jan Morris has pointed out (and as Kipling himself plainly realized), 'the start of the British Empire's decline'.[31] He was bringing the Navy home and taking it apart, but he was also reassembling it as a European weapon to play its role in the Armageddon that Kipling had long prophesied.

Looking at the Navy through Beresford's eyes, Kipling managed to convince himself that it was in an appalling state requiring his assistance. 'We are running the navy reduction scare for all it is worth,' he told a correspondent at the Cape. 'It is the one thing on which one can raise a panic in England ...' As usual Gwynne was mobilized – the *Standard* became especially virulent about Fisher – and was subsequently told by his master that he deserved a statue for his efforts.[32] But this time the cause demanded that Kipling himself should take an active hand. Building on the success of his oratory in Canada, he made speeches praising Beresford and denigrating the reforms. At the Naval Club in October 1908 he spoke on 'The Spirit of the Navy', deriding the view that the country simply needed 'more *Incredibles* or *Insupportables*, or whatever the latest fancy pattern of war-canoe' happened to be. A fleet depended on things besides guns and armour, which were 'only ironmongery after all'.

Isn't the morale of a Service a thousandfold more important than its material? Can't we scratch up a fleet of *Impossibles* or *Undockables* in a few years for a few millions; but hasn't it taken thirty generations to develop the spirit of the Navy? And is anything except that spirit going to save the nation in the dark days ahead of us?[33]

McAndrew would have scoffed at the sentiment just as he had at the 'Viscount loon' who asked him, 'Don't you think steam spoils romance at sea?'

Kipling's anxieties about British defences were stimulated by fear of Germany and its intentions. Distrust had begun with Kaiser Wilhelm's telegram to Kruger, had continued with the early announcements of naval construction, and had been periodically reinforced ever since. In 1900, when German troops left for China as part of the international force raised to combat the Boxer insurgents, the Kaiser told them to give no pardon and to take no prisoners. They must conduct themselves like Attila's Huns a thousand years earlier and behave with such ferocity that for the next thousand years no Chinaman would dare look a German in the face.[34] Kipling treasured the speech that gave him the opportunity two years later to introduce 'Hun' into the vocabulary of poetic Germanophobia.* Lord Lansdowne, the Foreign Secretary who had been attempting to improve Anglo-German relations, regarded the offending poem, 'The Rowers', as 'an outrage'. But unhelpful though it may have been to the diplomats, it was not an excessive response to an atrocious pronouncement.

A relatively restrained period followed with Kipling only privately accusing Germany of bribing the Liberal Party and (also privately) referring to the 'unfrei' peoples of Central and Eastern Europe as 'the Middle Ages with the modern guns'. Once, in an interview with *Le Figaro*, he even confessed he might have overstated his anti-German case: from the proofs of the piece he removed references to Germany's lack of achievement in industry, trade and science, and cancelled the claim that he owed nothing to German literature: in fact, as he admitted, he owed a good deal to Heine.[35]

---

*See above, p. 117.

A renewed spasm of ship-building, specifically Germany's decision to construct Dreadnoughts in 1908, set him going again. In that year he predicted that the conflict with 'the Teuton' was not far away, and a visit to the Continent in 1910 convinced him that the Europeans were getting ready for war while the British were 'camping comfortably on the raw edge of a volcano and telling each other that the danger of a German explosion' was over.[36] Watching French troops in 1910, he consoled himself with the thought that at least they could march, and an inspection the following year revealed that French gun-handling and horsemanship were superior to Britain's. But he was doubtful about the crucial figure, the French infantryman, 'a filthy looking brute' who did 'pretty much' as he pleased.[37] In the summer of 1911 he planned a holiday in Normandy 'if the Kaiser permits' and by the end of the year he was observing that 'the Teuton has his large cold eye' on Britain and was ready to attack whenever he felt 'good and ready'. His consolation this time was the reflection that the Teuton only knew 'about war as it should be waged scientifically'[38] – a bizarre solace since in Kipling's lifetime Germany had trounced, scientifically or not, the imperial armies of Austria and France, while Britain's wonderfully unscientific approach had led to numerous defeats at the hands of Boer farmers.

Kipling was not a solitary Cassandra over the German military threat. The Government's flamboyants, Churchill and Lloyd George, might once have sniggered at alarmist scaremongers, but by 1911 even they had been sobered by Germany's naval programme and its clumsy diplomatic behaviour. Long before then the War Office and the Admiralty had accepted the probability of a war with Germany. Their main disagreement, predictably, had been over whether Britain's effort should concentrate on the high seas or whether a sizeable contribution should be made to a European conflict on land. Kipling believed that Britain – regardless of imperial issues – was and always would be a Continental power obliged to fight in Europe when necessary.[39] It was strange, therefore, that he should have opposed the man who created the British Expeditionary Force even more than he criticized the finest British admiral since Nelson.

R.B. Haldane was a lawyer and an intellectual whose long and earnest speeches in the House of Commons caused stampedes to the tearoom. He was not a traditional Gladstonian but a Liberal with 'collectivist tendencies' who believed that the great social problems in Britain could only be solved by government 'interference ... with people's liberties'.[40] That was enough to damn him in the eyes of Kipling, who increasingly believed that Liberals were closet socialists. So was Haldane's love for Germany, which he once injudiciously referred to as his 'spiritual home': he translated Schopenhauer, read Hegel on trains, walked in Goethe's footsteps and harangued the Cabinet on Germany's contribution to civilization. But he was also on the right wing of his party on matters of defence and foreign policy and, a fact that might have redeemed him in Kipling's eyes, he was the Liberals' most conspicuous defender of Milner. In 1904 he had provoked the hostility of colleagues by abstaining on the Chinese Labour Ordinance and two years later he worked to ensure that the backbench censure motion was unsuccessful.

Haldane had hoped to become Lord Chancellor. He had spoken rarely in military debates and was a surprising choice to follow three inept Unionists – Lansdowne, Brodrick and Arnold-Forster – at the War Office. Yet the Boer War had convinced him that the Army needed extensive reform, and he was determined to provide it despite the opposition of Radicals as well as Unionists and some very tepid support from his own Front Bench. Campbell-Bannerman, a former War Secretary under Gladstone and Rosebery, had subsequently refined his military policy to a sentence of eight words: 'Leave the army alone and don't make war.'[41]

Like Fisher, Haldane knew that he had to reduce in order to modernize. His Unionist critics saw the negative side, bewailing the reductions as a concession to 'Little Englanders' in his party without admitting the advantages of creating a general staff, the Territorial Army and an expeditionary force that could be ferried rapidly across the Channel to obstruct Germany. Other Unionists were more sensible. Roberts, the former Commander-in-Chief, respected Haldane's work while wishing it had gone further, and Lansdowne confessed he could think of no better alternative to the Territorial Army. Even the *Morning Post* admitted in March 1911 that the War Secretary had 'accomplished more in five years than any of his predecessors since Cardwell' in the 1870s.[42] Three months later, when Gwynne became its Editor, the newspaper would not have dared to acclaim one of Kipling's bugbears.

The squire of Bateman's reacted to Haldane's reductions like any Tory moss-back. The proposal to demobilize trained men was so absurd that he thought even the English, 'hopelessly and irreclaimably mad' as they were, might object. When they failed to do so, he predicted that Britain would return to the fifth century, after Honorius had withdrawn the legions, and that he would be required to pay for the consequent anarchy with his money and his skin. On learning that a friend was about to dine with Haldane, he remarked that he would do the state and the Empire a great service by shooting him.[43] And later, returning to the mood of 'The Islanders', he savaged the Government for squandering money on 'wastrels' (that is on social reforms) and leaving the country without adequate defences.

> Swiftly these pulled down the walls that their fathers had made them –
> The impregnable ramparts of old, they razed and relaid them
> As playgrounds of pleasure and leisure with limitless entries,
> And havens of rest for the wastrels where once walked the sentries;
> And because there was need of more pay for the shouters and marchers,
> They disbanded in face of their foemen their bowmen and archers.

> ('The City of Brass')

Haldane's second transgression was his opposition to national service, a cause for which Kipling remained an ardent advocate. In 1910 the War Secretary wrote an introduction to *Compulsory Service*, a book by General Sir Ian Hamilton, who believed that defence of the Empire required encouragement of the voluntary spirit. Hamilton had been an old friend of Kipling's from Simla and, perhaps because of that and his reputation as 'a Roberts man', he had escaped the poet's censure during the Boer War, even though his carelessness at Ladysmith had nearly led to the town's capture. But he could not be pardoned for opposing national service. Hamilton 'ain't my notion of a straight person', Kipling now told Dunsterville, adding that half the generals were backing 'Haldane's nonsense' and 'the state of the territorials would make [him] sick'. In a verse imitating Swinburne, which he sent to Stanley Baldwin, he suggested that Hamilton's promotion to Inspector-General of Overseas Forces and GOC in the Mediterranean (a position he did not deserve and which had unfortunate consequences at Gallipoli) had been a reward for the book.

> When Haldane's Hound upon Haldane's hobbies
> Writes a book which is full of lies

Then we find out what a first class job is
And how Inspector-Generals rise.[44]

But in Kipling's eyes the War Secretary's last and most insidious defect was his honest and rather tactless Germanophilia. A love of German philosophy might just have been acceptable, but it was going too far to invite the Kaiser to lunch (1911), to send (with six colleagues in the Cabinet) good will pledges to Germany (1912) and – above all – to believe that his native home and his spiritual home were not necessarily predestined to fight. Leo Maxse, the acerbic Editor of the *National Review* and another journalist friend of Kipling, used to refer to him as a member of the 'Potsdam Party'.* Kipling took the same view, anonymously publishing a poem, riddled with prejudice and malice, about one of Haldane's visits to Germany.

THE HALDANE IN GERMANY
[After the German of H.Heine]

I know now wherefore the Haldane
So muddled our Army away.
He has taken his work into Prussia,
At the Kaiser's feet to lay.

He brings him a loyal offering,
Of regiments newly-killed –
The Kaiser who has few of them
With loving kindness is filled.

Soulful the Kaiser receives him
(And gives him food beside!)
The Holy German People
Come out to see him ride.

The Holy German People
Line, by command, the street,

---

*Maxse had the ideal political credentials for close friendship with Kipling: pro-French, pro-Beresford, pro-National Service and pro-Tariff Reform; anti-German, anti-Fisher, anti-Balfour, anti-Lloyd George and anti-Irish nationalism. In addition he believed women's suffrage would be a calamity second only to a German invasion, and he nicknamed Lloyd George the 'Artful Dodger of the Carnarvon Boroughs' and Churchill (a Scottish MP since 1908) the 'Windbag of Dundee'.[45]

And having cheered at him several times,
Hasten to build up their fleet.

The Haldane amid Princesses
And other surroundings splendid,
Feels quite like a noble person –
Which is what the Kaiser intended.

The Haldane thinks of the Haldane,
And how he has climbed thus highly –
The Kaiser thinks of the Fatherland,
And winks at his generals slyly.

The Haldane is heavenly peaceful,
And righteously honoured because
The Kaiser will give him an Eagle
For clipping the Lion's claws.

So the Haldane wags his tail,
While the Kaiser pats his head,
And the English sit in their chapels ...
And there is no more to be said.[46]

14

In Defence of Privilege

THE YEARS BEFORE the First World War exhibit many of Kipling's virtues and nearly all of his unpleasantness. It was his decade of hating. He had of course learned to hate long before then, and he continued to hate right up until his death. But the political and imperial struggles during the Liberal Government provoked a crescendo of execration to reinforce a range of loathing that already stretched from the Germans to the Québécois, and from the Irish to the Indian National Congress. In England it encompassed trade unions, democracy, liberalism, Free Trade, socialism and bungalows.

Yet he was also a decent and very dutiful man, honourable in his personal relationships and his business dealings. Visitors to Bateman's who steered clear of political discussions saw only the devoted son, the faithful husband, the affectionate nephew and cousin, the loving father and the incomparable entertainer of other people's children. Some of them also observed the friend who remained loyal to his friends, and the writer who refused, whatever the provocation, to criticize fellow writers.

He remained close to his parents who were enjoying a mellow retirement in Wiltshire. Lockwood compensated for the years of monotonous Anglo-Indian cooking by enjoying Sunday lunches of roast beef, Yorkshire pudding, roly-poly and Wensleydale cheese. The Family Square was occasionally reformed, but the state of Trix's mental health made it impossible to recreate the cheerful spirit of

Simla and Lahore. Locked into a childless and unhappy marriage, Rudyard's nervous and highly sensitive sister had suffered some kind of psychotic breakdown after returning from India at the end of 1898. Although she recovered partially a few years later, the problem returned in 1911, after her parents had died of heart failure within two months of each other, and she went to live in a series of 'homes'. Her brother quickly burned their parents' papers.

For Elsie and John, their father wrote the *Just So Stories* and the Puck books. He also played with them and with other children – often friends' sons on a day out from nearby prep schools – paddling on the pond or covering himself in a hearthrug pretending to be a bear. An indulgent parent by the standards of the era, he was amused by his son's refusal to read his books and by his question, 'I say, daddy, did you ever hear of a man named Gray? He spent a dull night in a country churchyard and then wrote a rotten poem about it.'[1] But he became alarmed by John's failure to make academic progress at his public school, Wellington, and warned him about becoming a 'slacker'.

Kipling was even more anxious about possible threats to his children's virtue. When Elsie was 9 years old, her father was already gloomily eyeing the day when 'some ruffian of a young man' would abduct her. But at least that day was some way off, and in the meantime Elsie was living at home. John, however, was under threat from the moment he went to a school where the boys' houses, according to the father who sent him to one, were 'nests of all sorts of muck'. He was inexplicitly warned about homosexuality, which his parents called 'beastliness' practised only by 'swine' and 'sweeps' and 'scum'. 'Keep your tongue between your teeth,' he was told, 'don't criticise aloud ... and flee from Contaminating Swine!' But 'O Lord!', Kipling moaned to a correspondent, 'Who'd be a father! Wait till your time comes and you wander round (with all your guilty past on your back) trying vainly to safeguard your son's mind and morals *and* virginity.'[2] At least he recognized the inherent hypocrisy of the father's role.

Kipling enjoyed giving admonitory advice to friends about to marry. This was evidently based on personal experience and cannot have been very encouraging to his correspondents. Matrimony, he warned one man on his way to the altar, was the most difficult of all crafts. 'Study it humbly, prayerfully and incessantly and when in doubt (this advice is above all rubies) THROW UP YOUR

HANDS!'³ Lord Castlerosse, who used to visit him at Bateman's, described Kipling's married life as 'one of complete surrender ... [he had] handed himself over bodily, financially and spiritually to his spouse', obeying her commands without 'any signs of murmuring or even of incipient mutiny': Carrie was 'a mistress in the literal sense, a governess and a matron'. Other witnesses made similar observations. Nancy Astor invited Kipling to Cliveden and found him 'very poor company' because he sat on a sofa with his wife and never answered a question without asking her opinion first.⁴ Even their daughter described the marriage as 'bondage'.

Doubtless he felt subservience was a reasonable price to pay for a tranquil existence. As Elsie later remarked, Carrie permeated family life with a 'sense of strain and worry amounting sometimes to hysteria'. Her possessiveness, her 'uncertain moods' and her 'difficult temperament all reacted adversely' on Kipling and 'exhausted' him.⁵ It was better not to resist: surrender and withdrawal to his well-guarded study was the wiser policy. Yet dutiful attendance to his work did not stop him yearning for a little elbowroom. In his poem 'A Pilgrim's Way' the pilgrim says that he does not need to meet holy saints or devilkins on his way 'So long as I have leave and choice to meet my fellow-kind'. But after settling at Bateman's he seldom did have leave. His whole work, as P.G.Wodehouse later observed, 'depended on messing around and talking to people', but Carrie 'kept him rigidly excluded from the world'.⁶ Although occasionally he could escape to naval vessels or to Tisbury to stay with his parents by himself, he did not roam far. He had a few friends among the squires and retired military in East Sussex, though one of them, Colonel H.W. Feilden, thought him 'an awful little bounder' at their first meeting.⁷ But his literary acquaintanceships, such as they were, fell away. Rider Haggard, who gave good advice about apple trees, was allowed the unique privilege of working with Kipling in his study, yet Henry James was seldom seen, and no effort was made to encounter Conrad or Conan Doyle. Kipling was a wonderful talker, as Mark Twain had discovered at their first meeting in 1889, but he was now seldom given the chance to demonstrate his talent. As Castlerosse recorded,

> Sometimes in the evening, enlivened by wine and company, he would take a glass more than he was accustomed to and then those great big eyes of his would shine brightly behind his strong spectacles, and Rud would take

to talking faster and his views would become more emphatic. If Mrs
Kipling was with him, she would quickly note the change and, sure
enough, in a decisive voice she would issue the word of command: 'Rud,
it is time you went to bed', and Rud always discovered that it was about
time he went to bed.[8]

In 1902, the year he moved to Bateman's with his imperial halo at
its brightest, Kipling wrote 'The Song of Diego Valdez', an exhilar-
ating ballad about a pirate who becomes 'High Admiral of Spain'.
From a pinnacle of ageing respectability, Valdez recalls his comrades,
'old playmates on new seas', the life of plunder and freedom, the 'old
careening riot' and the 'tavern 'mid the palm trees' – and regrets his
new role, 'crowned by Fleet and People / And Bound by King and
Pope', a sailor sold to 'the bondage of great deeds', to the 'straiter
prison' and the 'heavier chain' of the Spanish admiralty. No one
aware of Kipling's domestic situation could fail to realize that he, the
squire of responsibilities and the apostle of Empire, was missing his
old playmates of boats and bazaars and barracks.

He still travelled, but with Carrie in smart motor cars and staying in
smart hotels. After the South African farewell the family spent the
Christmas holidays at Engelberg in Switzerland, skating amateurishly
in the mornings and skiing equally badly in the afternoons. They also
stayed in Pyrenean France, initially for Carrie's arthritis, later because
they had come to love the landscape. France rapidly became Kipling's
favourite country, the only foreign love that never disappointed. Its
inhabitants were, admittedly, 'incurably foul in their habits', but they
were hospitable, they read his books and – except for 'a *douanier* fortified with brandy against the terrible rain of the Nord' – he never on
the road encountered anything but kindness, even from gendarmes.
He admired Clemenceau, he believed in the Entente Cordiale and he
regarded French civilization as 'at least coeval with ours'.[9] In 'France'
he delivered a panegyric awarded no other country, not India or
Canada or South Africa – and certainly not England.

> Furious in luxury, merciless in toil,
> Terrible with strength renewed from a tireless soil;
> Strictest judge of her own worth, gentlest of man's mind,
> First to face the Truth and last to leave old Truths behind –
> France, beloved of every soul that loves or serves its kind!

Kipling was probably in a minority of foreigners who thought the French particularly strict judges of their own worth, but the central message of the poem would have found wider support: England and France had been rivals for nearly a thousand years but now they must, as the remaining heirs of Roman civilization, unite to preserve that civilization from barbarian threats.

For the rest of his life Kipling preferred to remain within the boundaries of the Roman Empire, but in 1907 he and Carrie travelled to Sweden to receive the Nobel Prize. It was a gloomy visit because King Oscar had died during the voyage and Stockholm was in mourning, but Kipling was delighted by the Ruritanian court. Less delighted by the business were the denizens of literary London who were aghast that the prize should have gone to Kipling while Swinburne, Meredith and Hardy were alive. It was a case, said one of them, of neglecting the goldsmiths and exalting the literary blacksmith.[10] Nor were the goldsmiths soon compensated: the next Nobel Laureate from Britain was Galsworthy, another farrier. In the quarter century between the triumphs of the two English smithies, Scandinavians won the prize seven times.

By now Kipling had made a distinction between purely literary and academic awards, which he accepted, and honours from the Government or national institutions which he refused. He accepted honorary degrees, including one from Curzon, the new Chancellor of Oxford University, as well as the Freedom of the City of London and the gold medal of the Royal Society of Literature. The British Academy and its American equivalent were a grey area straddling his demarcation line, but he justified refusing membership of the latter on the grounds that he had already turned down membership of the former. It was quite simple, however, to reject the Order of Merit, the Companionship of Honour, and attempts by Salisbury and Balfour to make him a knight – an honour, he explained, which 'must continue outside my scheme of things'.[11]

Detestation of the Liberal Government acquired a whole new dimension when Lloyd George, the Chancellor of the Exchequer, proposed to increase taxes on wealth. Kipling's first reaction to the 'People's Budget' of 1909 was to think of his savings: 'We must get every penny we can out of this country before the smash.' The budget was a 'Desolater' that would lead to misery and unemployment; Lloyd George was a 'Welsh thief' and his colleagues were socialists or, as the poet called them, 'soccers': 'There are no Liberals now'.[12]

The Chancellor's budget speech was very long and (for him) unusually dull; he stumbled through the text, misreading the punctuation and giving the impression that he did not understand his own proposals. But the content contrasted eloquently with the delivery. Needing to raise money for social reforms (including old age pensions) as well as for the Dreadnoughts demanded by his opponents, Lloyd George revolutionized taxation by introducing land taxes, super tax and taxes on petrol and motor cars. All of them, plus increases in income tax and duties on tobacco and spirits, required a certain amount of unbelting from Kipling.

The taxation proposals provoked an embarrassing display of aristocratic indignation. Lord Rosebery, Gladstone's successor, stated that the budget was not a budget but a revolution: the British people would have no more control over these 'vast changes' than if they had been Tartars or Lapps – a curious comparison considering that neither Tartars nor Lapps had voted in enormous numbers for the Government proposing these changes. Many territorial magnates combined even less logic with even more hysteria. A phalanx of dukes declared that the tax increases would oblige them to sack their labourers, cancel their subscriptions to football clubs and reduce their contributions to charity. Not all of the Unionist Party agreed with its peers: one MP publicly regretted that all the dukes had not been locked up for the duration of the debate.[13]

Kipling sided with the dukes. Lloyd George was a rapacious 'brute'; Britain had become Rome in its decline, and the Goths and Vandals were running about the premises. Two months after the budget he published 'The City of Brass', aimed not just at the Liberal 'policy' of disbanding the Army so that more money could be spent on 'wastrels', but also at the Labour movement and the class conflict which the Government was encouraging.

They said: 'Who has hate in his soul? Who has envied his neighbour?
Let him arise and control both that man and his labour.'
They said: 'Who is eaten by sloth? Whose unthrift has destroyed him?

He shall levy a tribute from all because none have employed him.'
They said: 'Who hath toiled? Who hath striven, and gathered
possession?
Let him be spoiled. He hath given full proof of transgression.'

The last two lines summed up 'the whole of the Lloyd George gospel' – or so he told Strachey of the *Spectator*, yet another editor on whom Kipling could exert influence, although he was less malleable than Gwynne and Blumenfeld and remained a devout Free Trader. Kipling hoped that Strachey would 'deal faithfully with the brute' who was inciting the mob to howl 'citizen so-and-so out of his motor or off his golf-links for the sin of owning a car or playing golf'. Another part of the Lloyd George 'gospel' could be defined by the question, 'Why should we be beggars with the ballot in our hands?' As the Welshman had taken advantage of Britain's 'thousand year old forms of decency to wage red war of confiscation', Strachey should 'get after him … with a stick' and point out the 'raging social hate of the man'. He was not a real Chancellor but a 'snubbed Welsh bailiff in possession of a house where, till now, he has had to wait outside'. The *Spectator*'s Editor sycophantically replied, suggesting that Lloyd George was an 'ill-tempered little goat' and assuring Kipling he was the 'most astonishingly suggestive person' he had ever met, that there were 'about a dozen leaders' in his letter, and that a point he had made about 'government by denunciation' was 'perfectly admirable … and worthy of Burke'.[14]

In November 1909 the budget naturally passed its Third Reading in the House of Commons and, by all the rules of tradition, should have been passed automatically by the Upper House: in neither of the previous two centuries had the Lords rejected a Finance Bill. But now Lansdowne, the Unionist leader in the Lords, moved that the House was not justified in giving consent to the budget until it had been submitted to the judgement of the electorate. His motion was predictably carried by the Lords' huge Unionist majority and, equally predictably, Asquith quickly announced the dissolution of Parliament. It was curious that two such instinctive compromisers as Lansdowne and Balfour should imagine that an assertion of aristocratic privilege might help them win an election or that it was worth risking the Lords' veto on non-financial matters for the sake of delaying the budget for a few months. But neither would have taken the step by themselves. It was the upper-class fury that 'encouraged' them.

Kipling had never wanted to be an active player in politics. He liked to be a coach on the sidelines, bellowing at the team and occasionally running on to the pitch, as in the 'Khaki' election of 1900 or the Cape elections of 1904. But after the 'People's Budget' he decided to participate a little more obviously.

He still regularly lamented the loss of Chamberlain, who had had no 'understudy' because Balfour and the 'Inner Caste of Conservatism' had 'stifled and hampered the young bloods'. Gwynne was exhorted to find 'a young 'un and enthuse him',[15] but in the meantime they had to make do with Balfour. Kipling had been happy to see the Tory leader defeated in 1906 and was unenthusiastic about his return to the House of Commons: when Balfour won a by-election the following year, his critic failed to see why he was 'so damn necessary' to a party that needed a leader able to rouse his supporters with a 'fighting general's speech'. He soon despaired of finding a decent replacement for that 'strange evasive undulating man' incapable of reanimating the Tory spirit. The opposition, he reported a year later, was 'rotten-slack' and 'about as useful as a sick headache or a broken syringe'.[16]

On holiday in Switzerland during the first elections of 1910, Kipling remained confident that the 'socialists' would lose 110 seats and that his party could 'get 'em on the run yet'.[17] The first part of the prediction was accurate (the Liberals lost 104 seats ending up with only two more than the Unionists) but the Opposition could hardly 'get 'em on the run' when the Government could depend in a crisis on Labour and Irish nationalist MPs (40 and 82 respectively). In fact the Unionist advance merely restored Irish Home Rule to the political agenda.

Asquith returned to Downing Street as Prime Minister determined to end the Peers' veto but unsure how to do so and equally uncertain how to persuade King Edward to endorse whatever move he decided to make. The nature of the second dilemma was altered by the King's unexpected death in May, an event that seemed to drive Kipling beyond all reason. The Cabinet had killed him, he told Blumenfeld, urging his second favourite editor to call its members regicides: those 'vanity-drugged little beasts [had] killed him as surely' as if they had thrown a bomb.[18] What weapon they had used was not explained, but presumably it was Asquith's intention to ask the King to create hundreds of new peers to overcome the Unionist majority in the House of Lords. One unfortunate consequence was 'The Dead King', a dreadful poem implying that Edward had been a selfless and hard-working monarch. It was one of the few works Kipling wrote that suggested he might have made a suitable poet laureate.

Although the Lords passed the budget without a division in April 1910, the Prime Minister declined to accept this as a sufficient atonement. Instead he announced proposals that would prevent them from vetoing future money bills and restrict them to a suspensory veto of two years to delay other legislation. Reluctant to embarrass George V, the ill-trained and untried new monarch, Asquith hoped to persuade the Lords to accept his proposals in the shape of a Parliament Bill without having to obtain a Liberal majority in the House by flooding it with new peers. Only when negotiations between the two parties broke down in November did he ask the King for private guarantees that, if the Liberals were returned to power at another election, a sufficient number of peers would be created to ensure the passing of the Bill. Dissolution quickly followed, but the subsequent election left the Commons in an almost identical stalemate. A worse result for the Unionists was only averted by Balfour's promise to submit 'food taxes' – an inescapable consequence of Imperial Preference – to a referendum.

The Unionist leader's emasculation of Chamberlain's programme did not deter Kipling from participating in the campaign. Gwynne had extracted a promise from him to make a speech at the hustings and suggested that he do so at Ashton-under-Lyne for Max Aitken, the Canadian adventurer who, although he had never made a speech and knew nothing about politics except the 'Empire issue', had decided to 'pick out a good, sound, Liberal seat and turn it over to the Unionist Party'.[19] An oration from Kipling, argued the ingratiating journalist, would have a 'great effect' throughout Lancashire and probably gain several seats for the Unionists. Kipling duly spoke, Aitken was duly elected, and the new MP duly received rather patronizing advice about the House of Commons and the limited role it should be allowed to play.

Don't mind if you find the House, at first, about as stimulating as a Fundy fog-bank and as easy to handle as a mud-fence in thaw. *All* the chaps, except the abject fools, feel that at the first go. Then they get their second wind. Of course the whole secret of Government is to prevent that damned House doing anything at all: but in these days alas! that is not possible so one tries to minimise the harm it does.[20]

Kipling also campaigned in Sussex, canvassing and speaking several times for his local candidate: on Election Day he motored about in 'simply hellish weather picking up half-drowned voters' and taking them to the polls. The result did not depress him because, despite 'the ignorance of the elector and the bribes' he had been offered, the 'British character' had stood reasonably firm. A 'feeling in the air', he told Milner, made him more optimistic that their enemies had 'done their utmost' and could now be held 'with a little bit in hand'. It was 'the sort of feeling that came sometimes at the end of what looked like a wasted day's fight in S.Africa'. Even so he had a 'horrible fear' that the Lords would now compromise and behave like 'gentlemen' from 'some vague idea of saving the country, playing the game, pleasing the King or some other Devil's excuse for selling the pass'.[21]

In June 1911 Kipling reluctantly put on court dress to attend the Coronation in Westminster Abbey. Afterwards he amused himself by penning sketches of two of his least favourite politicians.

Haldane looked like a Toby dog strayed from a Punch and Judy show as he scuttled up the aisle in his unadjusted peer's robes,* and all the Winstonism of Churchill simply blazed up against that background of decent ritual. He looked like an obscene paper backed French novel in the Bodleian.[22]

As usual Kipling warned against a triumphalist celebration of a great imperial ceremony, advising Blumenfeld not to run a campaign to transform the King into the 'Emperor of the British'. He had a superstitious feeling that talk about emperors would lead to imperial collapse. The Empire might be 'on the verge of collapsing' anyhow, but Blumenfeld's proposal would only 'unite against the imperial idea all

* He had gone to the House of Lords a few weeks earlier and became Lord Chancellor the following year.

the weak, idle, inefficient, malignant persons' for whom the idea of Empire was an abomination. More suitable subjects for the *Daily Express* might be hand signals for cyclists around corners, an alleged revolt against trade unionism by 'harassed working men' and an inquiry into the decline of women's 'more charming characteristics' as a result of their 'enlarged participation in the work of the world'.[23]

Monarchical celebrations were soon followed by aristocratic bloodletting over the Parliament Bill. As the Liberals possessed few peers, they had little influence over the Bill's fate in the Lords where the issue was causing a civil war among Unionists: 'Diehards' or 'Ditchers' who yelled defiance at the Government, versus 'Hedgers' who thought it more sensible to accept the reduced powers offered by Asquith rather than risk a constitutional conflagration. Kipling was by now an automatic Diehard. So was Gwynne, who had just moved to the *Morning Post*, where his proprietor Lady Bathurst clamoured for the Bill's outright rejection.[24]

Both men were confident that the noble Diehards would win. Kipling no longer feared that the Lords would behave like gentlemen, 'playing the game' and 'selling the pass'. Three days before the vote Aitken informed him that the excitement and interest were over: the Diehards would assuredly be victorious. Gwynne was also exultant, convinced that the result would mean the 'political death' of Balfour, which he greatly desired and helped to hasten – though the death lasted only a few years and was succeeded by a protracted resurrection.[25]

The affair culminated in August on the hottest day ever recorded in Britain. Curzon wound up for the moderates, arguing that the Bill's defeat would result in the destruction of the Lords and the making of a new constitution. In the final speech Selborne attempted to insert the Diehards into the tradition of Gothick romanticism: it was better, he declared, to die 'in the light, killed by our enemies' than to 'perish in the dark by our own hand'.[26] Curzon won the debate, persuading thirty-seven Unionists to side with the Liberals and thirteen bishops to defeat the Diehards by seventeen votes. The majority of the Unionist peers abstained in accordance with the advice of Lansdowne and Balfour.

Kipling was aghast, railing with Haggard against the 'ratting of the peers'. For him it marked the end of constitutional government, though he thought the English might be too 'thick-headed' to comprehend it.[27]

Never before had Kipling shown enthusiasm for inherited privilege. The self-made Antony Gloster was more worthy than his effete heir; the 'Viscount loon' had been ridiculed by McAndrew. In 'The Sons of Martha', written in 1907, the men who work and take risks are exalted above the 'sons of Mary', who enjoy grace and privilege because Jesus sided with their mother when Martha asked her to help serve the dinner (Luke 10: 38–42). Nor had Kipling ever found the aristocracy personally very appealing. An encounter with duchesses in 1902 had left him raging at their tone and manner: 'Lord! Lord!' he had exclaimed. '*Why* are they so gratuitously and incurably and unconsciously offensive?'[28]

A decade later he was enjoying the 'giddy world' of a dinner party with duchesses and other aristocrats, relishing their titles and jewellery in a letter to his mother-in-law – even Carrie wore a tiara.[29] Yet despite occasional country house weekends with the Astors, the Curzons and the Desboroughs, he did not often attend such functions; and certainly, except at Westminster, he remained a champion of the sons of Martha. But his years in rural England, his telling of its history through Puck, and his obsessive hatred of the Liberals, helped him discern the historic values of the House of Lords at a moment when its future was threatened. Before the advent of the 'Welsh Manchu dynasty',[30] he could not have declaimed his paean to the House of Lords in Brighton in November 1910.

> Achievement which benefits the kingdom; heredity which gives responsibility and incentive to renewed achievement; independence which inspires fearless advice – these things were vitally important when England was in the making: and surely we have in these things the beginning of the House of Lords. Generation after generation, that assembly has been recruited from proven capacity in every walk of life to serve the needs of the day according to the standards of the day ...
>
> Yet, in essence, the House of Lords is what it was from the first – a body of democratic aristocrats, chosen after trial and observation out of an aristocratic democracy to guard the permanent life of the nation – that inner political life of the race which is very little affected by legislation.[31]

The few politicians Kipling genuinely admired, however, were invariably self-made men: Chamberlain, Rhodes and Milner and the two Scottish Canadians, Max Aitken and Andrew Bonar Law. Aitken, who had amassed a fortune by merging companies in Canada, also enjoyed making money for his friends and frequently gave Kipling advice on his investments. In 1911 he was knighted in the Coronation honours for no obvious reason except that he could afford to give money to Unionist funds; but Kipling, so quick to sniff corruption and nepotism among his enemies, found this no obstacle to close friendship. He became godfather to Aitken's second son (Peter Rudyard) and offered plenty of advice to the new MP. 'With your brains and my voice,' Aitken gratefully acknowledged in September 1911, 'I made a first rate speech on Thursday night.' A few weeks later he begged the poet to give him 'something to say' in a speech on Tariff Reform in the Free Trade Hall in Manchester. And the following year Kipling returned to Ashton-under-Lyne to warn Aitken's constituents that Britain was 'utterly unprepared' for the coming conflict with Germany.[32]

The Kipling family spent the Christmas of 1911 with the Aitkens at their home in Leatherhead. Also staying was the new Unionist leader, Bonar Law, with whom Kipling now cemented a friendship that endured until the politician's death twelve years later. In contrast to the buccaneering Aitken, Law's lugubrious personality did not invite friendship. His background (a daunting amalgam of Glasgow, Ulster and New Brunswick Presbyterianism), his childhood (when he learned to take 'politics with his porridge'[33]) and his early career (as an iron dealer he acquired his debating skills at a Glasgow bankruptcy court) no doubt encouraged a certain inherent gloominess. But so did his tastes and habits – anti-social, teetotal and unappreciative of art or nature: social life was in fact a torment to him unless its chief ingredients were bridge, chess, a good cigar and political conversation. Even his politics were gloomy: bereft of Tory romanticism, imperial vision and any leanings towards social reform, they concentrated, as he admitted, on Tariff Reform and the retention of Ulster inside the United Kingdom. Yet his sturdy character and his single-mindedness convinced Kipling that he would make an admirable leader.

The 'Balfour Must Go' campaign, spearheaded by Maxse and Gwynne, had become irresistible by the autumn of 1911. Three election defeats and tortuous indecisiveness over the Parliament Bill had left Balfour with so few admirers that he decided the party needed a 'slower brain' which did not 'see all the factors in a situation'.[34] His resignation, he claimed, made him one of the two happiest men in London and should have been celebrated by inviting the other, Leo Maxse, to dinner.

As the Unionists polarized behind Austen Chamberlain, supported by Diehards and Tariff Reformers, and Walter Long, the choice of Hedgers and Free Traders, Kipling hoped for the selection of the outsider, Bonar Law. The problem with Chamberlain, he thought, was that he was really only the son of his father. The problem with Long, a worthy exemplar of Tory squiredom, was that as leader he would be 'more immaculately useless and genteely incompetent than anything else in sight'. So he went 'bald-headed' for Law and was encouraged by Aitken to convert Gwynne, a Chamberlain supporter 'trying to remain neutral and doing badly'. Kipling promised to do his best 'quietly', informing the journalist by wire that Law was the 'best imperial asset of the three with fewest enemies soundest knowledge Tariff Reform and specially acceptable to Canada at present'. In the interests of party unity both principal candidates withdrew in favour of Law, an outcome that pleased Kipling so much that he promptly renewed his local political subscriptions.[35]

The reanimated activist soon submitted his thoughts on the state of the party. In a lengthy memorandum to Aitken, which was passed on to Law, he recommended that the Central Conservative Organization should be immediately 'taken to bits and reassembled' with a press office established to prepare and distribute information to newspaper editors. After Law had demonstrated gratitude for this early elucidation of the spin-doctor's art, Kipling congratulated him on his early performances as leader: the public was feeling that 'relief that steals over an angry and puzzled meeting of shareholders when a man who really understands figures gets up and straightens out the situation'. But 'best of all' was Law's 'form of attack', a method of combat already shaking the nerves of the 'Revolutionary Committee' (in other words, the Liberal Government).[36]

In fact Law's form of attack was simply knuckle-duster aggression. While Asquith and Balfour could conduct a gentlemanly debate after sharing a bottle of champagne, Law (who would have been unable to entice the Prime Minister to his supply of milk and ginger ale) denounced the Liberals as gambling cheats and Gadarene swine. Asquith never resorted to such language and, although Lloyd

George's speeches were often savage, they were tempered by humour. Law's leadership, by contrast, exhibited a viciousness – at least until 1914 – calculated to appeal to the worst instincts of his party. It certainly appealed to Kipling who admitted, 'I love [Law] because he hates.' Following that Christmas with the Aitkens, he increasingly respected his leader's 'deadly accuracy, his absence of illusions and his *conviction*'. Furthermore, the 'soccers' loathed and feared him, which was a 'good sign'.[37]

Kipling did not confine his targets to the 'soccers' on the Liberal benches. During these years, when his views were at least as savage as Law's, he frequently aimed at democracy, trade unions, socialism, Irish nationalism and the women's suffrage movement. He remained convinced that the interests of the working classes were badly served by Free Trade (which depressed wages and caused unemployment), trade unions (which damaged the economy) and a paternalist state which encouraged 'shirkers' to live off its charity.[38] The coal-miners and their unions achieved demonic status when they went on strike in 1912.

Double-barrelled tactics were retained for political and social issues. The first shot, fired instantly from the hip, carried furious instructions to friendly journalists and politicians. With the second he showed more restraint, waiting for the moment to write a poem or a story and, surprisingly often, to convert propaganda into art.

Gwynne and Blumenfeld remained the usual recipients of the first barrel, though the aim was sometimes shifted to Maxse or Strachey or J.L.Garvin of the *Observer*. In 1912 Gwynne was instructed to find out how much foreign influence was behind the coal strike and also to produce an article on the benefits the average working man would receive from joining a trade union. It appeared to Kipling that the working man was 'confiding his cash to the only bank in the world whose cashiers may embezzle without punishment'. At the *Express* Blumenfeld received different suggestions for dealing with the miners: he should, for example, describe their wages not as 57/- (shillings per week), which looked 'humble' without a £ sign in front, but as £148 (per annum) which looked 'much more' – though less in fact than Kipling could earn from a single story. At a higher level Blumenfeld was told to stress the need for finding a substitute for coal. 'Keep the *Express* going on that tack – talk, even, about harnessing the tides. Some lunatic may stumble on that secret which ...

is not near so impossible as was the telephone half one generation ago.'[39] Prescient and reactionary together, the mechanic and the environmentalist continued to compete inside the same head.

Kipling's artistic assaults on socialism include, besides 'The City of Brass', 'The Mother Hive', one of his more successful animal fables, in which a 'progressive' wax moth insinuates herself into a beehive and manages through propaganda to destroy its society. 'The Benefactors', published by Maxse at the *National Review*, is a more pedestrian fiction in which a coal-miner boasts of his power, claims 'the Unions are the government' and is untroubled by the shades of people who have died of cold, hunger or suicide during the strike. Kipling regarded it as a 'little loving idyll of organised Labour' and, given its political content, required no payment.[40]

The anti-suffragist cause was one of Kipling's least time-consuming crusades though it did inspire one of his most notorious poems. It was not primarily a misogynist movement: politicians who adored women such as Asquith and Curzon supported it because they shared Gladstone's fear that emancipation would 'trespass upon [women's] delicacy, their purity, their refinement, the elevation of their whole nature'.[41] Kipling did not of course adore women but he too believed that those who worked would lose their charm. Perhaps because he had been born among Anglo-Indians, he never liked the idea of a woman earning a living among men. 'She's too good for that job,' he used to say, and besides she had better things to do. Congratulating a friend's daughter on her engagement, he advised her to 'chuck poetry and literature' because they didn't 'make for married happiness on the she-side'. Later he asked her father to send him something she had written although he was 'loath to see [her] successful in literature now that she [was] adopting a real profession'.[42]

Many years earlier a story in *Stalky* contained the observation that 'the reserve of a boy [was] tenfold deeper than the reserve of a maid, she being made for one end only by blind Nature, but man for several'.[43] He returned to the theme in 'The Female of the Species' (1911).

> But the Woman that God gave him, every fibre of her frame
> Proves her launched for one sole issue, armed and engined for the same;
> And to serve that single issue, lest the generations fail,
> The female of the species must be deadlier than the male.

The verses contain one redeeming couplet, a justification for being deadlier.

> She who faces Death by torture for each life beneath her breast;
> May not deal in doubt or pity – must not swerve for fact or jest.

But this is followed by the delimitation of her role in the world.

> She can bring no more to living than the powers that make her great
> As the Mother of the Infant and the Mistress of the Mate!

Women – and men – naturally objected to the bad taste, bad insight and bad psychology of the poem. Kipling laughed away their criticism and claimed that the work, although provocative, was 'based on the facts of human nature'.[44]

More bad psychology and even weaker observation inspired his views on the suffrage issue. He was concerned less with the suffragists' window-smashing antics than with the need to 'dive into the matter physiologically', to explain that the movement was largely supported by Britain's surplus women (one and a half million according to him) who did not 'care a curse for politics' but who were desperate for closer proximity to men; later that 'same surplus' would for the same reason 'agitate for admission into the Church and so on'.[45] Other views contradicted the theme of 'The Female of the Species'. Kipling told Gwynne that even limited female suffrage in Britain would endanger India and Egypt and indeed 'all the East', while to Mrs Humphry Ward, a leading anti-suffragist, he stressed how confidently Germany counted on England's 'feminism' in the coming conflict.[46] Yet if British women were really as deadly and as uncompromising as 'Himalayan she-bears' and Red Indian 'squaws', it is not clear how they would have jeopardized their country's defensive capability in the Empire and against Germany.

Nothing that happened in the decade before the First World War persuaded Kipling to reconsider his rejection of the principles of democracy. He still believed that 'the people' did not exist, that there were 'men and women and interests and communities' but no entity with monolithic feelings and desires. Although 'the people' were a delusion, the age required constant genuflection to the Baal of Demos. Yet far from being a tabernacle, democracy was just a 'crowd on the move', the sort of 'helpless thing' that 'overturns pleasure-boats by rushing from port to starboard'. It was a system that, as he had seen in India, encouraged incompetent men (that is, MPs from London) to overrule those well qualified (in other words, the ICS) to administer the country. The 'only serious enemy to the Empire, within or without, was that very Democracy' which depended on the Empire for its own comforts.[47]

After six years of Liberal rule Kipling fondly imagined that people were fed up with 'the people', sick and tired and above all bored with the whole charade of democracy. Now that Demos had revealed himself to be more powerful than kings or popes, mankind would sooner or later 'quietly push him aside' as it had done individual tyrants. By 1913 everyone was so 'fed up with being fed with silky words' that he believed Demos might get bored himself before achieving the country's destruction.[48]

In 'Regulus', a late Stalky story, a schoolmaster voices his creator's belief that democracy is 'eternally futile ... in all ages and climes'. But Kipling usually preferred to mock his enemy with satire. In 'Little Foxes' a high-minded but ignorant Liberal MP is humiliated when he tries to interfere with the administration of an African colony: 'he knows less than a buffalo', says Abdul, his interpreter, who describes 'Demah-kerazi' as 'a devil inhabiting crowds and assemblies'. A more ponderous satire, 'As Easy as A.B.C.', is placed in the year 2065, when war, nationalism, politics and democracy have all been abolished. Some people, nevertheless, hanker after the 'old Voodoo-business of voting with papers and wooden boxes', their crosses later 'counted with certain mystic ceremonies and oaths'. They wanted a kinder, nobler world 'based on the sanctity of the Crowd and the villainy of the single person'.

As usual, his political criticism was more effective in verse than in fiction, but curiously he chose to keep one remarkable poem private. In Sir Charles Oman's copy of *Puck of Pook's Hill* he inscribed 'The Coin Speaks', a set of verses dated June 1907 which makes the analogy that absorbed him, the similarity between contemporary Britain and the Roman Empire in decline, and then in lines of powerful frugality castigates democracy, Parliament and the Government's betrayal of South Africa and the armed forces.

Singers sing for coin: but I,
Struck in Rome's last agony,
Shut the lips of Melody.

Many years my thin white face
Peered in every market-place
At the Doomed Imperial Race.

Warmed against and worn between
Hearts uncleansed and hands unclean,
What is there I have not seen?

Not an Empire dazed and old,
Smitten blind and stricken cold,
Bartering her sons for gold;

Not the Plebs her rulers please
From the public treasuries
With the bread and circuses.

Not the hard-won fields restored,
At the egregious Senate's word,
To the savage and the sword;

Not the People's Godlike voice
As it welcomes or destroys
Months-old idols of its choice:

Not the legions they disband,
Not the oarless ships unmanned,
Not the ruin of the land,
These I know and understand.[49]

If the principle of democracy was wrong, worse was its practice and still more deplorable were its practitioners. MPs should not be paid; they should be manacled and marched round the world so that they might learn something about the Empire. Politics, remarks the narrator in 'The Village that Voted the Earth was Flat', was 'a dog's life without a dog's decencies'. And one could no more 'prevent a Liberal from lying', he told Gwynne in April 1912, than one could stop a dog lifting his leg against a lamp-post.[50] The Marconi Scandal, which emerged later in the year, provided some ammunition for the theory.

In March 1912 Godfrey Isaacs, the Managing Director of the

Marconi Company in Britain, negotiated a contract with Herbert Samuel, the Government's Postmaster-General, to erect a series of wireless stations round the Empire. The following month shares in the American Marconi Company were secretly bought by three Liberal ministers, Lloyd George, Alexander Murray (the Chief Whip) and Rufus Isaacs (the brother of Godfrey), who was the Attorney-General. Soon rumours were rumbling about insider trading and corruption over the Government contract: scurrilous articles appeared with exaggerated charges (the contract itself was above board) fuelled in certain cases by anti-semitism. But the ministers were not entirely innocent. In the Commons debate in October Isaacs successfully economized with the truth by denying he owned shares in 'that company' (that is, the British one), thereby giving the impression that he had no Marconi shares at all. He later refused to tell the Select Committee, appointed to investigate the matter, about his shares in the American company; and he only revealed them, in the course of a libel action against a French newspaper, when it became apparent that Leo Maxse had learned about the transaction.

The Liberal majority on the Select Committee overruled its own chairman and produced a highly partisan report that acquitted the ministers of any wrongdoing. Until then, the summer of 1913, Kipling had been silent, despite an overpowering belief in the men's guilt. Hilaire Belloc and Cecil Chesterton (G.K.'s brother) had worked hard to discredit the ministers; and *The Times* devoted six leaders to the issue in a single month. But Kipling contented himself, according to a neighbour, with following 'the fight with interest of such a kind that it almost precluded his thinking of anything else'. He spent a weekend with Strachey and admitted they talked of nothing except Marconi. The whole thing 'stank pretty much', especially when it was rumoured in July 1913 that Isaacs would become the next Lord Chief Justice.[51] This insensitive appointment, made in October, duly inspired 'Gehazi', one of the greatest of all hymns of hate.

The Select Committee's exoneration and the Opposition's feeble reaction infuriated Kipling, who accused the 'tomfool' Unionist Party of stupidity and incompetence. Churchill privately agreed that the Tories had let the ministers off lightly: 'Some of them were too stupid', he remarked, 'and, frankly, some of them were too nice.' Kipling did not believe in being nice in politics. Gwynne was

exhorted to fight about the chief justiceship and Aitken, who controlled the *Globe* (one of London's seven evening newspapers), was
urged to take his paper off the fence (which was 'very crowded
already') and become more 'bitter' and 'savage': only the *Morning Post*,
Kipling grumbled, had the 'courage to hammer at Murray and the
Marconis'.[52]

'Gehazi' was tentatively offered to Gwynne and refused to Aitken,
who wanted the verses in 'garbled form'. Kipling was nervous about
the possibility of libel, but he hoped that 'one day – please the Lord'
he could get it published.* The idea of Isaacs as Gehazi originated
with Arthur Steel-Maitland, the Chairman of the Unionist Party, and
the inspiration came from the Old Testament.[53] Elisha, a 'man of
God' from the Second Book of Kings, cures Naaman of leprosy but
refuses to accept the patient's proffered payment; Gehazi, Elisha's
servant, then runs after Naaman, pretending his master has changed
his mind so that he can embezzle the money himself; but Elisha, on
realizing what Gehazi has done, punishes his servant by transferring
Naaman's leprosy to him and his seed for ever.

> 'Whence comest thou, Gehazi,
>   So reverend to behold,
> In scarlet and in ermines
>   And chain of England's gold?'
> 'From following after Naaman
>   To tell him all is well,
> Whereby my zeal hath made me
>   A Judge in Israel.'
>
> Well done, well done, Gehazi,
>   Stretch forth thy ready hand,
> Thou barely 'scaped from judgment,
>   Take oath to judge the land,
> Unswayed by gift of money
>   Or privy bribe, more base,
> Of knowledge which is profit
>   In any market-place.

---

*It was not in fact published until 1919 in *The Years Between*, but in the meantime the
verses 'circulated'. Isaacs, who became Lord Reading in 1914, did not sue for libel.

Search out and probe, Gehazi,
　　As thou of all canst try,
The truthful, well-weighed answer
　　That tells the blacker lie –
The loud, uneasy virtue,
　　The anger feigned at will,
To overbear a witness
　　And make the Court keep still.

Take order now, Gehazi,
　　That no man talk aside
In secret with his judges
　　The while his case is tried.
Lest he should show them – reason
　　To keep a matter hid,
And subtly lead the questions
　　Away from what he did.

Thou mirror of uprightness,
　　What ails thee at thy vows?
What means the risen whiteness
　　Of the skin between thy brows?
The boils that shine and burrow,
　　The sores that slough and bleed –
The leprosy of Naaman
　　On thee and all thy seed?
　　　Stand up, stand up, Gehazi,
　　　　Draw close thy robe and go,
　　　Gehazi, Judge in Israel,
　　　　A leper white as snow!

The poem has often been condemned as evil and anti-semitic. It is neither. The Old Testament frequently inspired Kipling's moral teachings, and its characters were evoked not because they were Jewish but because, as in the case of Elisha and Gehazi, they could be used to illustrate Good and Evil. Kipling's judgement, if not his vitriol, was in any case partly justified by the circumstances. The ministers invested in a company that was bound to benefit from its sister company's contract with the Government; they intentionally deceived the House of Commons about this investment and only disclosed it under pressure a year later; and Isaacs did indeed 'talk aside / In secret with his judges', informing two Liberal MPs on the Select Committee about the American shares so that they could ward off awkward questions from the Tories. More reprehensibly still, the Chancellor of the Exchequer – of all public servants – had been surreptitiously gambling with shares in very dubious circumstances. Both ministers (Murray had by then resigned and fled to Bogotá) were lucky to survive.[54]

Part Four

Jeremiah's Laments

15

Egypt and Ulster

NATIONAL ISSUES ABSORBED Kipling's mind in the years preceding the First World War. At last he seemed weary of the Empire and disheartened by its prospects. The Victorian proconsuls had departed, leaving their realms to be mismanaged by inept successors and their Liberal masters, men, he considered, who had betrayed South Africa after Milner, pandered to Egyptian nationalists after the departure of Lord Cromer, and 'played ball' with India after Curzon by introducing some modest political concessions that seemed designed to alienate Muslims, Rajahs and the Indian Army.[1]

Even the dominions, even the beloved 'eldest daughter', were now letting him down. Laurier's Liberals had proposed a Canadian navy of eleven warships; Borden's Conservatives had aimed to trump this and present three Dreadnoughts to the Royal Navy. Yet fearful of public opinion, neither had done anything: on the eve of the World War Canada's navy consisted of two elderly British cruisers on opposite coasts of the world's second largest country. Kipling despaired. When he read, he told a Canadian friend, 'of grave fat men who have done nothing but make money all their lives, talking about paying "tribute to England" if they help build a battleship, I do not know whether to vomit or laugh'. There had never been an empire, he reflected, offering such 'opportunities to all men', and there had never been one 'whose people took less advantage of those opportunities'.[2]

Of course he remained watchful of international events that, even if not especially encouraging, might still teach useful lessons. The Ottomans' loss of nearly all their European possessions in the Balkan War of 1912–13 demonstrated how swiftly 'Allah puts an end to empires of which he is weary'. Turkish power in Europe had lasted 459 years and was defeated in nineteen days. 'There's a moral for some nation I know of. On that basis we'd get about five weeks.'[3]

One happier development, a project that Kipling both inspired and assisted, was the establishment of the Boy Scout Movement. Robert Baden-Powell, the cheery saviour of Mafeking, had returned from South Africa to develop his scheme to improve the physique and morale of working-class youths from the towns, thousands of whom had been found unfit to join the Army. In promoting his idea Baden-Powell asked and received Kipling's permission to use the memory game from *Kim* in *Scouting for Boys*, which he published in 1908. The following year he asked for an anthem, the sort of request that normally ended up in the wastepaper basket at Bateman's. But Kipling responded with the 'Boy Scouts' Patrol Song', each of the six verses enjoining the boys to 'look out' for dangers within and without. Its hortatory repetitions proved rather austere for the campfire, however, and Scouts preferred to recite some of the bard's lines from 'The Feet of the Young Men'.[4]

> Who hath smelt wood-smoke at twilight? Who hath heard the birch-log
> burning?
> Who is quick to read the noises of the night?
> Let him follow with the others, for the young men's feet are turning
> To the camps of proved desire and known delight!

Kipling was delighted by the success of the Scouts: their movement was 'the best thing for boys outside boarding schools that [had] ever been invented'. Baden-Powell, who repeatedly assured him that he was the spirit behind the whole project, regularly asked permission to quote from his work and regularly received it: Kipling even allowed him to rewrite (very badly) the *Jungle Books* for use as morality lessons for junior Scouts, the Wolf Cubs, who had to be deterred from becoming sneaks, cowards and other forms of the monkey-folk. In 1922 he attended a jamboree in the grounds of Alexandra

Palace where 20,000 Cubs gave what the *Manchester Guardian* estimated as 'probably the biggest howl in history' – chucking up their chins and screaming at the Prince of Wales, 'AKELA* – We-e-e-e-e-e'll do-o-o-o ou-u-u-r BEST.'[5]

At the beginning of 1913 the Kiplings travelled to Egypt, their only journey outside Europe between leaving South Africa in 1908 and visiting Algiers in 1921. It was meant to be a holiday of sun and ruins, but a visit to such a vital strategic point could hardly fail to arouse an imperialist's curiosity.[†] Nor could the 'Laureate of the Empire', unless well disguised, expect to avoid officials anxious to give him information about imperial issues.[6]

The encounter with the East, his first for over twenty years, tore at Kipling's emotions. On the voyage out he felt again the Anglo-Indian sense of exile, the reminder of homesickness and separations, the young man's realization that Port Said marked the line dividing home and familiarity from loneliness and the unknown. The bazaar smells of old Cairo awakened nostalgia for India of an intensity that he had not expected and with which he could barely cope. Egyptian garments, the call to prayer and the cadence of certain street-cries might differ a little from those of Lahore, yet he felt overwhelmed by similarities of aspect and smell and association. 'This', he noted, 'is my real world again.'[7]

Carrie and he chugged up the Nile past the statues of Rameses at Abu Simbel ('like a novel by Rider Haggard!' he told his children) and into the northern Sudan, which was ruled by an Anglo-Egyptian Condominium. As Egypt reminded him of India, so the Sudan left him pining for South Africa: meeting the train from Khartoum on a 'hot dust-smelling night' made him think of Salt River Junction; and sometimes the 'desert play[ed] at being Karoo', a trick 'disturbing to those whose heart [was] at the other end of the continent'. But he was much excited by being in that vast territory, administered by a

---

*Kipling's 'Head-wolf'. His creator instructed the Chief Wolf Cub Commissioner how to howl his name.

†Egypt was in theory a tributary state of the Ottoman Empire ruled by its Khedive. In reality it was a part of the British imperial system run by a Consul-General and civil servants with the support of a small army; Alexandria was one of the Royal Navy's most important bases. Theodore Roosevelt, pro-British again after the Alaska boundary dispute with Canada had been settled in America's favour in 1903, praised the 'great work for civilization' that Britain was doing in Egypt.

handful of officials from the Sudan Political Service, the closest relations in any continent to the ICS, men whose combination of athletic
prowess and university education earned the Sudan its sobriquet,
'the Land of Blacks ruled by Blues'. It was 'good for the soul', he
reported to Milner, to be in 'a land sanely and decently administered';
he felt as if his own soul 'had been washed with ammonia in the
bath'.[8]

Egypt and the Sudan provided lessons for readers at home and
also for Americans shouldering the white men's burden in the
Philippines. It was a 'glorious experience', he told Cameron Forbes,
the Governor in Manila, to see colonialists at work, to hear the 'old
talk again' and to observe the progress of the land. The Sudan, until
recently 'a hysteria of blood and fanaticism', had been pacified, and
its people were being led, 'kinder-garten fashion', towards the light.
The situation would not last, of course, because before long the
newly protected, newly prosperous, newly educated Africans would
forget the tyrannies of their previous oppressors and start agitating
for the extension of local government, 'Soudan for the Soudanese'
and so on until the whole cycle had to be 'retrodden'. Kipling had
seen the process in Egypt, what 'Western wine in Eastern bottles
[was] doing for the gippy', and he hoped it would not happen to the
Filipinos. 'My fear', he told their Governor, '(not that it's any of my
business but we're all white men together) is that some fool
Democratic spasm may land your people with a full-blooded
modern constitution ... May Allah preserve your land from this fate
and enable you to continue your works in peace. After all, a man only
wants to be left alone at his job.'[9]

Thirty years after he had advocated minimal Government interference with the customs and lives of Indians, Kipling preached the
same treatment for Egyptians. They should be preserved – as they
now were – from 'murder and mutilation, rape and robbery', but
otherwise allowed to live as they wished in their 'silent palm-shaded
villages' without 'Western Civilisation' barging in and insisting on
measures of social reform. Yet recently Kitchener, the current
Consul-General, had introduced just such a measure – an agrarian
law which, while intended to protect small farmers, effectively prevented them from borrowing money to improve their land. Kipling
did his research, spoke to officials and was duly incensed. Typically
he dispatched indignant letters to Gwynne and to Strachey, who

agreed that Kitchener had 'no more grasp of economic subjects than a babe unborn'.[10]

On their return to Cairo at the end of their holiday, the Kiplings went to tea with Kitchener and were vastly unimpressed by this 'fatted Pharaoh in spurs'. He had 'gone to seed awfully', Gwynne was informed, and 'seemed garrulously intoxicated with power'. Kipling found him arrogant, spiteful, minatory and untruthful, a figure who thought himself a 'second Ramses' but reminded his audience of 'a sort of nebulous Rhodes without grip or restraint'[11] – not an encouraging report of a man who the following year became War Secretary at the most critical juncture of his nation's history.

The Egyptian voyage was an interlude in a period during which Kipling's commitments to the Unionist Party and Ulster took precedence over his writing. In January 1913 a Canadian Liberal MP, angry at Kipling's interference in his country's affairs, mocked the 'hired versifier and Poet Laureate of the Unionist Party', thereby prompting his target to plot libel actions if the remark was quoted in a British newspaper.[12] Kipling resented with some reason the persistent attacks on his politics: Tory writers such as Swift and Johnson had held intemperate views without being subject to endless criticism. Yet at this time he was very closely connected with the Unionist Party, which he referred to as 'our party' and 'the more stupid of the two', consoling himself with the belief that people were 'getting weary of clever scallawags'.[13] He was a friend and an influential adviser of Bonar Law, Aitken and several of the leading Tory journalists. And he was so identified with their cause that various constituencies were eager to have him as their parliamentary candidate. In 1914 he turned down Bordesley on the grounds that Westminster was not his 'line of country', that he could be 'more useful outside the House of Commons than in', and that the party should be looking for a working-class candidate in that seat. Attempts by Steel-Maitland to enlist him for other places during the Great War were equally unsuccessful.[14]

Kipling was not a philosophic Tory. He was no Burke or Hume or Bolingbroke. Abstract ideas had minimal appeal for him; so did most theories and doctrines. Even his scepticism did not manage to provide a philosophical framework, as it had done with Salisbury and other Tory thinkers. Kipling's political ideas were innate, intuitive, passed on by Lockwood or formed by experience. He was an extremist in politics, but his hatred of 'isms' made him seldom doctrinaire. Tariff Reform was one of the few doctrines that inspired zealotry and intolerance. What was the sense, he demanded in 1909, of choosing Lord Robert Cecil as a parliamentary candidate? 'What earthly good is a rabid Free Trader among Unionists today?'[15]

Kipling's extremism was at its most evident over Ireland, a subject that convulsed him and his party for years. Introduced in the House of Commons in 1912, passed by a large majority but rejected by an even larger one in the Lords, the Home Rule Bill was a devolutionary measure proposing substantial domestic autonomy to a parliament in Dublin while reserving certain areas, notably defence and foreign affairs, to Westminster. The Unionists had accepted a similar principle when dealing with the dominions, but its application to Ireland drove some of them, including their leader and their versifier, to open sedition.*

Kipling admitted that ancestral prejudice might have influenced what he humorously called his 'fine impartial outlook on Ireland'. Certainly it did not prompt him to dissuade Fletcher from disclosing in their book that the Irish had spent seven hundred years stealing cows and killing each other, and would have carried on like this for another seven hundred 'if the English Government had not occasionally interfered'. In fact he later adopted this version of history as his own. He had hunted 'high and low,' he wrote in 1919, 'for any data that would present Ireland as a nation,' but he had 'never come across any more than records of small caterans killing cattle and destroying their neighbours, and ... writing most dreary poems about it all'.[16]

Direct observation reinforced the disparagement. The southern Irish, he told a correspondent in 1901, were 'the Orientals of the West'[17] – whatever that was meant to mean. A visit with Carrie ten years later began badly because Dublin had no taxis, 'only horse-drawn nuisances' which made the place smell of manure and stable blankets and 'took one back to the middle ages'. The whole city

---

*The Bill was passed three times in the House of Commons (January 1913, July 1913 and May 1914) and rejected twice by the House of Lords (January and July 1913). As the Parliament Act restricted the Lords' veto to two sessions, Home Rule would have been enacted in the normal course of events in September 1914. But at the beginning of the War it was suspended by the Government. Lloyd George passed a very different measure in 1921 after a ferocious campaign by the IRA.

(apart from the enclave of Trinity College) 'looked and smelt' like a debauched America and the countryside was no better. The Irish might not be able to 'spoil the green or the sombre superb autumn colouring' but they could depress him with their plantless, 'damnably inartistic' cottages and their 'personal aridity of culture'. Allah had evidently made them poets because he had 'deprived them of love of line or knowledge of colour'.[18]

It was a relief to drive into the North, a country of 'decent folk', where human talk and human appearances and even the 'roar and rush of Belfast' comforted him. The Celtic threat of 'constant mob violence' did not disturb him there.[19]

A month before their visit to Ulster, Sir Edward Carson, the leader of the Irish Unionist Party, had assured 50,000 supporters that with God's help they would defeat 'the most nefarious conspiracy' that had ever been hatched against a free people. Kipling endorsed the Orange cause without qualification: nothing, he insisted, could justify subjecting loyal Ulstermen to the rule of Dublin and the Pope. In April 1912, on the day that Bonar Law addressed 100,000 Ulstermen outside Belfast under what was reportedly the largest Union Jack ever made, Kipling's 'Ulster' appeared in the *Morning Post*, accompanied by a leader recommending its 'stirring lines' as a 'fitting expression to the feeling aroused by this attempted betrayal'. Prefaced by a quotation from Isaiah about 'works of iniquity', the poem was intended to deal 'a really hard blow' at Home Rule, whose consequences were, to him at least, already apparent.

> Rebellion, rapine, hate,
> Oppression, wrong and greed
> Are loosed to rule our fate,
> By England's act and deed.

Disinterested readers might have pencilled a few question marks in the margins of Gwynne's paper. Where was the rapine to be found in granting autonomy to Dublin? If anyone was in rebellion, was it not perhaps the Ulster Protestant community now commencing an interminable epoch of drilling and marching?

> The blood our fathers spilt,
> Our love, our toils, our pains,
> Are counted us for guilt,

And only bind our chains.
Before an Empire's eyes
The traitor claims his price.
What need of further lies?
We are the sacrifice.

The pencil here might have queried the idea that John Redmond, the moderate, rather Anglophile leader of the Irish nationalists, could be regarded as a traitor for desiring the kind of autonomy that Gladstone had proposed many years earlier and which the dominions had long since acquired.

We know the war prepared
On every peaceful home,
We know the hells declared
For such as serve not Rome –
The terror, threats, and dread
In market, hearth, and field –
We know, when all is said,
We perish if we yield.

Here again a reader might have wondered whether the Irish Cardinal Logue, despite his denunciation of Parnell in 1890, was really a sort of Torquemada intent on persecuting non-Catholics.[20]

While the verses were quoted with approval by Carson and other speakers in Belfast, they understandably gave offence elsewhere. One outraged Liberal MP, Joseph Martin, asked the Attorney-General (Rufus Isaacs) to prosecute Kipling for sedition, but the future Gehazi declined to do so. In response to Martin, the poet suggested to Aitken that Unionist MPs should recite lines from his poem to disrupt the Government in the Commons. 'What need of further lies? / We are the sacrifice' could be chanted at ministers while, if Redmond intervened, he should be greeted with, 'Before an empire's eyes / The traitor claims his price.'[21] Yet even MPs on his own side were affronted by the poem: Mark Sykes condemned it in the *Morning Post* as 'a direct appeal to ignorance and a deliberate attempt to foster religious hatred'.[22]

A few months later Bonar Law, the Leader of the Opposition, publicly embraced sedition by declaring to a large audience in the grounds of Blenheim Palace that he could 'imagine no length of resistance' to which the people of Ulster would go, in which he would not be ready to support them. Shortly afterwards, at Belfast Town Hall, a quarter of a million Ulstermen signed a Solemn League and Covenant to resist Home Rule.

The gathering rebellion in Ulster in 1913 gave Kipling hope – and not just for Ireland. This was not merely a skirmish among politicians but the 'first move in the revolt of the English', the 'beginning of the counter-revolution' against the Liberal radicals and everything they had achieved since 1906.[23] At the end of the year he told Gwynne that

> if a thorough and unscrupulous and determined opposition ... to Home rule is put up *now* there is just a chance that we may pull through. If it isn't, if there is any compromise on any point, we lose the game ...
>
> If by any means the present Government can be visibly shown that Home Rule is more dangerous to their own hides and positions than leaving it alone would be, they will leave it alone. But if we give them cause to think (and I admit our past record is against us) that we shall be turned aside by considerations of 'loyalty', 'the Empire' and so forth then we and the empire are lost. It's a naked trial of strength that is forced on us and all the talking in the world won't make it anything else. For goodness sake stick to that line, old man. If we fight we may win. If we don't fight we *must* lose.[24]

This was stronger than anything his parliamentary leaders were saying privately. Carson and Bonar Law were already groping towards a compromise over Ulster, a four-county, six-county or possibly even nine-county exclusion from Home Rule. But Kipling rejected partition as a betrayal of the South just as a united Ireland would be a betrayal of Ulster. He even convinced himself that a betrayed Ulster would look to Germany for support just as in 1690 it had relied on a Dutch king for survival: '*an Ulster or an Ireland handed over to the Celt means an appeal for outside intervention* as in 1688'. Home Rule 'in *any* shape', he told Milner, would mean Teuton intervention, 'a change of dynasty' and '1688 or 1066 over again'.[25]

Milner was a sympathetic audience for such deranged thinking. Ulster had brought him back into politics, and he was touring England making speeches for the cause. In March 1914 he helped organize a 'British Covenant', published in *The Times* and signed by, among others, Kipling, Roberts, Elgar and himself. These distinguished signatories duly joined the ranks of the seditious by declaring that, if Home Rule became law without endorsement at a general election or in a referendum, they would feel 'justified in taking or supporting any action that may be effective to prevent the armed forces of the Crown from being used to deprive the people of Ulster of their rights as citizens of the United Kingdom'.[26]

A week later Asquith suggested that Ulster might opt out of Home Rule for six years, a futile compromise that Carson defined as 'sentence of death with a stay of execution'. The proposal made Kipling happy because he knew it was too absurd for Ulster to accept. Still adamantly opposed to any kind of compromise, he insisted that the choice was only between civil war and a complete surrender by the Government. The repeated references to 'civil war' in his correspondence in the spring of 1914 suggest that he relished the prospect.[27]

Kipling's eagerness for confrontation was stimulated by reports of the well-drilled Ulster Volunteer Force, recently recruited and now, thanks to a brilliant gun-running operation in April, well armed as well. Some time earlier, when requested to write songs for Irish Unionists, he had replied that they 'needed drilling a damned sight more than doggerel'. But now they had both. Although he had not actually seen the volunteers, he was convinced they were a fine body of men, 'perhaps the only efficient *manhood* army we have in England now'.[28] In May he wrote a sonnet for the *Covenanter*, the journal of the League of British Covenanters, which carried the defiant motto, 'Put your trust in God and keep your powder dry'. The same month he went to Tunbridge Wells and, to an audience of 10,000 people, made the most fanatical speech of his life.

Kipling's oratorical thesis was based on the premiss that the Government's policies were directed not by conviction or idealism but simply by corruption. The Liberals had passed the Parliament Bill so that their ministers could stay in power and enjoy their salaries; they had decided to pay MPs so that their followers would not be tempted to revolt and jeopardize those salaries; and they had passed Home Rule as a bribe to Irish MPs to support them in Parliament and thus allow them to keep their salaries for several years to come. Members of the Cabinet were 'outlaws', 'conspirators' who had 'met to arrange the massacre of decent citizens ... men who would bombard an open town of loyal subjects sooner than risk the loss of thirteen guineas a day while they ask the electors for leave to kill'.

The iniquities of the Government were matched by the evils inherent in Irish nationalism.

> The Home Rule Bill broke the pledged faith of generations; it officially recognised sedition ... conspiracy and rebellion; it subsidised the secret forces of boycott, intimidation, outrage and murder.

And at the heart of the issue was the primordial matter of betrayal.

> A province and a people of Great Britain are to be sold to their and our enemies. We are forbidden to have any voice in this sale of our own flesh and blood; we have no tribunal under Heaven to appeal to except the corrupt parties to that sale and their paid followers.

But the betrayal would not go unanswered.

> Ulster, and as much of Ireland as dares to express itself, wishes to remain within the Union and under the Flag of the Union. The Cabinet, for reasons which I have given, intend to drive them out. The electors of Great Britain have never sanctioned this ... Civil War is inevitable unless our rulers can be brought to realise that, even now, they must submit these grave matters to the judgement of a free people. If they do not, all the history of our island shows that there is but one end – destruction from within or without.[29]

Kipling's concentration was not broken by the death of Joseph Chamberlain on 2 July or the assassination of a Habsburg archduke four days earlier at Sarajevo: the old hero had been incapacitated since 1906, and the Balkans were always giving trouble. 'Hard' though it was to 'have to envisage civil war in one's declining years,' Kipling was doing so and preparing for it 'in all sorts of directions – legal and illegal chiefly the latter'. So was Carrie, busy assembling stocks of clothing for the Ulster refugees who would be flocking across the Irish Sea 'when civil war comes'.[30]

16

Armageddon

<hr>

IN HER DIARY entry of 4 August 1914 Carrie recorded that she had a cold. Her husband added laconically, 'Incidentally Armageddon begins. England declares war on Germany.'[1]

The civil war Kipling had been predicting for two years had not come. But the wider conflict, which he had been prophesying for a generation, had finally arrived. In 1902 he had published 'The Captive' in which a general refers to the Boer War as 'a first-class dress-parade for Armageddon'. Ten years later he told Max Aitken's constituents that Britain was living 'under the very shadow of Armageddon', for which it was 'utterly unprepared'.[2] And now the shadow had acquired substance in the shape of the 'Furor Teutonicus' tramping through Belgium.

Kipling and his family were staying on the East Anglian coast in a house belonging to Rider Haggard. After suspecting that the Liberals would 'wriggle out of the mess', he was relieved to learn that they had for once done the right thing and declared war. But he did not rush home. Rather than add to the confusion by 'lugging' his family about when the railways were needed for troops, he remained for a few days in Norfolk watching warships patrolling the coast.

On returning to Sussex his first priority was to arrange a commission for his son, who was not quite 17. John had been destined for the Navy from the age of 6 when he swaggered about wearing a plaited lanyard. Ten years later he opted for the Army but failed a physical examination because he had inherited his father's bad eyesight. Kipling, who had hoped that his son might fool the examiners by wearing pince-nez rather than glasses, took him for another examination at the outbreak of the war, but the result was the same. Insisting that the Army was being pedantic, he then approached the aged Lord Roberts, who obliged him by obtaining a commission for John in the Irish Guards.[3] In September the boy joined his battalion and began training at Warley Barracks in Essex. For the next year his parents watched his progress proudly, stoically and with understandable anxiety.

Kipling was soon busy. He made speeches; he encouraged the village rifle club; he urged Curzon, the Chancellor of Oxford, to close down the university and give its undergraduates military training.[4] During the autumn he visited Indian and Canadian troops as well as British bases in southern England before writing a series of articles for the *Daily Telegraph* called 'The New Army in Training'. In a speech at Brighton he urged enlistment so as to 'check the onrush of organised barbarism' and prevent 'the lights of freedom' from being extinguished throughout the world. At the Mansion House in London he pleaded that battalions should have musical bands as an aid to recruitment and an encouragement of morale. Despite the huge numbers of young men flocking to enlist, the issue of compulsory service continued to irk him, especially when he witnessed how the voluntary system allowed the 'shirkers' or 'black sheep' to enjoy a 'good time with the other fellows' jobs and the other fellows' girls'.[5]

Germany's invasion of Belgium, whose neutrality had been guaranteed by Britain, France and Prussia in 1839, was for Kipling the inevitable culmination of a process that the Kaiser had begun two decades earlier by congratulating Kruger on the outcome of the Jameson Raid: it was what Wilhelm had always wanted and what he and his generals had long planned. But Kipling was not a scholar of political nuance or complexity of motive. In fact the Kaiser, a less resolute figure than his critic believed, did not want a war at that moment and begged the Tsar of Russia not to mobilize his forces after Austria-Hungary declared war on Serbia. The Tsar was also anxious to avoid a conflict, as were the Austrian Emperor and the Sultan of Turkey. Indeed the war was not desired by any of the leaders of the empires that were destined to disappear. All of them were pushed into it by their generals and ministers.

Kipling's war predictions were as accurate as anyone's. In the early months he forecast that the struggle would last three years and would not end until Germany had suffered about five million casualties; in fact it lasted four years, by which time Germany had lost six million dead and wounded. Even earlier, less than three days after the war began, he had prophesied that the aggressors would make a 'ghastly "example"' of Belgian civilians. As the invasion swept across Belgium, a progress absurdly depicted by H.G.Wells as 'flagwagging Teutonic Kiplingism', the massacres unfolded: 384 civilians shot and bayoneted in the town square of Tamines, 612 killed at Dinant, 209 murdered and 42,000 expelled from the university town of Louvain. To his correspondents, especially in America, Kipling may have repeated some exaggerated stories of terror but he did not magnify the scale of the atrocities. Germany, he told his American publisher, was running the war 'without the faintest regard for any law human or divine'.[6]

Rage and grief soon harshened his language. There was 'no crime', he told a meeting at Southport in 1915, 'no cruelty, no abomination that the mind of man can conceive, which the German has not perpetrated, is not perpetrating, and will not perpetrate if he is allowed to go on'. There were now 'only two divisions in the world . . . human beings and Germans' – and the former desired 'nothing more than that this unclean thing should be thrust out from the membership and the memory of the nations'. Dehumanization had begun. Huns and Teutons were at least people, but from now on 'the German' was often neutered (referred to as 'it'), transformed into a wild beast or represented as 'Evil Incarnate'.[7]

The rape of Belgium galvanized Kipling's political verse-making. The enemy, he told his readers, had long been preparing their 'arsenals of death'.

> Through learned and laborious years
> They set themselves to find
> Fresh terrors and undreamed-of fears
> To heap upon mankind.

('The Outlaws')

There could be only one response to this 'crazed and driven foe'. On 1 September 1914, as the British Expeditionary Force was forced to retreat from Mons, *The Times* published 'For All We Have and Are'.

For all we have and are,
For all our children's fate,
Stand up and take the war,
The Hun is at the gate!
Our world has passed away,
In wantonness o'erthrown.
There is nothing left to-day
But steel and fire and stone . . .

. . . No easy hope or lies
Shall bring us to our goal,
But iron sacrifice
Of body, will, and soul.
There is but one task for all –
One life for each to give.
Who stands if freedom fall?
Who dies if England live?

The chief target of the poem is not 'the Hun . . . at the gate' but the politicians who have allowed him to get there and kill British lads. The Tommies and their officers fought well at the Mons-Condé Canal and at the First Battle of Ypres in the autumn. They had even learned some tactical lessons from the Boer War, though these were mysteriously unlearned by 1916 when General Haig sent 20,000 soldiers almost elbow to elbow to their deaths on the first morning of the Somme. But even in 1914 the casualties were enormous. As Kipling reported in October, all the young men whom Elsie had danced with during the 'Season' were now dead or wounded. They and their troops had been 'sacrificed almost to a man' to give Britain time to build proper armies. The 'wantonness' of the politicians, their neglect of Britain's defences, had made it 'necessary to throw up a barricade of the dead bodies of the nation's youth behind which the most elementary preparations could be begun'.[8] The theme continued to permeate his war poetry, most trenchantly in his 'Epitaphs of the War' ('If any question why we died, / Tell them, because our fathers lied'), and most harrowingly in 'The Children'.

That flesh we had nursed from the first in all cleanness was given
To corruption unveiled and assailed by the malice of Heaven –
By the heart-shaking jests of Decay where it lolled on the wires –

To be blanched or gay-painted by fumes – to be cindered by fires –
To be senselessly tossed and retossed in stale mutilation
From crater to crater. For this we shall take expiation.
But who shall return us our children?

In November Lord Roberts died, mourned by the Unionist press as 'the man whose warning the nation did not heed'. Kipling dedicated a third poem to his old friend – which placed him as subject matter on a par with Rhodes (though one of the poems was unpublished) and Lord Ripon (though each was derogatory). The verses inevitably eulogized the 'war-wise face' that 'pleaded and was not heard!' Kipling did not relish the role of the 'I told you so!' but he was justified in making the point. If Britain, as Theodore Roosevelt informed him, had built up its Army to something approaching Continental levels, there might have been no war. Yet an increase in the size of the Army, however desirable it may have been, was a political impossibility during the Edwardian years – for the Unionists as well as for the Liberals. A more coherent policy, however, a more definite political attitude in the summer of 1914, might have averted the conflict. If the Government had made it clear sooner that it would fight with France, if it had given Germany the clarification of position Berlin requested at the end of July, then perhaps the Kaiser and his Chancellor might have been able to resist their bellicose military leaders, Moltke and Falkenhayn.

One of the principal duties Kipling assigned to himself was the instruction of America on the nature of the conflict. His feelings for the United States remained consistently ambivalent. He continued to believe that it was fundamentally uncivilized and he had got hold of the theory, developed in his story 'The Edge of the Evening', that the real America had been killed by Lincoln 'from the highest motives' and its survivors swamped by so many immigrants that the country now possessed (in the words of one of his characters) 'a Government of the alien, by the alien, for the alien'. But he could still be enthused by the ideal of sharing the White Man's Burden. His friendship with Forbes, the Governor of the Philippines, convinced him that imperialism was flourishing in the Pacific, and he even hoped America might 'take hold' of Mexico and administer it *more asiatico* – as the British ruled India.[9]

He was disillusioned again by America's decision to make 'no sign' while the 'Hell-dance' in Europe went on in September 1914. Woodrow Wilson, who combined a devotion to the poem 'If'* with an ambition to be the American Gladstone, proclaimed neutrality and urged Americans to be neutral in thought as well as in deed – an arrogant and almost totalitarian instruction that implied no moral difference between the combatants. The British, Kipling told Roosevelt, were 'aghast at there being no protest from the US against the Belgian dealings'. Even neutrality should not preclude a condemnation of the horrors of 'Louvainism'.[12]

Kipling understood the value of propaganda, suggesting to Gwynne that the *Morning Post* 'might hint' that the Germans were 'not respecting the honour of American women' in Europe. He was not sure this was true (though he had a 'pretty strong notion' it was), but it was the 'one thing that fetches the US out of its boots'.[13] Yet the points in his enormous American correspondence were usually more solid. Conceding with reluctance that there was little to be done for the moment about neutrality, he urged Americans to build up their armed forces for a possible future role. If, as he warned

---

*In 1920 Wilson told the American journalist Edward Bok that he had 'derived constant inspiration' from 'If' and had 'often consciously tried to live up to its standards'. He frequently used its phrases in his speeches and, after one political setback, declared, 'I fight on, in the spirit of Kipling's "If"'. Although he also quoted from other poems and compared the American Constitution to the mechanical parts in 'The Ship that Found Herself', 'If' was his favourite work. According to a close ally, a newspaper clipping of the poem was one of Wilson's 'treasured possessions', and in 1920 the retiring President was so delighted when a friend gave him a facsimile of the text in Kipling's handwriting that he planned to invite the author to a housewarming party for his new mansion outside Washington.[10] Ironically, the poem seems to have fortified the prim and schoolmasterly self-righteousness that Kipling so deplored in the American leader.

'If' has had a much greater effect on soul-searching and self-improvement than any of Kipling's other poems. The Spanish fascist leader, José Antonio Primo de Rivera, hung a copy on the wall of his office, while the Duke of Alba kept one in a gold frame by his bedside in Madrid. The King of Siam, 'a very great admirer', told Somerset Maugham he had been moved to translate it into Thai, and 'a devil of a job he found it ... to get the rhythm and metre to his satisfaction'. Mr T.A.Brocklebank put a tiny copy of the poem into his watch while attempting to climb Mount Everest, but unfortunately in a high wind the 'watch sprang open and the ms flew away'. More relevant to this chapter, a Canadian soldier at the Front was so moved to hear the poem sung to the music of Chopin that he gave up drinking and gambling; and Australian officers were presented with a copy by General Sir Henry 'Rawly' Rawlinson and told to learn it and think it over.[11]

Roosevelt, the Germans won and dominated the Eastern Hemisphere, the United States with 'its present fleet and no army'* would be unable to prevent their seizure of the Western Hemisphere as well, and the Monroe Doctrine would become 'a scrap of paper not worth tearing up'. Self-interest alone dictated armament. The Allies were 'shedding their blood ... for every ideal' that the United States stood for; and if they lost, America would have to 'conform to the conqueror's ideals'.[14]

If Roosevelt had still been in power, the history of the war might have been different. Yet by standing as an independent in 1912 and splitting the Republican vote, he had let Wilson into the White House, and his influence was much reduced. He proposed enlarging the armed forces and interfering on behalf of Belgium, but he 'purposely abstained' from specifying the form such interference should take. As he explained to Kipling, there was no point advocating everything he believed in because it would do 'no good among our people'. Americans were so shortsighted that they did 'not understand international matters'. Nor did the man supervising them, Secretary of State William Jennings Bryan, a three-time loser in presidential elections whom Roosevelt unfairly regarded as 'the most ridiculous creature that we have ever had in a high public office in this country'. As for Wilson, he was a 'scholarly arid pacifist of much ability and few scruples' and – a detail which Kipling relished because it seemed to explain the President's behaviour – he came from a Virginian family 'none of whose members fought on either side of the Civil War'.[15]

In the autumn of 1914 Kipling sent many thousands of words across the Atlantic to a variety of influential people. The messages were always the same yet nearly always distinctively expressed: that the Allies were fighting for America's ideals, that if they lost the United States was 'next in the firing line', that 'for her conscience's sake, for the sake of her record in history and her position as the one untouched civilised power', America must take a moral stand on the German atrocities. He only became angry if his horror stories were doubted. 'Any people,' he told Bok, that could pass 'over in official silence the horrors in Belgium', must – if it were to 'continue to live

---

*When America entered the war in April 1917, its army consisted of 130,000 officers and men. By August of the following year over a million American soldiers were in Europe.

with itself' – believe that those horrors were exaggerated or even fictitious.[16] He had visited Belgian refugees, rape victims and wounded soldiers in the makeshift hospitals of southern England – and he *knew* they were true. Carrie reported one example in a letter to her mother.

> Rud tries to see as often as he can a poor young Belgian refugee who was a teacher at Liège ... Such a charming young fellow who they fear will go crazy. He saw the Germans cut the throat of his father and mother and sister of 12 after they had raped the latter and he cannot be got to close his eyes because he says then he can see it all again.[17]

It is impossible to estimate the effect of Kipling's transatlantic letters, to measure how much they persuaded, energized, irritated or were ignored. We know that some of the correspondence was shown to Woodrow Wilson,[18] but we cannot tell if it had any effect, subliminal or otherwise, on presidential policy. Perhaps the 'arid pacifist' finally decided to go to war after reciting 'If' at his shaving mirror.

Kipling's pen was much in demand in Britain partly because he had a well-deserved reputation for finding the right word to express the right sentiment, and partly because he had been proved right about the aggressiveness of Germany and the inadequate size of the Army. Much of the demand went unsatisfied. It was pointless going to GHQ to write a book about the Battle of Ypres based on the evidence of generals; it was equally pointless, so he thought early in 1915, to travel to the Front as a war correspondent when one was 'not allowed to say anything that matters'.[19] Later in the struggle he rejected an idea of Milner's to 'run round the whole of the Eastern theatres of war ... with a look-in in Arabia' and write a morale-inspiring account. Suggestions from people he disliked were also ignored or turned down: Churchill's hope that he would write a series of articles on the supply of munitions; the proposal from Godfrey Isaacs that he should record the 'heroism and endeavours' of wireless operators during the war; and the request from Downing Street, when Lloyd George was Prime Minister, that he describe 'the heroic deeds' of the Serbian Army – despite the fact that he had never been to Serbia and knew nothing about the country.[20] When Aitken became Minister of Information in 1918 he offered his friend an official post.* Kipling predictably refused though he gave plenty of advice.

But he did accept certain assignments even though their purpose was propagandist and the source material was necessarily restricted. He wrote three series of articles on the French Army, the Italian Army and the Indian soldiers on the Western Front, each intended to show how well they were all doing. He also compiled a good number of articles on the Navy, including a series on the Battle of Jutland, which he based on official dispatches at the Admiralty. He justified the exercise on the grounds that, by contrast with Serbia, he had lengthy first-hand knowledge of the subject.[21]

In August 1915 he changed his mind about being a war correspondent and went to the Front with Perceval Landon, a journalist friend from the Boer War who had taken a cottage at Bateman's. At least on his French travels he did not have to make a distinction between public and private thoughts. He could tell readers of the *Daily Telegraph* how the 'exquisite quality of the French soul' was a 'marvel' to him; but he could also rave to his friends and his family about the excellence of the French Army and the 'glorious spirit of France'. It was as stimulating to see Clemenceau, 'that amazing human explosive', in Paris, as it was to be in a trench a few yards from 'the Boche' among the hills of Alsace.[22] To his son, whose battalion had just arrived in France, he sent some dubious advice for the trenches: 'Don't forget the beauty of rabbit netting overhead against hand grenades. Even tennis netting is better than nothing.' John found the tip 'rather quaint' and, after it had been repeated several times, pointed out that there was a standing order never to place anything on top of a trench, even rabbit wires: 'If the Bosch comes, he has you like rabbits underneath it.' Somewhat tactlessly he added that, while his father had only been allowed to see specimen trenches, his CO had a great deal of experience and 'what he doesn't know about the game isn't worth knowing'.[23]

At the beginning of September the British Expeditionary Force went on to the offensive in Artois and was defeated at the Battle of Loos. To the Germans' astonishment, massed infantry advanced towards them as if on parade and were cut down in their thousands

---

*Aitken was now Lord Beaverbrook. Lloyd George had ennobled him in December 1916, to the mystification of many people, including a querulous George V.

by machine guns: the slaughter was so great that the defenders refrained from firing at the retreating survivors.[24] Before the next dawn the Second Battalion of the Irish Guards joined the attack and in Kipling's words 'lost seven of their officers in forty minutes'. Some years later, after assessing the evidence as the regimental historian, he wondered why an inexperienced battalion, which had not slept and had hardly eaten for forty-eight hours, had been sent across terrain packed with machine guns after a mere ninety-minute bombardment.[25]

Loos was Second Lieutenant Kipling's first and only battle. He was reported to have been wounded at 'Chalk Pit Wood' late in the afternoon and to have crawled into a building subsequently occupied by German soldiers. His father, displaying 'splendid pluck' according to Gwynne, clung to the official verdict, 'wounded and missing', and was furious when the *Morning Post* reported John as 'missing, believed killed'. Hoping that his wounded son might have been captured and was now in a German hospital or prison camp, he asked American diplomats to help trace him. By November he admitted he was probably dead, 'wiped out by shellfire', but since there was no corpse or definite evidence of death, he and Carrie continued to hope he was alive in Germany.[26]*

The Kiplings had never had illusions about their son's chances of survival. Asked the previous summer how they had the courage to send John away to fight, Carrie had replied that

> one can't let one's friends' and neighbours' sons be killed in order to save us and our son. There is no chance John will survive unless he is so maimed from a wound as to be unfit to fight. We know it and he does. We all know it, but we all must give and do what we can and live on the shadow of a hope that our boy will be the one to escape.[28]

She and Rudyard were proud of their son. He had been a hardworking subaltern at Warley and had gone off to the war, days after his eighteenth birthday, looking (as his mother recorded) 'very straight and smart and brave and young'. In his solitary action he was

---

*Since his body was not found, John Kipling's name appeared on the memorial to the missing at Loos. In 1992 the Commonwealth War Graves Commission claimed to have found his grave and had his name carved on the headstone. Recent research, however, suggests that the grave may belong to another officer of the Irish Guards.[27]

reported to have shown courage and verve. It had been a short life, his father wrote to Dunsterville, now commanding a brigade on the North-West Frontier. 'I'm sorry that all the years' work ended in that one afternoon but – lots of people are in our position and it's something to have bred a man.'[29] As in the case of Josephine, Kipling did not mention his child's death in his autobiography. But he commemorated him in 'A Nativity', a poem interpolating the birth and death of Christ with the despair of a grieving mother who knows not where her son 'is laid'.

> '*My* child died in the dark.
>   Is it well with the child, is it well?
> There was none to tend him or mark,
>   And I know not how he fell.'

And in 'My Boy Jack' he added a pathetic note of pride to the feelings of desolation.

> 'Have you any news of my boy Jack?'
>   *Not this tide.*
> 'When d'you think that he'll come back?'
>   *Not with this wind blowing, and this tide . . .*
>
> 'Oh, dear, what comfort can I find?'
>   *None this tide,*
>   *Nor any tide,*
> *Except he did not shame his kind –*
>   *Not even with that wind blowing, and that tide.*

John Kipling did not shame his kind.

Kipling tried to keep his spirits afloat with the thought of the nation united against Evil. Sometimes he even believed 'a better and more brotherly world' would be the outcome of the conflict. But his own feelings of brotherliness did not extend to politicians. 'There is *nothing* lower', he wrote, 'than an English politician in peace – except the same animal in war.'[30]

Predictably he believed that Asquith was even more drunk and incompetent as a war leader than he had been in peacetime. When

King George, a modest drinker, set an example by giving up alcohol for the duration of the war, Kipling wished the Prime Minister would try 'signing the pledge for three days'.[31] In May 1915 Asquith formed a Coalition Government with the Unionists but he became no more palatable to many of his erstwhile opponents. Both Law and Aitken assisted in his removal in December the following year and his replacement by Lloyd George. But Kipling approved the removal rather than the substitution: for him no Liberal was better than another, and Lloyd George was the most obnoxious of all. His view of the new Prime Minister scarcely brightened at the moment of victory – and it certainly dimmed soon afterwards. He never regarded him as the man who got the guns made or the man who beat the Germans. In August 1918 he grudgingly admitted he was 'the best we have for the purpose' but, 'at a time when a Lincoln' was needed, Britain was saddled with a liar who couldn't 'get out of his own immoral skin'. Lloyd George's mendacity as a politician was as transparent as colour blindness in an artist or an engine driver.[32]

Leo Maxse, the Editor of the *National Review,* had followed up his 'Balfour Must Go' with 'Haldane Must Go', a campaign that Kipling thoroughly approved of. As Lord Chancellor, Haldane was hardly a vital target in wartime, but the public hysteria that encompassed all things German naturally pursued the man who had called Germany his spiritual home. Blumenfeld understandably did not share the paranoia about German names – his father came from Nuremberg – but his *Express* joined the *Morning Post* and the *National Review* in demanding an end to the 'Haldane fetish'. The former War Secretary was discarded in cowardly manner by Asquith at the formation of the Coalition, but retirement did not spare him from Kipling's attempts at persecution through his cronies in the press. The following February Gwynne was scolded by his mentor for 'neglecting Haldane again' with the 'inevitable result' that the former minister was allegedly going around appointing 'reconcilers' with Germany to 'high places' in the Church. Unless the *Morning Post* kept Haldane 'in a funk, he [would] begin to do evil'.[33]

Later in the year Blumenfeld received the latest of Kipling's suggestions for the enlargement of journalism's vocabulary: 'Boschialist' and 'Hunnomite'. The former was a 'Socialist with Hun leanings' while the latter was a 'lower grade' of the same species. 'Hunnomite' was a 'beautiful word' with the advantage that it 'verges on the obscene'. Lord Haldane was 'indubitably a Hunnomite'.[34]*

Kipling visited munitions works in Wales and the North where he was impressed by the vast new factories and the quantity of weapons they were producing. But he declined to acknowledge that their success had any connection with the fact that Lloyd George was in charge of them for a crucial period in the middle of the war. Contemptuous of politicians, and secretly suspecting that the generals were another set of bungling Bullers, he put his trust in the British spirit.

Clichés about the British character were reinforced and expanded by Kipling's pen. The English were too polite; they did not know how to hate; they were useless when they were winning because they thought it was their duty to be conciliatory. Yet so long as the current 'grumbling and ostentatious pessimism' went on, things were all right. At the beginning of the war he prophesied that, since Germany was devoting itself to the 'cult of making hatred', even the English would learn how to hate. A year later he told his old friend Mrs Hill that, although it was not 'in the English nature to hate after the Prussian manner', his countrymen were now 'a little annoyed'. Another year on and the 'slow learners' had discarded their annoyance in favour of a deeper emotion. The Hun had 'taken two years to teach the English how to hate, which is a thing we have never done before, and it will take us two generations to stop'.[36] Kipling articulated the mood in a mediocre poem ('The Beginnings' with its refrain, 'When the English began to hate') accompanying 'Mary Postgate', a brilliant and chilling story in which the eponymous lady seems to refuse help to a dying German airman and – in a highly audacious piece of writing – gives herself an orgasm by leaning on a poker while he dies.

By now, apparently, the British had learned to hate so much that they wanted Germany to be destroyed and 'very little Hun left' at the end of the war. But by the autumn of 1916 hatred itself was redun-

---

*Later in the war Kipling offered Blumenfeld 'Bolshewhiggery' as a 'useful word for popularization' and in 1933 he suggested that the cartoonist of the *Morning Post* should refer to the National Government as the 'Socional' Government.[35] Kipling bequeathed as many phrases to the English language as any man since Shakespeare, but mercifully they do not include his political terms.

dant. After all one could only hate *people*, and the Hun was now 'outside any humanity': he had become like 'the germs of a malignant disease'.[37]

Kipling's optimism about the war's outcome was based on historical parallels and the indomitability of the British spirit. Napoleon had won 'all the victories [*sic*]' but had ended up on St Helena; Germany was winning all the battles, but the Allies would win the war. The 'solidarity of common effort and the spirit of calculated and implacable resolve' would see Britain through.[38]

It was not easy to find grounds for optimism in 1916 or in 1917, especially on the Western Front. In his *History of the Irish Guards*, written after the war, Kipling was 'scrupulous', as he put it, 'to avoid debatable issues of bad staff-work or faulty generalship'. But his criticisms are powerful even in their understated language. The Battle of Neuve Chapelle in March 1915, he wrote, 'proved' that 'unless artillery utterly root out barbed-wire trenches, machine-gun posts and fortified houses, no valour of attacking infantry can pierce a modern defensive line'. But it did not prove this to Sir John French or Sir Douglas Haig. Nor did Loos, John Kipling's battle in the autumn, which proved to the temporary historian that 'direct Infantry attacks, after ninety-minute bombardments, on works begotten out of a generation of thought and prevision, scientifically built up by immense labour and applied science, and developed against all contingencies through nine months, are not likely to find a fortunate issue'.[39] The same unsubtle tactics, the same straight, upright lines of infantrymen advancing shoulder to shoulder against machine guns and barbed wire, were used the next year at the Somme and cost Britain 420,000 casualties, the greatest carnage in the nation's history. At the Third Battle of Ypres in 1917 (the second greatest carnage) Haig decided to use them again and to go on doing so in the Flanders mud until another 240,000 dead and wounded had 'proved' they were still not working.

The strengthening of imperial ties was a by-product of the war, and Kipling was delighted to observe 'rivalries' between the dominions 'washed out in blood'. At the end of 1917 the new Lord Beaverbrook asked him to intervene once again in a Canadian election by sending a personal message requesting more troops for the Front and by drafting an appeal, to be signed by officers in Europe, asking 'New Brunswick folks at home' for reinforcements. Kipling obliged with a message in the British and Canadian press stating that without reinforcements Canada, 'after all her sons' mighty sacrifice in the last three years, must gradually go out of the war. The enemy will be encouraged, the war for liberty will be prolonged, the world's misery will increase.'[40] He was writing less than a month after Haig had pointlessly sacrificed 15,600 Canadians at Passchendaele – a slaughter that so enraged Borden, their Prime Minister, that at a meeting of the Imperial War Cabinet he seized Lloyd George by his lapels and shook him.[41]

Few things made Kipling angrier than the prolonged neutrality of the United States. Wilson's offer to mediate a 'peace without victory' rewarding neither side, together with his proposal for a post-war league of nations, infuriated Kipling almost as much as his later 'idiotic' Fourteen Points on the principles of a post-war settlement. The Americans, he insisted, had forfeited their right to give advice; they had committed 'moral suicide' by refusing to take sides or condemn atrocities; they were now simply 'descending from one unplumbed deep to another'.[42]

Cameron Forbes saw Kipling in the spring of 1916, a few months after John's death, and noticed that he looked older and greyer and more visibly lined. The former Governor of the Philippines reported that he was 'most bitter' about the United States, declaring that American orators could never again stand up and talk of liberty and democracy. Kipling even warned his friend that Canada might become a threat to his countrymen: without a proper army the Americans would be unable to resist '500,000 contemptuous Canadians, thoroughly trained, coming back from the war' if England 'happened to have a grievance'.[43]

In his poem 'The Neutral' he substituted sorrow for bitterness. America is speaking of the Allies:

> If it be found, when the battle clears,
>   Their death has set me free,
> Then how shall I live with myself through the years
>   Which they have bought for me?
>
> Brethren, how must it fare with me,
>   Or how am I justified,
> If it be proven that I am he
>   For whom mankind has died...?

Kipling changed the title to 'The Question' after Germany's use of unrestricted submarine warfare provoked America to join the conflict in April 1917. He was so relieved by the declaration of war that he did not carp about its tardiness or the reasoning behind the change of policy. 'Don't take the lateness ... to heart,' he told Forbes. There was still plenty of work to do, and America's 'value in the scheme of civilisation' would be to 'put in the *coup de grâce*'. When American troops eventually reached Britain, he welcomed them with speeches and an article entitled 'The Second Sailing of the "Mayflower"'; the Americans had 'returned' to Europe in order to help save their place of origin.[44] In another poem, 'The Choice', the 'American spirit' joins 'Freedom's brotherhood' and thanks God 'Who bade us choose that the Flesh should die / And not the living Soul!'

The euphoria soon shrivelled. A very Kiplingesque method of acquiring information was to sit in the No. 2 Buffet at Charing Cross Station and listen to soldiers on leave from the Front. The stories of the American troops, he told Lord Crawford, a member of the Government, would make the 'flesh of America creep with horror and indignation'. The soldiers themselves were good men but badly trained and incompetently led. Their C-in-C, General Pershing, was such a disaster that, according to Crawford, Kipling proposed to write a 'serious epoch-making indictment'.[45]

The timing of the American entry provided a more rankling and enduring grudge. In collected editions of his verse Kipling did not change the title of 'The Question' back to 'The Neutral'; but he made the same point by inserting an explanation: 'Attitude of the United States of America during the first two years, seven months and four days of the Great War'.[46] In 1922, exasperated by President Harding's isolationism, he was reported in a New York newspaper to have complained that the United States

had come into the war two years, seven months and four days too late. America had forced the Allies into making peace at the first opportunity instead of insisting upon finishing in Berlin. America quit the day of the armistice, without waiting to see the thing through ... 'They have got the gold of the world,' he said, 'but we have saved our souls! Do you think that any one of us who have fought the war – who have lost children in the war – would change with one of them for all their happiness and prosperity?'[47]

The reporter was Clare Sheridan, a cousin of Winston Churchill, the daughter of a friend and the woman he had long ago advised to 'chuck poetry and literature' when she married.* Kipling was outraged by the appearance of the 'interview' and upset by the uproar it caused on both sides of the Atlantic. Somewhat naïvely he believed he had been talking to her privately as a friend, and the betrayal of friendship prompted him to deny the quoted opinions. This may have been understandable and legitimate, but they were nonetheless authentic.

Besides his American and domestic correspondence, Kipling's written war work consisted of over 300,000 published words. A minute fraction of these were reserved for epitaphs and inscriptions, a trio of fine stories and half a dozen memorable poems. Nearly all the rest were divided between newspaper articles and the two-volume *History of the Irish Guards*.

The articles on the Royal Navy are not among his best journalism. Written at the request of the Admiralty and the Ministry of Information, they were compiled almost entirely from confidential reports. Those essential ingredients of Kipling's newspaper work, the vividness of sights and smells, were on this occasion mainly limited to the East Coast Patrol at Harwich. He wrote a series of articles about Jutland, but he had not been within 500 miles of the battle.

More interesting to himself – and to his readers – were his articles on Italy in 1917. The British Ambassador in Rome had asked him to write about the Italian Front because he found it 'maddening' that the British seemed to think Italy was 'not pulling her weight'.[48] Kipling required a second invitation before he agreed, perhaps because he was not as enthusiastic about Italy as he was about France. He regarded the Italians as an untrustworthy nation who had only entered the war to grab the South Tyrol from Austria. Yet he did not have to adulterate his reports. Setting off again with Landon, he discovered that the Italians were wonderful hosts and 'Princes among Road makers'; their architecture, as he told Carrie, was also 'most adorable'. After inspecting the Italian Army, he told Fletcher he had seen the 'Exercitus Romanus' reborn and alive as it was under the Republic and the best of the Caesars. Even the generals had the same heads as their Classical counterparts: 'wide browed, bull

---

*See above, p. 227.

necked devils, lean narrow hook-nosed Romans – the whole original gallery with a new spirit behind it'.[49]

Considering that these were his private views – and that he was writing before his Romans were routed at Caporetto – it was not difficult for him to praise the 'New Italy' in the *Daily Telegraph* and to predict a great future for this 'oldest and youngest among the nations'. The 'excitable Latin', he had realized, was merely a 'Boche legend'. The Italians were a hard people, fighting yard by yard through the mountains: they were as 'fine as the steel-wire ropes' and as 'implacable as the mountain' itself.[50]

Although the war had provided English literature with a vast dimension of new subject matter, Kipling predicted that writers would quickly return to a world of curates, roses and small talk.[51] But that world was entirely absent from his own work, with its themes both spiritual and macabre, and its style increasingly complex and allusive. He had intended to publish *A Diversity of Creatures* in 1914 but kept the collection back until 1917 when he added two stories of the war to the end. 'Swept and Garnished' describes a delirious German woman trying to clean her home of the imagined blood of Belgian children; and the protagonist of 'Mary Postgate' appears to exult in the death of the German aviator in what Oliver Baldwin, Kipling's cousin, called 'the wickedest story ever told'. Yet multiple readings of these and later tales suggest multiple possible meanings, none of them very wicked. In fact the aviator may not have been German at all, he may not even have existed, and the bomb with which he is supposed to have killed a child may also belong to Miss Postgate's imagination. Far from being a piece of anti-German propaganda, the story is an outstanding psychological study of a repressed woman experiencing fluctuating feelings of love and hate.

Since verse remained Kipling's favourite medium for expressing his views, propaganda and politics are only occasionally absent from his wartime poetry. But one poem at least places him in the front rank of war poets.

> The Garden called Gethsemane
>   In Picardy it was,
> And there the people came to see
>   The English soldiers pass.

We used to pass – we used to pass
  Or halt, as it might be,
And ship our masks in case of gas
  Beyond Gethsemane.

The Garden called Gethsemane,
  It held a pretty lass,
But all the time she talked to me
  I prayed my cup might pass.
The officer sat on the chair,
  The men lay on the grass,
And all the time we halted there
  I prayed my cup might pass –

It didn't pass – it didn't pass –
  It didn't pass from me.
I drank it when we met the gas
  Beyond Gethsemane.

'Gethsemane' requires no comment except one that Kipling himself made: 'What makes war most poignant is the presence of women with whom one can talk and make love only an hour or so behind the line.'[52]

For his political verse Kipling derived much comfort from John Bunyan, whose prescience and perceptiveness two centuries earlier were rewarded with a poem.

> *A TINKER out of Bedford,*
>   *A vagrant oft in quod,*
> *A private under Fairfax,*
>   *A minister of God –*
> *Two hundred years and thirty*
>   *Ere Armageddon came*
> *His single hand portrayed it,*
>   *And Bunyan was his name!*

('The Holy War')

Miraculously Bunyan (who was Kipling's most direct spiritual ancestor) had anticipated the dubious characters of the Great War, the 'Perseverance-Doubters', the 'Present-Comfort shirks' and the 'brittle intellectuals / Who crack beneath a strain' – John Bunyan 'met that helpful set / In Charles the Second's reign'. According to Kipling, he would have 'thoroughly … understood the Hun and the Pacifist mind', an insight that would also have enabled him to appreciate 'Russia to the Pacifists', a poem described by its author as 'practically a dirge over a dead Nation', a work attributing the Russian Revolution to the 'intellectuals and pacifists' whose efforts had 'directly produced the disease called Bolshevism'.[53]

In July 1917 Kipling had returned to an earlier mode with the angriest poem he had written since 'Gehazi', a set of verses so critical of senior officials that the *Daily Telegraph* would not publish them – they ended up with faithful Gwynne and the *Morning Post*. In 1915 the British had embarked on an ill-judged and badly planned campaign against the Turks in Mesopotamia. Advancing too far up the Tigris, 14,000 men of the Indian army under General Townshend were defeated at Ctesiphon, forced to retreat down river and then compelled to surrender at Kut el-Amara. An imperial humiliation to rival Yorktown and Kabul, Kut was the consequence of military blunders which, allied to medical incompetence, provoked condemnation from a Royal Commission and then from Rudyard Kipling.

> They shall not return to us, the resolute, the young,
>> The eager and whole-hearted whom we gave:
> But the men who left them thriftily to die in their own dung,
>> Shall they come with years and honour to the grave?

Kipling's fury was distilled and directed at the officials blamed by the report who managed to stay in their posts or be transferred to equivalent positions.

> … But the idle-minded overlings who quibbled while they died,
>> Shall they thrust for high employments as of old?
>
> Shall we only threaten and be angry for an hour?
>> When the storm is ended shall we find
> How softly but how swiftly they have sidled back to power
>> By the favour and contrivance of their kind?
>
> … Their lives cannot repay us – their deaths could not undo –
>> The shame that they have laid upon our race:

> But the slothfulness that wasted and the arrogance that slew,
>> Shall we leave it unabated in its place?

('Mesopotamia')

The poet explained privately that his targets were all the men who had escaped punishment for their share in the débâcle. But he had one figure above all in mind – the Viceroy, Lord Hardinge. Austen Chamberlain, the Secretary of State for India, resigned, but the much more culpable Hardinge slipped back into his old post as head of the Foreign Office and later became Ambassador to Paris.

The great absentee of Kipling's war verse is Tommy Atkins. But the old volunteer shillin'-a-day Tommies no longer existed. As their champion and interpreter pointed out, they had 'passed away in the mud of Flanders' – 90,000 casualties in the British Expeditionary Force by the end of 1914.* And it was impossible for Kipling to immortalise their young replacements, because they died too soon to be recognized. One could write about Tommy taking his 'chanst among the Kyber 'ills', but one could not write about his successors given no chance by Haig among the treeless downs of the Somme.

The longest and most laborious part of Kipling's war work was the *History of the Irish Guards*. Requested to write it by the Commanding Officer of his son's regiment, he agreed to do so for mixed reasons of duty, therapy and atonement. He spent five and a half years on the task and produced two volumes of relentless chronological history.

The poet Edmund Blunden complained in a review that the book conveyed neither the atmosphere of the trenches nor an understanding of the 'pandemonium and nerve-strain of war'. But Kipling had

---

*They were magnificently commemorated in A.E. Housman's 'Epitaph on an Army of Mercenaries'.

> These, in the day when heaven was falling,
>> The hour when earth's foundations fled,
> Followed their mercenary calling
>> And took their wages and are dead.

> Their shoulders held the sky suspended;
>> They stood, and earth's foundations stay;
> What God abandoned, these defended,
>> And saved the sum of things for pay.

Kipling regarded the poem as 'the high-water mark of all War verse'.[54]

not set out to describe the atmosphere. He only aimed to do a 'fairly conscientious bit of historical spade-work', and compile a methodical work of restrained prose and narrative detail.[55]

He finished the first volume in September 1921, the second in July the following year. He admitted it had been a dispiriting task, a 'weary, weary job of stale records of lost work'. Carrie recorded that at the end of it he looked exhausted, 'yellow and shrunken'.[56]*

---

*In 1918 Kipling published a less sombre work on the regiment, 'The Irish Guards', a poem that good-humouredly contrasts the Irish 'wild geese', who fought for France against England in the eighteenth century, with their descendants who fought for France *and* England in the Great War. He gave a cheque for £350 plus the poem's copyright to the regiment's charitable funds. But by the time the *History* was published in 1923, he was too disgusted by the Anglo-Irish dénouement to include such amiable verses.

17

The Pain of Peace

Towards the end of 1917 Lord Lansdowne published a courageous letter in the *Daily Telegraph* arguing that a compromise
peace should be negotiated with Germany. After three years of
slaughter, in which he had lost his second son, he believed the pro-
longation of the war would 'spell ruin for the civilised world'.[1]

The estimable old statesman, whose ministerial and proconsular
career had lasted nearly half a century, was abused publicly by the
press and privately by Kipling, who dismissed him as 'ga-ga' and suggested that an unspecified 'female ... in the Liberal interest' had
'worked upon' the 'old imbecile'.[2] Lansdowne thus joined the band
of neutrals and compromisers whom Kipling detested and despised.
The worst of them was Pope Benedict XV, whose failure to take
sides was duly denounced in verse. 'A Song at Cock-Crow', one of
the bitterest of all his poems, connects Peter's denial of Jesus to the
Vatican's failure to condemn German aggression.

Kipling's response to the compromising pessimists in his own
country was a speech at Folkestone demanding a fight to the end.
One of his main arguments was predictable but untrue – that 'nine-
tenths of the atrocities Germany has committed have not been made
public' – and another must have surprised anyone familiar with his
views on representative government: if the Germans won, he said,
'the whole idea of Democracy – which at bottom is what the Hun
fights against – will be dismissed from men's minds, because it will

have been shown incapable of maintaining itself against the Hun'.[3] Lansdowne and Germany had conjured a temporary democrat.

A few weeks later the stalemate on the Western Front finally ended. Reinforced by divisions no longer needed against Russia, the German Army broke through the British lines at the end of March 1918. Ludendorff followed his onslaught with four further offensives until in August the Allies counter-attacked and drove their exhausted and demoralized opponents back to their defensive barrier, the Hindenburg Line. Within weeks Germany's allies were dropping out of the war, first Bulgaria, then Turkey, and finally Austria (whose empire disintegrated in October) requesting an armistice. On 10 November the Kaiser abdicated, and the following day Germany also signed armistice terms.

Astonished by the rapidity of the collapse, Kipling and his country-men sat 'stupefied ... among the wrecks of Empires'. As the 'gigantic landslide' came crashing down, their feelings were numb, their responses deadened. 'The last four years', he wrote on 2 November, 'have slain all our faculty for emotion and there isn't a sign of jubilation anywhere.' There were celebrations after the German Armistice, but Kipling did not take part in them: he 'bolted' home from London and had his 'dark hour alone'. Like many bereaved parents, he and Carrie soon realized that the loss of their son was even harder to bear in peacetime: 'The pain gets acuter when peace comes because then one thinks what might have been ...' It was difficult trying to reconstruct lives with a generation missing – especially as it was the generation for which he had written *Puck* and the *Jungle Books*.[4]

The pain of peace was sharpened by the feeling that the Allies had been cheated of a decisive victory. The Hun had been 'let off' when they had him at their mercy and could have crushed him. The terms of the 'Amazing Armistice' made Kipling uneasy; so did the 'desperate Hun peace-offensive' at the end of 1918.

Kipling had long argued that peace must be accompanied by justice, reparation and as much retribution as possible. Besides paying for their 'moral misdeeds', he had written in 1916, the Germans would have to pay for all the material damage they had caused; and repayment should be 'spread across generations' in order to 'keep the Hun busy and harmless'. Two years later his 'main preoccupation' was that 'the Hun [should] be made to suffer' and

'*after* justice' to be 'exposed to the hate of the whole world'.[6]
Retribution was also a personal matter: Kipling directed his own
longings at the Kaiser in 'A Death-Bed', a set of verses in which it
was hoped that the man responsible for the war would die of throat
cancer. Less vicious but equally harsh was 'Justice', which demanded
that Germany must relearn the laws of Civilization.

> A people and their King
> > Through ancient sin grown strong,
> Because they feared no reckoning
> > Would set no bound to wrong;
> But now their hour is past,
> > And we who bore it find
> Evil Incarnate held at last
> > To answer to mankind.
>
> For agony and spoil
> > Of nations beat to dust,
> For poisoned air and tortured soil
> > And cold, commanded lust,
> And every secret woe
> > The shuddering waters saw –
> Willed and fulfilled by high and low –
> > Let them relearn the Law.

Kipling hoped for peace terms so 'drastic' (as he put it without
specifying them) that he was bound to be disappointed even by a
treaty that humiliated Germany. Versailles was far too lenient for
him. After winning the war, he announced in 1920, 'England pro-
ceeded to dissipate the results and no one now knows whether she
has won or lost.' Commenting on reparations the following year, he
declared it an 'open question whether we won the war'.[7]
Yet he was less anxious about the scale of financial atonement
than about Germany's potential for resurrection. He had become
'rather a one-idea person', he admitted in the last July of the war,
looking for Germans 'under every bush'. The paranoia did not abate
in peacetime. Throughout 1919 he was assuring correspondents that
the undefeated enemy was still capable of great harm. The fighting
might be over but the war was 'in full blast between a rather wearied
humanity and a Devil' trying to persuade people he was 'not so black

as he is painted'.[8] The Devil's new weapons were underground and insidious: agents were being used to sap British morale and promote civil strife. In December 1919 he asked the Minister for Agriculture (Lord Lee) for a list of all farms where foot-and-mouth disease had recently broken out; and on the same day he asked the War Secretary (Churchill) for a list of all camps where German prisoners had been held during the war. The requests were connected: the inquirer believed that the disease had been spread by scraps of infected 'Hun beef' sent in food parcels to the prisoners from Germany.[9]

Kipling allowed himself a brief period of optimism over the future role of the United States. Large numbers of American troops had 'returned' to Europe to play a crucial part in defeating and demoralizing Ludendorff and his armies. Surely the experience would encourage America to assume a permanent international role, not just to share the burden of benighted places like the Philippines, but also to help rebuild and look after a shattered world? Despite his reservations about Wilson, the Fourteen Points, the talks at Versailles and the embryonic League of Nations, Kipling wanted the Americans to take up a political role in the Eastern Hemisphere. He hoped they would accept a mandate for Constantinople or Armenia and that 'national pride in achievement' would induce them to stay 'in the game'.[10]

The right man to carry out the extension of America's responsibilities to Europe and Asia was of course Roosevelt. Kipling believed that 'in all human probability' he would become president again at the end of Wilson's term. But Roosevelt died within two weeks of this prediction – and was commemorated in 'Great-Heart', one of the inferior elegies. 'He was the greatest of your people's line of great men,' Kipling told Cabot Lodge, who might have hoped to share the accolade. In his last letter to his elegist Roosevelt declared that the war had given him a 'greatly increased sense of admiration' for the British Empire.[11]

Kipling mourned for the man as well as for the politician he regarded as the only American capable of visualizing a role for the United States in the Near East. Wilson was a complete contrast, a man who liked to 'give lofty advice and return to his national fireside'.[12] Kipling had met him at dinner at Buckingham Palace at the end of the war and had been unimpressed. But he still hoped the American people would realize that victory over 'the Hun [was] merely the first step in the business, and that they must help now to keep him down and under'.

> I am hoping and praying that the U.S.A. will come into the game to stay. It isn't as if she wasn't being offered every inducement to do so. Never before in history has a people been tearfully besought to take over the keys of the world and jingle them on her chatelaine ... But the main hitch of course is that there is no sense in making a League of Nations if you don't put down an adequate force of police to watch the chief offender, and up to the present the U.S.A. don't seem inclined to help police the Hun border, and the Hun is the last tiger in the world with whom paper safeguards are effective.[13]

Wilson tried to come 'into the game' because he wanted to make the world 'safe for democracy'. He went to the Peace Conference, he supervised the drafting of the League's Covenant and, despite deep anxieties over reparations and territorial changes, he signed the Treaty in the Hall of Mirrors in Versailles. Then he returned to Washington to persuade Congress to accept the Treaty and the League. But just as he had irritated European leaders with his Fourteen Points and his 'sermonettes', so he antagonized the Senate with further preaching and displays of self-righteous rigidity. During his frenetic campaign for ratification he suffered two strokes – and lost the campaign. A compromise over admission to the League was possible, but Wilson preferred a defeat that left his principles intact. Americans were thus kept out of the organization by the inflexibility of its chief architect and advocate.

Kipling viewed Wilson's performance at the conference with derision, wishing that Doubleday, his American publisher, could send a 'battleship and take him home' so that the other delegates could 'get to business'; to the same correspondent he later expressed the desire to dispatch the American President and the British Prime Minister to enjoy each other's company in the Sahara Desert. He was still harsher about Wilson's compatriots, even though one could not 'expect people whose forbears went west to avoid trouble to stand up to responsibility in a far land for no immediate cash return'.[14] But worse than a simple withdrawal into isolationism was the manner in which the United States claimed international moral leadership while declining to incur the costs or responsibilities of upholding the ideals it shared with Britain and France. Kipling perceived decadence in the United States and, consistent with his belief that the real America had died at Gettysburg, ascribed it to Jewish and southern European immigrants who were corrupting the 'national fabric' and even the national literature. These cuckoos were 'throwing the eggs of [American] thought out of the nest'. By 1926 their country disgusted him so much that he instructed Gwynne to tell his readers that the country had been 'specially exempted from the processes of Evolution'.[15]

Equally exempt from the evolutionary flow were Liberal MPs, ministers and of course Lloyd George. But Kipling could no longer attack them as the versifier of the Opposition because his party now formed the bulk of Lloyd George's Coalition, and Bonar Law, Baldwin and Beaverbrook were all ministers.* Kipling reacted by flirting with organizations of the far Right, supporting the resentful Diehards of the short-lived National Party in 1917 and joining Rider Haggard's even shorter-lived Liberty League, formed in 1920 to 'combat the advance of Bolshevism' in Britain and the Empire.[16]† But he remained sharp enough to write 'The Gods of the Copybook Headings', a humorous attack on the 'political correctness' of the day in which he contrasts the eternal truths of the title with the false truths of fashion. The targets are the usual collection but they sound better in verse than in correspondence: the 'Cambrian' Lloyd George and Liberal disarmament – 'When the Cambrian measures were forming, They promised perpetual peace. / They swore, if we gave them our weapons, that the wars of the tribes would cease'; female

---

*In Lloyd George's governments Bonar Law was Chancellor of the Exchequer (1916–19) and Lord Privy Seal (1919–21); Baldwin was Financial Secretary to the Treasury (1917–1921) and President of the Board of Trade (1921–2); and Beaverbrook was Chancellor of the Duchy of Lancaster and Minister of Information (February–October 1918).

†Haggard and Kipling were the leading signatories of a letter to *The Times* (3 March 1920) announcing the birth of the League. Next day a commentator in the *Daily Herald* nicely caught the spirit of the two disgruntled reactionaries with a short poem that began

'Every Bolsh is a blackguard,'
Said Kipling to Haggard
– 'And given to tippling,'
Said Haggard to Kipling.

emancipation – 'On the first Feminian Sandstones we were promised the Fuller life / (Which started by loving our neighbour and ended by loving his wife)'; and trade unionism (specifically the coal-miners) – 'In the Carboniferous Epoch we were promised abundance for all, / By robbing selected Peter to pay for collective Paul.'[17]

Kipling's most ferocious post-war eruptions were caused by Lloyd George's policies on India and Ireland. The Subcontinent had experienced little constitutional development since he had last been there nearly three decades earlier. Indian political aspirations had made no headway under Curzon, and the Minto-Morley reforms of 1909, which had increased the number of Indians on provincial councils, had been not much more than a gesture of benevolence. But the current Secretary of State, the Liberal Edwin Montagu, visited India in 1917 and came back with a scheme, later known as the dyarchy, whereby elected Indians in each province would run ministries of health, education and agriculture, while the local governor would retain control over matters such as finance and the police. The appearance of Montagu's Report in the summer of 1918 prompted Kipling to denounce it to Gwynne as 'systematic lunacy' and, in a rare burst of anti-semitic hysteria, to accuse the *Spectator*'s Strachey of being an 'archetypal trimmer' for suggesting that the Jewish (though strongly anti-Zionist) Montagu wanted to preserve the British Empire. 'Racially,' he fulminated, the minister did not 'care for it any more than Caiaphas cared for Pilate: and psychologically he [couldn't] comprehend it'. Carrie recorded her husband's attitude after Montagu's proposals had been passed by Parliament: 'We get off all our Indian securities to be sold. Rud deeply distrusting the future of India.' Kipling continued to urge Strachey to 'get after Montagu' and showed his feelings about Parliament, the Government and perhaps India itself by contributing to a fund for General Dyer, the officer condemned by the House of Commons for the massacre of more than 300 Indians at Amritsar in April 1919.[18]

Ireland proved to be an even more volcanic issue than India. During the war Kipling had allowed himself to become complacent about the island, at least after the Easter Rising of 1916. Ireland had 'made herself a bore to all the world', he declared the following year, and everyone was 'quite fed up with her and her tantrums'. He was irritated by Irish opposition to the Military Conscription Act of April 1918 and believed it was a German plot. Reading a book about 'pernicious little' Ireland left him 'with a sense of confirmed hopelessness and despair – the sort of bored terror one has of a woman of 50 who explains that she has never been understood since she was born'.[19]

Ireland had changed rather more swiftly than India in recent years. By the spring of 1920 the republicans of Sinn Fein had destroyed the moderate nationalists; Britain's newly recruited Black and Tans were on the rampage; and the IRA was rapidly developing its skills in terrorism. Faced by a lethal guerrilla campaign, Lloyd George had to negotiate an arrangement – and he had to do so with gunmen rather than with the gentlemanly Redmond. The Government of Ireland Act resurrected much of the Home Rule Bill (plus a compromise on Ulster), which was accepted in the North (where King George opened a parliament in Belfast), but ignored in the South. In the autumn of 1921 Lloyd George offered Sinn Fein more – the same constitutional status as Canada – and bullied its delegates into accepting a treaty that extricated Britain from the South and provoked a bloody civil war within Sinn Fein.

Politics as 'the art of the possible' was a notion that Kipling was never able to assimilate. For him no crisis could justify negotiations with the Irish gunmen. He was not an historian, he reminded his guru Fletcher, but he doubted whether England had 'ever made a deal with so flagrant a type of assassin'. To other correspondents he accused the House of Commons of conniving at murder and 'encouraging assassination' in Ireland 'by constitutional revisions'. The Government, he claimed, had used bribery and control of the press to force acceptance of 'their surrender to the Irish gunmen'.[20]

Since Ulster had been at least temporarily retained inside the United Kingdom, his rage can be explained only by his belief that the Anglo-Irish Treaty was symptomatic of a vast and sinister process. The 'Irish betrayal' was not just an Irish or even a British matter but an event of imperial consequence, another step – like Montagu's – in the Empire's 'recessional'. The Government, he told his French translator André Chevrillon, was breaking it all up, though this was quite an undertaking and mercifully the whole thing could not be 'wrecked in one administration'.[21]

Carrie found her husband more depressed by the treaty than he had ever been during the war. The Irish Free State, he believed, was the precursor of 'Free States of Evil' throughout the Empire, wherever the Government wanted to set them up. India was no doubt next on the list. Fortunately Kipling soon managed to relegate Ireland as a topic of correspondence, though he continued to make little cracks, referring to the Free State as the 'Free Hell' and describing Irish nationalism as 'Bolshevism in Erse'.[22]

One casualty of the treaty was the friendship between Kipling and Beaverbrook. They had remained on good terms until the end of the war: Kipling had supplied the new peer's motto and had been invited to join 'the Beaver's' Ministry of Information. But soon afterwards the friendship foundered. In the 1950s Elsie Kipling instructed her father's official biographer to explain that the relationship 'began to cool' because 'there were many things which they no longer saw in common'. Charles Carrington, who was under constant pressure from Elsie during his work, complied even though Beaverbrook had told him that it was specifically his support for the Irish treaty that had caused the rift. Once at a Madrid hotel the former friends met by accident when Beaverbrook was travelling with Tim Healy, the first Governor-General of the Free State. 'Kipling showed deep resentment, directed entirely against Healy. Tough things were said.' Beaverbrook, who was not always a reliable storyteller, claimed that he tried several times to re-establish the friendship and once even attempted to introduce Kipling to Lloyd George. He always failed.[23] In 1930, commenting on Beaverbrook's plans for a United Empire Party, Kipling wrote, 'It don't pay to build dams with the Beaver. But I knew *that* ages ago.'[24]

Much of Kipling's most memorable war work was done at the end of the struggle and in the early years of the peace, in his literary epitaphs, his inscriptions for memorials and his service with the Imperial War Graves Commission.

As late as October 1916 he claimed that he could not write for monuments. In any case he believed that the only suitable inscription for a soldier who fell in action was 'He died for his country'.[25] Reluctance was overcome as appeals mounted up and he discovered that he was after all well suited to the task. His style and training helped him achieve the concision required to evoke different categories of dead in a handful of words. After most of the memorial had been taken up by the Glory of God and the identity of the fallen, there were seldom more than seven words to differentiate, for example, the men of the Harwich Mine-Sweeper Fleet, who had died 'that the seas might be made free', from the Merchant Navy and Fishing Fleets, 'who have no grave but the sea'.

Kipling's work for the War Graves Commission,* which he joined in 1917, involved more than writing inscriptions. He attended its meetings, contributed to its booklets and visited the cemeteries as they were formed and developed along the line of the Front. He also argued strenuously the points he felt strongly about, the need for 'distinctive regimental headstones' and 'equality of treatment' for the fallen. It was natural, he admitted, for the bereaved to want 'to do something special and particular for their own dead'; and the richer they were, the more likely they would be to want something ornate or imposing to distinguish their graves from others. But the poorer mourners clung to the idea of 'equality of treatment', to uniform graves, because that accepted the principle of 'equality of sorrow'. Kipling took their side. The wealthy, he argued, should not be permitted to 'proclaim their grief above other people's grief' simply because they had larger bank accounts: if his son's body had been found and marked by an expensively designed gravestone, he would not have been able to face the people of his village, who had lost fifty young men of their own. 'Lord knows I'm no democrat', he exclaimed, but everyone's sons had died for a common cause: the movement for special graves was unacceptable because it was a demand for 'privilege in the face of death'.[26] The point was made in 'Equality of Sacrifice', the first of his 'Epitaphs of the War'.

> *A.* 'I was a "have."' *B.* 'I was a "have-not."'
> (*Together*). 'What hast thou given which I gave not?'

In April 1920 Kipling defended the principle of 'equality of treatment' before the Army Committee of the House of Commons, but

---

*The Imperial (now Commonwealth) War Graves Commision was set up to oversee the burial and commemoration of the war dead of the British Empire. It operated on a number of principles: that the dead should be buried as close as possible to where they had fallen; that there should be no private memorials; that officers and men should be buried together; and that, although the fallen should be honoured by individual graves, they should have the same headstones, differentiated only by their name, their regimental badge and the symbol of their religion.

he did not attend the parliamentary debate on the matter. He had been 'fairly shocked by the bitterness' of those demanding special memorials, and he was relieved that MPs had voted in support of the Commission's policy. The Cecil family had been particularly critical of the Commission and of Kipling's role in it. Certainly they had a legitimate concern – five of the late Lord Salisbury's ten grandsons had been killed in the war – but their High Church intolerance was ill suited to ecumenical and inter-religious ideas of commemoration. Lady Florence Cecil, the Bishop of Exeter's wife who lost three of her four sons, demanded crosses on the graves instead of head-stones, while her eccentric brother-in-law, the MP Lord Hugh Cecil, attacked the idea of erecting a mosque and a Hindu temple for the Indians who had died in France. The combative politician also attacked the Commission for employing Kipling, 'not a known relig-ious man', to choose its inscriptions.[27]

But even Lord Hugh, a liturgical gendarme who spent much of his career making it more difficult for people to divorce or remarry, would have been unable to deny that Kipling's choice of inscriptions was appropriate. On the stones of remembrance he chose five words from Ecclesiasticus – 'Their Name Liveth for Evermore'. He selected seven more from the same source for those whose burial places had been destroyed by shelling: 'Their Glory Shall Not Be Blotted Out'. And on those graves for which a name could not be found, he chose nine of his own: 'A Soldier of the Great War Known unto God'.

In 1920 the Kiplings made their first journeys to the cemeteries on the Western Front. They visited thirty of them near the battlefields of Loos and the Somme and made a pilgrimage to Chalk Pit Wood 'about the hour that John fell'. After his first sight of the devastated areas, Kipling felt the 'entire inadequacy of words to express' what he had seen. They returned the following spring after visiting Algiers and travelling up from Provence. The French were the 'most marvel-lous nation on the planet', he proclaimed in Hyères. They had been ravaged, 'kicked through Hell' and deprived of 'half' their young men, but they still had 'the civilisation and the poise' that the British could only strive after.[28]

In late April the Kiplings crossed the Rhine into occupied Germany. It was a distressing experience, as he must have foreseen. He could never pass a wounded man in England 'without remembering the sources and the authors of the evil'. Now that he saw those authors in the flesh, he surprised himself by the depth of hate 'caused merely by seeing them alive when so many were dead'. It was galling to drive through the 'sleek and prosperous' German countryside, to look at geese and oxen and new houses, to see 'fat children', girls with plaited hair and old men smoking pipes. 'And they were alive!' It was even more harrowing to return to Rheims along a route of 'utter desolation' and 'insupportable sorrow', a landscape of 'skinned chalk hills' and 'glaring trenches' and 'furlongs of heaped barbed wire'.[29]

A year later he was back among the graves to attend a ceremony near Boulogne with George V and Haig. He had composed a speech for the King, who duly declared that there could be no 'more potent advocates of peace upon earth than this massed multitude of witnesses to the desolation of war'. He also wrote a poem about the monarch's visit, 'The King's Pilgrimage', in which he inserted a political point of his own. The dead, he suggested, would not 'grudge their death'

> Save only if they understood
> That, after all was done,
> We they redeemed denied their blood
> And mocked the gains it won.

Although the local mayor talked too much and put the wreath in the wrong place, the ceremony was a success. Carrie curtsied graciously, George V said 'seemly' things to her husband, and the bard congratulated his sovereign on the delivery of his speech – 'which was also seemly'. After conversing about politicians, he detected that the King shared his views on the breed.[30]

Kipling continued to tour those foreign fields that are forever gardens of Britain. He reported on the condition of the cemeteries; he made recommendations to the Commission; he badgered the Prime Minister, his cousin Stanley, to force the Treasury to release large sums of money for the maintenance of the graves. The cemeteries impressed him by the individuality of their design and the grandeur of the whole scheme. Taken together, he remarked, they formed the vastest piece of 'concrete work since the Pyramids' and the 'largest bit of landscape gardening undertaken in any country'.[31]

One day in March 1925 Kipling was at Rouen, inspecting graves and doing 'penance at where Joan [of Arc] was burned'. That evening he began writing a story, 'The Gardener', which he finished the following week in Lourdes. In the diary he sporadically kept on his travels he noted on finishing that it was 'not so badly done'. In fact it was one of the best things he ever did, a wonderfully compassionate tale about the grieving mother of an illegitimate boy killed in the war. Helen Turrell pretends to her village that her son is her nephew, the village pretends to believe her, and the social hypocrisies of English life are thus gently satisfied. She continues to pretend until she goes to France and searches for her 'nephew's' grave. Unable to find it among so many others, she approaches the cemetery gardener, who looks at her with 'infinite compassion' and says, 'Come with me ... and I will show you where your son lies.' The 'gardener' is of course the resurrected Christ, and Helen is a Mary Magdalene who sins, who loves and who is forgiven. It is a tender and magnificent tale that makes one wonder how the same man could have written 'The Female of the Species'. As tender and magnificent is 'The Burden', the poem that accompanies it in the volume *Debits and Credits*. The first three verses unveil the agony of Helen Turrell; the fourth reveals the consolation of Mary Magdalene.

> *One grave to me was given —*
> *To guard till Judgment Day —*
> *But God looked down from Heaven*
> *And rolled the Stone away!*
> *One day of all my years —*
> *One hour of that one day —*
> *His Angel saw my tears*
> *And rolled the Stone away!*

Bateman's was never a rural retreat from the tribulations of life. It was life itself, the wheat and the tares. It had remained superficially peaceful because there was no telephone and because the War Office had declined Kipling's offer to use it as a hospital. But its administration was taxing and sometimes noisy: the departures of servants and gardeners were frequent and invariably accompanied by grumbles from Carrie about 'base ingratitude'.

The land provided sporadic solace. Carrie complained that the world viewed her husband as 'a sort of stage farmer' instead of a 'busy man' who happened to live in the country. But he loved to proclaim his agricultural role, even if it really belonged to his wife. He was pretending to write poems, he told Oliver Baldwin in 1918, but 'at heart' he was a farmer and a haymaker. Difficult though it was to farm in wartime with only 'a sprinkling of female labour', it was worth the trouble. The Guernsey cows, which the Kiplings bought to supply Bateman's with milk and butter, were not economical, but at least they won prizes at the Tunbridge Wells Cattle Show. And even if one lost money on field crops, there were 'worse things in the world than trying to do one's duty by the land'.[32]

Kipling still appreciated the survival of rural lore. He admired the way that village boys could make a grass blade between their thumbs sound like a frightened rabbit and thus draw a stoat or a weasel into the open. He appreciated too the skills of carters, ditchers and woodmen, and deplored the fact that 'modern progress' was turning country folk into 'meritorious menials'. Despite his love of the motor car and other technology of the age, he was appalled by their inevitable accompaniments. The coast at Rottingdean, he complained in 1925, was 'all one dirty mess of bungalows'. The following year he observed that England had become 'pockmarked' with these little horrors and now possessed 'no lanes free from tar and motor-traffic'.[33]

For the last twenty years of his life Kipling was frequently ill and in much pain; unable to eat well, he often weighed less than nine stone. In 1918 Haggard encountered him looking 'thin and worn and aged' and suffering 'fits of pain in his inside'. The testimony of Carrie's diary and the observations of visitors form a lengthy catalogue of sickness and anguish. He was treated for 'gastritis' from 1915, but it was not until 1933, when he acquired 'a fresh vet', that a French doctor diagnosed what his English counterparts had failed to discern; that he had long been suffering from a duodenal ulcer.

Depression caused by almost constant illness was exacerbated by the loneliness of Bateman's. After fathering three children in the 1890s, Kipling would have expected, in the normal course of events, to have had grandchildren by 1918. No one would have been a better grandfather. But two of the children were dead, and the third was childless. In 1924 Elsie married George Bambridge, a semi-invalid Guards officer who spent much of the inter-war period as an honorary attaché at embassies in Europe.

Deprived of young descendants, Kipling turned to other people's children. He wrote them letters signed 'Uncle Rud'; he compiled reading lists; he invited them to stay at Bateman's, especially at half-term when he provided a paddleboat, a shooting competition and a 'rabbit stalk' in the evening. While staying with friends, he once heard his hosts shooing their grandchildren away so as not to disturb the distinguished guest. 'Don't send them away,' he pleaded, 'they are very precious.' Then he added wistfully, 'You don't know how fortunate you are to have grandchildren.'[34]

More constant companionship was provided by his dogs, though he knew the sorrow 'of giving your heart to a dog to tear'. Long after the death of his Aberdeen terrier, he missed the sound of its feet clipping along the floor as it followed him from room to room. But he soon acquired a new puppy, a Scottie who cheered and amused the household. After dinner his dogs had a special hour even when visitors were staying: their master turned the carpets up and rolled around with them on the floor with a ball.[35] The Aberdeen starred in his work more than any human mortal. As a male it became 'Boots', the narrator of *Thy Servant a Dog*, a delightful book that sold 100,000 copies in the two months before the Christmas of 1930; and as 'Dinah' in 'The Woman in his Life', it helps her owner, a former officer traumatized by the trenches, to recover from a breakdown.

The 1920s was the only decade in which Kipling did not compose a mass of political poetry. The Government produced no new 'Gehazi', nor Ireland a 'Mesopotamia', nor the slackness of British society a sequel to 'The Islanders'. He was not interested in a proposal from Robert Bridges, the Poet Laureate, who had been 'earnestly exhorting' him to write 'patriotic verses for the rising generation'. Nor was he tempted to follow the current god of the market place: he remained an 'infidel' about free verse 'except as a cheap way of putting down one's notes'.[36] Like Robert Frost, he would 'as soon play tennis with the net down'.

Kipling's short stories, by contrast, enjoyed a revival. Liberalism, Ulster and the war had created a semi-desert after the publication of *Actions and Reactions*, his weakest collection, in 1909. *A Diversity of Creatures* appeared in 1917 but the best of his late stories were not published in book form until 1926 in *Debits and Credits*. Apart from 'The Gardener' and 'The Eye of Allah', the later collection included 'The Wish House' and 'A Madonna of the Trenches', two further brilliant and compassionate tales exploring the connections between love and pain and redemption.

The Sicilian writer, Giuseppe Tomasi di Lampedusa, used to enjoy categorizing writers as *grassi* ('plump ones' like Shakespeare) and *magri*, 'lean ones' like Stendhal who, by concision and implication, make readers labour to interpret them. The style of Kipling's later stories, the hints, the excisions, the intricate use of symbol and allusion, place their author among the champions of the *magri*. They are not alas relevant to the themes of this book, but the four mentioned in the previous paragraph are at the summit of Kipling's art.

The study at Bateman's was a place for reading as well as writing. Kipling admitted he was a 'hasty and ... gluttonous reader' – as he had been ever since Westward Ho! Jane Austen, whom he read aloud to Carrie, was his favourite author, slightly ahead of Walter Scott, whose appreciation of ballads matched his own. But his appetite demanded new fare, as young as Galsworthy and as old as Horace, whose work he learned by heart and subtly incorporated into later stories such as 'The Church that was at Antioch'. Before leaving for long sea voyages in 1929 and 1930, he asked Heinemann, the publisher, to send him a 'packet of books', topographical, biographical and technical, 'with a dash of long novels or tales'.[37] He enjoyed reading 'lives' yet he regarded them with suspicion and desperately hoped that posterity would spare him the attentions of a biographer. The genre was 'a bit too near the Higher Cannibalism' for him. 'Ancestor worship' was all very well, but the way biographers served their subjects up, 'filleted or spiced, or "high" ', was too much.[38]

One biography he did not enjoy reading was the manuscript of Ian Colvin's life of Dr Jameson. According to Carrie's diary, he spent days 'trying to tidy up' the 'disappointing' effort before he and Milner decided it needed rewriting altogether.[39] A more intriguing challenge was the typescript of *Seven Pillars of Wisdom*, the work T.E.Lawrence had been writing about his wartime exploits in Arabia and Syria. Kipling regarded Lawrence as a romantic figure, a maker of Arab kings, an unfettered Stalky let loose among the Bedouin. In 1922, as biographers of both men have recorded, Lawrence asked him to read his work; but it does not seem to be realized that Kipling had at least partly inspired the project several years earlier. According to an almost illegible draft letter at Harvard in Lawrence's handwriting, the two met in 1918, sat up for two nights while the desert hero 'talked very much' until Kipling, 'wanting perhaps to go to bed, told [him] to go and write a book. Well,' Lawrence exclaimed four years later, 'I did it.'[40]

Lawrence's first draft was stolen on a train, and the second was not ready until the summer of 1922. Kipling agreed to read it on condition that Lawrence never disclosed the fact, but he did not much care for the book. Nor did he appreciate Lawrence's criticisms of the French, who had partitioned Syria after the war and ejected the king-maker's new king (Feisal of the Hejaz) from Damascus. Nor did he like Lawrence himself, though he softened his hostility on learning that the 'poor chap' was illegitimate. It was 'perfectly amazing', he told Doubleday, and explained the 'whole uneasy soul of the man'. It made Kipling 'like him much better than before' and confirmed one of his 'pet theories that the wrong side of the blanket doesn't breed the worst sort'.[41]

Kipling's post-war public duties were not onerous. In 1922 he became Rector of St Andrews University and went to Scotland the following year to give his address. Although he grumbled about having to make a speech, 'the sad duty of a rector', he admitted that he had a 'most wonderful week' in the town. Two years later he resigned as a Rhodes trustee because he disapproved of the trust's new Secretary, Philip Kerr, who 'did not fight in the war' and whose views on imperial unity he did not share. Ill and disheartened, Kipling was grateful for an excuse to resign. He had in any case become rather a negative trustee, opposing candidates who were married (and so could not benefit from the atmosphere of an Oxford college) and those who had not fought in the war. The appointment of a shirker, he argued, seemed to be contrary to the benefactor's requirement that a Rhodes scholar should be a 'sports-man'.[42]

Kipling remained a natural rejectionist of official posts and distinctions. He appreciated an honorary fellowship at Magdalene College, Cambridge, but he stuck to his rule about honours and he also declined to succeed Balfour as president of the London Library. One curious 'honour' he was unable to refuse was the foundation of the Kipling Society by an obsessed admirer, Mr J.H.C.Brooking. Regretting that he had not tried to suppress the project at its conception in 1922, Kipling begged Dunsterville, who became the Society's first president, not to start it up till he was dead. When the attempt failed, Kipling refused for a while to answer Stalky's letters. By 1927 he was exasperated, complaining to his old friend that his 'damn society' made him feel 'naked as well as ridiculous'. Worse still, it encumbered his correspondence with 'silly questions' and demands for information. The whole thing was 'utterly repugnant' to him, but at least he could refuse Brooking's request to inspect articles submitted to the *Kipling Journal*.[43]

After the war he did not quite become the surly recluse of hostile legend. He made no new friends and hardly any new acquaintances; he admitted he could count the people he really cared for on his fingers. But he still enjoyed the company of those few. One frequent visitor to Bateman's, to whom he loved to read his stories and poems, was his friend and neighbour, Violet Milner, a sister of Leo Maxse, a former daughter-in-law of Lord Salisbury and a widow after Milner's death in 1925. Another was Rider Haggard, who found talks with Kipling 'one of the greatest pleasures' left in his life and who believed, probably rightly, that he was the only person, apart from Carrie, to whom he 'opened his heart'.[44]

The Visitors' Book at Bateman's reveals a regular flow of guests, some of whom later made snide remarks about the quality of comfort and cuisine. The Kiplings also saw people outside Sussex. 'Mother thrives on social life,' he wrote to Elsie in 1929 on the day that he met 'a charming man' called P.G.Wodehouse. The dinners and dances of his daughter's 'giddy season' before the war were not repeated, but there was plenty of aristocratic hospitality. Kipling's correspondence with Elsie reveals a series of meals with duchesses as well as visits to grand country houses. In 1923 he and Carrie even had lunch with Lord Lansdowne, the 'old imbecile' who six years earlier had proposed a compromise peace with Germany. Visiting Bowood, Lansdowne's home in Wiltshire, was 'an amazing experience' because the house covered the area of a small village.

Kipling had once told Henry James that one must either live 'frankly in the middle of fields' – as he did – or else in the middle of London. He enjoyed his trips to the capital, which he usually made by motor-car – perhaps to avoid the disrespect shown him at the ticket office at Etchingham Station.* He especially appreciated his

---

*Accused once of jumping the queue, Kipling angrily asked the ticket clerk, 'Do you realise who I am?' The man shouted back, 'I know who you are, Mr Rudyard Bloody Kipling, and you can bloody well take your place in the queue like everybody else.'[45]

clubs, partly no doubt because he could hold forth without Carrie butting in to finish his stories. He loved the Beefsteak, a 'very nice human pot house', and Grillons, where he heard 'more good *talk* and more political tosh' than in most places. He found dining clubs congenial though their seating arrangements made them hazardous. At one dinner of 'The Club', he moaned to Elsie, 'God gave me Haldane on my right'. Later he promoted the idea of a Horace Club with a dozen members carefully selected to avoid such mishaps.[46]

More metropolitan entertainment was provided by the theatre, especially Noël Coward's *Hay Fever* which was a 'really funny modern play'. The cinema was usually shunned, but during the 1920s Kipling saw enough Hollywood epics to capture their tone in 'Naaman's Song', in which he returned to the story of Elisha and the general but omitted Gehazi.

There rise her timeless capitals of Empires daily born,
Whose plinths are laid at midnight, and whose streets are packed at morn;
And here come hired youths and maids that feign to love or sin
In tones like rusty razor-blades to tunes like smitten tin.

('Naaman's Song')

Realistic enough to know that the cinema was not going to disappear, Kipling decided to co-operate with the film-makers. The work was artistically (though not financially) unrewarding because, although he was advising on a screenplay for 'Without Benefit of Clergy' as early as 1920, very few of his stories were filmed in his lifetime – mercifully he died long before Walt Disney's *Jungle Book*. In his last year he was corresponding sternly about making *Soldiers Three* and 'The Man Who Would Be King', grumbling about substituting 'blinking' for 'bloody' and bewildered by complaints about the almost biblical phrase, 'giving the breast', unless there was an 'old maid' among the censors. When he thought of the 'multitude of practically nude whores who caper and sprawl and languish through the "acceptable" films', he felt a 'bit sickish' over objections to the filming of his naked soldiers fording the river at Lungtungpen.[47]

In spite of their infirmities, the Kiplings still travelled during the 1920s, usually in search of winter warmth. A visit to Algiers in 1921 reminded him of India, and the sight of Algerian *tirailleurs* reassured him that they could properly take care of 'the Hun' in occupied Germany. Experience of Andalusia the following year revealed that Spain was a 'heavenly Oriental land' whose inhabitants should not bother to disguise themselves in petticoats and trousers. It also demonstrated that the Spaniards were poor colonists: they were having 'one hell of a time in their Morocco' where, without visiting it, he decided they did 'nothing at all ... except dish out medals'.[48]

Sicily in 1928 provided beauty and wild flowers, but Holland had little chance with its tourist because its prince consort was a German, its inhabitants were European Boers and it had remained neutral during the war; even so he was impressed by the way the Dutch worked and how they handled the river traffic on the Scheldt. More enjoyable was a voyage to Brazil, which produced eight articles, a glimpse of the Rio Carnival and an insight into the possibilities of racial harmony. Kipling thought the Brazilians a 'wonderful breed' who had 'managed to knock out the Colour-Question altogether!' The mixture of 'Red, Black and White' had created 'a type and a very subtle intellect'.[49]

France remained the favourite and most visited destination because he adored the landscape and admired its people. But he no longer much liked the Riviera. The motor car had turned it into a 'noisy smelly' Hell which was not ameliorated by the sight of Cannes 'in all its seasonal whoredom'. 'That dam' Monte [Carlo]' was very much out of his 'line of country', but it was 'internally convenient' despite the overwhelming 'incursion of Huns' who got drunk, infested the restaurants and displayed their wealth with women, cigars, champagne and motor cars. The incursion provided one evening's consolation when Kipling 'watched a Boche ... lose sixty thousand francs in three minutes' at the Casino.[50] And if the smelly traffic became too much, he could always escape to the scented, pine-wooded, less frequented coastal roads, 'indescribably lovely *and* fierce' and reminding him of the landscapes of Turner. By then, also, he had learned to avoid the haunts of English expatriates, the 'mid-Victorian survival' hotel, the 'plain, nourishing food', the 'committees to run everything' from bridge to the golf course that consumed precious local water.[51]

In 1929 and 1931 the Kiplings returned to the Near East to travel up the Nile and to inspect the cemeteries of Allenby's army. Egypt's recent independence, circumscribed though it was in practice by the British High Commissioner, convinced him of the danger of 'premature releases' of imperial control; Palestine confirmed his view that Britain's Zionist policy, sponsored by Balfour and Lloyd George, had created a 'cheap Hell' in the Holy Land. After returning from Palestine he was surprised to find himself 'being bombarded' with Zionist propaganda, a campaign that only reinforced his feeling that the Arabs were in the right.[52]

Between their visits to the Eastern Mediterranean the Kiplings made their final – disastrous – voyage across the Atlantic. After a holiday in Jamaica they intended to stay for a few days in Bermuda before returning home. But Carrie fell ill in Jamaica with stomach pains that were later diagnosed as appendicitis. Unimpressed, apparently, by the island's medical facilities, Kipling insisted on taking her to Bermuda where he installed her in the hospital and himself in the Hotel Bermudiana. He ate alone, reading newspapers that made him 'savage', getting indigestion in the process and trying to avoid people who wanted to 'kodak' him and make him sign books. Besieged in his hotel, he was forced to witness the effect of Prohibition on American citizens – 'rather an unpleasing exhibition on the social side', he complained with restraint to the Canadian doctor who had looked after Carrie on board ship. Writing to Elsie he called his hotel a 'Howling Caravanserai of Rich Drunks', the destination of hundreds of 'Yanks' escaping Prohibition on 'big ocean booze-hounds' from New York. The exhibition upset him, especially the 'crapulous flushed women': he hated seeing a woman 'coopered' in public. When Carrie was well enough to travel, after two and a half months on the island, her husband insisted on returning via Montreal rather than via the 'barrage of barbarians to Southward' in New York.[53]

18

Bonfires on the Ice

I N THE SPRING of 1921 ill health forced Bonar Law to resign from
Lloyd George's Government and from the leadership of the
Unionist Party. Urged by his doctor to recuperate in the south of
France, he repaired to Cannes where he played bridge and chess and
one set of tennis a day. The Kiplings, who had been visiting Algiers,
found him there and moved into his hotel.

The poet was not impressed by the sight of a 'demobbed' politician. His friend was 'dead-stale and tired-out' and bereft of inner
resources to sustain his compulsory idleness. His conversation illustrated the enervating effect that a political career had on a man's
character: even a 'straight and good politician' like Law was more
concerned with means than ends and talked more about the personalities 'in his game' than about his convictions.[1]

Two springs later, Kipling again encountered Law in France: this
time he was so appalled by the state of his friend's health that he tele-
graphed Beaverbrook, with whom he was no longer on speaking
terms, to rush out to Aix-les-Bains.[2] During the two years separating
his attempted recuperations, Law had returned to politics, destroyed
the Coalition Government, regained leadership of the Unionists,
become Prime Minister and won a General Election. He was now
dying of throat cancer.

Soon after Kipling's return to England in May 1923, Law was succeeded as Prime Minister by Stanley Baldwin. The succession was a

curious event. Largely on the advice of Balfour, the King rejected the claims of Curzon, the Foreign Secretary, in favour of the less talented Baldwin, who had disappointed his colleagues as President of the Board of Trade and who had hardly distinguished himself during his few months as Chancellor of the Exchequer. But the selection was not confined to credentials. Apart from the advantage of being in the Commons while Curzon was in the Lords, Baldwin was better suited to deal with the circumstances of post-war Britain. T.P. O'Connor, the irrepressible Irish journalist and MP, observed that in politics and speech Curzon personified those imperial feelings that Kipling expressed in poetry and prose.[3] The statesman and the poet were essentially late Victorians, already uncomfortable in the Edwardian Age and far more so in the Britain of 1923, a bruised and traumatized nation uneasy with greatness, tired of imperial responsibilities and wishing to turn inwards and deal with its social and economic problems. As it later showed, the country was relieved to have a leader so different from Lloyd George, a rather humdrum, pipe-smoking, reassuring politician with an ear for the concerns of ordinary people and a conciliatory approach to the Labour movement.

Kipling admired Curzon's intellect and politics but preferred Baldwin's character and personality. The former proconsul, he observed to Haggard, was a 'machine of necessary industry', but his talents were marred by vanity and self-pity. Cousin Stanley was more congenial, modest about his achievements – as at the time he had every reason to be – and lacking the swagger of a man born to the purple. As a Cabinet minister, noted Carrie, he had been rather pompous and humourless, but as premier he was soon in 'excellent form'. He and his wife had been the first guests at Bateman's in 1902 and were among the most regular visitors for the next thirty years. In return they entertained the Kiplings at Downing Street, Chequers (recently designated as the Prime Minister's country residence) and their home in Worcestershire. Kipling was not sure about Baldwin's politics, which were indeed somewhat opaque, yet he helped him with his speeches, he had him elected to 'The Club', and he offered him an honorary degree at St Andrews. To Rider Haggard he remarked that the new Prime Minister was 'reasonably sincere and honest' – high praise for a politician outside the pantheon of Rhodes, Milner, Chamberlain and Roosevelt.[4]

In November 1923 Baldwin asked the King to dissolve Parliament only a year after Bonar Law had won an election that gave the Conservatives (as the Unionists called themselves again after the Anglo-Irish Treaty) an overall majority in the Commons of 75. Against the advice of Curzon, who predicted an electoral disaster, he had insisted on appealing for a mandate to introduce tariffs as a means of combating unemployment. The disaster duly occurred, Baldwin resigned, and the first Labour Government, led by Ramsay MacDonald and tacitly supported by the Liberals, took office.

On learning the electoral result, Kipling urged his cousin not to compromise or form a coalition but to 'drive Labour to take the helm'. Since Labour MPs occupied less than a third of the parliamentary seats – and could be voted out if they misbehaved – the Conservatives were in a strong position to 'try them out'. Yet he was nervous about the experiment. As he confessed to his friend Chevrillon, the English had the 'insane' idea that everyone should be given a chance, 'as tho' the affairs of the Empire were a cricket match'. MacDonald's ministry would be 'Bolshevism without bullets' – a mysterious deduction – but at least the 'excited orders and instructions from Moscow' would show people who was really in charge of the Labour Party.[5]

The following autumn the Liberals turned MacDonald out and in the ensuing election – the third in less than two years – they lost three-quarters of their seats. Kipling was delighted by the size of his cousin's victory – an overall majority of 223 – but knew that this did not reflect the real balance of forces in the country. He himself tended to exaggerate the strength of Labour and the Trades Union Congress. As early as 1919 he had claimed that the effective government of the country was in the hands of the TUC as much as medieval Europe had been in the hands of the Papacy.[6] He did not change his view. Nor did he amend his conviction that industrial strikes were being financed by the Bolsheviks. During the General Strike of 1926 he urged the *Morning Post* to produce lists of trade union leaders with details of their affiliation to Moscow; more sensibly he advocated, as an 'elemental' need, a secret ballot of union members before striking. Yet the Strike, he concluded after it had been defeated by Baldwin, had been a salutary experience because it had damaged the 'sacred prestige' of the unions and had shown 'the revolutionary' that 'we don't much care for Revolutions as a nation'.[7]

By the time Labour formed another minority government in 1929,

Kipling was less inclined to 'try them out'. MacDonald, again Prime Minister, was 'unintelligent and unintelligible'; his mind was 'tosh'; he was a 'false fellow from his boots to his quiff'. His party had gained power by bribing the electorate and was exercising it by cooking up a 'hell-broth' for India and a 'débâcle' for Egypt. Every step the Government took, he told Gwynne, was 'a sort of echo of the Soviet lead', and he urged his friend to hammer away in the *Morning Post* at the relationship between 'the Soviet and our gang'. In the summer of 1931 he invited Gwynne to Bateman's where they spent an evening in a mood of deepening depression. 'We each drove the other', he reported, 'to beyond the bottom – to the absolute zero – of pessimism.'[8]

One particularly depressing subject was personal taxation. Kipling could never understand why he should be obliged to surrender a large chunk of his income to provide for people who were thereby 'freed from the necessity of doing any work at all'. Land taxes were 'simply insane', while death duties would ensure that most of the land at Bateman's would eventually be covered by pink and mauve villas costing £595 apiece. At the end of 1931 he was wondering where, after paying taxes, he could afford to go on holiday. He exaggerated his impoverishment, but not excessively. The following year his income tax and super tax amounted to £17,000, over half his income.[9]

Yet for Kipling the most obnoxious act committed by the second Labour Government was the advice to foreign officials that they need not feel obliged to lay wreaths at the Whitehall Cenotaph or on the Tomb of the Unknown Warrior. Incensed by the administration's subsequent explanation that it aspired to the 'eradication of memories of the Great War', Kipling published 'Memories', a poem that resonated within those who believed the Government to be pacifist and unpatriotic. Prefaced by the words, *The Socialist Government speaks*, the verses describe Labour's reasons for not honouring the dead and its tactics for reducing the influence of Remembrance Day.

> Wisely, but yearly, filch some wreath –
> Lay some proud rite aside –
> And daily tarnish with Our breath
> The ends for which They died.

Distract, deride, decry, confuse –
(Or – if it serve Us pray!)
So presently We break the use
And meaning of Their day!

During MacDonald's ministry Kipling gave moral support to his cousin against onslaughts not from Labour but from Conservative malcontents and from the country's two most powerful press barons, Lords Beaverbrook and Rothermere. Baldwin's opponents held the view (which Kipling increasingly came to share) that the Conservative leader was inept and uninspiring. Many of them also believed (as Kipling did) that the correct response to unemployment and the Tory defeat was protectionism. In the summer of 1929 Beaverbrook launched his 'Crusade' for Empire Free Trade – an intentionally confusing term* – and the following year he was supported by Rothermere in his attempt to destroy Baldwin and supplant him in person.† The press barons fanned each other's megalomania. In the summer of 1930 Rothermere announced that his newspapers would not support Baldwin unless he was given the names of the next cabinet in advance. This amazing display of arrogance finally goaded the Tory leader into defending himself. He repudiated 'with contempt', he declared in a speech to his MPs, the most 'preposterous and insolent demand' ever made to the leader of a political party.

In the autumn of 1930 Kipling wrote a sympathetic letter to Baldwin about the iniquities of the press barons. They were damaging the Tory leader, the country and the Empire while merely gaining the recognition of 'gangster' journalism, of 'putting men "on the spot" if they don't happen to suit the political racketeer'. It was an exact parallel to Chicago. 'I hope and pray', he added, 'you'll be able to down 'em and, after that, to keep 'em in their places.'[11]

At the time – and for several months after – it looked improbable

---

*Years later Beaverbrook was asked by the historian Robert Blake why he had used this slogan for a cause promoting tariff reform. His 'reply was that the British public was addicted to free trade and fond of the Empire; they would only swallow protection if suitably described'.[10]

†The unusual alliance between the proprietors of the *Daily Express* and the *Daily Mail* can be partly attributed to the fact that they had enormous shareholdings in each other's companies.

that Baldwin would be able to 'down 'em'. On the day he received Kipling's letter, the official Conservative was defeated by a candidate put up by Beaverbrook at a by-election in South Paddington. The following February the Tory was beaten into third place by an Empire Crusader in the Labour seat of East Islington. And as a third by-election humiliation loomed in March, in the St George's Division of Westminster, Baldwin surrendered to pressure within the party and decided to resign. Dissuaded at the last moment by two of his supporters, he denounced Beaverbrook and Rothermere in one of his most memorable speeches. Their newspapers, he declared a week before St George's went to the polls, were not newspapers but 'engines of propaganda' for the 'personal likes and dislikes of two men' whose journalism consisted of half-truths, misrepresentation and direct falsehood.

> What the proprietorship of these papers is aiming at is power, and power without responsibility – the prerogative of the harlot throughout the ages ... this contest is not a contest as to who is to lead the party, but as to who is to appoint the leader of the party.

The speech was a triumph; so was the result, a large and unexpected majority for the Conservative candidate, Duff Cooper. The success of both is thought to have owed much to the phrase, 'the prerogative of the harlot throughout the ages', which has invariably been attributed to Kipling. It sounds quite like Kipling, and it sounds not at all like Baldwin, but the claim that the former was the author rests merely on family tradition among the Baldwins that the poet had 'lent' the phrase to the politician. Nevertheless, Kipling had been helping his cousin on another speech a few days earlier, and he had used the words 'power without responsibility' about Rothermere the previous year in a letter to his Aunt Edith Macdonald. Yet, for all its arresting sonority, the phrase seems to make little sense. Harlots are not usually more powerful and irresponsible than their customers.

The St George's victory ended the threat to Baldwin's leadership. It also marked the end of a lengthy period of cousinly appreciation. In response to the financial crisis of the summer of 1931, Baldwin joined MacDonald in the Cabinet of a National Government consisting of four Labour ministers, four Conservatives and two Liberals. Scoffing at the new administration, in which Baldwin served under MacDonald, Kipling told Gwynne that his cousin was a 'socialist at heart', of 'one kidney' with 'Mac'; it was all the fault of mixing with the 'academic socialist crowd' when he was at Cambridge.[12] Baldwin, who regarded himself as a progressive Conservative, was not of course a socialist: if in the 1920s he did not confront Labour as vigorously as Kipling wanted, it was because he hoped the party would become a moderate and constitutional force in national politics. His cousin could not sympathize with the project and seemed incapable of understanding it.

The Labour Party did not follow its leader into the National Government. Indeed it expelled MacDonald and his ministerial colleagues and fought the General Election against a coalition of Conservatives, Liberals and 'National Labour'. The result was so overwhelming that even Kipling was briefly pleased. Labour was reduced to 52 seats, while the National Government held an astonishing 554; the Conservative tally of 473 MPs was the highest won by any party in the history of Westminster. Yet Kipling sobered himself with the reflection that the Government would be led by sentimentalists eager not to victimize or hurt the feelings of the 'overwhelmed Bolshies'. Two months after the election he told Aunt Edith that the administration appeared to have a 'strong Labour-Liberal-Socialist thrust'. The following year he defined the 'so-called' National Government as 'a sort of Higher Socialism tempered with hot air'.[13]

Kipling's criticism of the Mac Stan condominium was directed at its position on Europe and the Empire. Yet there was little cause to scold it as far as the dominions were concerned. He might complain that the British were throwing away their Empire 'in lumps' (although they had not even begun to do so). He could despair that the Australian motor car market was dominated by Americans rather than by Morris of Cowley. But in the early 1930s he could not suppress a sense of optimism about the future of the dominions, especially Canada. The diamond jubilee of the Canadian Confederation in 1927, celebrated at Westminster Abbey to the strains of 'Recessional', had been a heartening experience, a 'step on the threshold of a new life and self-knowledge for the Dominion and the Empire'. Canada was 'awake, aware and resolute' and continued to be so during the subsequent decade. It was a 'miracle' that she had been able to 'find herself' and 'pursue her own destiny' despite the 'moral disorder' of her enormous southern neighbour. Above all, what a relief that she was not following the wrong Roosevelt's 'pernicious example' of setting up some kind of New Deal.[14]

The main imperial preoccupation was India. In 1928 the Indian National Congress, a more considerable organization than it had been when Kipling reported its conference forty years before, reaffirmed its aim for dominion status within the British Empire. The following year the Viceroy, Lord Irwin, declared that dominion-hood was also Britain's intention, a statement approved by the Government and endorsed by Baldwin without consulting his Shadow Cabinet. Imperialist Conservatives were appalled. An outraged Churchill savaged the policy and warned that the 'loss of India would mark and consummate the downfall of the British Empire'.[15]

Kipling thus acquired a fellow Cassandra, though not one whom he was ever able to admire. Churchill's misdemeanours as a Liberal, his well-timed return to the Conservatives in 1924, his unamended Free Trade views as Baldwin's eccentric choice for the Exchequer — the combination helped preserve him as one of Kipling's least favourite politicians. Yet their views on India were virtually identical. They saw the Subcontinent through the eyes of the nineteenth century, which was when they had last seen it; they insisted that Indians were unready to govern themselves; and they believed that British withdrawal would lead to sectarian conflict and the tyranny of the Hindus. Irwin's release of Gandhi of 1931 (he had been jailed during the civil disobedience campaign the year before), followed by the ex-prisoner's interview with the Viceroy, enraged the Tory diehards. Lord Lloyd, a former Governor of Bombay and a friend of Churchill and Kipling, was amazed at the sight of the Delhi Government 'drinking tea with treason and actually negotiating with sedition'. Churchill was 'nauseated' by the spectacle of a 'fakir, striding half-naked' to parley on equal terms with the Viceroy. And Kipling reacted by urging the *Morning Post* to publish a leader or a cartoon depicting the 'betrayal of 300,000 Irish loyalists as a rehearsal for the betrayal of 300,000,000 wretched peasants'.[16]

Like Churchill, Kipling believed that with a little firmness Britain could crush Congress, restore order and rediscover its sense of imperial mission. Other powers, he suggested, would destroy the nationalist movement with a six-week dose of repression. But Britain's gentlemanly ways, its exasperating kindness, its actions governed by the 'highest motives', were simply convincing nationalists that the imperial power was losing the will to protect its interests. 'Hideously worried' by the situation, and believing that a Hindu government would restore suttee and other evils, he joined the Indian Defence League and became one of its vice-presidents. But although he contemplated a public damnation of the Government, in the end he rejected appeals to take part in a campaign. Despite his opinion that Britain's Indian policy was a 'tangle of ignorance', he did nothing more active than request his old paper, the *Civil and Military Gazette*, to feed the *Morning Post* with items of significance.[17]

The culmination of the National Government's policy was the India Act of 1935 that proposed a federal structure for the whole of the Subcontinent, including the princely states. Churchill opposed it strenuously, although it was a hopeless cause and one that blunted the effectiveness of his simultaneous campaign for rearmament against the threat of Nazi Germany. Like Kipling, he saw imperialism as a static idea, unsuited to even the mildest evolution. Their view remained unshaken by the Great War, the Fourteen Points and the League of Nations. In 1931 Parliament had passed the Statute of Westminster enshrining the change from the idea of an imperial enterprise directed by Britain to the concept of a Commonwealth of Nations, the dominions and the 'mother country' in free association and with equal status. Churchill regarded it as 'repellent legislation'. Kipling hated it because it gave the world the impression that England was 'putting up her imperial shutters'. It was also demonstrably premature: how could the dominions be autonomous and equal in status when they were dependent on British strength for their defence? 'There's no point', he observed, 'in giving boys latchkeys till they have a house with a door that locks.'[18]

As he approached his seventieth year, Kipling became ever more virulent about the National Government and his cousin's role in it. He was in 'immense form', reported Violet Milner after a visit to Bateman's in November 1934, reading a story, reciting a poem and talking about the 'ghastly failure of Baldwin'. The Government, he liked to insist, was socialist, led by an 'international socialist' with a 'philosophical socialist' (Baldwin) as his 'cat's-paw' nominally representing a large number of voters who had no influence over policy. It was little consolation when the cat's-paw exchanged places with

MacDonald and became Prime Minister for the third time in June 1935.[19]

On European issues, as on India, the Government's chief adversary was Churchill. Again his views coincided almost entirely with Kipling's, and again they made no difference to the poet's estimation of his admirer. Until the end of his life Kipling regarded him as the most untrustworthy man in British politics and, as late as February 1935, told his son-in-law that he would prefer Neville Chamberlain as Prime Minister to anyone else. For once his long-sightedness was defective. Not only did Chamberlain become the evangelist of appeasement; he also proved an even more inadequate war leader than Asquith.

All Kipling's European views were predicated on the security of France and the maintenance of the Anglo-French Entente with sufficient strength to counter the inevitable resurgence of Germany. After the war he became Vice-President of The Friends of France and at a banquet at the Sorbonne, where he was awarded an honorary degree, he described Britain and France as the 'twin fortresses of European civilisation'. The 'whole weight of the world', he declared at other times, lay on the necks of the two nations and required them to form an alliance.[20]

Britain and France disagreed, however, over the treatment of defeated Germany. The French Prime Minister, Poincaré, who was determined to weaken their opponent still further, encouraged separatist movements in the Rhineland and the Palatinate. He was also intransigent over the collection of reparations, refusing a moratorium even when the German currency was collapsing, and in January 1923 he ordered his troops to occupy the Ruhr and collect them by force. While the British regarded the occupation as counter-productive for everyone, they were not prepared to break the Entente on the issue. They therefore took up a position of neutrality that may have been respectable but was politically ineffectual.

Kipling saw nothing respectable in neutrality and was outraged that France should be regarded as 'militaristic'. The French, he insisted, had every right to strengthen themselves at the expense of Germany: a twice-burned nation was justified in taking steps to deter a third catastrophe. Large areas of France had been 'stamped into dust' and their 'guts trampled out' – and 'the Hun' was still sitting across the frontier, 'developing new gases of extraordinary potency'.

It was absurd of the United States and Britain, protected by seas, to lecture a country that had been 'half killed' and was 'naturally a little concerned that next time she should be wholly slain'.[21]

Kipling's Francophilia was now so ardent that he even managed to like Poincaré, the most fractious and unsympathetic of French leaders. And he liked him, as he admitted to his son-in-law, 'precisely' because Poincaré did not like the *'Albionistes perfides'* – 'and I don't blame him', he added. Less inexplicably, he also admired Clemenceau, whom he fawned on, reverentially reporting their meetings in Paris and addressing him in their correspondence as 'Master'. But his admiration did not extend to Briand or to the next generation of French politicians. By 1933, after years of political instability, he was hoping for a restoration of the monarchy or a dictatorship.[22]

Since he believed that no reasonable person could fail to see the justice of France's position, Kipling ascribed anti-French hostility to bribery, propaganda and political extremism. People in England who called France 'militaristic' were avowedly the 'enemies of all order and the friends of the Boche and the Bolshevik and the Irish'. An international campaign to malign the French must, he presumed, have had 'an enormous amount of Hebrew and Hun money' behind it. To one correspondent he attributed pro-German feeling to the pull of Absolute Evil. Whenever 'there was a taint of perversion in any mind, it seems to have turned as automatically towards the Hun as a flower turns to the light'.[23]

Kipling's views on European security were based on a single premiss: that Germany is irredeemable. The Boche never changes. He wages peace as he wages war – by creating a desert all around him. He defaults on his reparations because, so he pretends, he cannot afford to pay them, though in reality it is because he wants the money to buy guns. But he must be forced to pay up so that he simply cannot afford to rearm. He must remember (as we seem to have forgotten) that 'he's the Leading Gangster of the World'.[24] And he's going to start another world war.

Such an opinion naturally prevented Kipling from seeing any merit in Germany's attempts at international rehabilitation. The efforts of Gustav Stresemann, the remarkable Foreign Minister between 1923 and 1929, were seen as window-dressing. Germany might agree to pay reparations, renounce Alsace-Lorraine, fulfil its Versailles obligations, even join the League of Nations, but it was still

Germany. It was still the 'resurrected heathen who came into Christianity a thousand years or so after the rest of Europe and who at heart follows the dark Gods of the North with the ferocity and darkness of the were-wolf his ancestor'.[25]

Before the end of the Great War Kipling had developed the theory that every race betrays its essential characteristics in its folk tales. For the rest of his life he argued publicly and in private that Germany's wickedness was illustrated by the legend of the werewolf. In 1921 he had told his Sorbonne audience about the phenomenon, the murderous beast that became a man and reverted whenever he pleased. Following years of killing and devastation, the German wolf had decided to become a human being. But in 1932, when Hitler won over thirteen million votes in a presidential election, he changed shape again. After twelve years as a man, after accomplishing all that he could achieve by peaceful means, it was the beast's turn to make further gains. The next war, the 'real war', Kipling announced as he surveyed the rise of the Nazis, had begun on 11 November 1918.[26] He did not accept that it might have started a year later at Versailles or that the vindictive conditions of the peace treaty had assisted the Nazis' rise to power.

Like Churchill, Kipling did not divide Europe into fascists versus democrats or Bolsheviks versus Nazis. For both of them the essential struggle was between Germany and Western Europe, between barbarism and civilization. They did not bracket Mussolini with Hitler because it seemed absurd and dangerous to do so: what was the point of converting an ally of the last war into an enemy in the next one? Kipling might argue that Liberalism was 'the mother of Destruction the world over' but he was not a fascist. His limited and temporary admiration for Mussolini was based on the belief that the Duce was a strong man who got things done. At the time of the General Strike he envied the way that Mussolini had dispensed with industrial unrest. And during his visit to Algeciras in 1924 he was glad that 'the Spaniard' was 'being Mussolinied for his own good' by General Primo de Rivera.[27] Yet he had no time for fascist doctrines or for jackboots and the rest of the paraphernalia; nor did he sympathize with Oswald Mosley ('a bounder and an *arriviste*') and his Blackshirts. By the mid-1930s he had come to regard Mussolini as a crazy and irrational megalomaniac.[28]

Kipling thought the Italian invasion of Abyssinia was a mistake:

the soldiers would die of disease, mechanized troops would be useless, it was futile to bomb mountainous country from the air. But he did not regard the onslaught as a crime. He was not by nature inclined to condemn the imperial impulse, however debased (unless it was German), although he regarded Italy as an inappropriate colonizer and once remarked that he had mistrusted it ever since the Middle Ages.[29]

His sympathy for the Italian position grew when the League of Nations imposed economic sanctions in response to the attack on Abyssinia, a member of the League. Almost anything the League did was bound to annoy Kipling. Sceptical about the organization from the beginning, he labelled it 'dangerous', mocked its ideals and wished it would lie down and die.[30] Now, with British support, it was surpassing itself by antagonizing Italy and propelling Mussolini into the arms of Hitler on the eve of a global conflict. Sanctions, he believed, were a 'dam-silly ... racket'. Britain was not rich enough in friends to provoke a new enmity not only in Europe but also on the route to India in the Red Sea and the Horn of Africa. Enraged by an 'unusually silly' cartoon about Gorgonzola in *Punch*, he asked friends whether it was 'even moderately expedient' to be 'funny' at the expense of a 'long-memoried and vindictive race' that would not forgive Britain for three generations.[31] In December 1935 he sent *The Times* a poem that was doubtless pungent on the subject of sanctions; but he managed to suppress and destroy it on learning of the Hoare-Laval plan, an agreement between Britain and France to hand over the fertile half of Abyssinia to Italy.

In May 1932 Kipling published 'The Storm Cone', a powerful but oblique warning of the approaching Götterdämmerung.

> This is the midnight – let no star
> Delude us – dawn is very far.
> This is the tempest long foretold –
> Slow to make head but sure to hold.

Two months later the Nazi Party won 230 seats in the Reichstag. Kipling decided to become slightly less oblique: his last major writings are complicated but unambiguous forewarnings of the Second World War.

In 1933 Hitler became Chancellor and quickly established his dictatorship. 'The Hitlerites are out for blood', noted Kipling: 'the Hun [was] stripped naked for war' while the British, still running down their defences, were displaying less forethought than 'incubated chickens'.[32] Kipling was so disgusted by the Nazis and the sight of their flag that he removed the swastika, a Hindu symbol of good luck, from his bookbindings. It had been his trademark for nearly forty years but it was now 'defiled beyond redemption'.[33]

On 12 November Germany held an 'election' in which the people were given the choice of voting for or against a single Nazi list for the Reichstag; and a plebiscite to support (or not) Hitler's decision to withdraw from the League of Nations because Germany was not being treated as an equal by the other Powers. Nearly all Germans voted, and nearly all of them voted for Hitler. At the concentration camp in Dachau 97 per cent of the prisoners voted for their gaolers.[34]

Kipling's commentaries on the events were well timed. Primed by his master, Gwynne had been issuing warnings of the Nazi threat and earlier in the year he had printed a letter from Kipling arguing that civilization depended on Britain and France standing together against a Germany that had learned nothing from the previous war. Now, on the fifteenth anniversary of the Armistice, the *Morning Post* published Kipling's 'The Pleasure Cruise', a dialogue between dead soldiers who have been killed because their generals were no good and because they had only been trained to play cricket; returning to England, they find that everyone has forgotten them and that Demos and demagoguery are again leaving the country unprotected. This prose return to the spirit of 'The Islanders' was printed the day before the plebiscite. On the day after the vote the *Morning Post* published, alongside news of the result, 'Bonfires on the Ice', a poem in which Kipling chose to tell self-evident truths in the language of political cliché and platitude.[35]

> We know that Ones and Ones make Twos
> (Till Demos votes 'em Three or Nought)
> We know the Fenrys wolf is loose. *
> We know what Fight has not been fought.
> We know the Father to the Thought

---

*Wolves were much on Kipling's mind. Fenrys or Fenrir was a monstrous wolf in Norse mythology chained by Gods who know that he will break loose on Doomsday and try to devour them. Hitler was a suitably lupine anthropoid.

> Which argues Babe and Cockatrice
>   Would play together, were they taught.
> We know *that* Bonfire on the Ice.

Comrade Mac and Cousin Stan were building *that* bonfire for Britain.

Kipling found comfort in the sheer obviousness of Hitler's intentions. The 'Boche' was 'our best friend' because he was unable to conceal his motives, his ambitions and even his nature. Hitler was so plainly the Fenrys wolf that 'not even the deafest of pacifists' could fail to understand him. Nor, presumably, could anyone fail to detect his programme: it was nothing else but 're-armament preparatory to war for plunder'. The only uncertainty was the starting date. In 1934 Kipling hoped it could be delayed for three years.[36]

Yet as obvious as Germany's intentions was Britain's unreadiness to counter them. The armed forces were in a pitiful state, worse than in 1914, Kipling claimed, with the Navy cut by half and the Army outnumbered by civil servants. The country was simply inviting the Germans to attack it. All this was obvious to him and to Churchill and to many other people, including admirals and generals, but it was not obvious to the Cabinet or its supporters in the country. At Grillons Club in 1935 Kipling met Sir John Simon, the Foreign Secretary, and thought him extraordinarily naïve about Ribbentrop, the architect of the most infamous Nazi treaties. The British people were refusing to take precautions because they wanted to be 'fair to their enemies', to regard them as innocent if they were merely flourishing their pistols rather than firing them. According to Kipling, they had connived at the 'wrecking' of the armed forces and had accepted disarmament as a process of nature. But they still deserved to be protected. 'Yell', he commanded Gwynne, for protection from air raids. Tell the Government that if it refuses to let us defend ourselves, it must build shelters and give us a chance to live. Dated January 1934, it was one of Kipling's most prescient and pathetic appeals.[37]

In March 1935 Kipling published 'Hymn of Breaking Strain', one of his last poems, a prayer for help from a mysterious God.

> Oh veiled and secret Power
>   Whose paths we search in vain,
> Be with us in our hour
>   Of overthrow and pain;

> That we – by which sure token
> We know Thy ways are true –
> In spite of being broken –
> *Because of being broken –*
> *May rise and build anew.*
> *Stand up and build anew!*

Two months later, on the day of the King's Silver Jubilee, he gave a résumé of the international situation at a dinner of the Royal Society of St George. In much of the Eastern Hemisphere, he declared, administration was carried out by 'State-controlled murder and torture ... State-engineered famine, starvation, and slavery ... [and] State-prescribed paganism'. Germany, he pointed out, had won its place in civilization by means of three well-planned wars and, although checked in the fourth, had been planning for many years for the fifth. Yet although these developments had been perfectly obvious, the British had decided they were not threatened and that their country had more important things to do than worry about them. While concentrating on improving living standards,

> we chose not to provide that reasonable margin of external safety, without which even the lowest standard of life cannot be maintained in this dangerously congested island ... [Thus the German's] path was made easy for him. Stride for stride with his progress towards his avowed goal, we toiled, as men toil after virtue, to cast away a half, and more than a half, of our defences in all three elements, and to limit the sources of their supply and renewal. This we did explicitly that we might set the rest of the world a good example.[38]

It was a stark message, and its truths were soon revealed. Kipling did not live to see Munich or the Anschluss or even the German reoccupation of the Rhineland, but none of these events would have surprised him. During his final month, however, he flickered briefly into optimism. In January 1936, as the Government was belatedly rearming, he thought Britain might pull through. Things were even improving in the 'European lunatic asylum', though it was 'depressing to live with lunatics'. Civilization was 'appealing on the ground of reason and sanity' to two megalomaniacs, Hitler and Mussolini, who had 'parted with both a long time ago'. But the explosion was not due yet, and every year gained, every month even, increased the prospects of the sane.[39]

Kipling was resentful that Hitler had denied him a peaceful old age. But his last years were not entirely miserable, and at least his health was better. Both Kiplings had been persistently ill since John's death, he from his undiagnosed ulcer (and the effects of taking the wrong medicines for years), Carrie from diabetes, rheumatism and hysteria exhibited by extreme possessiveness and the recurrent threat that she would jump out of the window if her husband did not do what she wanted. At the beginning of 1932 they felt better after a stay in Bath where Kipling was able to sleep properly for the first time in years. But by early summer he was again in great pain. Violet Milner, still a regular visitor, noted that he was almost always ill and recorded a 'very depressing' lunch at Bateman's with Rudyard ill and 'very low' and Carrie 'almost beside herself with nerves'.[40]

Physical collapse, preceded by vomiting and haemorrhages, finally drove Kipling to acquire a new doctor, a French specialist who found the ulcer and expelled the medicine bottles. After a few days in the hands of his 'fresh vet', Kipling felt buoyant and at last free of pain. He had a relapse in July 1934 but recovered so quickly that 'Rud in great form' was soon spattering the pages of Lady Milner's diary. Cutting down on cigarettes and munching a diet of 'farinaceous flap-doodle' were annoying, but the compensation of restored health was immense.

Bateman's and its land still gave him pleasure. He loved the songs of nightingales in the yew hedges; he enjoyed the work on the farms, the supervision of hedging, ditching and shoring up his riverbank. Such things kept him occupied and happy: on his seventieth birthday he announced that they interested him more than anything else.

Beyond the perimeter of Bateman's the countryside gave less pleasure. The rabbit hutches of suburbia were appearing; corncrakes were disappearing; hikers were invading footpaths and making him nervous about his bulls. Pastoral Sussex no longer features in his late collections of stories, *Debits and Credits* and *Limits and Renewals* (1932): in 'The Wish House', as Professor Bodelsen has observed, the county is 'pointedly de-romanticised' with heavy traffic and football crowds. Kipling advised Dunsterville to spend his retirement in the

West Country, which was comparatively free of bungalows, and told another friend it was pointless to build a house in Majorca because the island would soon be covered by tourists and cocktail bars.[41]

One of the late solaces of his life was his friendship with George V. Kipling was the only writer whose company the King enjoyed, and consequently he dined at Buckingham Palace and was invited to Balmoral. In return he lent the monarch books and helped him with his speeches, a time-consuming favour he extended to Prince George and the Prince of Wales. In 1932 he agreed to write the King's first Christmas message for the wireless and wept as he heard his own words broadcast to the Empire: 'I speak now from my home and from my heart to you all; to men and women so cut off by the snows, the desert or the sea, that only voices of the air can reach them.' The following year he performed the same service, but the draftsmanship was subsequently taken over by Archbishop Lang.[42]

Since the King believed the Navy could teach a prince all he needed to know, the Senior Service logically became the chief subject of conversation between the poet and his sovereign. Kipling much admired King George and was convinced that his knowledge of men stemmed from his years as a youthful sailor. In July 1935 he watched the Navy Review, part of the Silver Jubilee celebrations, and published one of his worst poems, 'The King and the Sea', a eulogy attributing the King's sense of duty and strength of character to his naval upbringing. Later in the year the monarch sent a telegram congratulating him on his seventieth birthday.[43]*

At New Year 1936, a fortnight before his death, Kipling claimed to have no fear of dying: he knew that God (who had played a minor and intermittent role in his life) did not abandon His people at the end of their days. He had known for a couple of years that little time remained and the previous August he had begun writing his short, brilliant and severely self-censored autobiography, *Something of Myself*. All trains, he observed to friends, had to stop at one station or another, and he was lucky to have seen the distant signal in time. But

---

*Although it arrived a month early, this was a comparatively minor mistake. At the time of Thomas Hardy's seventieth birthday, Asquith's private secretary rang up Buckingham Palace and suggested a telegram should be sent to 'old Hardy'. The scheme was regarded as a 'jolly good idea', and Mr Hardy of Alnwick, who made the King's fishing rods, was duly 'astonished to receive royal congratulations on attaining an age he had not attained on a day which was the anniversary of nothing'.[44]

he wished the station did not have to be 'such an ugly and lonesome place'.[45]

On 12 January Kipling visited his son-in-law, who was in bed with bronchitis. Bambridge had not seen him as happy or as healthy for years: freedom from pain had made his 'talk and thoughts quick as lightning & splendid to listen to'.[46] A few hours later Kipling's ulcer burst, and he was rushed from his Piccadilly hotel to the Middlesex Hospital. In the small hours of the 13th he told a surgeon that 'something has come adrift inside', and an operation on his perforated duodenum was quickly performed. Uncertainty about his chances of recovery continued for several days, but on the 16th he deteriorated. He lost consciousness late on the following day and after midnight he died. It was his forty-fourth wedding anniversary. Two days later George V also died. 'The King has gone', it was said, 'and taken his trumpeter with him.'[47]

Rudyard Kipling was cremated at Golders Green and his ashes buried at Poets' Corner in Westminster Abbey. The pallbearers reflected the imperial rather than the literary side of his career: they included the Prime Minister (Baldwin), a Field Marshal, an Admiral of the Fleet, and his disciple and closest surviving friend, Taffy Gwynne.* The congregation sang 'Recessional' and 'Abide With Me', and the Dean of Westminster gave the Blessing, specially composed for the occasion.

> In thankfulness to Almighty God for the life and work of one who has been allowed to speak as a prophet to many generations of men, his own generation and those which are yet to come – unto God's gracious mercy and protection we deliver him. The Lord bless him and keep him, and the blessing of God Almighty be upon you now and always.

Kipling's death prompted numerous tributes, to his teachings and his inspiration and to his literary genius and his laureateship of the Empire. A bleaker yet sadly accurate note had been sounded the previous month when an American newspaper predicted that Kipling's seventieth birthday would be the anniversary of a ghost: the bard's life had become so secluded and remote that to most Englishmen he belonged to the 'folklore of his country – a silent, shadowy figure of the past'. Although

---

*J.M.Barrie was invited to be a pallbearer and accepted. But according to Elsie, the author of *Peter Pan* 'got the jitters and backed out of it at the last minute!'[48]

several of his greatest stories had been written in the 1920s, he had long been treated, as Peter Keating has remarked, as a 'dead Classic'.[49]

At the time of his death – and often afterwards – it was said that Kipling was born out of his time. It is not true. He was very much a child of his time; he represented the epoch of his youth better than anyone. But the times changed, as they usually do, and Kipling did not change with them. Much the same can be said of Churchill, although he was transmuted into a Liberal before reverting in the 1930s to a Victorian imperialist or, as Baldwin put it, 'the subaltern of hussars of '96'. Until Hitler revived his career, Churchill seemed to be a Classic who was almost dead.

In his prime as an imperial bard, Kipling seemed to embody both the hopes and the fears of his countrymen. But he did more than that. His was a voice that people loved not just beause it articulated their thoughts but because it also managed to express their feelings and illuminate their lives. It was the voice of Simla and the ICS, of Tommy Atkins in India and South Africa, of McAndrew and the naval engineers, of millions of individuals from New Zealand to New Brunswick who were part of the imperial experience.

Kipling's imperial prime lasted until about 1905, when the Liberals came to power, leaving him three decades to acquire the status of a 'dead Classic' before he actually died. Near the end of his life Kipling accosted a young barrister, John Maude, and barked, 'I hate your generation.' On being asked the reason, he explained, 'Because you are going to give it all away.'[50] Kipling was right, of course, though at the time few people believed him. Pessimists and reactionaries make the best prophets because they are without illusions, because they can see behind as well as beyond contemporary viewpoints. Sir Robert Vansittart, who at the Foreign Office in the 1930s had pressed for rearmament, recognized that Kipling had 'glimpses of the future', that he was 'armed to his discomfort with flashes of the insight which usually eludes statecraft'.[51]

Glimpses of the future made Kipling bitter. Human progress, he believed, was chiefly mechanical. 'Internally and spiritually,' he once said, 'we are about where our Neolithic ancestors were'.[52] It may have been regrettable that he did not subscribe to the ideals of the League of Nations, but he knew more about human nature than Woodrow Wilson. The choice, says the medieval Abbot in 'The Eye of Allah', a brilliant late story, lies between two sins: 'To deny the world a Light which is under our hand, or to enlighten the world before her time.'

He is referring to a rudimentary Arab microscope, brought from Spain, which he decides to destroy because the invention is premature. But there were no abbots to destroy contemporary killing machines, products of human ingenuity rather than of human progress.

Kipling was a prophet whose prophecies were fulfilled too often to be coincidences: the Boers and apartheid, the Kaiser and a war, Hitler and another war, the Hindu-Muslim strife whenever Britain decided to withdraw from India – these and many other things were predicted by Kipling years, sometimes decades, before they happened.

Prophets, as the Old Testament reveals, say unpalatable things and say them in provocative and unpleasant language. So did Kipling. Some of these pages chronicle opinions that are repellent and often inexplicable; many people, even admirers, will hate them. But there was an excuse for his bitterness, as there was with Jeremiah: he *knew* what was going to happen. Other people accepted that the Empire was in transition or in decline, but Kipling knew it was going to disappear; almost alone of his contemporaries, he would have been unsurprised to learn that the whole thing, the famous red quarter of the globe, would have gone within a generation of his death.

Nearly everything he valued, nearly everything to which he had dedicated his life outside his art, was threatened by decline or extinction in January 1936. Even Britain's survival was in doubt. The pessimism and the anxiety were justified, although in the end the nation – and he always had more faith in its people than in its leaders – managed to pull through.

The spirit of Dunkirk and the Battle of Britain owed much to Kipling. From Churchill, the new Prime Minister, to the non-commissioned officers and the ranks, he had remained an inspiration. According to Sir Lewis Namier, the great historian, his spirit infused a vigorous new Government no longer dominated by appeasers. 'After sterile years of an empire-weary generation,' wrote Namier, 'when the time came for new work and sacrifices for the Empire', it was the 'Kipling imperialists'* who 'were called in to bring back to us the creed of an older generation'.[53] They duly brought it back, they used it to win the War and, although they were unable to preserve the Empire for long, they kept their country alive.

---

*Those specified by Namier in this category were Winston Churchill, Leo Amery and Lord Lloyd.

Notes

ABBREVIATIONS

CK	=	Carrie Kipling
Gazette	=	*Civil and Military Gazette*
K	=	Rudyard Kipling
KJ	=	*Kipling Journal*
KP	=	Kipling Papers at the University of Sussex
Letters 1, 2, 3 and 4	=	the four volumes of the *The Letters of Rudyard Kipling*, edited by Thomas Pinney
SOM	=	*Something of Myself* (Kipling's autobiography)

PREFACE

1. Esher to Knollys, 2 June 1909, KP 20/11.
2. Chaudhuri, 'The Finest Story about India – in English', in Gross, *Rudyard Kipling*, p. 29; Carrington to Mrs Hill, 17 March 1953, Rice Collection.
3. *Letters* 4, p. 574.
4. Link, *The Papers of Woodrow Wilson*, Vol. 66, pp. 352–3.

CHAPTER 1: EJECTIONS FROM PARADISE

1. See correspondence from K to Sunderland, 1932–4, KP 17/35.
2. K diaries, Macmillan Archives; correspondence from K to Sunderland, 1932–4, KP 17/35; *Letters* 2, p. 244.
3. *Letters* 4, p. 599.
4. *KJ*, April 1942, p. 13; *KJ*, April 1942, p. 13; K to Saintsbury, 20 Sept. 1921, KP 17/29; K to Mrs Hussey, 21 Sept. 1921, KP 16/11.
5. *Letters* 4, p. 59.
6. Baldwin, *The Macdonald Sisters*, p. 32.
7. L.Kipling to E.Plowden, 13 Nov. 1893, Baldwin Papers.
8. K to Lady E.Cecil, 2 Dec. 1908, Kipling Collection, Syracuse.
9. Baldwin, *The Macdonald Sisters*, p. 44; Baldwin Papers 1/20; Rivett-Carnac, *Many Memories*, p. 226.

10. K to Bates, 9 June 1931, KP 14/13; K, *Souvenirs of France*, pp. 6–7; *Letters* 4, p. 13.
11. *Letters* 4, p. 582.
12. *Letters* 4, p. 583; *SOM*, p. 3; K to Sykes, 4 Jan. 1930, KP 17/36.
13. *Letters* 4, p. 583; Lawrence, *The India We Served*, pp. 58–9.
14. Ankers, *The Pater*, p. 63.
15. Baldwin, *The Macdonald Sisters*, p. 114; Lycett, *Rudyard Kipling*, pp. 28–9; Birkenhead, *Rudyard Kipling*, pp. 12–13.
16. *Letters* 4, p. 583; see Ricketts, *The Unforgiving Minute*, p. 12.
17. See Mason, *Kipling*, p. 33, and Stewart, *Rudyard Kipling*, p. 18; Curzon Papers, 112/363.
18. Tomkins, *The Art of Rudyard Kipling*, p. 8.
19. *Letters* 3, p. 156; *Letters* 4, p. 584; *SOM*, pp. 9–10.
20. *Letters* 2, p. 339; *Letters* 4, p. 584; K to Baker, 17 March 1934, KP 14/7; K to L.Baldwin, 3 Oct. 1909.
21. K to Baker, 17 March 1934, KP 14/7; *SOM*, p. 183.
22. K to Snow, 16 April 1932, Kipling Collection, Syracuse; K to Dunsterville, 20 Jan. 1927, KP 14/52; Gross, *Rudyard Kipling*, p. 14.
23. A.Kipling to Price, 24 Jan. 1878, Baldwin Papers.
24. K to Dunsterville, 11 July 1917 and 20 Jan. 1927, KP 14/52; *SOM*, p. 16; *Letters* 1, p. 118; 'The United Idolaters'.
25. *SOM*, p. 271; *Letters* 4, p. 577; *Letters* 1, p. 18; Beresford, *Schooldays with Kipling*, p. 14.
26. E. Hill diary, Kipling Collection, Cornell; *Letters* 4, pp. 39–40; Birkenhead, *Rudyard Kipling*, p. 56
27. *SOM*, p. 183.
28. L.Kipling to E.Plowden, n. d. 1883, KP 1/10; K to Marker, 22 July 1913, Dunscombe Colt Collection.

CHAPTER 2: A NEWSMAN IN LAHORE
1. E.Hill memoir, Kipling Collection, Cornell.
2. Brown, *Rudyard Kipling*, p. 21.
3. *SOM*, pp. 53–4.
4. *SOM*, p. 27.
5. *Letters* 1, p. 70.
6. *From Sea to Sea*, Vol. 1, p. 232; E.Hill diary, Kipling Collection, Cornell; *Letters* 1, p. 120.
7. *Letters* 1, pp. 169–97.
8. Seymour-Smith, *Rudyard Kipling*, pp. 45–77 *passim*.
9. *Letters* 1, p. 126; diary in Houghton Library, Harvard; see Ricketts, *The Unforgiving Minute*, pp. 71–3.
10. *Letters* 2, p. 98; Orel, *Kipling* 1, p. 108.
11. Beames, *Memoirs of a Bengal Civilian*, pp. 62–3.
12. Minute of 27 Aug. 1900, Curzon Papers.
13. Hamilton to Curzon, 4 July 1901, Curzon Papers.
14. Rutherford, *Early Verse*, p. 250.
15. Dewey, *Anglo-Indian Attitudes*, p. 163; Thompson diaries, *c.* 1898, in Thompson Papers.
16. Birkenhead, *Rudyard Kipling*, p. 62.
17. *SOM*, pp. 31–2.
18. Gopal, *British Policy in India*, p. 147.
19. Bennett, *The Ilberts in India*, p. 29; Gopal, *The Viceroyalty of Lord Ripon*, p. 93.
20. L.Kipling to E.Plowden, n. d., KP 1/10; Ankers, *The Pater*, p. 93.
21. *Letters* 1, p. 35.
22. *SOM*, p. 31.

23. Rutherford, *Early Verse*, pp. 184–5.
24. *Gazette*, 27 March 1886.
25. *Gazette*, 28 and 29 Jan. 1887.
26. *SOM*, p. 201.
27. *From Sea to Sea*, Vol. 1, p. 146.
28. *SOM*, p. 28; *Letters* 1, p. 116.
29. K to Wheeler, 1 Feb. 1897, KP 17/49; Orel, *Kipling*, pp. 69–82.
30. *Letters* 1, pp. 126–7.

CHAPTER 3: THE ANGLO-INDIAN CHRONICLE
1. *Plain Tales*, p. 320; *SOM*, p. 35.
2. Gilmour, *Curzon*, pp. 148, 204–6.
3. Lawrence, *The India We Served*, pp. 80–2; introduction to Lawrence diaries, Lawrence Papers 143/26.
4. *Letters* 1, p. 39; unpublished ms by E.Hill, Kipling Collection, Cornell.
5. *Letters* 1, pp. 83–4; *Gazette*, 9 July 1885.
6. *Letters* 1, p. 136; Ankers, *The Pater*, p. 129.
7. L.Kipling to E.Plowden, 27 July 1885, KP 1/10; Rutherford, *Early Verse*, p. 19; Carrington, *Rudyard Kipling*, pp. 64–5.
8. *Letters* 1, p. 222.
9. Bence-Jones, *The Viceroys of India*, p. 146.
10. E.Hill diary, 1888, Kipling Collection, Cornell.
11. *Letters* 1, pp. 164, 221, 225, 244, 281.
12. E.Hill diary, April 1888, Kipling Collection, Cornell; *Letters* 1, pp. 184–6, 209–10.
13. *Letters* 1, p. 120.
14. *Letters* 1, p. 136.
15. Orel, *Kipling*, Vol.1, p. 74.
16. Green, *Kipling: The Critical Heritage*, pp. 38–41; *Letters* 1, pp. 193, 265; Rutherford, *Early Verse*, p. 404.
17. *Letters* 1, pp. 83–4, 142.
18. Green, *Kipling: The Critical Heritage*, p. 104.
19. Cornell, *Kipling in India*, p. 163.
20. 'The Rescue of Pluffles'.
21. 'At the Pit's Mouth'.
22. 'Wressley of the Foreign Office'.
23. *Letters* 1, p. 98.
24. 'In the Rukh'; *SOM*, p. 38.
25. Pinney, *Kipling's India*, p. 285
26. *Gazette*, 8 July 1892.
27. 'A Little Prep'.
28. Orel, *Kipling*, p. 110.
29. Orel, *Kipling*, p. 72.
30. Fraser, *Sixty Years in Uniform*, pp. 139–44.
31. *Letters* 1, p. 380; K to Cooke, 10 Dec. 1893, Kipling Collection, Syracuse.
32. *KJ*, June 1998, p. 46.
33. 'The Madness of Private Ortheris'.
34. Gilmour, *Curzon*, p. 193.
35. Ballhatchet, *Race, Sex and Class*, pp. 82–3; Gilmour, *Curzon*, pp. 193–4; Hyam, *Empire and Sexuality*, pp. 126–7.
36. Kitchener's Memo, Oct. 1905, Kitchener Papers, PRO 30/57.
37. Ballhatchett, *Race, Sex and Class*, p. 59.
38. Birkenhead, *Rudyard Kipling*, p. 226.

39. Letters from Dowdall to his family, Oct.–Nov. 1890, Dowdall Papers.
40. Carrington, *The Complete Barrack-Room Ballads*, p. 5.
41. Longford, *Wellington*, Vol. 1, p. 322.
42. K to Cooke, 10 Dec. 1893, Kipling Collection, Syracuse.
43. Brown, *Rudyard Kipling*, p. 139.
44. Fraser, *Sixty Years in Uniform*, p. 145.
45. Younghusband, *A Soldier's Memories*, p. 187.
46. Ellman, *Oscar Wilde*, p. 286.
47. Woolf, *Growing*, pp. 46, 151.
48. *Letters* 1, p. 183; Curzon to Queen Victoria, 23 March 1899, Curzon Papers; Kincaid, *British Social Life*, p. 230.
49. Pinney, *Kipling's India*, pp. 190–1.
50. Brock, 'Rudyard Kipling in Politics', p. 110.
51. Curzon to Dawkins, 2 July 1902, and Dawkins to Curzon, 25 July 1902, Curzon Papers.
52. Green, *Kipling: The Critical Heritage*, p. 40.
53. Du Cane to Du Cane, 30 May 1885, Du Cane Papers; Macmunn, *Kipling's Women*, p. 20; Pearse, unpublished ms, Pearse Papers.
54. Conchman to Phelps, 30 Oct. 1894, Phelps Papers.
55. Bonus to Phelps, 10 Jan. 1889, Phelps Papers.

CHAPTER 4: CITIES OF DREADFUL NIGHT
1. *Gazette*, article dated 3 July 1885.
2. 'Miss Youghal's Sais'.
3. *From Sea to Sea*, Vol. 2, p. 305.
4. *Letters of Travel*, p. 236.
5. Orel, *Kipling*, Vol. 1, pp. 72, 82.
6. E. Hill, unpublished ms, Kipling Collection, Cornell. A shorter version appeared in the *Atlantic Monthly*, April 1936.
7. *Letters of Travel*, p. 237.
8. See Islam, *Kipling's Law*, p. 36.
9. Pinney, *Kipling's India*, p. 178; *Letters* 1, p. 121.
10. *Letters* 1, p. 99.
11. *Letters* 2, p. 75.
12. *Letters* 1, pp. 99–101.
13. *Letters* 1, p. 121.
14. Chandra, *Enslaved Daughters*, pp. 38–40.
15. Chandra, *Enslaved Daughters*, pp. 162, 201.
16. *Gazette*, 18 March and 9 April 1886, 11 March, 14 and 16 April 1887.
17. *Gazette*, 28 Jan. 1887.
18. *Gazette*, 16 April 1887.
19. *Gazette*, 1 July 1887.
20. *Gazette*, 5 May 1886, 24 Feb. 1886.
21. *Letters* 1, pp. 121–2.
22. *Gazette*, 17 June 1887, 10 Dec. 1886, 28 March 1887; *Pioneer*, 1 Jan. 1887.
23. Gopal, *British Policy in India*, p. 117.
24. See the correspondence of Du Boulay and Francis in the Phelps Papers.
25. *Gazette*, 14 April 1886.
26. *From Sea to Sea*, Vol. 2, pp. 280–1, 323–4.
27. K to Gwynne, 26 Nov. 1930, KP 15/15.
28. *Pioneer*, 1 Jan. 1889.
29. *Contemporary Review*, Vol. 58. Sept. 1890.
30. Maconochie to Phelps, 23 Nov. 1891, Phelps Papers.

31. Curzon to Wedderburn, 17 April 1900, Curzon Papers 111/181.
32. *Gazette*, 18 Sept. 1886.
33 *Letters* 1, p. 151.
34. *From Sea to Sea,* Vol. 1, pp. 33–4, 44, 52, 70; see Moore-Gilbert, '*Letters of Marque*: Travel, Gender and Imperialism', *KJ*, March 1991, pp. 12–24.
35. See Edward Said's introduction to *Kim*, pp. 28–9, and Williams, '*Kim* and Orientalism' in Mallet, *Kipling Considered*, p. 42.
36. Forster to Annan, see *KJ*, June 1986, p. 45.
37. Kinkead-Weekes, 'Vision in Kipling's Novels', in Rutherford, *Kipling's Mind and Art*, p. 233.
38. Gilbert, *The Good Kipling*, p. 119.
39. 'The Mother-Lodge'.

CHAPTER 5: A SENSE OF EMPIRE
1. E. Hill diary, April 1888, Kipling Collection, Cornell; *Letters* 1, p. 158.
2. E. Hill diary and unpublished ms, Dec. 1887, Kipling Collection, Cornell.
3. Bayly, *The Local Roots of Indian Politics*, p. 84.
4. *Letters* 1, pp. 260, 287, 291.
5. E. Hill diary, May 1888, Kipling Collection, Cornell.
6. *Letters* 1, p. 171.
7. *Letters*, pp. 219, 238, 240, 245, 251.
8. *From Sea to Sea*, Vol. 1, p. 208.
9. *From Sea to Sea*, Vol. 2, p. 202; E.Hill, upublished ms, Kipling Collection, Cornell.
10. Orel, *Kipling*, Vol. 1, p. 66, *SOM*, p. 45.
11. Lycett, *Rudyard Kipling*, p. 171; Carrington, *Rudyard Kipling*, p. 132.
12. *Letters* 1, pp. 292, 297.
13. E. Hill diary notes, 1889, Kipling Collection, Cornell; *From Sea to Sea*, Vol. 1, pp. 220–1, 232.
14. *Gazette*, 4 June 1892.
15. E. Hill diary notes, 1889, Kipling Collection, Cornell.
16. *From Sea to Sea*, Vol. 1, p.253.
17. *Letters* 1, p. 217.
18. *Gazette*, 9 Oct. 1886; Rutherford, *Early Verse*, pp. 338–9.
19. *Gazette*, 28 March 1887.
20. *Gazette*, 28 March and 25 April 1887.
21. Bauer, *Rudyard Kipling*, p. 32.
22. *Letters* 1, pp. 91–3, 98.
23. 'His Private Honour' in *Many Inventions*, and 'India for the Indians: A Glimpse at a Possible Future' in *St James's Gazette*, 31 Dec. 1889.
24. *Letters* 2, p. 235.
25. Philips, *Historians of India*, pp. 391–2.
26. *Letters* 1, p. 98.
27. Pinney, *Kipling's India*, p. 34.
28. *Gazette*, 7 Nov. 1885.
29. Quoted in Woodruff, *The Guardians*, p. 68.
30. *From Sea to Sea*, Vol. 1, pp. 71–2.
31. Ankers, *The Pater*, pp. 146–7.
32. *Letters* 2, p. 205.
33. 'On the City Wall'.
34. Maconochie to Phelps, 17 Sept. 1890, Phelps Papers.
35. Sandison, 'Kipling: The Artist and the Empire' in Rutherford, *Kipling's Mind and Art*, p. 149

36. 'India for the Indians: A Glimpse at a Possible Future' in *St James's Gazette*, 31 Dec. 1889.
37. 'Without Benefit of Clergy'.
38. K to Davis, 3 Jan. 1893, Pierpont Morgan Library.

CHAPTER 6: THE LONG TRAIL HOME
1. Note by E. Hill, Kipling Collection, Cornell; *From Sea to Sea*, Vol. 1. pp. 270–376 *passim*.
2. E. Hill diary notes, 1889, Kipling Collection, Cornell; *Letters* 1, p. 312; *From Sea to Sea*, Vol. 1, pp. 472–97 *passim*, and Vol. 2, pp. 59–72 *passim*.
3. K to Barr, 5 Oct. 1897, KP 14/12; K to Hopkins, 7 March 1896, Cabot Holbrook Collection.
4. E. Hill diary notes, 1889, Kipling Collection, Cornell.
5. Hill to Paterson, 26 April 1947, Kipling Collection, Cornell.
6. 'In Partibus'; *SOM*, pp. 48, 53.
7. *Letters* 1, p. 366.
8. K to Booth, 21 Feb. 1932, Kipling Collection, Austin.
9. Morris to Rodd, 20 Oct. 1889, Kipling Collection, Syracuse.
10. Quoted in Green, *Kipling: The Critical Heritage*, p. 159.
11. K to Gosse, 6 Dec. 1890, KP 15/13; *Letters* 1, p. 29.
12. *SOM*, p. 50.
13. Guedalla, *Men of Letters*, pp. 62–3.
14. K to Frierson, 6 March 1925, KP 15/11.
15. Green, *Kipling: The Critical Heritage*, p. 68.
16. CK diary, 11 November 1893, KP 1/8.
17. *Letters* 1, pp. 303–4, 358.
18. *SOM*, p. 128.
19. *Letters* 1, p. 372.
20. Cecil, *Max*, p. 55.
21. *Book of Words*, p. 3; Gross, *Rudyard Kipling*, p. 13.
22. Robert Conquest, 'A Note on Kipling's Verse' in Gross, *Rudyard Kipling*, p. 103; Green, *Kipling: The Critical Heritage*, p. 280; *Book of Words*, p. 72.
23. *Letters* 1, p. 373.
24. Porter, *The Nineteenth Century*, p. 346.
25. *SOM*, p. 55.
26. *SOM*, p. 54.
27. Tennyson to K, 6 April 1891, KP 22/26.

CHAPTER 7: THE AMERICAN YEARS
1. Seymour-Smith, *Rudyard Kipling, passim*.
2. Carrington, *Rudyard Kipling*, p. 183.
3. K to Canton, 3 Feb. 1892, Berg Collection.
4. Green, *Kipling: The Critical Heritage*, p. 68.
5. Letter from Miss Morton, 14 July 1898, British Library, RP1874.
6. Seymour-Smith, *Rudyard Kipling*, pp. 188, 200–1.
7. *Letters* 2, p. 107.
8. Carrington, *Rudyard Kipling*, p. 516.
9. See Mason, *Kipling*, pp. 230–1.
10. K to Canton, 3 Feb. 1892, Berg Collection; CK diary, 15 April 1892, KP 1/8.
11. *Letters of Travel*, pp. 16, 21; *Letters* 2, pp. 86, 249.
12. *Letters of Travel*, p. 103.
13. CK diary, 3 Aug. 1893, KP 1/8.
14. Gwynn, *The Letters and Friendships of Cecil Spring Rice*, Vol. 1, p. 173.
15. L. Kipling to anon, n.d., Kipling Collection, Cornell.

16. *Letters* 2, pp. 134, 145, 155, 195.
17. Kipling to Bok, 9 Dec. 1897, Carpenter Collection.
18. Kipling to Murray, 4 Feb. 1897, British Library, RP2097 (ii).
19. Kipling to Mrs Dodge, 5 March 1893, Dodge Collection.
20. Green, *Kipling: The Critical Heritage*, p. 69.
21. Melville to Kipling, 3 Dec. 1894, KP 22/45; K to Melville, 4 Dec. 1894, Kipling Collection, Syracuse.
22. Green, *Kipling: The Critical Heritage*, p. 69.
23. Green, *Kipling: The Critical Heritage*, p. 187.
24. *From Sea to Sea*, Vol. 2, p. 172.
25. Carrington, *Rudyard Kipling*, p. 224.
26. I am grateful to Herbert Agar's brilliant account in *The Price of Union*, pp. 604–5.
27. *Letters* 2, pp. 215, 221.
28. K to Finney, 13 Jan. 1896, Kipling Collection, Dalhousie; *Letters* 2, p. 226.
29. Quoted in McAveeney, *Kipling in Gloucester*, pp. 78–9.
30. CK to Norton, 29 June 1896, KP 17/14.

CHAPTER 8: THE PROPHET'S BURDEN
1. *Letters* 2, pp. 263, 266; K to Fraser, n.d., Kipling Collection, Cornell.
2. Quoted in Lowry, *The South African War Reappraised*, p. 32.
3. Kipling to Baker, 13 Jan. 1934, KP 14/7.
4. *Letters* 2, pp. 305–6.
5. Marsh, *Joseph Chamberlain*, pp. 440–1; Roberts, *Salisbury*, p. 695.
6. K to Blumenfeld, 22 Aug. 1918, KP 14/19.
7. Salisbury to Curzon, 9 Aug. 1902, Curzon Papers, 111/224.
8. Gosse, *Life of Algernon Charles Swinburne*, p. 277.
9. Cecil, *The Cecils of Hatfield House*, p. 240.
10. *Letters* 2, p. 186.
11. K to Mrs Tree, 4 March 1897, KP 17/43.
12. Thurston Hopkins, *Rudyard Kipling*, p. 73; Birkenhead, *Rudyard Kipling*, p. 187.
13. K to Horder, 23 April, 1905, Kipling Collection, Austin.
14. Orwell, *Collected Essays*, Vol. 2, pp. 215–16.
15. Information from Ramachandra Guha; Gilbert, *The Good Kipling*, p. 16.
16. See C.E.Carrington in *KJ*, Dec. 1967, p. 14.
17. K to Editor of the *Times*, 16 July 1897.
18. See *KJ*, June 1936; Cohen, *Rudyard Kipling to Rider Haggard*, p. 34; *Letters* 2, p. 305.
19. K to Dschzessop, 15 Dec. 1897, Kipling Collection, Cornell.
20. Carrington, *Rudyard Kipling*, pp. 266–7; Ricketts, *The Unforgiving Minute*, p. 237; Green, *Kipling: The Critical Heritage*, pp. 195, 211, 225, 260, 275.
21. Neider, *The Autobiography of Mark Twain*, p. 287.
22. H.G.Wells, *The New Machiavelli*, p. 128.
23. Cohen, *Rudyard Kipling to Rider Haggard*, p. 35; Green, *Kipling: The Critical Heritage*, p. 256; *Letters* 2, p. 373.
24. Paterson, *American Foreign Relations*, pp. 20–4
25. *Letters* 2, p. 335.
26. *Letters* 2, p. 344; K to Zogbaum, 6 Feb. 1899, Kipling Collection, Syracuse.
27. *Letters* 2, pp. 345–8.
28. Carrington, *Rudyard Kipling*, p. 278.
29. The scrapbook is in the Kipling Collection at Dalhousie University.
30. Robb, *Victor Hugo*, p. 371.
31. Keating, *Kipling the Poet*, pp. 119–20.
32. Speech in the House of Commons, 12 Dec. 1826.

33. Quoted in Lowry, *The South African War Reappraised*, p. 218.
34. 11 Feb. 1889.
35. Green, *Kipling: The Critical Heritage*, pp. 236–44.
36. Longford, *A Pilgrimage of Passion,* p. 335.
37. *Truth,* 9 Feb. 1889.
38. Le Gallienne, *Rudyard Kipling,* pp. 30, 63–4, 130, 133, 155–61.
39. Ellman, *Oscar Wilde,* p. 292; Cecil, *Max*, pp. 139, 251, 321, 367.

CHAPTER 9: RHODES AND MILNER
 1. K to Baker, 22 Feb. 1934, KP 14/7; *Letters* 3, pp. 196, 384.
 2. Cohen, *Rudyard Kipling to Rider Haggard*, pp. 35–7.
 3. *SOM*, p. 87; K to Cornford, 26 Feb. 1898, Dunscombe Colt Collection.
 4. Roberts, *Cecil Rhodes*, pp. 1, 154; Thomas, *Rhodes*, pp. 2, 13.
 5. *Letters* 3, pp. 22, 101.
 6. K to Baker, 17 March 1934, KP 14/7.
 7. K to Baker, 15 Dec. 1932, KP 14/7; *SOM*, p. 101.
 8. Rhodes to K, n.d., KP 21/29.
 9. Trevelyan, *Grey of Fallodon*, p. 61.
 10. Quoted in Wilson, *The Strange Ride of Rudyard Kipling*, p. 224.
 11. Wrench, *Alfred Lord Milner*, pp. 190–1.
 12. *Letters* 3, pp. 31, 34.
 13. Spender, *Campbell-Bannerman*, Vol. 1, p. 264.
 14. Pakenham, *The Boer War*, p. 584.
 15. Porter, *The Nineteenth Century*, p. 615; Marlowe, *Milner*, p. 99.
 16. See Lowry, *The South African War Reappraised, passim;* Porter, *The Nineteenth Century*, p. 23.
 17. Roberts, *Salisbury*, p. 725.
 18. Roberts, *Salisbury*, p. 717.
 19. Pakenham, *The Boer War*, pp. 65; Roberts, *Salisbury*, pp. 722, 729.
 20. Roberts, *Salisbury*, p. 732.
 21. Roberts, *Salisbury*, p. 743.
 22. *The Times*, 29 Sept. 1898.
 23. K to Sullivan, 27 May 1900, Gilbert and Sullivan Papers; Newton, *Retrospection*, pp. 203–4; *Letters* 4, p. 227.
 24. K to Shingler, 8 Jan. 1900, University of Cape Town.
 25. K to De Forest, 15 Jan. 1900, KP 14/46.
 26. Najder, *Joseph Conrad*, pp. 176, 261.
 27. *Letters* 3, p. 42.
 28. *SOM*, p. 97.
 29. K to Duchess of Sutherland, 8 Nov. 1901, Kipling Collection, Dalhousie; *Letters* 3, p. 16.
 30. Lowry, *The South African War Reappraised*, pp. 123, 134–5; Marlowe, *Milner*, p. 92; *Letters* 3, p. 56.
 31. K to Gillon, 22 Oct. 1899, Howell Wright Papers; K to Buckle, 31 Oct. 1899, Kipling Collection, Dalhousie; K to De Forest, 15 Jan. 1900, KP 14/46; K to Duchess of Sutherland, 8 Nov. 1901, Kipling Collection, Dalhousie.

CHAPTER 10: LESSONS FROM THE BOERS
 1. K to Lawrence, 14 Aug. 1898, Kipling Collection, Syracuse; K to Duchess of Sutherland, 31 Dec. 1899, Kipling Collection, Dalhousie; K to De Forest, 15 Jan. 1900, KP 14/46.
 2. Pakenham, *The Boer War*, p. 191; Roberts, *Cecil Rhodes,* pp. 277–8.

3. CK diary, 3 April 1900, KP 1/9.
4. Keating, *Kipling the Poet*, p. 134.
5. Ralph, *War's Brighter Side*, p. 83.
6. Keating, *Kipling the Poet*, pp. 134–5.
7. Quoted in Birkenhead, *Rudyard Kipling*, pp. 207–8.
8. K to Ward, 4 June 1912, Bodleian, Ms Autogr b. 11.
9. *SOM*, p. 88.
10. *KJ*, Dec. 1985, pp. 59–60.
11. Ralph, *War's Brighter Side*, pp. 185, 259.
12. K to Miss Otty, 28 Dec. 1899, Dunscombe Colt Collection.
13. Clark, *History of Australia*, pp. 406–7; Lowry, *The South African War Reappraised*, p. 193.
14. *Letters* 3, p. 53.
15. *Letters* 3, p. 53.
16. K to Baldwin, 25 Nov. 1901, Kipling Collection, Dalhousie; *Letters* 3, p. 38.
17. Marsh, *Joseph Chamberlain*, p. 499; Pakenham, *The Boer War*, p. 492.
18. *Letters* 3, p. 23; K to De Forest, 15 Jan. 1900, KP 14/46.
19. Lowry, *The South African War Reappraised*, p. 197; Pakenham, *The Boer War*, pp. 73–4, 80; *Letters* 2, p. 352; *The Times*, 3 Oct. 1911.
20. Salisbury to Curzon, 23 Sept. 1901, and Curzon to Hamilton, 4 Jan. 1900, Curzon Papers.
21. *Letters* 3, pp. 108–9; K to Strachey, 17 Oct. 1901, Strachey Papers.
22. K to Bell, 5 Oct. 1899, Dunscombe Colt; *Letters* 3, p. 18.
23. See Pakenham, *The Boer War*, pp. 96, 153–5, 165, 484; *Letters* 3, p. 70.
24. K to Conland, 23 Aug. 1901, Pierpont Morgan Library; *Letters* 3, p. 26.
25. *Letters* 3, pp. 41–2
26. *Letters* 3, pp 41–2; K to Conland, 23 Aug. 1901, Pierpont Morgan Library.
27. Roberts, *Salisbury*, pp. 802–5; Marlowe, *Milner*, p. 111.
28. *Letters* 3, pp. 87–9.
29. *Letters* 3, pp. 177–9; K to Baker, 15 Dec. 1932, Rhodes Papers; CK to Baker, 25 Nov. n.d., KP 14/7.
30. *Letters* 3, pp. 87–9.
31. Pakenham, *The Boer War*, pp. 597–9, 608.
32. K to Lady E. Cecil, 17 July 1902, Kipling Collection, Syracuse.
33. *Letters* 3, p. 106.
34. *Letters* 3, pp. 125–33; Amery, *Life of Joseph Chamberlain*, Vol. 4, p. 375; Chamberlain to K, 10 March 1903, KP 22/6.
35. See Pinney's introduction to *The Jungle Play*.
36. 'Spartan Mothers' in Austin, *Songs of England*, pp. 83–4.
37. Quoted in Keating, *Kipling the Poet*, p. 351.
38. *The Times*, 4, 7 and 9 Jan. 1902.
39. L. Kipling to Cornford, 12 Jan. 1902, Baldwin Papers; Beresford, *Schooldays with Kipling*, p. 60; *Book of Words*, pp. 95–6.
40. Cohen, *Rudyard Kipling to Rider Haggard*, pp. 46–7.
41. Ellman, *Oscar Wilde*, pp. 38, 47–8; Longford, *A Pilgrimage of Passion*, p. 293.
42. Orwell, *Collected Essays*, Vol. 2, pp. 219–20.
43. Mangan, *The Games Ethic*, pp. 35–6, 45.
44. Orwell, *Collected Essays*, vol. 2, p. 88.

CHAPTER 11: THE DISCOVERY OF ENGLAND
1. Cohen, *Rudyard Kipling to Rider Haggard*, p. 51; *Letters* 3, pp. 150, 281.
2. *Letters* 3, p. 113; K to Mrs Almy, 15 May 1924, Rice Collection.
3. H. James to W. James, 11 Oct. 1903, Kipling Collection, Syracuse.

4. *Letters* 3, p. 113; K to MacDougall, 22 March 1930, Kipling Collection, Dalhousie.
5. K to Fröhlich, 21 July 1909, Kipling Collection, Dalhousie.
6. *Letters* 3, p. 458; *SOM*, p. 106.
7. K to Strachey, n.d. [*c.* 1904–5], Strachey Papers.
8. *Letters* 3, p. 73.
9. K to Mrs Strachey, 16 Oct. 1904, Strachey Papers.
10. Sutcliff, *Rudyard Kipling*, p. 52.
11. Mackail and Wyndham, *Life and Letters of George Wyndham*, Vol. 2, pp. 552–3.
12. K to Matthews, n.d., Brander Matthews Collection; *Letters* 3, p. 329.
13. *SOM*, p. 121; K to Matthews, 4 Dec. 1912, Brander Matthews Collection.
14. K to Chisholm, Sept. 1900, Dunscombe Colt Collection; *Letters* 4, p. 80.
15. Sutcliffe, *The Oxford University Press*, pp. 158–62.
16. Amis, *Rudyard Kipling*, p. 103.

CHAPTER 12: THE COLONIAL SISTERHOOD
1. K to Edwardes, 10 Dec. 1901, Kipling Society Library; K to Strachey, 17 Oct. 1901, Strachey Papers; *Letters* 3, p. 68.
2. K to Strachey, 17 Oct. 1901, Strachey Papers; K to Gwynne, 2 Feb. 1905, KP 15/15; *Letters* 3, pp. 144–5; K to Ward, 8 Oct. 1905, Bodleian, Ms Autogr b. 11.
3. K to Baldwin, 7 March 1904, KP 11/3.
4. Arnold-Forster diary, 29 June 1904, 27 Feb. and 5 April 1905, Arnold-Forster Papers; Ridley and Percy, *Letters of Arthur Balfour*, p. 73.
5. Quoted by Pinney in *KJ*, March 1994, pp. 44–5.
6. Porter, *The Nineteenth Century*, pp. 339–40, 356.
7. *Book of Words*, p. 33; K to Macmechan, 22 Jan. 1902, Kipling Collection, Dalhousie.
8. K to Strachey, 3 Aug. 1913, Strachey Papers.
9. See Gallagher and Robinson, 'The Imperialism of Free Trade', *Economic History Review*, VI, 1 (1953).
10. Roberts, *Salisbury*, p. 682.
11. Porter, *The Nineteenth Century*, p. 357; Marsh, *Joseph Chamberlain*, p. 555.
12. Marsh, *Joseph Chamberlain*, p. 563.
13. K to Baldwin, 6 June 1903, KP 11/1.
14. K to Aitken, 23 Nov. 1911, Beaverbrook Papers.
15. K to Strachey, n.d. [*c.* 1904–5], Strachey Papers; CK diary, 8 April 1901, KP 1/9.
16. K to Hargreaves, n.d., Kipling Collection, Cornell.
17. Porter, *The Nineteenth Century*, p. 75.
18. *Letters* 3, p. 351.
19. K to Lady E. Cecil, 29 Sept. 1902, Lady Milner Papers.
20. K to Levily, n.d., Kipling Collection, Cornell; K to Gwynne, 7 Feb. 1906, KP 15/15.
21. K to Gwynne, n.d. [*c.* spring 1907], KP 15/15; K to Ford, n.d. [*c.* 1908], KP 15/7.
22. *Letters of Travel*, pp. 179–205 *passim*.
23. K to Macmechan, 22 Jan. 1902, Kipling Collection, Dalhousie.
24. *Letters of Travel*, pp. 119–21; A. Kipling to E. Plowden, 25 November 1907, KP 1/10; K to Frewen, 4 Dec. 1907, Kipling Collection, Cornell.
25. *Letters* 3, pp. 330, 275; *Letters of Travel*, p. 122.
26. *Letters of Travel*, pp. 126, 134; *SOM*, p. 116.
27. K to Gwynne, 20 June 1904, Kipling Collection, Dalhousie; K to Maxse, 10 Dec. 1908, Maxse Papers; *Letters* 3, p. 279.
28. *Letters* 4, pp. 46–7.
29. McNaught, *Canada*, p. 211.
30. CK to Lady E. Cecil, 23 Sept. 1911, Lady Milner Papers; *Letters* 4, p. 50; Aitken to K, 3 Oct. 1912, Beaverbrook Papers.

31. K to Bell, 21 July, 1905, Dunscombe Colt Collection; *Letters* 3, p. 196; Gilmour, *Curzon*, p. 310; Dilks, *Curzon in India,* Vol. 2, p. 189.
32. K to Lawrence, 22 Sept. 1899, Kipling Collection, Syracuse, Box 3.
33. *Letters* 3, p. 206.
34. Balfour to Selborne, 21 Sept. 1905, Balfour Papers.
35. K to Gwynne, 7 Feb. 1906, KP 15/15; *Letters* 3, p. 215.
36. *Book of Words*, p. 26.

CHAPTER 13: LIBERAL TREACHERIES
1. *Letters of Travel*, p. 119.
2. 'The Comprehension of Private Copper' in *Traffics and Discoveries.*
3. Wilson, *CB*, p. 151.
4. *Letters* 3, p. 279.
5. K to Aitken, 17 Sept. 1911, Beaverbrook Papers.
6. *Letters* 4, pp. 122–4, 218.
7. *Letters* 4, p. 89; K to Garvin, 1 Feb. 1912, Kipling Collection, Austin.
8. Koss, *The Pro-Boers*, p. xxix.
9. *Letters* 3, p. 200.
10. K to Gwynne, 24 Jan. 1906, Kipling Collection, Dalhousie.
11. Marlowe, *Milner*, pp. 172–3.
12. Pakenham, *The Boer War*, p. 492.
13. Marlowe, *Milner*, p. 170.
14. K to E. and G. Bambridge, 13 July 1926, 14 Feb. 1935, KP 12/15 and 24.
15. *Letters* 3, pp. 254, 337.
16. *Letters* 3, pp. 231, 235–6.
17. *Standard*, 27 July 1906.
18. *Letters* 3, p. 300.
19. K to Fitzpatrick, 22 April 1924, National English Literary Museum, Grahamstown.
20. *Letters* 3, pp. 310–15.
21. K to Macphail, 10 Feb. 1908, National Archives of Canada; K to Ford, 15 Sept. 1906, 3 April 1907 and n.d. [*c.* 1908], KP 15/7; K to Gwynne, 6 May 1908, KP 15/15; *Letters* 3, pp. 308, 347.
22. *Letters* 3, p. 436; K to Baker, 29 July n.d., Rhodes Papers.
23. Marlowe, *Milner*, pp.174–5.
24. *SOM*, p. 97.
25. K to Gwynne, 20 Feb. 1907, KP 15/15; K to Cornford, 24 May 1908, National Maritime Museum; K to Ralling, 13 June 1908, Library of Congress.
26. Ferguson, *The Pity of War*, pp. 83–7.
27. Ferguson, *The Pity of War*, pp. 83–7; Kennedy, *The Rise and Fall of the Great Powers*, p. 203; Keegan, *The First World War*, pp. 231–2.
28. Ferguson, *The Pity of War*, p. 86.
29. *Letters* 3, pp. 156, 374; K to Aitken, 1 Nov. 1914, Beaverbrook Papers.
30. Koss, *Lord Haldane*, p. 66.
31. Morris, *Fisher's Face*, p. 124.
32. K to Murray, 9 Nov. 1907, Kipling Collection, Syracuse; *Letters* 3, pp. 227, 374.
33. *Book of Words*, pp. 58–9.
34. Roberts, *Salisbury*, p. 772.
35. K to Baldwin, 8 Dec. 1904, KP 11/1; *Letters* 3, pp. 158, 193.
36. K to Bateson, 14 April 1910, Kipling Collection, Austin; K to Dunsterville, n.d. [*c.* 1911], KP 14/52.
37. K to Ford, 19 April 1910, KP 15/7; *Letters* 4, p. 40.
38. *Letters* 4, pp. 75–6.

39. K to Fullerton, 28 April 1913, Kipling Collection, Harvard.
40. Koss, *Lord Haldane*, p. 19.
41. Koss, *Lord Haldane*, p. 45.
42. Koss, *Lord Haldane*, p. 61
43. K to Ford, 10 July 1908, KP 15/7; K to Hopman, 11 March 1908, Kipling Collection, Cornell; *Letters* 3, p. 392; K to Harris, 26 Nov. 1908, British Library, RP 2225.
44. *Letters* 4, pp. 25, 40.
45. Donaldson, *The Marconi Scandal*, p. 89.
46. Anonymously published in the *Daily Express*, 7 Dec. 1914.

CHAPTER 14: IN DEFENCE OF PRIVILEGE
1. I.. Kipling, excerpt from undated letter to anonymous recipient, Kipling Collection, Cornell.
2. K to Morris, 10 Jan. 1905, *Notes and Queries*, July 1976, pp. 296–7, *Letters* 3, p 107; *Letters* 4, pp. 107, 118; K to Marker, 22 July 1913, Dunscombe Colt Collection.
3. K to Morris, 10 Jan. 1905, *Notes and Queries*, July 1976, pp. 296–7.
4. *Sunday Express*, 24 Dec. 1939; Sykes, *Nancy*, pp. 100–1.
5. Carrington, *Rudyard Kipling*, p. 516.
6. *KJ*, March 1998, p. 58.
7. *KJ*, Dec. 1997, p. 47.
8. *Sunday Express*, 24 Dec. 1939.
9. *Souvenirs of France*, pp. 25, 32.
10. Gardiner, *Prophets, Priests and Kings*, p. 293.
11. K to Balfour, 7 Nov. 1903, Dunscombe Colt Collection.
12. *Letters* 3, p. 381; K to Poynter, 26 Dec. 1909, Baldwin Papers.
13. Grigg, *Lloyd George: The People's Champion*, p. 198; Jenkins, *Mr Balfour's Poodle*, pp. 88–9.
14. K to Strachey, 26 Oct. 1910, and Strachey to K, 26 Oct. 1910, Strachey Papers.
15. *Letters* 3, p. 204.
16. K to Gwynne, 7 Feb. 1906 and n.d. [June 1907?], KP 15/15; K to Drummond Chaplin, 24 July 1908, National Archives of Zimbabwe; K to Drummond Chaplin, 8 May 1908, Michael Silverman Catalogue, No. 3, 1990.
17. K to Poynter, 26 Dec. 1909, Baldwin Papers.
18. K to Blumenfeld, 8 May 1910, KP 14/19.
19. Chisholm and Davie, *Beaverbrook*, p. 75.
20. K to Aitken, 9 March 1911, Beaverbrook Papers.
21. K to Aitken, 12 Dec. 1910, Beaverbrook Papers; K to Milner, 14 Dec. 1910, Milner Papers.
22. *Letters* 4, p. 39.
23. K to Blumenfeld, 27 July 1910, Kipling Collection, Austin.
24. Koss, *The Rise and Fall of the Political Press*, Vol. 2, pp. 179–80.
25. Aitken to K, 7 Aug. 1911, Beaverbrook Papers; Koss, *The Rise and Fall of the Political Press*, Vol. 2, p. 182
26. Gilmour, *Curzon*, pp. 392–3.
27. Cohen, *Rudyard Kipling to Rider Haggard*, p. 72; K to Blumenfeld, n.d., KP 14/19.
28. *Letters* 3, p. 94.
29. *Letters* 4, pp. 124–5.
30. K to Aitken, 23 Nov. 1911, Beaverbrook Papers.
31. *Book of Words*, pp. 65–6.
32. Aitken to K, 30 Sept. and 20 Nov. 1911, Beaverbrook Papers.
33. Adams, *Bonar Law*, p. 9.
34. Mackay, *Balfour*, p. 238; Dugdale, *Arthur James Balfour*, Vol. 2, p. 86.
35. *Letters* 4, p. 67; Chisholm and Davie, *Beaverbrook*, p. 112; K to Aitken, 10 Nov. 1911, Beaverbrook Papers; K to Gwynne, 10 Nov. 1911, Bonar Law Papers.

36. *Letters* 4, p. 74.
37. *Letters* 4, pp. 90, 139.
38. K to Cornford. n.d. [December 1905], Library of Congress.
39. K to Gwynne, 21 April 1912, KP 15/15; K to Blumenfeld, 28 Nov. 1912 and n.d., KP 14/19.
40. K to Maxse, 1 June 1912, Maxse Papers.
41. Grigg, *Lloyd George: The People's Champion*, p. 165.
42. K to Blumenfeld, 25 July 1910, Kipling Collection, Austin; *Letters* 3, p. 252; K to C. Frewen, 5 July, and to M. Frewen, 6 Oct. 1910, Kipling Collection, Cornell.
43. 'The Flag of Their Country'.
44. *Letters* 4, p. 83; K to Doubleday, 18 March 1919, Doubleday Collection.
45. *Letters* 4, p. 70.
46. K to Gwynne, 21 June 1910, KP 15/15; K to Mrs H. Ward, 2 Feb. 1912, Kipling Collection, Dalhousie.
47. Portion of unaddressed letter n.d., Ray Collection, MA 45000K; *Letters of Travel*, pp. 155, 205.
48. *Letters* 4, p. 73; K to Doubleday, 6 March 1912, Doubleday Collection; K to Blakeney, 29 Sept. 1913, British Library, Add ms 48979.
49. *KJ*, June 1991, pp. 16–17.
50. K to Aitken, 15 Nov. 1913, Beaverbrook Papers; *Letters of Travel*, p. 143; K to Gwynne, 21 April 1912, KP 15/15.
51. Ward, *G.K. Chesterton*, p. 307; *Letters* 4, pp. 193, 195.
52. K to Aitken, 12 Aug. and 14 Nov. 1913, 15 Jan. 1914, Beaverbrook Papers; Cooper, *Old Men Forget*, p. 46.
53. K to Gwynne, 26 Sept. 1913, KP 15/15; K to Aitken, 14 Nov. 1913, Beaverbrook Papers; *Letters* 4, pp. 194–5.
54. Grigg, *Lloyd George: From Peace to War*, pp. 48–66; Donaldson, *The Marconi Scandal, passim*.

CHAPTER 15: EGYPT AND ULSTER

1. *Letters* 3, p. 377.
2. Aitken to K, 3 Oct. 1912, Beaverbrook Papers; Porter, *The Nineteenth Century*, p. 543; *Letters* 4, p. 228; *Letters* 3, p. 336.
3. K to Doubleday, 5 Nov. 1912, Doubleday Collection; K to Blumenfeld, n.d. [1912], KP 14/19.
4. Brogan, *Mowgli's Sons*, pp. 29–36.
5. K to Dawson, 28 Feb. n.d., Kipling Collection, Dalhousie; Brogan, *Mowgli's Sons*, pp. 41–9.
6. K to Cecil, 12 March 1913, Lady Milner Papers.
7. *Letters* 4, p. 231; *Letters of Travel*, pp. 212, 222, 236–7.
8. K to Milner, 3 March 1913, Milner Papers.
9. K to Forbes, 9 April 1913, Kipling Collection, Harvard; *Letters of Travel*, pp. 277–84.
10. *Letters of Travel*, pp. 247–9; Tignor, *Modernization and British Colonial Rule in Egypt*, p. 239; *Letters* 4, p. 173; K to Strachey, 14 March 1913, Strachey to K, 24 March 1913, Strachey Papers.
11. CK diary, 13 Feb. 1913, KP 1/10; *Letters* 4, pp. 173–5.
12. *Letters* 4, p. 149; K to Gwynne, 25 Jan. 1913, KP 15/15.
13. *Letters* 4, p. 203.
14. K to Amery, 7 June 1914, KP 14/3; K to Chamberlain, 10 June 1914, KP 14/33; KP 21/1.
15. K to Gwynne, 13 June 1909, Kipling Collection, Dalhousie.
16. Fletcher and Kipling, *A History of England*, p. 69; *Letters* 4, pp. 59, 596.
17. K to Mrs Guthrie, 16 Nov. 1901, Dunscombe Colt Collection.

18. *Letters* 4, p. 59.
19. *Letters* 4, p. 59; K to White, 25 Dec. 1912, KP 17/50.
20. I have benefited from Edward Pearce's comments on this poem in his *Lines of Most Resistance*, p. 402.
21. *Letters* 4, p. 105.
22. 11 April 1912; Michael Brock: '"Outside his Art": Rudyard Kipling in Politics' in *Essays by Divers Hands*, Vol. 45. pp. 115–16.
23. *Letters* 4, pp. 203, 211.
24. K to Gwynne, 26 Nov. 1913, KP 15/15.
25. *Letters* 4, pp. 211, 222, 225.
26. *The Times*, 3 March 1914.
27. *Letters* 4, pp. 215, 224–6; K to Frohlich, 14 March 1914, Kipling Collection, Dalhousie.
28. Falls, *Rudyard Kipling*, p. 45; *Letters* 4, p. 226.
29. KP 28/9.
30. *Letters* 4, pp. 239–40.

NOTES TO CHAPTER 16: ARMAGEDDON

1. *Letters* 4, p. 132.
2. *Letters* 4, p. 249; K to Feilden, 7 Aug. 1914, KP 15/2.
3. K to Harding, 2 Sept. 1903, Kipling Collection, Harvard; *Letters* 4, pp. 182, 253.
4. K to Curzon, 24 Aug. 1914, Curzon Papers.
5. KP 29/9; K to Blumenfeld, 23 Dec. 1915, Kipling Collection, Austin; *Letters* 4, p. 351.
6. K to Doubleday, 31 Aug. 1914, Doubleday Collection; *Letters* 4, pp. 250–4, 277; Hugh Brogan, 'The Great War and Rudyard Kipling' in *KJ*, June 1998, pp. 18–34; Keegan, *The First World War*, pp. 92–3.
7. *Morning Post*, 22 June 1915; K to Blumenfeld, 22 Aug. 1918, KP 14/19.
8. K to Doubleday, 5 Oct. 1914, Doubleday Collection; *Book of Words*, pp. 123, 182.
9. *A Diversity of Creatures*; *Letters* 4, p. 231.
10. Link, *The Papers of Woodrow Wilson*, Vols. 15, 23, 24, 30, 38, 43, 66, 67 *passim*.
11. *Morning Post*, 13 Nov. 1933; Neruda, *Memoirs*, p. 249; Maugham to K, 24 Feb. [1934], KP 22/40; Godfrey to K, 31 March 1919, KP 22/40; K to Lewin, 20 Jan. 1933, Dunscombe Colt Collection; Winter, *Haig's Command*, p. 294.
12. *Letters* 4, pp. 254–5.
13. K to Gwynne, 12 Aug. 1914, Kipling Collection, Dalhousie.
14. *Letters* 4, pp. 256, 261.
15. Roosevelt to K, 4 Nov. 1914, copy in Milner Papers.
16. K to Doubleday, 11 Sept. 1914, Doubleday Collection; K to Matthews, 20 Sept. 1914, Brander Matthews Collection; K to Johnson, 11 Sept. 1914, Kipling Collection, Dalhousie; K to Martin, 7 Oct. 1914 and K to Barret Wendell, 28 Oct. 1914, Kipling Collection, Harvard; *Letters* 4, pp. 263–5.
17. CK to Mrs Balestier, 28 Oct. 1914, Dunham Papers.
18. Memo by Forbes, 8 Nov. 1915, in Kipling Collection, Harvard.
19. CK diary, 29 March 1915, KP, 38/40; K to Lawson, 22 May 1915, KP 16/20.
20. Milner to Carson, 11 Nov. 1917, Churchill to K, 27 Jan. and 6 Feb. 1918, Isaacs to K, 4 Dec. 1918, Davies to K, 23 May 1917, all in KP 22/1; K to Davies, 25 May 1917, KP 14/45.
21. K to Davies, 25 May 1917, KP 14/45.
22. K's articles in *Daily Telegraph*, Sept. 1915; K to Dunsterville, 27 Aug. 1915, KP 14/52.
23. Gilbert, *'O Beloved Kids'*, pp. 200–13.
24. Keegan, *The First World War*, pp. 217–18.
25. *History of the Irish Guards*, Vol. 2, pp. 20–8.
26. *Letters* 4, p. 336–45, 402–3.

27. Holt and Holt, *My Boy Jack?*, pp. 205–22.
28. CK to Mrs Balestier, 28 Oct. 1914, Dunham Papers.
29. *Letters* 4, pp. 344–5.
30. K to Macmechan, 2 Nov. 1914, Kipling Collection, Dalhousie; *Letters* 4, p. 291.
31. K to Lady E. Cecil, 9 April 1915, Lady Milner Papers.
32. K to Strachey, 31 Aug. 1918, Strachey Papers; K to E. MacDonald, 30 Dec. 1930, KP 11/10.
33. *Letters* 4, p. 360.
34. Ricketts, *The Unforgiving Minute*, p. 332.
35. K to Blumenfeld, 22 Aug. 1918, KP 14/19; K to Gwynne, 13 April 1933, KP 15/15.
36. K to Barrett Wendell, 28 Oct. 1914, Kipling Collection, Harvard; *Letters* 4, pp. 310–11, 380, 395.
37. K to Dunsterville, 11 Sept. 1916, KP 14/52; *Letters* 4, pp. 392, 405.
38. *Letters* 4, pp. 345, 355; K to Adam, 28 March 1917, Kipling Collection, Cornell.
39. *History of the Irish Guards*, Vol. 1, pp. 26, 86, Vol. 2, p. 28.
40. *Letters* 4, pp. 355, 478–9; Beaverbrook to K, 28 Nov. and 6 Dec. 1917, Beaverbrook Papers.
41. Keegan, *The First World War*, pp. 392–5; Winter, *Haig's Command*, pp. 108–9.
42. *Letters* 4, pp. 370–3; K to Frewen, 28 Jan. 1917, Morton Frewen Collection.
43. Memo by Forbes, 5 April 1916, Kipling Collection, Harvard.
44. K to Forbes, 28 Aug. 1917, Kipling Collection, Harvard; *Daily Telegraph*, 17 Aug. 1918.
45. Vincent, *The Crawford Papers*, pp. 396, 502; *Letters* 4, p. 517.
46. Keating, *Kipling the Poet*, p. 200.
47. *New York World*, 10 Sept. 1922.
48. Rodd to K, 15 May 1915, KP 23/10.
49. *Letters* 4, pp. 457–8, 464.
50. *Daily Telegraph*, 16 June 1917.
51. K to Matthews, 4 November 1919, Brander Matthews Collection.
52. *Letters* 4, p. 544.
53. *Letters* 4, p. 542.
54. K to Barry, 21 Dec. 1935, KP 38/2.
55. Green, *Kipling: The Critical Heritage*, p. 332; K to Macphail, 12 Feb. 1921, National Archives of Canada.
56. K to Fletcher, 22 Sept. 1921, KP 15/5; CK diary, 27 July 1922, KP.

CHAPTER 17: THE PAIN OF PEACE
1. Newton, *Lord Lansdowne*, pp. 463–8.
2. *Letters* 4, p. 474.
3. 15 Feb. 1918, KP 28/9.
4. *Letters* 4, pp. 515, 520; CK diary, 11 Nov. 1918, KP; K to Hannay, 18 Jan. 1919, Kipling Collection, Dalhousie; K to Mrs Gerould, 1 May 1920, Princeton, Gen ms misc CO140.
5. *Letters* 4, pp. 520, 524; K to Matthews, 4 Nov. 1919, Brander Matthews Collection.
6. K to Forbes, 19 Sept. 1916, Kipling Collection, Harvard; *Letters* 4, p. 515.
7. K to Drummond Chaplin, 15 July 1920, National Archives of Zimbabwe; K to Gwynne, 30 Oct. 1921, Kipling Collection, Dalhousie.
8. K to Colvin, 2 July 1918, Kipling Collection, Syracuse; K to Mrs Stoddard, 6 Dec. 1935, Library of Congress.
9. *Letters* 4, p. 601; K to Churchill and to Lee, both 17 Dec. 1919, KP.
10. *Letters* 4, p. 515; K to Doubleday, 22 April and 27 Aug. 1919, Doubleday Collection.
11. *Letters* 4, pp. 540, 528.
12. *Letters* 4, p. 528.
13. K to Forbes, 1 March 1919, Kipling Collection, Houghton; K to Doubleday, 22 April

1919, Doubleday Collection.
14. *Letters* 4, pp. 556, 578, 594.
15. K to Matthews, 23 Oct. 1921, Brander Matthews Collection; K to Gwynne, 20 March 1926, Kipling Collection, Dalhousie.
16. Lycett, *Rudyard Kipling*, p. 476; Cohen, *Rudyard Kipling to Rider Haggard*, pp. 111–13.
17. See Keating, *Kipling the Poet*, pp. 220–2.
18. K to Strachey, 22 Aug. 1918 and 18 Dec. 1920, Strachey to K, 12 March 1919, Strachey Papers; CK diary, 11 Nov. 1920, KP 38/40.
19. *Letters* 4, pp. 470, 596; K to Doubleday, 21 Aug. 1918, Doubleday Collection.
20. K to Fletcher, 22 Sept. 1921, KP 15/5; K to Crewe, 28 Nov. 1921, East London Museum; K to Chevrillon, 31 Dec. 1921, KP 14/37.
21. K to Chevrillon, 31 Dec. 1921, KP 14/37.
22. CK diary, 7 Dec. 1921, KP; Birkenhead, *Rudyard Kipling*, p. 294; K to Bambridge, 31 March 1924, KP 12/13; K to Fletcher, 4 Oct. 1922, KP 15/5.
23. Carrington to Beaverbrook, 4 Nov. 1954, Beaverbrook to Carrington, 18 Nov. and 8 Dec. 1954, Beaverbrook Papers.
24. K to Bates, 18 June 1930, KP 14/13.
25. K to Mrs Sington, 6 Oct. 1916, Kipling Collection, Syracuse.
26. K to Lewin, 26 April and 3 May 1920, Dunscombe Colt Collection.
27. K to Lewin, Oct. 1920; Longworth, *The Unending Vigil*, pp. 47–8; Rose, *The Later Cecils*, pp. 270–1.
28. CK diary, 25 July 1920, KP 38/40; K to Sedgwick, 29 April 1920, Massachusetts Historical Society; K to Matthews, 27 March 1921, Brander Matthews Collection.
29. K to Dawson, 30 Dec. 1919, Duke University; Kipling diary, 28 April and 1 May 1921, Macmillan Archives.
30. Carrington, *Rudyard Kipling*, p. 458.
31. K to Robinson, 25 June 1928, Kipling Collection, Syracuse.
32. CK to Adcock, 14 Aug. 1924, Kipling Collection, Cornell, Box 5; K to Baldwin, 17 June 1918; Orel, *Kipling*, Vol. 2, p. 341; K to Macphail, 12 Feb. 1921, National Archives of Canada.
33. K to Mrs Reed, 22 May 1932, Kipling Collection, Harvard; *SOM*, p. 119; K to Ridsdale, 9 Nov. 1915, Baldwin Papers; K to De Forest, 22 May 1926, letter, the possession of Thomas Pinney.
34. K to U. Stanley, 8 June 1928, and R. Gwynne, 21 June 1932, Kipling Collection, Syracuse; G. Strutt to author, 22 Sept. 1997.
35. K to R. Gwynne, 22 Dec. 1930, Kipling Collection, Syracuse; Orel, *Kipling*, Vol. 2, p. 320.
36. K to E. Bambridge, 24. Aug 1925, KP 12/15; K to Matthews, 21 July 1920, Brander Matthews Collection.
37. K to Frere Reeves, 24 Jan. 1929 and 27 Jan. 1930, Kipling Collection, Syracuse.
38. K to Cockerell, 6 Oct. 1932, Pierpont Morgan, MA 3687.
39. CK diary, July and Aug. 1921, KP 1/12.
40. Lawrence notebook, Houghton Ms Eng 1252 (355).
41. K to Lawrence, 20 and 25 July 1922, British Library, RP 2174; K to Doubleday, 1 Nov. 1927, Doubleday Collection.
42. K to Beit, 22 June 1925, KP 21/29; K to Gilmour, 8 Dec. 1918, and K to Parkin, 18 Nov. 1919, Milner Papers; *Letters* 4, p. 595.
43. K to Dunsterville, 20 Nov. 1927, KP 14/12; K to Brooking, 20 July 1927, KP 21/27.
44. Cohen, *Rudyard Kipling to Rider Haggard*, pp. 101, 106–7.
45. Cobb, *Something to Hold Onto*, p. 85.
46. K to Bates, 2 Feb. 1932, KP 14/13; K to E. Bambridge, 19 Feb. 1925, KP 12/14; K to Courtauld, 12 Feb. 1932, Samuel Courtauld Papers.
47. K to Rawlinson, 11 Jan. 1935, Berg Collection.
48. K to Bambridge, 6 March 1921, KP 12/13; K to Pawling, 2 April 1922, Doubleday

Collection; K to Dunsterville, 30 April 1922, KP 14/52.

49. K to Bates, 6/7 Feb. 1925, KP 14/13; K to Forbes, 3 May 1927, Kipling Collection, Harvard.

50. K to E. Bambridge, 19 Feb. 1933, KP 12/22; K to Spink, 26 March 1932, KP 38/13; K to Dawson, 9 March 1932, Dawson Papers.

51. K to Baker, 17 March 1934, KP 14/7; K to Mrs Hussey, 28 March 1921, KP 16/11.

52. K to Roosevelt, 16 April 1932, Theodore Roosevelt Jr. Collection; K to Lawrence, 20 July 1922, British Library, RP 2174; K to Jarvis, 21 Jan. 1930, KP 16/14.

53. K to Bates, 4 and 12 May 1930, KP 14/13; K to MacDougall, 22 March 1930, Kipling Collection, Dalhousie; K to E. Bambridge, 22 March 1930, KP 12/19; K to Macphail, 19 May 1930, National Archives of Canada; Pinney, 'Kipling in Bermuda, 1930', *KJ*, Dec. 1997.

CHAPTER 18: BONFIRES ON THE ICE

1. K to Feilden, 9 April 1921, KP 15/2; K to Macphail, 15 April 1921, National Archives of Canada.

2. James, *Memoirs of a Conservative*, p. 149.

3. *Daily Telegraph*, 21 March 1925.

4. Cohen, *Rudyard Kipling to Rider Haggard*, pp. 132, 163–4; CK diary, 7 Oct. 1922, KP 1/12.

5. K to Baldwin, 9 Dec. 1923, Baldwin Papers; K to Chevrillon, 10 Jan. 1924, KP 14/37.

6. K to Smith, 27 Aug. 1919, Kipling Collection, Syracuse.

7. K to Gwynne, 12 and 16 May 1926, KP 15/15 and Kipling Collection, Dalhousie; K to De Forest, 22 May 1926, McGill University.

8. K to Gwynne, 14 Nov. 1929, 26 Nov. 1930, 19 Feb. 1932 and n.d., KP 15/15; K to Bates, 13 Aug. 1931, KP 14/13.

9. K to Dunsterville, 20 May 1927, KP 14/52; *Letters from Rudyard Kipling to Guy Paget 1919–1936*, privately published; K to E. MacDonald, 31 Dec. 1931, KP 11/10; CK diary, Feb. 1933, KP 38/40; Birkenhead, *Rudyard Kipling*, p. 344.

10. Chisholm and Davie, *Beaverbrook*, p. 280; Blake, *The Conservative Party from Peel to Churchill*, p. 233.

11. K to Baldwin, 29 Oct. 1930, Baldwin Papers.

12. K to Gwynne, 26 Aug. and n.d. 1931, KP 15/15.

13. K to Bates, 29 Oct. 1931, KP 14/13; K to E. Macdonald, 31 Dec. 1931, KP 11/10; K to Hughes, 18 July 1932, KP 16/10.

14. K to Macphail, 26 March 1922, National Archives of Canada; K to Morris, 18 and 23 Oct. 1926, National Library of Australia; K to Larkin, 1 July 1927, National Archives of Canada; K to Macphail, 2 Jan. 1934, National Archives of Canada; K to Roosevelt, 18 Sept. 1935, Theodore Roosevelt Jnr. Collection; K to Barry, 13 May 1935, KP 38/2.

15. Rose, *Churchill*, p. 233.

16. Charmley, *Lord Lloyd*, pp. 176–7; K to Bates, 12 Feb. 1931, KP 14/13.

17. K to Gwynne, 26 Nov. 1930 and n.d. [Sept. 1933], KP 15/15; K to Curry, 28 June 1932, Kipling Collection, Cornell; Orel, *Kipling*, Vol. 1, p. 90; K to E. Bambridge, 23 Feb. 1935, KP 12/24.

18. K to Allen, 24 Dec. 1935, Kipling Collection, Dalhousie; K to Bates, 30 May 1935, KP 14/13.

19. Lady Milner diary, 5 Nov. 1934, Lady Milner Papers; K to Bambridge, 26 Feb. 1935, KP 12/24.

20. *Books of Words*, pp. 186, 202; K to Northcliffe. 4 Nov. 1922, Kipling Collection, Dalhousie.

21. K to Chevrillon, 31 Dec. 1921, KP 14/37; K to Fletcher, 22 Sept. 1921, KP 15/5; Cohen, *Rudyard Kipling to Rider Haggard*, p. 170; K to Crewe, 28 Nov. 1921, East London Museum; K to Wister, n.d., Owen Wister Collection.

22. K to E. Bambridge, 25 and 29 Dec. 1926, 21 March 1933, KP 12/15 and 22; K to Clemenceau, 30 June 1926, Kipling Collection, Cornell.
23. K to Chevrillon, 22 Dec. 1921, KP 14/37; K to Northcliffe, 4 Nov. 1922, Kipling Collection, Dalhousie; K to Owen, 7 May 1921, Dunscombe Colt.
24. K to Doubleday, 24 Dec. 1931, Doubleday Collection.
25. K to MacDougall, 2 Jan. 1934, Kipling Collection, Dalhousie.
26. *Book of Words*, pp. 201–4; K to Gwynne, 11 June 1932, KP 15/15; *Souvenirs of France*, p. 41.
27. K to Dunsterville, 1 May 1926, KP 14/52; K to Gwynne, 10 April 1926, KP 15/15; K to Fletcher, 30 March 1924, KP 15/5.
28. K to Bambridge, 20 March 1931 and 29 April 1934, KP 12/20 and 23; K to MacDougall, 2 Jan. 1936, Kipling Collection, Dalhousie.
29. K to Barry, 14 Sept. and 30 Dec. 1935, KP 38/2; K to Bambridge, 21 March 1933, KP 12/22.
30. K to Wister, n.d., Owen Lister Collection; K to Hughes, 24 Sept. 1933, KP 16/10.
31. K to Hughes, 15 Nov. and 9 Dec. 1935, KP 16/10.
32. K to Doubleday, 17 March 1933, Doubleday Collection; K to Hughes, 19 Dec. 1933, KP 16/10.
33. K to Bok, 1 Nov. 1935, and to White, 28 Dec. 1935, Kipling Collection, Syracuse.
34. Shirer, *The Rise and Fall of the Third Reich*, p. 212.
35. *Morning Post*, 13 Nov. 1933; Keating, *Kipling the Poet*, pp. 237–8.
36. K to Fullerton, 16 May 1935, Kipling Collection, Harvard; K to Chevrillon, 1 June 1935, KP 14/37; K to Courtauld, 12 April 1933, Samuel Courtauld Papers; K to Hughes, 28 July 1933, KP 16/10; K to Gwynne, 31 July 1933, 12 Jan. 1934, KP 15/15.
37. Kipling to Gwynne, 2 and 12 Jan. and 4 March 1934, KP 15/15; K to Gwynne, 23 Sept. 1935, Kipling Collection, Dalhousie; K to Bates, 6 June 1935, KP 14/13; K to Chevrillon, 1 June 1935, KP 14/37; K to Barry, 15 Dec. 1935, KP 38/2.
38. *Morning Post*, 7 May 1935.
39. K to Lewis, 1 Jan. 1936, Lewis Papers; K to MacDougall, 2 Jan. 1936, Kipling Collection, Dalhousie.
40. Lycett, *Rudyard Kipling*, pp. 564 ff.; Lady Milner diary, 27 Oct. 1932, Lady Milner Papers.
41. K to Courtauld, 1 Jan. and 16 May 1935, 23 Oct. 1933, Samuel Courtauld Papers; Bodelsen, *Aspects of Kipling's Art*, p. 40n.
42. Rose, *King George V*, p. 394.
43. Rose, *King George V*, p. 59; K to E. MacDonald, 25 July 1935, KP 11/10.
44. KP 20/3; Jones, *An Edwardian Youth*, p. 113; Rose, *King George V*, p. 313.
45. K to E. MacDonald, 2 Jan. 1936, KP 11/10; K to Baker, 13 Jan. 1934; K to Snow, 26 Dec. 1934, Kipling Collection, Dalhousie.
46. Bambridge to Knoblock, 30 Jan. 1936, Kipling Collection, Syracuse.
47. Birkenhead, *Rudyard Kipling*, pp. 357–8; Carrington, *Rudyard Kipling*, pp. 504–6.
48. KP 20/5.
49. Unidentified newspaper cutting in KP 28/8; Keating, *Kipling the Poet*, p. 215.
50. Maude to author, January 1978.
51. Vansittart, *The Mist Procession*, pp. 131, 365.
52. K to De Forest, 22 May 1926, McGill University.
53. Rose, *Lewis Namier and Zionism*, p. 109.

Bibliography

MANUSCRIPT COLLECTIONS

Arnold-Forster, H.O., British Library
Baldwin, Earl, University of Sussex
Balfour, A.J., British Library
Beaverbrook, Lord, House of Lords Record Office
Berg, New York Public Library
Blakeney, E.H., British Library
Carpenter, William, Library of Congress
Chandler, Admiral L.H., Library of Congress
Courtauld, Samuel, private collection
Curzon, Marquess, British Library
Dawson, Geoffrey *see* Robinson
Dodge, Mary Mapes, Princeton University
Doubleday, F.N., Princeton University
Dowdall, Thomas Percy, British Library
Du Cane, Sir Edmund, Bodleian Library
Dunham, University of Sussex
Dunscombe Colt, H., University of Sussex
Eton College Library
Frewen, Moreton, Library of Congress
Gilbert, W.S., and Sullivan, A., Pierpont Morgan Library
Hill, Edmonia, Cornell University
Holbrook, F. Cabot, Marlboro College
Kipling, Lockwood, University of Sussex
Kipling, Rudyard, Cornell University
———Dalhousie University
———Harvard University
———Library of Congress
———Syracuse University

Bibliography

——University of Sussex
——University of Texas at Austin
Kitchener, Lord, Public Record Office
Law, Andrew Bonar, House of Lords Record Office
Lewis, W.H., private collection
Macmillan Archive, British Library
Macphail, Sir Andrew, National Archives of Canada
Matthews, Brander, Columbia University
Maxse, Leo, West Sussex Record Office
Milner, Lady, Bodleian Library
Milner, Lord, Bodleian Library
Pearse, General George, British Library
Phelps, Reverend Lionel, Oriel College
Ray, Gordon, Pierpont Morgan Library
Rhodes, Cecil, Rhodes House
Rice, Howard, Marlboro College
Robinson, Geoffrey (Dawson), Bodleian Library
Roosevelt, Theodore Jnr., Library of Congress
Scribner, Charles, Princeton University
Selborne, Earl of, Bodleian Library
Stein, Aurel, Bodleian Library
Strachey, John St Loe, House of Lords Record Office
Strutt, Guy, private collection
Thompson, Sir John Perronet, British Library
Wharton, Edith, Yale University
Wister, Owen, Library of Congress
Wright, Howell, Yale University

PUBLISHED SOURCES

(The editions listed are not necessarily the earliest but those which have been consulted.
The place of publication is London unless otherwise stated.)

Adams, R.J.Q., *Bonar Law*, John Murray, 1999
Advani, Rukun, *E.M. Forster as Critic*, Croom Helm, 1984
Agar, Herbert, *The Price of Union*, Houghton Mifflin, Boston, 1949
Amery, J., *The Life of Joseph Chamberlain*, Vol. 4, Macmillan, 1951
Amis, Kingsley, *Rudyard Kipling*, Thames and Hudson, 1986
Ankers, Arthur R., *The Pater: John Lockwood Kipling, His Life and Times*, Pond View Books, Otford, 1988
Austin, Alfred, *Songs of England*, Macmillan, 1900
Bailey, R.V., 'The Poet's Trade and the Prophet's Vocation: Development and Integration in the Poetry of Rudyard Kipling', Oxford Ph.D. thesis, 1982
Baldwin, A.W., *The Macdonald Sisters*, Peter Davies, 1960
——*My Father: The True Story*, George Allen & Unwin, 1955
Baldwin, Stanley, *On England*, Philip Allan, 1926
Ballhatchett, Kenneth, *Race, Sex and Class under the Raj*, Weidenfeld & Nicolson, 1980
Bauer, Helen Pike, *Rudyard Kipling: A Study of the Short Fiction*, Twayne, New York, 1994

Bibliography

Bayly, C.A., *The Local Roots of Indian Politics: Allahabad 1880–1920*, Oxford University Press, 1975

Beames, John, *Memoirs of a Bengal Civilian*, Eland, 1990

Bence-Jones, Mark, *The Viceroys of India*, Constable, 1982

Bennett, Mary, *The Ilberts in India, 1882–1886*, BACSA, 1995

Beresford, G.C., *Schooldays with Kipling*, Gollancz, 1936

Birkenhead, Lord, *Rudyard Kipling*, Weidenfeld & Nicolson, 1978

Blake, Robert, *The Conservative Party from Peel to Thatcher*, Methuen, 1985

—— *The Unknown Prime Minister*, Eyre & Spottiswode, 1955

Bodelsen, C.A, *Aspects of Kipling's Art*, Manchester University Press, 1964

Braddy, Nella, *Son of Empire: The Story of Rudyard Kipling*, Collins, 1964

Brock, Michael, ' "Outside his Art": Rudyard Kipling in Politics' in *Essays by Divers Hands*, Vol. LXV, Royal Society of Literature

Brogan, Hugh, *Mowgli's Sons: Kipling and Baden-Powell's Scouts*, Jonathan Cape, 1987

Brown, Hilton, *Rudyard Kipling*, Hamish Hamilton, 1945

Brown, Judith M., and Louis, Wm. Roger (eds.), *The Twentieth Century*, Oxford University Press, 1999

Buck, Edward J., *Simla Past and Present,* The Times Press, Bombay, 1925

Carrington, Charles (ed.), *The Complete Barrack-Room Ballads of Rudyard Kipling*, Methuen, 1973

——*Rudyard Kipling: His Life and Work*, Macmillan, 1955

Cecil, David, *The Cecils of Hatfield House*, Cardinal, 1975

——*Max: A Biography of Max Beerbohm*, Atheneum, New York, 1985

Chandra, Sudhir, *Enslaved Daughters: Colonialism, Law and Women's Rights*, Oxford University Press, Delhi, 1999

Charmley, John, *Lord Lloyd and the Decline of the British Empire*, Weidenfeld & Nicolson, 1987

Chesterton, G.K., *Heretics*, John Lane, 1905

Chisholm, Anne, and Davie, Michael, *Beaverbrook*, Hutchinson, 1992

Clark, Allan (ed.), *A Good Innings*, John Murray, 1974

Clark, Manning, *History of Australia*, Pimlico, 1995

Clarke, Peter, *Hope and Glory: Britain 1900–1990*, Penguin, 1997

Coates, John, *The Day's Work: Kipling and the Idea of Sacrifice*, Associated University Presses, 1997

Cobb, Richard, *Something to Hold Onto*, John Murray, 1988

Cohen, Morton (ed.), *Rudyard Kipling to Rider Haggard: The Record of a Friendship*, Hutchinson, 1965

Cooper, Duff, *Old Men Forget*, Rupert Hart-Davis, 1953

Cornell, Louis L., *Kipling in India*, St Martin's Press, New York, 1966

Daiches, David, *Some Late Victorian Attitudes*, André Deutsch, 1969

Darling, Malcolm, *Apprentice to Power*, Hogarth Press, 1966

Dewey, Clive, *Anglo-Indian Attitudes: The Mind of the Indian Civil Service*, Hambledon Press, 1993

Dilks, David, *Curzon in India*, 2 vols., Rupert Hart-Davis, 1969 and 1970

Dobrée, Bonamy, *Rudyard Kipling: Realist and Fabulist*, Oxford University Press, 1967

Donaldson, Frances, *The Marconi Scandal*, Rupert Hart-Davis, 1962

Dugdale, Blanche E.C., *Arthur James Balfour, First Earl of Balfour*, 2 vols., Hutchinson, 1936

Dunsterville, L.C., *Stalky's Reminiscences*, Jonathan Cape, 1928

Egremont, Max, *Balfour*, Collins, 1980

Eliot, T.S. (ed.), *A Choice of Kipling's Verse*, Faber & Faber, 1941

Ellmann, Richard, *Oscar Wilde*, Hamish Hamilton, 1987

Bibliography

Falls, Cyril, *Rudyard Kipling: A Critical Study* , Martin Secker, 1925

Ferguson, Niall, *The Pity of War*, Allen Lane, 1998

Feuchtwanger, E.J., *Democracy and Empire: Britain, 1865–1914*, Edwin Arnold, 1990

Foster, R.F., *Modern Ireland*, Penguin, 1989

Fraser, John, *Sixty Years in Uniform*, Stanley Paul, 1963

Gardiner, A.G., *Prophets, Priests and Kings*, Alston Rivers, 1908

Gilbert, Elliot L. (ed.), *O Beloved Kids, Rudyard Kipling's Letters to His Children*, Weidenfeld & Nicolson, 1983

——*The Good Kipling: Studies in the Short Story*, Manchester University Press, 1972

——*Kipling and the Critics*, Peter Owen, 1966

Gilmour, David, *Curzon*, John Murray, 1994

Gokhale, B.G., *India in the Eyes of the British*, Cross Cultural Publications, Indiana, 1991

Gopal, S., *British Policy in India, 1858–1905*, Cambridge University Press, 1965

——*The Viceroyality of Lord Ripon*, Oxford University Press, 1953

Gosse, Edmund, *The Life of Algernon Charles Swinburne*, Macmillan, 1917

Goulding, Colonel H.R., *Old Lahore, Civil and Military Gazette*, Lahore, 1924

Green, Roger Lancelyn, *Kipling and the Children*, Elek, 1965

——*Kipling: The Critical Heritage*, Routledge & Kegan Paul, 1971

Greene, Graham, *Collected Essays*, Bodley Head, 1969

Grigg, John, *Lloyd George: From Peace to War, 1912–1916*, Methuen, 1985

——*Lloyd George: The People's Champion*, 1902–1911, Eyre Methuen, 1978

Gross, John (ed), *Rudyard Kipling: The Man, His Work and His World*, Weidenfeld & Nicolson, 1972

Guedalla, Philip, *Men of Letters*, Hodder & Stoughton, 1927

Gwynn, Stephen (ed.), *The Letters and Friendships of Sir Cecil Spring Rice*, 2 vols., Constable, 1929

Hamilton, Ian, *Listening for the Drums*, Faber, 1944

Harbord, Reginald (ed.), *The Readers' Guide to Rudyard Kipling's Works*, privately printed, Canterbury and Bournemouth, 1961–72

Holt, Tonie and Valmai, *My Boy Jack? The Search for John Kipling*, Pen & Sword Books, Barnsley, 1998

Hopkins, R. Thurston, *Rudyard Kipling: A Character Study*, Simpkin, Marshall Hamilton, Kent & Co., 1921

Hopkirk, Peter, *The Great Game*, John Murray, 1990

——*Quest for Kim: In Search of Kipling's Great Game*, John Murray, 1996

Hyam, Ronald, *Empire and Sexuality: The British Experience*, Manchester University Press, 1991

Islam, Shamsul, *Kipling's Law: A Study of His Philosophy of Life*, Macmillan, 1975

James, Robert Rhodes (ed.), *Memoirs of a Conservative: J.C.C.Davidson's Memoirs and Papers, 1910–1937*, Weidenfeld & Nicolson, 1967

Jenkins, Roy, *Mr Balfour's Poodle*, Collins, 1989

Jones, L.E., *An Edwardian Youth*, Macmillan, 1956

Kanwar, Pamela, *Imperial Simla*, Oxford University Press, Delhi, 1990

Keating, Peter, *Kipling the Poet*, Secker & Warburg, 1994

Keegan, John, *The First World War*, Hutchinson, 1998

Kemp, Sandra, *Kipling's Hidden Narratives*, Basil Blackwell, Oxford, 1988

Kennedy, Paul, *The Rise and Fall of the Great Powers*, Unwin, 1988

Kincaid, Dennis, *British Social Life in India, 1608–1937*, George Routledge, 1938

The Kipling Journal, The Kipling Society, 1929–2001

Koss, Stephen, *The Pro-Boers: The Anatomy of an Antiwar Movement*, University of Chicago Press, 1973

Bibliography

——*The Rise and Fall of the Political Press in Britain*, Vol. 2, Hamish Hamilton, 1984
——*Lord Haldane: Scapegoat for Liberalism*, Columbia University Press, New York, 1969
Lamb, Richard, *The Drift to War, 1922–1939*, W.H.Allen, 1989
Laski, Marghanita, *From Palm to Pine: Rudyard Kipling Abroad and at Home*, Sidgwick & Jackson, 1987
Lawrence, Walter, *The India We Served*, Cassell, 1928
Le Gallienne, Richard, *Rudyard Kipling*, John Lane, 1900
Lewis, C.S., *They Asked for a Paper*, Geoffrey Bles, 1962
Link, Arthur S., *The Papers of Woodrow Wilson*, Vols. 15–67, Princeton University Press, 1973
Longford, Elizabeth, *A Pilgrimage of Passion: The Life of Wilfrid Scawen Blunt*, Weidenfeld & Nicolson, 1979
——*Wellington*, Vol. 1, Weidenfeld & Nicolson, 1969
Longworth, Philip, *The Unending Vigil: The History of the Commonwealth War Graves Commission, 1917–1967*, Leo Cooper, 1976
Lowry, Donald (ed.), *The South African War Reappraised*, Manchester University Press, 2000
Lycett, Andrew, *Rudyard Kipling*, Weidenfeld & Nicolson, 1999
McAveeney, David C., *Kipling in Gloucester: The Writing of Captains Courageous*, Curious Traveller Press, Gloucester (US), 1996.
McClure, John A., *Kipling & Conrad: The Colonial Fiction*, Harvard University Press, 1981
Mackail, J.L., and Wyndham, Guy (eds.), *Life and Letters of George Wyndham*, Vol. 2, Hutchinson, 1925
Mackay, Ruddock F., *Balfour: Intellectual Statesman*, Oxford University Press, 1985
Macmunn, Sir George, *Kipling's Women*, Sampson Low, n.d.
McNaught, Kenneth, *The Penguin History of Canada*, Penguin, 1988
Mallett, Philip (ed.), *Kipling Considered*, Macmillan, 1989
Mangan, J.A., *The Games Ethic and Imperialism*, Viking, 1986
Marlowe, John, *Milner: Apostle of Empire*, Hamish Hamilton, 1976
Marsh, Peter, *Joseph Chamberlain: Entrepreneur in Politics*, Yale University Press, 1994
Mason, Philip, *Kipling: The Glass, the Shadow and the Fire*, Jonathan Cape, 1975
——*A Matter of Honour*, Papermac, 1974
Middlemas, Keith, and Barnes, John, *Baldwin*, Weidenfeld & Nicolson, 1969
Moon, Penderel, *The British Conquest and Dominion of India*, Duckworth, 1989
Moore-Gilbert, B.J., *Kipling and 'Orientalism'*, Croom Helm, 1986
Morris, J., *Fisher's Face*, Viking, 1995
——*Pax Britannica*, Penguin, 1979
——*Stones of Empire*, Oxford University Press, 1987
Moss, Robert, *Rudyard Kipling and the Fiction of Adolescence*, Macmillan, 1982
Najder, Zdzislaw, *Joseph Conrad*, Cambridge University Press, 1983
Neider, Charles (ed.), *The Autobiography of Mark Twain*, Chatto & Windus, 1960
Neruda, Pablo, *Memoirs*, Souvenir Press, 1977
Newton, Lord, *Lord Lansdowne*, Macmillan, 1929
——*Retrospection*, John Murray, 1941
Nicolson, Adam, *The Hated Wife: Carrie Kipling, 1862–1939*, Short Books, 2001
O'Brien, Terence, *Milner*, Constable, 1979
O'Dwyer, Michael, *India as I Knew it: 1885–1925*, Constable, 1925
Orel, Harold (ed.), *A Kipling Chronology*, G.K.Hall, 1990
——*Kipling: Interviews and Recollections*, 2 vols., Macmillan, 1983
Orwell, George, *Collected Essays, Journalism and Letters*, Vol. 2, Penguin, 1971

Pafford, Mark, *Kipling's Indian Fiction*, Macmillan, 1989
Page, Norman, *A Kipling Companion*, Papermac, 1984
Pakenham, Thomas, *The Boer War*, Weidenfeld & Nicolson, 1979
Paterson, T.G., Clifford, J.G., and Hagan, K.J., *American Foreign Relations*, Vol. 2, D.C. Heath, Lexington, 1995
Pearce, Edward, *Lines of Most Resistance: The Lords, the Tories and Ireland, 1886–1914*, Little, Brown, 1999
Philips, C.H. (ed.), *Historians of India, Pakistan and Ceylon*, Oxford University Press, 1961
Pinney, Thomas, *In Praise of Kipling*, University of Texas, 1996
——*Kipling's India: Uncollected Sketches, 1884–1888*, Macmillan, 1986
——*The Letters of Rudyard Kipling*, 4 vols., University of Iowa Press, Iowa City, 1990–9
Porter, Andrew, *The Nineteenth Century*, Oxford University Press, 1999
Ralph, Julian, *War's Brighter Side*, C. Arthur Pearson, 1901
Ricketts, Harry, *The Unforgiving Minute: A Life of Rudyard Kipling*, Chatto & Windus, 1999
Ridley, Jane, and Percy, Clare (eds.), *The Letters of Arthur Balfour & Lady Elcho*, Hamish Hamilton, 1992
Rivett-Carnac, J.H., *Many Memories*, Blackwood, Edinburgh, 1910
Robb, Graham, *Victor Hugo,* Picador, 1997
Roberts, Andrew, *Salisbury: Victorian Titan*, Weidenfeld & Nicolson, 1999
Roberts, Brian, *Cecil Rhodes: Flawed Colossus*, W.W.Norton, New York, 1988
Roberts, Lord, *Forty-one Years in India*, 2 vols., Richard Bentley, 1897
Rose, Kenneth, *King George V*, Weidenfeld & Nicolson, 1983
——*The Later Cecils*, Harper & Row, 1975
Rose, Norman, *Churchill: The Unruly Giant*, The Free Press, New York, 1994
——*Lewis Namier and Zionism*, Oxford University Press, 1980
Rutherford, Andrew (ed.), *Early Verse by Rudyard Kipling, 1879–1889*, Oxford University Press, 1986
——*Kipling's Mind and Art*, Oliver & Boyd, 1964
Said, Edward, 'Introduction' to *Kim*, Penguin, 1987
——*Orientalism*, Routledge & Kegan Paul, 1978
Seymour-Smith, Martin, *Rudyard Kipling*, Queen Anne Press, 1989
Shanks, Edward, *Rudyard Kipling: A Study in Literature and Political Ideas*, Macmillan, 1940
Shirer, William L., *The Rise and Fall of the Third Reich*, Book Club Associates, 1972
Silkin, John, *Out of Battle: The Poetry of the Great War*, Oxford University Press, 1972
Spender, J.A., *Life of the Right Hon. Sir Henry Campbell-Bannerman G.C.B.*, 2 vols., Hodder & Stoughton, 1923
Stewart, J.I.M., *Rudyard Kipling*, Gollancz, 1966
Sutcliff, Rosemary, *Rudyard Kipling*, Bodley Head, 1960
Sutcliffe, Peter, *The Oxford University Press*, Oxford University Press, 1978
Sykes, Christopher, *Nancy: The Life of Lady Astor*, Collins, 1972
Thirkell, Angela, *Three Houses*, Oxford University Press, 1931
Tignor, Robert L., *Modernization and British Colonial Rule in Egypt, 1882–1914*, Princeton University Press, 1966
Thomas, Antony, *Rhodes: The Race for Africa*, Penguin, 1997
Tompkins, J.M.S., *The Art of Rudyard Kipling*, Methuen, 1959
Trevelyan, G.M., *Grey of Fallodon*, Longman, 1937
Vansittart, Lord, *The Mist Procession*, Hutchinson, 1958
Vincent, John (ed.), *The Crawford Papers*, Manchester University Press, 1984
Ward, Maisie, *Gilbert Keith Chesterton*, Sheed & Ward, 1944
Welldon, J.E.C., *Recollections and Reflections*, Cassell, 1915
Wells, H.G., *The New Machiavelli*, John Lane, 1911

Bibliography

Wilson, Angus, *The Strange Ride of Rudyard Kipling: His Life and Works*, Secker & Warburg, 1977
Wilson, John, *CB: A Life of Sir Henry Campbell-Bannerman*, Constable, 1973
Winter, Denis, *Haig's Command*, Penguin, 1992
Woodruff, Philip, *The Guardians*, Jonathan Cape, 1963
Woolf, Leonard, *Growing*, Hogarth Press, 1964
Wrench, John Evelyn, *Alfred Lord Milner*, Eyre & Spottiswode, 1958
Young, Kenneth, *Arthur James Balfour*, G. Bell, 1963
Young, W. A., *A Kipling Dictionary*, Routledge, 1911
Younghusband, George, *A Soldier's Memories in Peace and War*, Herbert Jenkins, 1917

EDITIONS OF KIPLING'S WORKS CITED IN THE TEXT AND NOTES

Actions and Reactions, Macmillan, 1909
Barrack-Room Ballads and Other Verses, Methuen, 1917
A Book of Words, Macmillan, 1928
The Brushwood Boy, Macmillan, 1910
'Captains Courageous', Macmillan, 1924
The Day's Work, Macmillan, 1924
Debits and Credits, Macmillan, 1965
Departmental Ditties and Other Verses, Methuen, 1904
A Diversity of Creatures, Macmillan, 1917
The Five Nations, Methuen, 1927
A Fleet in Being, Macmillan, 1899
From Sea to Sea, 2 vols., Macmillan, 1912 and 1914
A History of England (with C.R.L.Fletcher), Clarendon Press, Oxford, 1911
The Irish Guards in the Great War, 2 vols., Spellmount, 1997
The Jungle Book, Macmillan, 1901
The Jungle Play, Allen Lane, 2000
Just So Stories, Macmillan, 1928
Kim, Macmillan, 1935
Land and Sea Tales for Scouts and Guides, Macmillan, 1923
Letters of Travel (1892–1913), Macmillan, 1920
Life's Handicap, Macmillan, 1913
The Light that Failed, Macmillan, 1953
Limits and Renewals, Macmillan, 1932
Many Inventions, Macmillan, 1940
The Naulahka: A Story of East and West (with Wolcott Balestier), William Heinemann, 1892
Plain Tales from the Hills, Macmillan, 1931
Puck of Pook's Hill, Macmillan, 1951
Rewards and Fairies, Macmillan, 1926
Rudyard Kipling's Verse: Inclusive Edition, 1885–1918, Hodder & Stoughton, 1919
Sea Warfare, Macmillan, 1916
The Second Jungle Book, Macmillan, 1950
The Seven Seas, Methuen, 1896
Soldiers Three etc., Sampson Low, Marston, 1893
Something of Myself, Cambridge University Press, 1991
Souvenirs of France, Macmillan, 1933

Bibliography

Stalky & Co., Macmillan, 1929
'They', Macmillan, 1905
Thy Servant a Dog, Macmillan, 1930
Traffics and Discoveries, Macmillan, 1904
Wee Willie Winkie and Other Stories, Macmillan, 1929
The Years Between, Methuen, 1919

Index

Index

Carnest